PRAISE FOR *OUTSIDERS IN A PROMISED LAND*

M000110718

"Outsiders in a Promised Land opens a view onto an unexplored but surprising landscape—the history of religious activism for social and political change in the Pacific Northwest. This region may be the nation's most unchurched corner, but it turns out that its religious leaders have had an outsized influence on its social character. Soden convincingly shows that religiously-motivated activists, both conservatives and liberals, leveraged their minority status into a sense of aggrieved outsiderhood and then used this leverage to exert a powerful impact on Northwest politics. The general patterns of religious protest mostly followed national trends—whether Civil Rights in the 1960s or Culture Wars in the 1980s—but local developments often diverged in fascinating and important ways. This is a significant and substantial book, original in conception and deft in execution, which should revise how we look at both religion and politics in Pacific Northwest history."

—Michael S. Hamilton, Professor of History, Seattle Pacific University

"Outsiders in a Promised Land vividly illustrates the degree and variety of religious activism in the Pacific Northwest from the nineteenth century to the present, a history that both works with and belies the notion of the region as a land of 'nones.' Soden's definition of activism is inclusive, his cast of characters memorable, and his analyses consistently fair and on point."

—Paul Harvey, Chair, Department of History, University of Colorado at Colorado Springs and author of *The Color of Christ: The Son of God and the Saga of Race in America*

"This fascinating and deeply informed study shows how religious activists have struggled, sometimes successfully, to shape the public culture of America's least religious region. In telling their story, Dale Soden has given us the essential history of religion in the Pacific Northwest."

—Mark Silk, Professor of Religion in Public Life at Trinity College and author of *Unsecular Media: Making News of Religion in America*

"Dale Soden restores religiously motivated Protestant, Catholic, and Jewish activists to the narrative of Pacific Northwest history. Anyone who wants to understand the building of social institutions in the midst of early Euro-American settlement, the Pacific Northwest's progressive and conservative political turns, its late twentieth century culture wars, or the stakes involved in the current contest over environmental protection needs to read this book."

—Patricia O'Connell Killen, Ph.D., coeditor of *Religion and Public Life in the Pacific Northwest: The None Zone* and *Selected Letters of A. M. A. Blanchet, Bishop of Walla Walla and Nesqualy, 1846-1879*

Steve and Bonnie,

Thank you for such a long and rich friendship.

Thank you for your support and encouragement — You are a model for living out your convictions for the good of others —

With affection and admiration,

Dale

OUTSIDERS IN A PROMISED LAND

RELIGIOUS ACTIVISTS IN PACIFIC NORTHWEST HISTORY

DALE E. SODEN

OREGON STATE UNIVERSITY PRESS   CORVALLIS

The paper in this book meets the guidelines for permanence and durability of the Committee on Production Guidelines for Book Longevity of the Council on Library Resources and the minimum requirements of the American National Standard for Permanence of Paper for Printed Library Materials Z39.48-1984.

Library of Congress Cataloging-in-Publication Data

Soden, Dale Edward, author.
Outsiders in a promised land : religious activists in
Pacific Northwest history / Dale Soden.
pages cm
Includes bibliographical references and index.
Summary: "Explores the role that religious activists have played in shaping the culture and communities of the Pacific Northwest from the mid-nineteenth century onward "—Provided by publisher.
ISBN 978-0-87071-778-9 (paperback) — ISBN 978-0-87071-779-6 (ebook)
1. Northwest, Pacific—Religion—History. 2. Religion and civilization—Northwest, Pacific. I. Title.
BL2527.N95S63 2015
305.6'709795—dc23
2015035068

TABLE OF CONTENTS

PREFACE

In October 1942, Reverend William Sherman Burgoyne moved to Hood River, Oregon, to serve as pastor of the Asbury Methodist Church. Only a few months earlier, just under five hundred individuals of Japanese descent had been forced to leave town on their way toward internment camps. Although interned, several Japanese Americans from Hood River either volunteered or were drafted into the US Army and served with distinction in the all–Japanese American 442nd Battalion. Back in Hood River, officials erected a billboard near the county courthouse with the names of all the community's residents, including sixteen Japanese Americans, who were serving in the war. However, the hatred toward persons of Japanese descent was so strong that in December 1944, the local chapter of the American Legion decided to remove the sixteen Japanese American names. At that point, Reverend Burgoyne formally complained in the *Hood River News* about the action of the American Legion and stated that "every person in Hood River County . . . is disgraced." He urged them to replace the names immediately.[1] In response, the city's former Chamber of Commerce president took out six large ads in the local paper in the form of "an open letter to W. Sherman Burgoyne." The first ad began, "So Sorry Please, Japs Are Not Wanted in Hood River." Burgoyne and his wife Doris were aghast. In response, he cofounded the League for Liberty and Justice, which supported Japanese Americans and countered propaganda and bigotry. In the end, Burgoyne succeeded in getting the names restored. As Japanese Americans slowly trickled back to Hood River, the League for Liberty offered to shop for local Japanese Americans, urged chain stores to accept Japanese business, and drove trucks to warehouses.[2]

Although severely criticized in Hood River, Reverend Burgoyne's efforts did not go unrewarded nationally. In 1947, the Methodist minister was selected in a national poll of five hundred civil liberties and service organizations and over a thousand editors to receive the

Thomas Jefferson Award for promoting democracy by the Council Against Intolerance in America, along with Frank Sinatra, former Georgia governor Ellis Arnall, and Eleanor Roosevelt.[3]

In spite of the national recognition for his efforts, Sherman Burgoyne felt like an outsider in his own community. What seems clear is that this deeply religious person felt compelled to take a stand that seemed in so many respects countercultural. Sherman Burgoyne's story is just one of thousands of individuals who, out of their religious identity or values, became active in the public life of the Pacific Northwest.

These stories have surfaced only occasionally in the most widely read histories of the region. With the exception of early missionary activity, which has been well documented, most historians have focused on economic, environmental, and social forces other than religion to explain the character and culture of what became Washington and Oregon. This book is an effort to bring forward stories of religious activism and to place them in their broader historical context. I make the case that religion has mattered more significantly than previously acknowledged and, interestingly, has helped shape the relatively liberal character of Washington and Oregon relative to the rest of the nation.

In one sense, the Protestant and Catholic missionaries, who came to the Pacific Northwest beginning in the 1830s, might be considered the earliest activists who were not Indian in the region. Both Protestants and Catholics attempted to convert Native Americans to Christianity and to persuade them to abandon traditional ways of living for Western culture. In their attempt to do so, Protestants and Catholics often became bitter rivals. While not all Indians resisted conversion, and indeed some tribes welcomed it, the larger project of assimilation was a failure. This complicated story of Indian and white engagement has been treated by numerous historians over the past several decades and is not the subject of this study.[4]

This book begins with the generation of religious activists that arrived in the second half of the nineteenth century. Most of them were only marginally interested in Native Americans. Instead, those activists, despite a number of differences theologically, were surprisingly united around a common concern: How could they make the region a safer place for women and children? Specifically, how could they develop a culture that reflected the values most closely associated with Victorian America? In raising these questions, religious activists helped initiate a cultural war against behaviors most often identified with younger and mostly working-class males.

This younger male culture was the natural outgrowth of economic forces that dictated much of Northwest life in the middle to late nineteenth century. Logging, fishing, and mining all attracted young men looking to work for a living wage—or better yet, strike it rich. Inevitably, small towns and emerging cities provided fertile environments for the requisite cheap amusements desired by working men in the form of saloons, gambling halls, and houses of prostitution. For many Catholics, Protestants, and Jews, who largely came by railroad to settle in these developing urban centers, changing this culture of alcohol and gambling proved to be a very important priority. These activists employed a variety of strategies and developed a wide range of institutions, many of which still exist more than a hundred years after their initial establishment. Religiously motivated women and men believed in the importance of common schools, colleges and universities, health-care institutions, public libraries, orphanages, and homes for unwed mothers. Virtually all of them were designed to provide either a social safety net or a means for developing moral character. New social organizations such as the Young Men's and Young Women's Christian Associations, Catholic and Jewish benevolent associations, and settlement houses became alternatives to the saloon. Alcohol abuse and prostitution focused the energy of religious activists for decades in Washington and Oregon. This grassroots activity gave rise to Prohibition laws in the far Northwest well before the Eighteenth Amendment was ratified, making the use of alcohol illegal across the nation.

In the early twentieth century, a significant number of Northwest pastors, priests, and rabbis participated in the Social Gospel and Progressive era reforms. However, after World War I a different spasm of religious activism emerged in the form of the Ku Klux Klan in Oregon and Washington. The Klan, often led by Protestant ministers, attempted unsuccessfully to eliminate the cultural influence of southern and eastern European immigrants who were mostly Catholic.

Beginning with the Great Depression in the 1930s and with World War II, religious activism in the Northwest took on a different emphasis. As was the case across the nation, more attention turned to issues of social injustice toward persons of color, women, homosexuals, and ethnic minorities; these issues were all too prevalent in the Pacific Northwest. In this era, religious activism started assuming the liberal character that would eventually prevail in the second half of the twentieth century. However, it was not that simple; conservative religious activists also surfaced in the years following World War II. Fears of secularism and Communism as well as liberalism itself motivated thousands of conservatives to become active in public policy issues in Oregon and Washington.

It was during the Civil Rights Movement of the 1960s that liberal activism reemerged as the salient feature of Pacific Northwest religious influence in the public square. Black and white religious clergy and their parishioners worked together to change hearts and to effect legislative reform. Grassroots activism energized thousands of individuals in the 1960s. Beginning in the 1970s and extending to the present, women's issues, gay rights, environmental causes, and peace initiatives all galvanized liberal religious communities in Washington and Oregon. However, conservatives responded with opposition to homosexuality, abortion, and feminism. Thus, religious activism contributed to a full-blown culture war, largely within the middle class in the Pacific Northwest. This same struggle persists well into the twenty-first century, as liberals and conservatives seldom find common ground, with few exceptions apart from environmental issues and human trafficking.

Much in this narrative will be familiar to the student of American religious and cultural history. Chronologically and topically, the general pattern of Protestant, Catholic, and Jewish involvement with public life mirrors much of the history of religious engagement with public life in the rest of the country. Social and political forces that shaped the nation—industrialization, urbanization, immigration, foreign policy, and waves of economic prosperity and depression, as well as fundamental issues of race, gender, and class—all influenced religious response to public life in the Pacific Northwest.

As was the case for the rest of the nation, most activists identified with the principal European religious traditions that had rooted themselves in the United States. In the late nineteenth century and first half of the twentieth century, Methodists, Presbyterians, Congregationalists, Episcopalians, Unitarians, Northern Baptists, and Quakers most frequently surfaced among the Protestant activists in the Northwest. In the second half of the twentieth century, several branches of the African American church as well as Lutherans joined those other faith traditions and became actively engaged in political and social issues.

A number of evangelicals took an active role in public life in the late nineteenth and early twentieth centuries, but it was beginning in the 1970s that nondenominational Protestants and evangelical Christians emerged more prominently on several issues. Throughout the history of the Northwest, Catholic priests and nuns as well significant numbers of laypersons can be found among the most active participants in public affairs, as can adherents of Reform Judaism. This pattern of involvement is similar to many other parts of the United States.

Nevertheless, several elements of religion and public life in the Northwest are different compared with the rest of the country. Geography surely has had a role in shaping the particular character of religious activism. It has been hard to escape the sense that the region felt and can still feel isolated from the rest of the country. Among the last of the lower forty-eight states to be settled, the far Northwest reinforced a sense of remoteness that was often overwhelming to those who ventured over the Rocky Mountains or made the trip by sea around South America to the Northwest coast. On one hand, the region's isolation made it attractive to utopian and communitarian groups who wanted to flee other parts of the country and be free to live according to their own beliefs and social norms.[5] But more subtle was the reality that geography contributed to a diminished loyalty to traditional religious denominations and institutions. As Northwest historian Carlos Schwantes put it, "Mountains contribute to the irregularity of natural and manmade landscapes in the Pacific Northwest. Unlike the prairie states, where rectangular fields of corn and soybeans extend to the horizon, the far Northwest gives the appearance of being rough and unfinished."[6] The physical landscape likely provided an impetus to abandon formal religion and a reason to innovate new religious practices. At an early symposium on religion in the Pacific Northwest in 1914, one commentator noted, "In the East they were faithful church members; now they are not even church [at]tenders. The ascent of the Great Divide seemed too steep for church letters. The air of the Northwest seemed too rare for prayer. . . . We hurried forth to conquer the wilderness, but we have been conquered by it."[7]

From the very beginning, traditional religious institutions found thin soil. The net result was to make the far Northwest comparatively the least-churched region in the country in terms of church affiliation. All of this presented both challenges and opportunities for those who wanted to engage in public life. On one hand, activists often felt little support from a religious community that was comparatively weak. On the other hand, activists undoubtedly felt less constrained by the religious establishment than in other parts of the country. Challenging the status quo had fewer social costs.

Historian Patricia Killen has done much to help interpret the reality of religious isolation in the Pacific Northwest. Her phrase, the "None Zone," references the fact that more people in Washington and Oregon claim "none" when asked their religious identification than in any other region of the United States. Perhaps most importantly, Killen and others have observed that no one religious tradition has emerged in Oregon and Washington to dominate the cultural and political landscape. Unlike Minnesota with its Lutherans, Oklahoma and Texas with their Southern Baptists, or Utah and Idaho with their Mormons, the far Northwest was and still is an open religious environment. That open environment fosters a degree of competition between various religious groups and individuals.[8]

My work builds on many of the observations made by Killen and others and asserts that while religious activists had a significant impact on the culture of the region, they did so as outsiders to the mainstream of Pacific Northwest society. A large part of the common feeling of being an outsider was the consequence of a lack of a unified majority religious tradition within the region. With apathy toward institutional religion the norm, religious activists on both the right and left have felt that they were running upstream against a culture hostile to formal religion.

This sense of being an "outsider" likely caused countless activists to believe that they were engaged in a life-and-death struggle for cultural influence. It encouraged powerful moral suasion in the form of sermons, marches, and picket lines, as well as prompted legislative coercion against certain behaviors. The sense of being an "outsider" likely fostered a greater degree of cooperation or collaboration with any allies that could be found. Although the Northwest has had its fair share of anti-Catholic episodes, nonetheless, the ecumenical cooperation between Protestants and Catholics has been as strong as if not stronger than in any other part of the country. And it can be argued that black and white religious leaders during the civil rights struggles of the 1960s were as united in the Northwest as anywhere in the country.

Historian R. Laurence Moore, in his book *Religious Outsiders and the Making of Americans*, suggests that religious groups who have considered themselves outsiders have provided a dynamism to American cultural life that has often gone unappreciated.[9] In a similar way, I am arguing that religious activists in the Northwest have exercised influence beyond their numbers on the cultural and public life of the region.

Writing about the role of religion in the western United States has always proved somewhat challenging. Noted historians Ferenc Szasz and Patricia Limerick both observed that the conventional narratives of the West have seldom found room for the religious activist. "In a story full of cowboys, sheriffs, saloon girls, outlaws, gunfighters, prospectors, and stagecoach drivers, the church was, at best, the place where the frightened townspeople gathered to sing hymns and await rescue by the all-too-worldly hero," wrote Limerick. "The church, after all, was aligned with the forces of respectability, the forces that would eventually tame the Wild West and end all the fun and adventure of the glory days." But both she and Szasz argued there was merit in recovering the stories of a "different kind of Western hero: the sustainable hero who can replace the old, exhausted, and depleted Western heroes."[10] For Limerick and for Szasz, a new history of the West and Pacific Northwest should have room for religious activists who sought to make the world a better place.

Outsiders in a Promised Land is not explicitly about the discovery of new heroes, although there are certainly individuals contained within this narrative who meet Limerick's test. My hope is to make visible the many ways in which religious activists, in this least-churched region of the country, have shaped the struggle to define the nature of public life.

It takes courage to engage in public debate, to march on a picket line, or to stand up to the American Legion as did Sherman Burgoyne. A democratic culture requires that its citizens be willing to articulate their deepest convictions and to engage peacefully in activity designed to persuade fellow citizens of a better way. Northwest religious activists engaged the public square passionately and mostly as outsiders who were trying to make the Northwest a better place, and this is their story.

CHAPTER 1

HERE COME THE VICTORIANS

On warm summer nights in Seattle in 1899, the area later known as Pioneer Square often teemed with recreational activities of all sorts. Only two years removed from the Klondike gold rush of 1897, downtown Seattle featured saloons, gambling halls, vaudeville theaters, and burlesque houses. Competition among proprietors was fierce for the mostly single males who came to patronize these establishments, where in addition to consumption of alcohol and opportunity to indulge in various sexual activities, one could find blackface minstrel shows and occasional prize fights. On most nights, local business owners employed musicians to play popular music in an effort to attract prospective customers into their respective establishments. But it also was not uncommon for a different kind of music to be heard in the streets of Seattle. In those years, the Salvation Army often had its own street band to bring its distinctive message to downtown customers. On one particular evening, although likely repeated on many occasions, musicians played their beckoning music on balconies that hung over the entrances to their street-level theaters. Anticipating their religious competitors, these performers readied themselves for what would seem bizarre by today's standards—a battle of the bands. According to one newspaper reporter, "At a given signal, as the Salvationists marched past, flags flying, torches smoking and sputtering, and musicians playing like mad, pandemonium would break loose. A musical free-for-all would take place in which the Salvationists were out-pointed two to one. But on they marched toward their Yesler Way barracks, righteously singing their hymn-book words grotesquely fitted to popular street melodies, happily unconscious of defeat."[1]

Just a few months later, on the other side of the state, readers of Spokane's *Spokesman-Review* opened their newspaper to the

■

front-page story that read, "Varieties are closed; Council also declares for suppression of gambling and other forms of vice." During the previous evening, scores of Spokane citizens had packed the city council chambers to give their opinion about whether variety theaters and box houses should be licensed. The box house, a saloon with a small theater, received its name because the balcony in such establishments was separated into alcoves where curtains could be drawn so that one could see the show without being seen. Women of the box house encouraged patrons to buy drinks and, depending on the particular establishment, engage in sexual activity. Popular and profitable, the saloon, box house, and theater culture drew the attention of the city council. The reporter for the *Spokesman* described the scene at the council as the "largest and oddest assortment ever gathered at one time and for the same purpose in the hall. Ministers in black coats and white lawn ties were jammed in between gamblers, saloon men, . . . nickel-in-the slot machine owners . . . a few lawyers, three or four physicians and . . . inside the railing sat seven or eight women from the churches." During the course of the evening, the audience heard various arguments both for and against the licensing of variety theaters with their box houses. After each presentation, loud applause would erupt and the audience would stomp the floor with their heels. "Gamblers and preachers rubbed elbows in alternate applause," as the debate raged on through the evening. In the end, at least on this occasion, the council sided with the ministers and those who opposed the theaters. And at least for a short time, the "moral" forces of Spokane prevailed.[2]

Whether as members of the Salvation Army or as local ministers and laypersons, religious activists by the turn of the century were often engaged in the fight over what kind of culture should prevail in the Pacific Northwest. But it was an uphill battle. Clearly outsiders to a prevailing culture, activists often felt isolated and relatively alone in a struggle that pitted them against economic forces and a culture that simply catered to the needs of single males.

Regardless of the occasional victories by religious individuals over certain activities, Spokane had a difficult time shedding her reputation as "one of the naughtiest cities in the West, rated next to San Francisco and Seattle for its wickedness." As one historian put it, "The demands of wealthy miners had created a café society that wined and dined in splendor, using champagne as well as fresh iced oysters by the barrel.

Hordes of lumberjacks, too, descended on the city every weekend, seeking refreshments for their thirst and solace for their loneliness."[3] Seattle and Spokane were little different than Portland and Tacoma, or for that matter Walla Walla, Eugene, or Bellingham when it came to the issue of how to manage a culture of cheap entertainment. No matter where one lived in the Pacific Northwest in the late nineteenth and early twentieth century, citizens debated over how best to control the behavior of mostly young males who patronized the saloons, box houses, and gambling establishments with great frequency. This was not strictly a debate between religious and nonreligious segments of the community. Nevertheless, many Protestants, and to a lesser extent Catholics and Jews, found themselves engaged in a bitter cultural battle with proprietors—and on occasion elected officials—over how to make a community more "respectable."

While this struggle was a familiar one throughout America in the nineteenth century, the Pacific Northwest proved to be a particularly fertile environment for such cultural conflict. Beginning in the middle decades of the nineteenth century, discoveries of coal, gold, and silver brought hordes of young men, nearly all between twenty and forty years old, rushing into the region looking to improve their fortunes. Soon to follow were logging camps in both Oregon and Washington Territory. Faced with long hours and dangerous and tedious work, these men sought some form of recreational escape. As small towns and budding urban communities developed, law enforcement seemed nonexistent. Rough and bawdy, wild and open, these towns on the frontier often resembled a Hobbesian state of nature. These communities were, according to historian Richard White, a libertarian's dream, where local government was extremely limited. Free enterprise prevailed; the principal social institutions were the saloon and the house of prostitution.[4]

The need to escape from the rigors as well as boredom of work tended to encourage the consumption of alcohol, which in turn often led to bad behavior. Historian Julian Rolph's observations about Montana certainly applied to the Pacific Northwest in general: "Men without the restraint of law, indifferent to public opinion, and unburdened by families, drink whenever there is nothing else to do. . . . Bad manners follow, profanity becomes a matter of course. . . . Excitability and nervousness brought on by rum help these tendencies along, and then to correct this state of things the pistol comes into play."[5] One historian described early Seattle residents as "tough men, alone, and with little sense of civic responsibility."[6] The box house was just one of many cheap and available amusements that catered to the needs of such "tough men." As another historian put it, the box house appealed "principally to lumberjacks and men of the woods who came to town with a half-year's pay in their jeans, ready to celebrate the 'splash' when the logs were sent down the river."[7]

With lots of young men and not very many women, drunkenness and violence marked the social environment of most communities in the West and the Northwest from the late nineteenth century well into the twentieth. Historian David Courtwright noted in his study of the culture of violence in America that from the end of the Civil War through the Great Depression, "a floating army of itinerant workers, variously known as tramps, hobos, navvies, shanty boys, and bindle stiffs, moved about the country seeking work in construction sites, lumber camps, canneries, threshing crews and other places where temporary or seasonal jobs were available." Courtwright observed that the money earned by those mostly single men did not go into savings or support for a family; instead, it was "dissipated in saloons, poker games, and brothels. Bachelor workers led a life of alternating work and spree until they finally either got out, burned out, landed in jail, or ended beneath the dissecting knife on the coroner's slab."[8]

This pervasive culture of inexpensive entertainment in Northwest communities posed a tremendous challenge to religious activists and other reformers. There were occasional successes, such as when the Tacoma City Council in 1899 passed, over the mayor's veto, an ordinance that excluded women from variety theaters;[9] or, for example, when the Fountain Theatre in Walla Walla closed in 1893 because of a "lack of patronage and the influence brought to bear by the Salvation Army."[10] For the most part, however, successes were limited to Sunday closings and occasional ordinances that tried to prohibit the employment of females in places where alcohol was sold.[11]

Christian reformers and activists struggled to convince single males that there was something more to life than drinking, gambling, and sexual gratification; they also struggled to convince an emerging business community of a bigger picture. One reporter in the *Spokesman-Review* in 1895 noted some of the challenges:

Undoubtedly there is a strong sentiment among the merchants in support of the theaters. Many business men say while they are opposed to all lawlessness or wild west hurrah business, they are also opposed to going to what they consider the extreme of closing up places of amusement where the line of entertainment upon the state is very similar to that presented by the average farce comedy company on the Auditorium stage.[12]

These early reformers and activists felt challenged by a social environment that seemed indifferent to "moral" concerns and bereft of any sense that the region might be a "respectable" place for families to plant roots. Most activists must have believed that they were on the outside looking in and that any success in changing the culture would be long in coming.

What made the cultural struggle in the late nineteenth and early twentieth century even more challenging was that the vast majority of educated Protestants broadly subscribed to a Victorian worldview. For most Victorian Christians, the purpose of culture and civilization was to impose order, to restrain the self, and to nurture higher ends for human beings beyond mere survival and the experience of pleasure—a tough sell on the frontier and in the nascent communities of the Northwest. Victorians believed that nothing should be done just for its own sake but for the larger purpose of advancing Western Civilization. Recreation and leisure (most notably drinking and gambling) rarely served to edify individuals. Instead, each of life's activities should contribute to the improvement of humanity. One should study architecture because it pointed to admired qualities of an earlier period and conveyed a moral purpose.[13] One should study the natural world because it pointed to God's ordered creation. Victorians prized reading, developed museums, staged world fairs, and built public libraries, all with an eye toward improving humankind and demonstrating that Western civilization was superior to all others. And, of course, sexual behavior was a particular focus of concern. Interaction between the sexes should be closely monitored. The purity of womanhood should be protected; sexual intercourse should be reserved for marriage. The traditional family was considered sacrosanct.

If Victorian Christians were sometimes the object of ridicule for seeming, even to their contemporaries, too judgmental and often arrogant about the superiority of their own culture, they nevertheless developed into a considerable social force throughout the Pacific Northwest. Hundreds of Victorian Christians came to the Northwest with the intent of changing the prevailing culture. Over several decades, Victorian Christians employed two fundamentally different strategies in an attempt to undermine the male culture of the region. As we have seen, they did what those individuals in Spokane were doing in 1899: they tried to regulate through legislation and ordinance those behaviors to which they objected, including prostitution, gambling, and excessive alcohol consumption. They persisted in trying to limit the number of recreational activities on the Sabbath. In addition to trying to regulate the box house, they attempted to restrict early forms of recreation such as dancing, cigarette smoking, the nickelodeon, vaudeville shows, boxing, movies, and amusement parks. And most importantly, as we will see in a subsequent chapter, they worked to eliminate alcohol. In this effort, they were moderately successful in both Oregon and Washington, particularly when it came to passing closing laws on Sunday, better known as blue laws.[14]

But Victorians also employed a second strategy that was more influential over the long term. This strategy focused on the establishment of a public and private educational system for young boys and girls. Victorian Christians hoped that schools would transform behavior and shape moral character. Education would serve as the antidote, first to frontier culture and subsequently to urban culture, in the budding communities of Oregon and Washington. For example, when the first school was established in Olympia in 1852, the local newspaper exclaimed that "the children heretofore roaming about our streets listless as the Indian, will begin to imbibe the knowledge requisite to make them good citizens, good republicans, good Christians, and, in short, prepare them to fill the position in which the death of their parents must soon place them."[15] For Victorian Christians, the school, both public and private, provided the hope for changing life in the Pacific Northwest.

Protestant ministers took the lead role in the establishment of the public or common school. Many of these clergymen who came to the Northwest had been educated at Andover Theological Seminary, Yale, and Princeton. They came with hopes of establishing not just churches but similar kinds of schools, colleges, and libraries that had been familiar to them on the East Coast. Often hostile to Catholicism, these ministers believed that the common school provided the best antidote to "Romanism, barbarism, and skepticism."[16]

But the Northwest in the mid to late nineteenth century was far from a hospitable place for these ministers. Isolated from virtually any kind of institutional support, these clerics found the region to be a particularly discouraging place. They frequently commented on the rootless character primarily among young men, as well as the general lack of social restraint in communities in which they lived.[17] These clergy hoped that attendance at school would provide the necessary environment for shaping male behavior on the frontier, but that was no easy task. According to one observer of early education in Washington Territory:

> Frequently a gang of ruffians, men grown but illiterate, would attend school intermittently for a few weeks in the winter when work was slack. The school afforded a warm rendezvous and a means of social diversion. The more they irritated the teacher and bullied the smaller pupils the more they exulted in their prowess. Sometimes they were not bad, simply unoccupied and spoiling for excitement; but sometimes they were real desperadoes, toting guns and bad whiskey, constant terrors to their neighborhoods.[18]

In response, the Washington territorial legislature in 1877 mandated a curriculum specifying that all subjects be taught in English and that in addition to reading, writing, arithmetic, geography, and grammar, "attention shall be given during the entire course to the cultivation of manners and morals."[19]

Protestant ministers assumed that the common school would reflect, broadly speaking, a Protestant view of manners and morals. "Missionaries saw the Sunday school and the common school as correlative institutions," according to historian David Tyack. "Just as children in rural areas went to 'church' in their schoolhouse, so they probably saw the 'weekday school' and the Sunday school as part of the same fabric of authority."[20] It was not unusual for children in Sunday school to be taught by the same teacher in the weekday common school classroom.

Methodists, Presbyterians, and Baptists may have competed for churchgoers on Sunday, but they declared a general truce when it came to the common school because they assumed that a universal moral law would be taught in the classroom. The belief that religious principles should be integrated into public school curricula was widely accepted. For example, in 1874, the *Rules and Regulations for the Government of Public Schools* stipulated that while Oregon teachers were prohibited from giving "sectarian or partisan instruction," they were encouraged to "inculcate in the minds of their pupils correct principles of morality."[21] In 1882, the superintendent of the Portland Public Schools was quoted in the *Journal of Education*: "The American public school has been built up, and is still upheld, by the great mass of sensible Christian people who believe in a vital connection between religion and morality, and value the schools largely for the influence and character of their teachers and the effect of their discipline on characters of their children."[22] Joseph Marsh, a professor from Pacific University in Forest Grove, Oregon, spoke to the Oregon State Teachers' Association in 1884 and emphasized that the church, the home, and the state were allies in training young people. He spoke for a generation of Victorians when he said, "There *must* be a *religious* basis to our educational system; an acknowledgment of our religious obligations, and the natural and common presentation of incentives to piety, must have their place in the common school, or it utterly fails of its mission, and will soon go the way of all effete institutions."[23]

Oregon's most important religious activist on the education front was George Atkinson. Born in Newburyport, Massachusetts, in 1819, Atkinson moved with his family to Newbury, Vermont, in 1830. Atkinson's father, a founding trustee of Newbury (Vermont) Seminary and a founding member of the board of directors of the Vermont Central Railroad, encouraged his son's educational pursuits. Atkinson graduated from Dartmouth College and Andover Seminary and determined that God was calling him to the mission field. He married Nancy Bates in 1846 and was ordained in 1847 in the Congregational Church. He nearly went to Africa under the auspices of the American Board of Commissioners for Foreign Missions, but instead he was persuaded by the American Home Missionary Society to serve in Oregon. In 1847, the Atkinsons sailed from Boston around Cape Horn for the Sandwich Islands (Hawai'i) and eventually landed in Astoria in 1848.[24] From the outset, Atkinson hoped to re-create his eastern common school experience in the Pacific Northwest. He told an audience in 1848, shortly after his arrival, that the Puritans had it right when they asserted that "a free school for every settlement and a grammar school for every hundred families" should be standard.[25]

Atkinson, like other Protestant ministers, carried a mandate from his sponsoring society to create "churches, schools, whatever would

benefit humanity—temperance, virtue; the industrial, mental, moral and religious training of the young, and the establishment of society upon sound principles by means of institutions of religion and learning."[26] He soon set to work lobbying for a school law with Joseph Lane, the territory's first governor. In 1849 Atkinson convinced both Lane and the legislature to pass a law that required sections sixteen and thirty-six of surveyed territorial land to be set aside for schools in each township. But Atkinson did not stop there. He helped establish the Clackamas County Female Seminary and served as the first school commissioner of Clackamas County. Beginning in

George Atkinson played a pivotal role in establishing educational institutions in Oregon's early history.

1863, after moving to Portland, Atkinson served as the superintendent of schools for Multnomah County for three terms of two years each. Atkinson also served as a trustee of Whitman College in Walla Walla and Pacific University, both Congregational in origin. In addition he helped found three private academies in Washington Territory.[27]

Atkinson embraced the common school as the best hope for shaping the character of young males on the frontier in the face of an ungoverned individualism that manifested itself in behavior that was often self-destructive and dangerous to others. He preached to his congregation that the "right training of children" was necessary for the success of God's Kingdom. He noted in his letters the frequency with which fathers went hunting on the Sabbath, and young men "lurched down the streets of town, cheeks flushed by 'the intoxicating cup,' and children running wild."[28]

In 1888, Atkinson addressed the National Education Association's national convention in San Francisco and forcefully argued for use of the Bible in the common school. He claimed that moral truths

■ ──

embedded in Scripture were essential to the proper moral upbring-ing of the current generation of students. "Of such quality are the Decalogue, the Proverbs, the aphorisms of Jesus in the Sermon on the Mount, and in His Parables," according to the Oregon minister, "that the maxims of political economy in the Hebrew commonwealth have never been surpassed or annulled in the experience of nations [that] have tried them."[29] Atkinson argued that "God's book of human rights and laws" should provide the source of authority in the public school. "Why not engrave the Ten Commandments at one end of every school-room and the Sermon on the Mount at the other end? Why not follow that pathway of light which prepared the way and predicted the coming of Him who should bring forth judgment to the Gentiles? Why not restore the word of God to the public school, and enrich the pupils with its treasure of wisdom and knowledge?" He finished his speech with a call for "the Bible our text book!"[30]

In the early 1880s, Atkinson and fellow Portland Unitarian minister Thomas Lamb Eliot found themselves embroiled in a major debate with the editor of the *Oregonian*, Harvey Scott, over the issue of whether public high schools should be supported entirely at public expense.[31] Scott and others feared that the increased level of taxation necessary to support a public high school would be oppressive. They also argued that a free public high school would harm business by taking young men and women out of the labor market, and that free education would undermine the character of young people by seemingly allowing them to get something for nothing. Atkinson and Eliot, on the other hand, argued relentlessly that public education was necessary to the moral and social well-being of the community.[32] Underscoring the role that public education played in creating a common culture, Reverend Eliot, who had become the superintendent of Multnomah County Schools in 1872, argued that the "justification of our public school system really lies where people seldom look for it, viz: In the necessity of a republic's preserving a homogeneous people; the necessity of having one institu-tion which effectually mingles and assimilates all classes, and so oppose the creation of classes and castes."[33] In the end, Atkinson and Eliot carried the day, and Portland residents voted to support a public high school system. And their efforts confirmed the importance of Protestant clergy in developing the public school movement in the Northwest.[34]

Victorian Protestants' belief that education could help transform the culture of male behavior was nowhere better reflected than in their commitment to establish colleges and universities throughout the Northwest. Missionary Jason Lee is given credit for helping found Willamette University in 1842. By 1866, Willamette had established the state's first school of medicine and by 1883 the state's first law school. In 1849, George Atkinson helped secure a charter for the Tualatin Academy, which eventually became Pacific University in Forest Grove, Oregon. Baptists founded a college at McMinnville, Oregon, in 1858, later renaming it Linfield College. In 1859, Congregationalists in Walla Walla founded Whitman Seminary, which became Whitman College in 1883. Presbyterians established the Albany Collegiate Institute in 1867, which later became known as Lewis and Clark College, and in Sumner, Washington, Presbyterians also founded an academy in 1884, which six years later was incorporated as Whitworth College. Methodists founded the University of Puget Sound in 1888 in Tacoma, and two years later Lutherans founded Pacific Lutheran University in South Tacoma. Free Methodists established Seattle Pacific College in 1891; that same year Quakers founded Pacific College, which later changed its name to George Fox College in Newberg, Oregon. Jesuits established Gonzaga College in Spokane in 1886 and Seattle University in 1891. Benedictines founded St. Martin's College, just north of Olympia, in 1895, and the Catholic Congregation of the Holy Cross established what became the University of Portland in 1901. A score of other religious colleges and universities were also begun in the nineteenth century but failed to survive.[35]

Each of these colleges and universities has a story of dedicated founders and committed church bodies who poured considerable energy and resources into these nascent institutions. Typical of the effort given to the establishment of both public and private educational institutions in the Northwest was Presbyterian minister George Whitworth. Born in England in 1816, Whitworth's formative experience came in Ohio and Indiana. At the relatively advanced aged of twenty-eight, he enrolled in seminary. Ordained four years later, he began serving churches in Indiana and Kentucky. By the early 1850s, Whitworth, inspired by missionary tales from the Northwest, decided that God was calling him to organize a group to head west along the Oregon Trail and establish a Presbyterian colony. He expressed his dream that "no child or youth, connected with the colony, shall ever be permitted to grow up without the benefit of a good English education, and thorough religious training."[36]

Arriving in Portland in 1853 following his trek across the country, Whitworth spent the next thirty years establishing some twenty Presbyterian churches in Oregon and Washington. Partly out of financial necessity, Whitworth became a lawyer, a farmer, a businessman, and a public servant, holding the post of chief clerk of the Indian Department of Washington Territory. Like Atkinson and other Protestant ministers, Whitworth believed in the common school and in higher education. He was elected superintendent of common schools for Thurston County in 1854 and served as president of the young University of Washington for two short terms in the 1870s. Whitworth helped write the common school law for the territory in 1876.

George Whitworth served as president of the University of Washington and later founded Whitworth College. Courtesy Whitworth University Archives, Spokane, Washington

In his mind, Whitworth came to the Northwest to civilize the region by promoting a broadly Protestant worldview. For him, that goal necessitated the establishment of an educational institution affiliated with the Presbyterian Church. In 1883, Whitworth convinced several other Presbyterian clergy and laity that an academy should be started in the small town of Sumner, some ten miles northeast of Tacoma, Washington. From the outset, founders paid significant attention to the moral and social environment that might shape their students. Alcohol was uppermost in the minds of administrators and faculty. An early catalogue tried to persuade readers—presumably parents and students—that "the normal tone of Sumner has a reputation above that of any city or town on the Pacific Coast. It is free from saloon influences and is surrounded by a very intelligent active and enterprising people."[37]

While each of these Protestant institutions reflected distinctive elements related to its respective religious traditions, virtually all of them shared similar core values and assumptions about the role of education in the promotion of intellectual and moral development. They all asserted the importance of Western civilization, the rationalist tradition, Judeo-Christian maxims, and Victorian culture.

Mostly established in and around the budding urban centers of the Northwest, these colleges offered a curriculum that emphasized the importance of moral character. These new schools stood in opposition to traditional vices. College trustees, administrators, and faculty had a palpable fear of what young males might do with young females in an unsupervised environment.

For example, founders of Whitworth College favored classical education for both men and women, but what is striking is the concern that Whitworth and other colleges exhibited over the social behaviors of men and women. Men at Whitworth and other colleges needed to present letters of introduction before they could date college women. Like other Christian colleges in the region, Whitworth's faculty identified character development to be the institution's key objective. An early Whitworth catalogue states,

> It must be kept in mind that knowledge is not the highest value sought, but culture, the discipline of the powers, the vitalizing of the faculties and the developing of self-activity. . . . But above all this the dominant principle in education and in the preparation for active life is the supreme importance of character. Christian education means the utilization of the best years of acquisition for founding deep broad principles of conduct. Expertness, capacity, knowledge, culture, all are valueless without character. There can be no true success, no real honor, no permanent good without character.[38]

The college made it clear that the dean of women would "have exclusive charge of the young women, and will accompany them when necessarily called to leave the College grounds."[39]

College curriculum and cocurricular activities reflected the importance of Victorian assumptions about culture for Protestants and Catholics. Typical of other colleges from this era, Whitworth adopted a curriculum where fully one-third of the credits centered on Roman and Greek history, politics, literature, and language. Campus life was dominated by literary societies, forensics, oratorical societies, and the evangelical YMCA (Young Men's Christian Association) and YWCA (Young Women's Christian Association). Colleges and universities offered young men and women myriad opportunities to participate in orchestras, bands, and archery, glee, and bicycle clubs. Sports—in particular football—were often portrayed as character-building activities designed to channel male aggression into healthier activities while appealing to "manly" competition.

It would be hard to overstate the degree to which each of these institutions of higher education in the Northwest placed a premium on controlling behavior—particularly male behavior. Smoking, dancing, and of course drinking were all banned. All forms of gambling were prohibited, along with the "writing of obscene words or drawing improper pictures in any part of the college premises."[40] At Lewis and Clark College in Portland, dancing and roller skating were forbidden. Social life centered on Friday night literary society meetings and singing marches. Rules and regulations governed the first men's literary society, Sigma Phi, which was organized in 1867, followed by the Erodelphian for women in 1871.[41] All of these measures helped cultivate Victorian culture.

The University of Puget Sound, a Methodist institution, offered another example of this emphasis on the supervision of female and male behavior. An early catalogue tried to assure parents:

> For young ladies care has been taken to provide cheerful and homelike surroundings. . . . Under [the preceptress's] careful guidance young women committed to our care will receive, as far as possible, the protection, training and environment of the best regulated home. The young men will have a well-situated dormitory . . . and a member of the faculty will live there and have oversight of affairs, thus providing that young lads away from home for the first time shall not be thrown alone into the midst of a large city, but shall have the moral restraint and influence consequent upon the presence of a respected superior.[42]

Lutherans in the Pacific Northwest were not to be outdone by other Protestant denominations. Six Lutheran colleges were established in the Northwest between 1890 and 1910, one by Swedes, one by Germans, and four by Norwegians. But according to historian Philip Nordquist, the region could probably have supported only one in an adequate manner.[43] Poulsbo, Everett, and Spokane all sported colleges, in addition to Parkland, where Pacific Lutheran took root and ultimately flourished, while the rest of the institutions failed. Like its sister institutions in the region, Pacific Lutheran stressed classical education and controlled behavior. The 1896 catalogue noted that attendance at daily chapel and Sunday services was required of all students. And just to be certain that there was no confusion about the intent of the institution regarding behavior, the catalogue indicated that the "government of the school may be characterized as parental. Patience and forbearance toward the weak and erring will not hinder the swift justice to the willful wrongdoer."[44]

Much the same story unfolded for Catholics. From the outset, Catholics had been a major force in the establishment of schools in the Northwest. As early as 1859, Catholic Sisters of the Holy Names established St. Mary's Academy in Portland, which remains Oregon's oldest continuously operating secondary school. By 1865, Holy Names schools operated in Oregon City, St. Paul, Salem, The Dalles, and Jacksonville. Likewise, as dioceses were established in the late nineteenth century in Washington state, Catholic schools sprang up throughout the region.

At the college and university level, Gonzaga, Seattle University, St. Martin's, and the University of Portland all were committed to maintaining a strong Catholic identity among their students, but they also reflected the same general commitment to the management of male behavior. For example, an early catalogue from Gonzaga emphasized that the "rules and regulations of the College are calculated to secure the order essential to the effectual pursuit of studies, to develop and strengthen character, and to promote gentlemanly deportment and good manners. They are enforced with paternal gentleness, combined with energy and firmness."[45]

Despite their churches' similarities of purpose, Catholic views on the consumption of alcohol were generally more tolerant than their Protestant counterparts. Despite this difference and a general ethos of competition and fear between Protestants and Catholics, the educational aims of these nineteenth-century religious institutions were similar in their several aims. Both Protestants and Catholics believed that education was moral in purpose. Spiritual discipline and intellectual rigor marked the ends pursued by priests and nuns throughout the Northwest. Philip Gleason, historian of Catholic higher education, makes clear how the cultivation of virtues such as "honor, fairness, honesty, truthfulness, self-reliance, [and] fortitude," as well as citizenship training, were all objectives espoused by Catholic educators throughout the country in the late nineteenth century.[46]

If any particular college president represented this effort to transplant Victorian culture into the "uncivilized" Pacific Northwest, it was Stephen Penrose at Whitman College in Walla Walla. As a young Congregationalist minister, Penrose arrived in Walla Walla in 1890. According to historian Tom Edwards, this preacher was one of six men—the "Yale band"—who were coming to preach in Washington's small towns.[47] Penrose took a pastoral call in the nearby town of Dayton, Washington, apparently intending not to stay very long. But during the next four years, Penrose regularly attended the Blue Mountain Chautauqua Literary Circle, taught Greek and Hebrew to a country editor, lectured to local audiences on topics ranging from astronomy to Whittier (the poet), played on a local baseball team, participated in public school programs, served as a city library director, and engaged in popular outdoor sports.[48]

Penrose embodied a Victorian worldview. He had studied philosophy at Williams College in Massachusetts and later received a master's degree in divinity from Yale. During Penrose's short term as pastor of the Congregational Church in Dayton, he attracted the attention of the board of trustees at Whitman and was soon offered the presidency in 1894, even though he was only thirty years of age.[49]

Penrose's impact on Whitman over the next three decades was remarkable. Like his counterparts, Penrose sought to establish the type of college he had experienced in the East, with an aim

Stephen Penrose helped bring Victorian cultural values to Whitman's early history. Courtesy Whitman College and Northwest Archives, Walla, Walla, Washington

toward transforming the culture of the region. He was fond of saying that the "primal purpose is to promote that Christian education which shall unite the resolute purpose which characterized Marcus Whitman with the lofty consecration of Cushing Eells [founder of Whitman College]. . . . Its aim is to give the most thorough education which it is possible for a student of the Northwest to receive, and to permeate that education with the finer spirit of Christ."[50] The

Whitman curriculum was classical in its focus, and Penrose himself taught Bible and philosophy. As was the case for all denominational colleges established in the region, Whitman's professors were hired not only to teach their subjects but to shape character. A professor at Whitman was responsible for admonishing those "who were lazy, untruthful, insubordinate, crude, or immoral."[51]

Penrose never wavered in his belief that education was as much about character as knowledge. In 1906, Penrose wrote, "It is the purpose of education, in my judgment, to help to live nobly. Training, technical training, helps to make a living. The State, according to our American system, cannot provide a complete education because at present time it omits the religious element."[52] Throughout Penrose's career, he believed that the Whitman faculty should comprise men and women of "Christian faith and character."[53]

If Penrose's commitment to Christianity and Victorian culture at Whitman was to be expected at a church-related institution, perhaps more surprising was the commitment of his counterparts at Washington State College and the University of Washington, who shared largely the same vision for education. At Washington State College, a key figure was Enoch Bryan, who served as president from 1893 to 1916. The son of a Presbyterian minister, Bryan grew up near Bloomington, Indiana. He graduated from the University of Indiana in 1878 and eventually became president of nearby Vincennes University. Like Atkinson, Penrose, Whitworth, and scores of other Victorians who came to the Pacific Northwest, Bryan believed in character training. On several occasions, beginning as early as the 1880s and extending through his early years at Washington State, Bryan lectured on "Character," which it appears was his favorite subject. He defined character as "an inward spiritual grace" involving "strength of mind and body as well as depth of soul."[54] In 1895, Bryan wrote letters to three parents and expressed "deep regret" that he had had to suspend their sons for visiting houses of prostitution in Moscow, Idaho, and getting drunk. "It is absolutely necessary," he wrote, "where a large number of young men are committed to our care to use every precaution to prevent debauchery and to insure good conduct."[55]

The early history of the University of Washington also reflects a strong dose of Victorian Christian culture, with an eye toward domesticating male behavior. In 1863, William Barnard, a graduate of Dartmouth, assumed the presidency. Prior to coming to Seattle,

Barnard had been a headmaster at several academies in New England. Once in his position at the University of Washington, Barnard expressed his disdain for Northwest culture, which he characterized as a disorganized society of "drunkenness, licentiousness, profanity, and Sabbath desecration."[56] Early on, he established a rule that "frequenting of saloons and attendance upon theaters and balls" would not be permitted. Barnard made sure that observance of the Sabbath and chapel services was part of the university program. Reading of the Scripture was announced as a daily exercise of the school. Students were required to be in their rooms at stated hours. Barnard's rules soon softened as attendance seemed to suffer, but the larger aim of managing male behavior and instilling Victorian values persisted.[57]

Atkinson, Whitworth, Penrose, Bryan, and Barnard, along with several Jesuit priests, all exerted significant influence over the character of education in the Pacific Northwest from the middle of the nineteenth century well into the twentieth, and in doing so, they sought to exert cultural influence over the emerging communities of the Northwest. These Christian educational leaders despised the lack of self discipline and the lack of order that exhibited itself in the saloon culture of the region. From the outset, they expected to use the legislative system to their advantage, but mostly they understood that education was the key to the advancement of their view of civilization.

As Victorians, Atkinson, Whitworth, Bryan, Penrose, and countless others clearly assumed that a civilized educated individual was punctual, neat, hardworking, and temperate—in the words of historian Louise Stevenson, "self-controlled."[58] They were outsiders to the prevailing Northwest culture that focused on satisfying the needs of single males in a social environment that privileged freedom and lack of restraint instead of self-discipline. To change the culture of the Northwest was a big task in the remote region that had been so attractive to the young itinerant male looking to escape poverty. One might marvel at the confidence these Victorians exhibited in their ability to bring "self-control" through the process of public and private schools.

In the end, the influence of Christians—both Catholic and Protestant—on the shaping of middle-class culture in the Pacific Northwest was significant. As more people arrived in Oregon and Washington in the late nineteenth and early twentieth centuries, education proved critical to the development of a professional middle class. Both explicit and implicit emphasis on Christian and Victorian values in the public schools waned as the twentieth century progressed. However, many private, religiously affiliated institutions survived, and some even flourished in the Pacific Northwest.

Male behavior, however, would continue to be a concern. And many women could not wait for a more domesticated Victorian male culture to evolve. Beginning in the late nineteenth century and extending well into the twentieth, religiously motivated women in the Pacific Northwest entered the public sphere for the purpose of transforming the region; they too focused on countering the results of a predominantly male-centered culture.

CHAPTER 2

WOMEN TO THE RESCUE

Valentine Prichard, like so many others in the mid-nineteenth century, migrated in a westerly direction with her family. Born in Massachusetts in 1862, she moved first to Illinois and then to California. Staunch Christians, Valentine's parents raised their daughter to find purpose and meaning in serving others. She first earned a degree in public health and then studied to be a kindergarten teacher. In 1898, she arrived in Portland, Oregon, and at the age of thirty-six assumed the position of kindergarten principal at St. Helens Hall. Shortly thereafter, she became the supervisor of kindergartens for all of Portland's public schools. But Valentine Prichard wanted to make a bigger impact. By 1904, with the help of Pastor Edgar Hill of the First Presbyterian Church, Prichard launched her dream: the People's Institute, a settlement house modeled after Jane Addams's Hull House in Chicago. A passionate Christian woman, Prichard became an activist and soon developed a multifaceted program that included an employment bureau for women, a dispensary that became the first free medical clinic in Portland, and an array of classes and services designed to assist the poor and recently arrived. At the end of her second year, she finished her annual report with her view of the role that Christianity was playing in the Pacific Northwest:

> The idea that the world is selfish, that one-half does not care how the other half lives, is all a fallacy. . . . It is true Christianity is everywhere becoming more and more practical in its application and work. It is a working together with God in this world for the uplifting and advancement of the human race. It is a seeking to lessen the pains and burdens of life

among the toilers and strugglers, and a reaching out after the children of poverty and want. It is the standing beside the lowly and ignorant with the hand of friendship extended. It is the giving of self with a heart of love, the preaching of Christ through the sympathetic word, the kindly deed, the thoughtful act. This is a Christianity which the world at large can understand and is ready to welcome.[1]

Prichard was only one of thousands of women who ended up in Washington and Oregon in the late nineteenth and early twentieth centuries who felt as she did. Christian and Jewish women met some of the most important social needs of the region. Without their tireless efforts, the Northwest would have been a much less livable place for virtually everyone. Certainly, whatever influence Northwest Christians and Jews achieved in changing the region's culture in this era was largely due to the efforts of unnumbered women.

The principal story focuses on an enormous effort to establish a safety net for the most vulnerable, to transform destructive male behaviors, and to create new social norms that broadly reflected a Christian and Jewish worldview; these reforms, women believed, were essential to the world in which they wanted to live and raise children. But it is also a story about women whose religious beliefs helped them see opportunity in the Pacific Northwest. Undaunted by the absence of established institutions or even the hint of a religiously friendly culture, these women were not confined by traditional roles or expectations. They leaned into a public sphere that was generally inhospitable to women, both politically and socially. In many ways, they were quintessential outsiders, not only to the prevailing culture of single men in the Northwest but also to a culture that protected white male privilege in the realm of public life.[2]

These religiously motivated women, however, were relentless in establishing their moral authority in the Pacific Northwest by address- ing issues that focused on the safety and well-being of women and children. Contrary to the prevailing mid-nineteenth–century "cult of domesticity" in which women were taught to stay out of the public sphere and confine themselves to the home and the raising of children, these women threw themselves into some of the era's most difficult social problems. Taking their lead from many of their female coun- terparts on the national scene, Northwest women tirelessly worked to transform the region's culture.

From the middle of the nineteenth through the early twentieth century, women in Washington and Oregon established rescue homes for prostitutes and unwed mothers, settlement houses, orphanages, asylums, libraries, and hospitals, as well as organizations such as the YWCA, the Council for Jewish Women, and various Catholic women's organizations. The vast majority of these institutions still exist today in communities throughout the region, and many of them still articulate mission statements based broadly on their religious roots. These women also spent countless hours pursuing the right to vote, as well as fighting to prohibit the use of alcohol. Even a cursory examination of the legacy of women who came to the Pacific Northwest reveals a remarkable degree of social commitment.

Perhaps the best-known religious women who arrived in the middle of the nineteenth century were the Sisters of Providence—most specifically, a woman known simply as "Mother Joseph." Her impact on the Northwest begins with the story of another noteworthy woman, Emmelie Gamelin. In one of those remarkable but not uncommon occurrences, Sister Gamelin, living in Montreal at the time, believed that God had provided her with a simple message that she should go and serve the poor. This mission from God surfaced after she had lost her husband and three children to illness in the 1820s.[3]

By 1843, now-Mother Gamelin had founded the international community called the Sisters of Providence. Soon these highly motivated women were working in the midst of typhoid epidemics and other diseases throughout Montreal. Mother Gamelin had heard that Augustin Magloire Alexandre Blanchet had become bishop in 1850 of the new diocese in Nesqually (originally bounded by the Columbia River on the south and the Cascade Mountains to the east), and her thoughts turned to the possibility of going west. Tragically, however, in 1851 she contracted typhus and died.[4]

Mother Gamelin's hopes and dreams were ultimately carried on by Esther Pariseau, who would later take the name Mother Joseph. Having been brought to Mother Gamelin's convent at age twenty in 1843, Esther Pariseau learned how to feed and clothe the poor and to wield a hammer and saw; but perhaps just as importantly, she learned how to organize and build institutions. By 1845, Esther Pariseau took the name Sister Joseph, the thirteenth Sister of Providence to take vows, and set about the task of fulfilling her vocation among the poor.[5]

In 1856, Bishop Blanchet asked the Sisters of Providence for help in the Northwest. Shortly thereafter, Sister Joseph, at thirty-three years old, was appointed superior of a group of five sisters and novices. Assigned to the Diocese of Nesqually, the sisters accepted the mission to serve the poor, sick, and non-Christian. The six Catholic women arrived by ship at Vancouver, just north of the Columbia River, in December 1856. With virtually nothing ready for them in a pioneer community still largely consisting of only a few wooden buildings, muddy streets, and enormous stands of Douglas fir, the sisters set out to meet the social needs of the community.[6] By spring 1857, their first school was ready to open. With an indefatigable

Mother Joseph and the Sisters of Providence left a lasting legacy of service throughout the Pacific Northwest. Courtesy of Archives of Roman Catholic Diocese of Spokane

spirit and boundless energy that would characterize the work of the sisters for the next several decades, they tended to the sick, spent nights with the critically ill, consoled families who lost loved ones, provided meals for the poor, and worked to educate orphans.[7]

By 1858, the sisters opened St. Joseph Hospital in Vancouver, which was the first permanent hospital in the Northwest. It still operates today as the Southwest Washington Medical Center. Mother Joseph and the sisters incorporated the Sisters of Charity of the House of Providence in 1859. This institution evolved into the parent corporation of the Sisters of Providence and is one of the oldest existing corporations in the Pacific Northwest. Shortly thereafter, the Sisters of Providence built a separate hospital for treatment of the mentally ill in Vancouver.

For Blanchet, the work of the sisters was critical in establishing a meaningful presence of the church in the Pacific Northwest. He repeatedly requested more sisters, and by 1877, fifty-three Sisters of Providence were working in the dioceses compared with seventeen priests. Over the next several decades, the sisters pushed northward to Puget Sound and into eastern Washington.[8]

The budding city of Spokane benefited tremendously from the work of Mother Joseph. In 1886, the Sisters of Providence arrived in town and began building the city's first hospital, Sacred Heart, which opened during the following year. Committed to serving the indigents of the city, the sisters provided food, housing, and work for many of the city's poor, in addition to hospitalization.[9]

By the time Mother Joseph died on January 19, 1902, the sisters operated seventeen hospitals and eight schools in Washington, Oregon, Montana, Idaho, California, and Alaska. But efforts did not cease with her death. The sisters continued to establish social service institutions in Everett, Medford, and Spokane. Called to serve the poor, the sick, and the needy, the sisters translated a simple mission into a vocation dedicated to establishing institutions that were staffed professionally and accessible to the poor.

Protestant women also provided significant health-care services in most of the communities in the Pacific Northwest. While not organized to the degree that the Sisters of Providence were, Protestant women nonetheless played a key role in the late nineteenth and early twentieth centuries. For example, in Spokane, historian Nancy Engle has detailed ways in which Protestant women felt responsible for creating local institutions that provided health care for the poor. These women believed that for Spokane to become "a respectable city," it needed to have adequate hospital care and sufficient homes for orphaned children. According to Engle, Protestant women strove for a "civic respectability imbued with their own sense of moral correctness."[10]

The story of Spokane's Deaconess Hospital illustrates the degree to which Protestant women made an impact on the city. The Deaconess movement began in 1888 at the national Methodist Episcopal General Conference. In the Pacific Northwest, the first Deaconess Board of Directors was organized in January 1892, through the efforts of Minnie Beard O'Neill of Spokane. Later that year, she and her husband gave the deaconesses a home to care for the city's sick and needy. In 1896, several individuals in Spokane, along with the recently arrived Dr. George Libby, agreed to establish the Maria Beard Deaconess Home of Spokane.[11] By 1900, the city was served by three hospitals, all of a religious character: Sacred Heart, founded in 1886; Deaconess, in 1896; and St. Luke's, in 1897. Clearly, the religious community created a foundation for what would be a signature identity for Spokane—health care.

While Catholic and Protestant women made a significant impact on health-care services, the most active grassroots women's organization in the late nineteenth and early twentieth centuries in the Pacific Northwest was the Woman's Christian Temperance Union (WCTU). Later generations often described the WCTU in caricatured terms as a group of pietistic women in blue stockings who, like the hatchet-wielding Carrie Nation, would stop at nothing to close down a saloon. A subsequent chapter will detail the union's efforts to achieve Prohibition, but the story of the WCTU in Washington and Oregon reveals a far more complex movement, and one that exerted a much broader influence than simply the effort to prohibit alcohol.[12]

The WCTU originated in Cleveland, Ohio, in 1874, in the aftermath of temperance efforts known as the "Woman's Crusade." Delegates elected Annie Wittenmyer as their first president, and she quickly focused her attention on a strict temperance program that emphasized education through moral persuasion. In 1879, Frances Willard succeeded Wittenmyer as president. She broadened the reach of the WCTU into a number of areas beyond temperance and pushed the organization to adopt political strategies. As president, Willard advocated female suffrage, birth control, "social purity," prison reform, and fair treatment of prostitutes and women in the courts. She urged the adoption of the eight-hour workday and a "living wage" for all workers.[13]

Willard's theology centered on the belief that individuals should work for the implementation of God's kingdom on earth. She wanted to link the WCTU with the National Prohibition Party and later the Progressive Party. She also pushed hard for the WCTU to become active in child labor issues and to advocate for women who were being exploited in the workplace. Willard's indefatigable spirit and relentless energy helped grow the WCTU membership from approximately 27,000 in 1879 to over 150,000 members by the time of her death in 1898.[14] According to one historian, by the end of the nineteenth century Willard had built the WCTU into "one of the most powerful vehicles in the United States for addressing women's issues and producing strong, independent women, who entered the public world, determined to change it."[15] This proved to be her legacy in the Pacific Northwest as well.

In Oregon, the WCTU officially began in 1880, and in the following year Rebecca Clawson organized the first local WCTU group in Portland.[16] But Frances Willard herself played a significant role in the initial development of the WCTU in the Pacific Northwest. In 1883, four years after being named president of the WCTU, Willard made a trip to California, Oregon, Washington, and Idaho—the latter two were still territories. Her presence helped organize WCTU chapters throughout the region.

The WCTU adopted the motto "Protection of the Home," and much of their work focused on protecting women from predatory male behavior. Local chapters or unions, as they were called, found working women, single women, and single mothers all feeling vulnerable to destructive male behavior, particularly in the urban West. In many Northwest communities, WCTU women initiated the "noon rest," where they would try to provide support services for any woman who was stranded in the city.[17] The WCTU often deployed matrons at railway stations who identified young women coming to the city looking for work without friends, family, or financial support.[18] The WCTU established homes and shelters for unwed mothers, hoping to instill domestic skills and Christian virtues among former prostitutes. The first such rescue homes were established nationally in 1882. By 1888, the first shelter, called the White Shield Home, was organized in Tacoma and became a major project of the WCTU for many years.[19] Portland's first home was founded in 1887 and two years later was reorganized into the Women's Refuge Home for Fallen Women.

Meanwhile, a parallel movement was developing out of a partnership between Francis Willard and philanthropist Charles Nelson Crittenton. A former businessman in the drug industry, Crittenton had been devastated by the death of his five-year-old daughter, Florence. He subsequently devoted his life to serving homeless and unwed mothers with infant children. In 1889, Crittenton provided modest amounts of money to support homes that would bear his daughter's name, and soon these efforts bore fruit in the Pacific Northwest. In Portland, a home was established in 1892, and it proved so successful that the state of Oregon appropriated $7,500 per year in support of these shelters. Soon, Crittenton's efforts extended throughout the Northwest and resulted in homes in Spokane and Seattle as well.[20] Training women mostly to be domestic servants, these homes provided shelter for a year or more and offered exposure to religious activity on a daily basis.

WCTU women believed that establishing a web of social institutions that would educate, protect, and provide alternatives to the gambling hall, saloon, and brothel was critical. In some Northwest communities, WCTU women organized town libraries and developed the first reading rooms; literacy was high on the union's agenda for social reform.[21] In both Oregon and Washington, WCTU chapters initiated kindergartens to aid working women who needed care for their children. In other communities, WCTU women worked to establish reform schools for juvenile delinquents. The Coffee Club, an idea nearly a century ahead of its time, proved to be popular in towns throughout the region as women sought to provide an alternative to the saloon for young men looking for a social gathering place.

Several women played critical roles in the organization of the union throughout the region. For example, Mary Bynon Reese provided remarkable leadership in the early years, and her story suggests some of the difficulty associated with working in the Pacific Northwest. Born in Allegheny, Pennsylvania, in 1832, Reese found herself caught up in the Woman's Crusade of 1874 when she was first arrested for her attempts to close down a saloon. From that point, her life's ambitions revolved around temperance work. Reese came to the Pacific Northwest in 1886 and began organizing local unions. She spoke to Nez Perce Indians through an interpreter, and she met with lumbermen in their camps. Reese estimated that she traveled over six thousand miles, "hundreds of which were by wagon, stage and private conveyance, some by canoe with the Indians, and some on horseback through otherwise inaccessible places."[22] Selected as the honorary president of the Western Washington WCTU, Reese remained in the Seattle area until she passed away in 1908.

African American participation in the WCTU was limited due in part to the small numbers of black women in the Northwest, but fifteen women in Seattle's First African Methodist Episcopal Church did organize the Frances Harper Colored Unit within the WCTU. Harper, an African American abolitionist, later organized black chapters within the WCTU. In Seattle, the first chapter president was a former slave, Emma Ray. Under Ray's leadership, the unit worked primarily in Seattle's red-light district in the Yesler-Jackson area of the city. Ray specifically ministered to prostitutes and those who were imprisoned.[23]

Women in the WCTU boldly criticized the largely male and often violent culture of the Northwest.[24] In address after address, pamphlet after pamphlet, women of the WCTU attempted to raise awareness of young males' use of violence against others; this violence had disastrous consequences for women and children. In March 1908, the

White Ribbon Bulletin: Official Organization of the Western Washington Chapter of the WCTU, stated,

> It must be held that the state cannot under the guise of a license delegate to the saloon business a legal existence, because to hold that it can is to hold that the state may sell and delegate the right to make widows and orphans, the right to break up homes, the right to create misery and crime, the right to make murderers, the right to produce idiots and lunatics, the right to fill orphanages, poorhouses, insane asylums, jails and penitentiaries and the right to furnish subjects for the hangman's gallows.[25]

WCTU leaders frequently lamented the double standard for men and women when it came to moral behavior. "We expect our girls to grow up in purity and honor; we demand it of them, and we hurl the anathemas of society against her who steps aside from the path marked out for her," proclaimed Margaret Platt, an early WCTU president from western Washington. "Why not expect and demand honor and purity of our boys as well[?] ...We condemn in unmeasured terms the moral fall of a woman—why do we condone the errors of her brothers and pass them over lightly as sowing of 'wild oats'[?]"[26]

Remarkably, union members found the means to organize themselves in ways that both challenged the existing social order and created a sense of identity as women. As historian Sandra Haarsager noted, "The WCTU fostered organized womanhood in the Pacific Northwest, developing among members a sense of connection, of personal and collective identity, of community service, and of power."[27]

Women from the WCTU spent tens of thousands of hours sending countless letters to legislators in Olympia and Salem, organizing thousands of marches and pickets, sponsoring essay contests, and pushing school districts to educate students on the health risks associated with drug and alcohol consumption and smoking, as well as the bad influence of certain literature and moving pictures.[28] In fact, the union in western Washington directed intensive lobbying on behalf of legislation that raised the age from twelve to eighteen before one could purchase cigarettes.[29] In Oregon, WCTU activists Bethenia Owens Adair and Anna Riggs helped introduce legislation that would raise the age of consent for sexual activity from fourteen years to eighteen. While initially defeated, voters eventually did raise the age.[30]

As will be seen in a subsequent chapter, the WCTU played a major role in the passage of legislation that made illegal the sale of alcohol in the Pacific Northwest. But the legacy of the WCTU is much deeper. In attacking a dominant male culture, women of the WCTU established what historian Barbara Epstein has called a "protofeminist culture throughout the organization."[31] In other words, the WCTU made it possible for many women in the Northwest to develop both skills and self-confidence in the political arena. Hundreds of women developed a female consciousness and a sense of connection to one another that helped create a powerful force within Pacific Northwest politics.[32] The WCTU helped break down spheres of influence that had separated men from women in the nineteenth century, and in doing so it helped create a dynamic that led to social changes in the emerging culture of the Pacific Northwest in the twentieth century.

The late nineteenth century was a fertile period in the American West for hundreds of women who sought to make an impact on their communities. As historian Peggy Pascoe has written, "Appalled by the overwhelming masculine milieu of western cities and influenced by the Victorian belief that women should be pious and pure moral guardians, [middle-class Protestant women] set out to 'rescue' female victims of male abuse."[33] In cities throughout the West and Pacific Northwest, women set about the task of trying to establish a "middle-class Protestant woman's vision of moral order in their new communities."[34]

While the WCTU in the Pacific Northwest emerged as a major player in the battle for cultural influence, the settlement house movement also established a toehold in Portland and Seattle and played a significant role in both assimilating immigrants and mitigating the role of male behavior. The most famous advocates of the settlement movement were Jane Addams and Ellen Gates Starr. Together they opened Hull House in 1889 in Chicago in an effort to assist European immigrants, as well as to provide protection for women and children. In Portland, the creation of a settlement house was mostly the work of the well-to-do Caroline Ladd and her daughter Helen Ladd Corbett. The aforementioned Valentine Prichard, who was the supervisor of the public school kindergartens in 1902, along with Reverend Edgar Hill of Portland's First Presbyterian Church, worked closely with Ladd and Corbett. The Ladd family donated property at Fourth and Burnside for what was called a Men's Resort, with the stipulation that space

Valentine Prichard stood out for her commitment to serving Portland's poor in the early twentieth century. Courtesy Oregon Health Sciences Historical Collections and Archives, Portland, Oregon

be provided for comparable work with women and children. Heavily supported by First Presbyterian, the women established what became known as the People's Institute in 1904. Modeled on Jane Addams's Hull House, the People's Institute filled a significant role in the lives of many Portland newcomers.

Prichard, meanwhile, scoured the neighborhood with her staff, visited more than five hundred homes trying to locate children who were in need of education, and quickly developed a kindergarten. Children in Prichard's Kitchen Garden and Little Housekeepers classes, from eight to twelve years old, were taught basic housekeeping skills such as washing, ironing, sweeping, dusting, scrubbing, making beds, and setting tables. The Girls' Cooking School offered basic culinary lessons and instruction on serving for girls twelve years old and older. There was also a cooking school for boys. The underlying concern for male behavior was always in evidence. The boys who belonged to the brigade pledged to forsake "swearing and bad language of every kind; the use of intoxicating liquors as a beverage; Sabbath breaking; places and company associated with evil; falsehood, dishonesty and meanness; dirty habits; [and] disobedience to parents and teachers."[35] Religious instruction at the institute included a Sunday school and children's choir program, and the Mother's Club, organized in 1906.[36]

The institute advocated for a number of public policies, including the inspection of dance halls and the early closing of stores that employed women. Working with the Juvenile Improvement Association, the institute helped establish censorship of motion pictures in Portland. With the Consumers League, it pushed for a new housing code and with the health board worked for better sanitation in the city. The People's Institute organized a Traveler's Aid Society, promoted rigid enforcement of the curfew law, worked for the licensing of newsboys, and secured a State Industrial School for Girls. The list of accomplishments included the organization of home nursing classes with the Red Cross and well-baby clinics with the Infant Welfare Society. Following the 1906 San Francisco earthquake, the People's Institute was transformed into an emergency hospital to care for the scores of hungry and ill refugees who poured into Portland. Volunteers met trains from 7:30 a.m. until 11:00 p.m. each day to greet the refugees, who were then fed, clothed, and given medical attention. In 1907 a free dispensary was added to the institute's projects.[37]

In the second decade of the twentieth century, the People's Institute continued to expand. In 1912 a large number of the clubs and classes were transferred to a site in Lower Albina (northeast Portland), where a branch of the institute had been opened in 1910. In 1913 another branch was opened in South Portland. From 1914 to 1918 the institute cooperated with federal and state agencies to address community needs. Their activities included making surgical dressings, weighing and measuring babies, establishing milk stations, and providing medical relief for World War I soldiers' families. Gradually, the People's Institute was replaced by other social service agencies, but without question it made a significant contribution to the social well-being of Portland in the first three decades of the twentieth century.[38]

Women in the Jewish community also influenced immigrant life in Portland and Seattle through settlement houses. Like the organizers of the People's Institute, Jewish women took their lead from Jane Addams's work in Chicago. In Portland, the Jewish settlement house, or "Neighborhood House" as it came to be called, was founded by Ida Loewenberg and Rabbi Stephen Wise in 1905.[39] The Neighborhood House became one of the most important social institutions in south Portland by providing classes, offering health services, and sponsoring athletic events. Organizers tried to inculcate a sense of self-reliance and civic responsibility among immigrant Jews. [40] However, the Neighborhood House also served other immigrant groups; approximately half of the students were non-Jewish. Growing demand for services dictated that by 1910 a new building was constructed, which housed a swimming pool, handball courts, a stage, boxing areas, and wrestling and weightlifting rooms. [41] The Neighborhood House published its own newspaper and continued to add athletic, social, music, and literary clubs, as well as an orchestra and theater group.

In 1906 in Seattle, Jewish women, led by Babette Schwabacher Gatzert, established their own settlement house after several years of raising money through rummage sales, luncheons, vaudeville performances, card parties, and dances. Two years later, Hannah Schwartz took over the leadership of the house and served for fourteen years. Settlement House, as it was called, offered an array of programs, including a free religious school, sewing classes, night school for English instruction, a branch library, citizenship classes, free baths (the first in Seattle), free medical care for the needy, a nurse to visit homes, and social clubs for young people. By all accounts, this institution became a vital part of the Jewish community and served the needs of countless immigrants. [42]

By far the most important of these Jewish organizations were the local chapters of the National Council for Jewish Women (NCJW). First established in Chicago in 1893, the NCJW came out of the Reformed Jewish community. The Seattle chapter of the NCJW, organized in 1900, played a major role in the establishment of the Settlement House mentioned earlier, and it also helped found the Caroline Kline Galland Home for the Aged in Seattle, which was still operating in 2015. [43] The Portland chapter of the NCJW, founded in 1896, grew into one of the city's most important social organizations. [44] It took on issues of prostitution and venereal disease. After World War I, the council pressed the Oregon state legislature for public kindergartens and advocated for pensions for widows, as well as increased welfare programs and improved working conditions for women. The net impact of Jewish activity on Portland's civic and social life was significant. These women, with little training or experience outside the home, drew the attention of politicians, business leaders, and community activists. Historian Steven Lowenstein called the Council for Jewish Women "a truly remarkable organization . . . [that] was the most effective and respected organization in the Jewish community addressing the major social and economic issues of the day."[45]

The same social forces that had moved Jewish women to become involved in the life of their respective communities also influenced the work of the Young Women's Christian Association (YWCA) in the Pacific Northwest. With roots going back to London, England, in 1855, the YWCA established its first chapter in the United States in New York City in 1858. The YWCA, like the Young Men's Christian Association, had a distinctly Protestant evangelical background, which in the mid-nineteenth century fostered a strong commitment to social justice and reform. Along with the YMCA, the YWCA emerged as one of the most important social institutions in the Pacific Northwest, becoming one of the most visible expressions of Christianity in budding urban communities.

Established mostly in the 1890s, the YWCA chapters in Seattle, Portland, Tacoma, and Spokane moved quickly to provide service and protection to single women who were looking to find work in the cities of the Northwest. The Portland YWCA offered ten-cent lunches and a safe refuge for women. The Traveler's Aid program was started in 1900 to meet the needs of hundreds of women arriving alone at urban docks and railroad stations. YWCA founders also created "female-only" space, where women could gather to hear the Gospel—a central facet of the YWCA's mission at that time. Meanwhile, social services continued to expand, including boarding rooms, a tea room, a cafeteria, and cooking and domestic science courses.[46]

In Seattle and other Northwest cities, a similar pattern unfolded. In 1894, Rees P. Daniels, who had been active in the YWCA in Washington, DC, helped organize the Seattle chapter. Again, protecting young women from predatory males was a central concern. The YWCA sponsored railroad matrons who patrolled train stations looking for any young woman who might be unclear as to her destination. One of numerous women who took on this task, Susan Stine, met as many as thirty-eight trains daily in Seattle and spent an average of thirteen to fourteen hours a day, 320 days a year, in order to help young women avoid men of questionable character.[47]

The Seattle YWCA established a noon rest hour for young women, along with the provision of ten-cent lunches. In 1906, the YWCA served the city's many homeless by providing food, shelter, and clothing to over two thousand refugees from the San Francisco earthquake. In 1914, the Seattle YWCA opened its own building, with a cafeteria, Turkish baths, swimming pool, gymnasium, hotel, clubrooms, and a vocational school. It offered classes in dressmaking, millinery, cafeteria work, tearoom management, practical nursing, manicuring, and salesmanship. Preparation for marriage and domestic work, with an emphasis on cooking, was the subject of the course in home economics. The YWCA worked closely with the business community, arranging job placements and lobbying for better working conditions for women.[48]

While the YWCA helped protect women, other Christians (mostly women) attempted to address concerns about the growing numbers of orphans in the Pacific Northwest. The earliest effort in the region to meet the needs of orphans seems to have occurred in 1847 when Tabitha Brown, who had come west on the Oregon Trail a year earlier, organized what she called the "Orphan Asylum" in Forest Grove, Oregon. She had witnessed firsthand a number of children who had lost their parents to hardship or disease on the trail. In 1848, with the onset of the California gold rush, many widowed men headed for the goldfields and left their children with "Grandma Brown" at the asylum. She, in effect, served as a teacher, manager, and housekeeper.[49] In that same year, a group of Congregational and Presbyterian ministers founded an academy at the site of the Tabitha Brown's Orphan Asylum, which eventually became Pacific University.[50]

Concern for orphans across the country had grown since the middle of the nineteenth century, when the Reverend Charles Loring Brace founded New York's Children's Aid Society. Brace hoped to rescue impoverished children from cities and "place them out West in good Christian families where they would be cared for, educated, and employed."[51] By 1890, an estimated eighty-four thousand children had been placed with families in the Midwest and West, but the need for placement continued to increase, and Brace could not keep up with the need. By that time, other organizations began to spring up, including the Children's Home Society in 1896.[52]

Two individuals made significant contributions: Methodist minister Reverend Harrison D. Brown and his wife, Libbie Beach Brown. They differed little from the thousands of Catholics, Protestants, and Jews who came to the region in the late nineteenth century, armed more with missionary zeal than with significant financial resources. Moved by many encounters with orphaned children, the Browns became convinced that the best strategy was to place children in homes and not in institutions.[53] Arriving first in Portland in 1895, the Browns encountered some resistance to their ideas. Undaunted, they moved to Seattle, where Reverend Brown took the pastorate at the Battery Street Methodist Episcopal Church. Shortly thereafter, the Browns' living room became the headquarters for the Children's Home Society.[54]

Their efforts were timely. In 1897, the Klondike gold rush frenzy exacerbated the problem of abandoned children just as the earlier California gold rush had done. In that year, Libbie Beach Brown took over as superintendent of the Children's Home Society. She assumed the principal role of identifying families in the community that would provide appropriate homes for the growing numbers of orphans. She visited homes and supervised the care to the best of her ability.[55]

By 1899, the need for homes for orphans outstripped the available supply, and the Browns sought help from the Washington State legislature. The couple lobbied for legislation that would allow the court to take children out of abusive situations and place them in organizations like their Children's Home Society. The legislature agreed, and the society was given authority to investigate child abuse and to remove children from what were determined to be "improper and vicious surroundings." The society, though, wanted additional protection for all children and worked for the establishment of a juvenile court, which the state legislature approved in 1905.[56]

Libbie Brown had other counterparts who were motivated by their Christian beliefs and felt a particular need to help children who were vulnerable to life's circumstances. Among the more well known was Olive Hannah Ryther, who came to be known simply as Mother Ryther. In 1867, Olive married Noble Ryther, a carpenter from Iowa. Active in the Methodist Church, the two soon had three children. Work must have been scarce, because Noble Ryther left the family in Iowa in 1874 as a consequence of the financial panic of 1873 and came to Seattle. Job prospects were not much better in the Pacific Northwest. Ryther lived at the City Mission on Seattle's waterfront, but he also took responsibility for ministering to indigent men by helping provide food and shelter. Whenever he could, Ryther built houses for other people and sent back part of his earnings to Olive. In 1881, Noble built a cabin and was able to send for the family.

In that same year, while caring for a neighbor who was about to die, Olive promised that she and Noble would adopt the woman's four children and raise them as their own. Aware that Seattle had a shortage of orphanage facilities, the Rythers promised never to turn an orphaned child away. Soon their cabin was filled with children, and they subsequently moved to a larger home in the Central Area neighborhood. Taking a job as cook at the City Mission, Olive Ryther focused her attention on the needs of prostitutes. Eventually, Seattle officials recognized her value and appointed her to be the women's jail matron. However, because the jail did not have separate facilities for women, the Rythers housed female prisoners in barricaded upstairs rooms in their own home. [57]

The Rythers responded to more unmet need by founding the City Mission Foundling Home in 1883 for unwed mothers and their babies. At about that time, more and more people began to refer to Olive as "Mother" Ryther in recognition of the way she tended to pregnant unwed women and prostitutes. Her philosophy centered on trying to make these women self-sufficient. She required all of those living in her home to do chores and care for infants and eventually provide day care for the children of other women who were able to work during the day.

As the 1890s unfolded, the Rythers increasingly focused on orphaned and abandoned children. Olive worked closely with Emma Ray, the aforementioned African American woman who was active in the WCTU. Between them, the two frequented the waterfront looking for orphans as well as donations.[58] According to historian Mildred Andrews, Ryther "worked tirelessly, caring for her children and nursing those who were sick or injured. In a house with no plumbing, she and members of her growing family cooked, gardened, cleaned, milked cows, and gathered eggs."[59] Ryther sought ways to send all of her orphaned children to the Seattle public schools, and she expected "her boys" to learn a trade by sixteen and girls to pursue a business degree. For years, she made her operation work by depending on her personal relationships with people throughout the Seattle area. Once the *Seattle Times* reported that when twenty-five of her children needed shoes, she marched into the local shoe store and asserted, "These children are staying here until you fit them all with shoes—that'll be your contribution to the Ryther Home."[60] By the time she died in 1934, it was estimated that she and her staff had cared for thirty-one hundred children over fifty-one years of service.

Another woman who contributed significantly to the well-being of children was Anna Clise. In 1899, she and her husband, James, and young son, Willis, moved to Seattle. At age five, Willis died of inflammatory rheumatism, and Anna learned firsthand that the health services in the city were inadequate for children. According to historian Emilie Schwabacher, "True to her Mennonite training, Anna Clise researched the potential of a children's hospital."[61] She traveled across the country, drawing from the lessons of existing children's hospitals in New York and Philadelphia. Inspired by what she saw, Anna Clise returned to Seattle and shared her vision of a hospital dedicated to the care of children with twenty-three of her female friends. In February 1907, in a small ward of an existing hospital, their shared vision became a reality. In its first year, the new hospital took care of thirteen children; the next year, the number increased to thirty-nine. Soon, the need for care exceeded their capacity. Clise found enough supporters to build a house on Queen Anne Hill, north of downtown Seattle, and named it "Fresh Air Cottage." Eventually Clise's efforts culminated in the establishment of the Children's Orthopedic Hospital, which became one of Seattle's most important health-care facilities.[62]

If one other woman helps reveal the many ways in which religiously motivated activists exercised significant influence over the public life of the Pacific Northwest, it is Lola Baldwin. Born in 1860 in Elmira, New York, Lola moved with her parents to Rochester. Eventually she became a teacher and then headed west in 1880 to Lincoln, Nebraska, where she met and married LeGrand Baldwin. She quit teaching and soon gave birth to two sons. But her biographer suggests that her upbringing in the "Burned-Over" district of New York, with its legacy of religious and social activism, left a deep impression. "Baldwin was inculcated from her youth with a zealous female reform impulse which seemed to be a definitive local trait," according to biographer Gloria Myers. "An above-average number of women from that region became involved in the most important social reform movements of the nineteenth century. Operating at first within the confines of church-based 'moral reform' societies, middle-class women began to attack the vices which they felt were threatening the home."[63]

Baldwin's commitment to the well-being of other women first emerged in her volunteer work for a Nebraska Rescue Home for unwed mothers. And while the Baldwins moved several times during the next ten years to cities that included Boston, Yonkers, Norfolk, and

Lola Baldwin not only served as Portland's first policewoman, but she embodied a commitment to the city's moral order. Courtesy Oregon Historical Society, Portland, Oregon

Providence, in each case she found herself engaged in volunteer work among women. In 1904, her husband's company, the E. P. Charlton Company of Fall River, Massachusetts, asked him to move to Portland to open a new merchandising outlet. Once again, Baldwin followed her husband and took up volunteer work, in this case with Portland's Florence Crittenton Home.[64]

When they reached Portland, preparations were well under way for Portland's first major tourist event—the centennial celebration of the Lewis and Clark Expedition. However, city leaders were worried about the possibility of unscrupulous men preying on innocent women who had come to the city either for employment or entertainment. The WCTU, the Council for Jewish Women, and the YWCA all had begun to rally around this concern and had created another arm of the Traveler's Aid Society. Rabbi Stephen Wise of Temple Beth Israel enthusiastically supported the idea not only because it was preventive and protective but also because of its ecumenical spirit.[65] At about that time, Baldwin became known to religious leaders in the city as a person who might be suited to lead the newly formed Traveler's Aid operation. She accepted the offer of $75 a month.[66]

Once the fair began, Baldwin made sure that volunteers from Traveler's Aid met virtually every train that came into the city. It often became a race to see who could be first to reach the young women who arrived by the scores each week—Baldwin's volunteers or the agents of Portland's many houses of prostitution. Baldwin committed herself to never leaving a girl alone "for an instant."[67] She and her workers offered the newly arrived women lodging and employment opportunities. By the fair's end in October 1905, it was estimated that 1,640 women and girls had been served in one way or another.[68]

Soon, Baldwin began lobbying Portland city officials for more resources to continue the work of protection from and prevention of violence against women in the city. Citing the amount of money designated for the city dog pound, she asked rhetorically whether authorities cared as much for the city's "straying daughters" as they did for "straying dogs." Largely due to her lobbying, the city council appropriated funds for a female detective in the police department. In 1908, the Portland Police Department swore in Lola Baldwin as the city's first policewoman. She happened to be the first policewoman in the United States to be hired with regular enforcement duties.[69]

Almost immediately, Baldwin began investigating rooming houses, fortune tellers, massage parlors, and businesses such as bowling alleys and shooting galleries that hired "pretty young girls."[70] But the issue that attracted much of her early efforts as Portland's policewoman was the regulation of dance halls. In many ways, the dance hall was an alternative to the saloon for women who spent ten to twelve hours working in often unsafe, tedious jobs in the growing industrial economy. The lure of "cheap amusement" and the possibility of being taken on a "date" by a man who might well expect sexual favors in return proved to be attractive to young working women, as well as to pimps, drunkards, and known prostitutes. Shocking to a Victorian world that emphasized the importance of sexual restraint and supervised relationships between the genders, dance halls reflected the complex struggle of the time between working-class women and Victorian culture.[71] In 1908, Portland judge John Van Zandt observed that most of the delinquent girls who were being prosecuted blamed the dance hall in some way or another as the place where they "went astray."[72]

From the time she assumed her duties in 1908 until the passage of the dance hall ordinance in 1913, Baldwin helped spearhead the effort to change the culture of the working class as well as the emerging middle class in Portland. As one might imagine, the ability to regulate or prohibit certain forms of dancing was fraught with difficulty, but in the end, Baldwin and other reformers prevailed by mandating that the waltz would become the only allowable form of dancing. Baldwin and her supporters influenced dance behavior in Portland for many years in an attempt to moderate sexual activity among young adults. In doing so, Lola Baldwin helped make the policewoman a censor.[73]

Baldwin's work and influence extended well beyond the dance hall. Vaudeville shows in the early twentieth century again proved to be a form of culture where Victorian mores clashed with immigrant working-class values, as well as those of the urban middle class. In 1910, Baldwin openly clashed with Sophie Tucker, the vaudeville star from the William Morris circuit. Although Baldwin's supervisor, a male chief of the Portland police force, ultimately saw nothing wrong with Ms. Tucker's stage interpretation, Baldwin had Sophie Tucker arrested for what she considered indecent behavior and precipitated a major public controversy.[74]

Throughout her fourteen years as a paid officer on the police force, Lola Baldwin relentlessly attempted to change cultural life in Portland. She persistently worked in areas related to the protection of underage females in saloons and movie houses. She worked to limit the distribution of pornography. She exposed charlatans who paraded under the guise of being "Christian" in hopes of avoiding the law.[75] Baldwin believed that Portland could become a morally redeemed city by her standards. She dedicated her work to the preservation of traditional standards. Baldwin believed that the Victorian affirmation of moral purity could be sustained only through a thoroughgoing commitment of governmental, religious, and educational institutions.[76] There are few better examples of the ways in which Christian women attempted to transform Northwest culture through the adoption of a Victorian way of life.

CONCLUSION

The legacy of activism on many fronts by religiously motivated women in the late nineteenth and early twentieth centuries is a rich one. The nascent urban environments were hardly hospitable toward their efforts. In almost every case, they faced significant obstacles in pursuit of their dreams. Yet these female activists persisted with almost herculean effort to protect vulnerable women and children. These women believed that they needed to restrain men from exhibiting immoral and destructive behaviors. While success is difficult to measure, there seems little doubt that these activists helped change the culture.

From Mother Joseph and Mother Ryther to Ida Loewenberg and Lola Baldwin, Protestant, Catholic, and Jewish women, out of deep religious conviction, transformed the social landscape of the region. From hospitals, schools, libraries, and orphanages to settlement houses, the WCTU, and YWCAs, women embraced and led the challenge of developing the Pacific Northwest into a place that would be suitable for men, women, and children. They challenged the prevailing norm that discouraged women from taking an active role in public affairs. Their early feminism in both advocacy for women and direct involvement in the public square identified them as outsiders to the prevailing culture, but they left a lasting mark on the culture of the region.

These women, however, were not alone. A significant number of male activists—mostly pastors, priests, and rabbis—joined in the effort to change the culture of the Northwest. They too centered much of their activity on trying to manage the behavior of males. In that effort, a remarkable consensus emerged around religious activism's role in the public square.

CHAPTER 3

THE SOCIAL GOSPEL

The streets in this part of the city literally swarm with men. . . .
Mills, factories, foundries, railroad terminal yards, wharves, river
and sea craft of all descriptions abound within and around this
locality. . . . Thousands of men pour into this part of town from
railroad, mining and logging camps from the farms and smaller
towns. In the main these men are under middle age, and many
are husky farm lads in their teens and twenties. Among them
are many foreigners. . . . The fact that more arrests are made
and more crimes are committed within these confines than in
any other part of the city is not to be wondered at when the
character of its institutions of vice is considered.

—*Eleventh Annual Report of the Men's Resort and People's
Institute*[1]

Written in 1907 by an anonymous observer, this description of
Portland city life could easily have described similar conditions
in Seattle, Tacoma, and Spokane in the early twentieth century.
While Northwest cities did not have the flood of European immigrants experienced by New York, Philadelphia, Boston, and Chicago, nevertheless the growth was considerable. Seattle's population
surged from 42,837 in 1890 to 237,194 in 1910; in those same two
decades, Portland's expanded from 46,385 to 207,214, and Spokane's
population increased from 19,922 to just over 104,000. Urbanization
in the Northwest presented both challenges and opportunities for
religiously motivated individuals and organizations. On one hand,
the growth of cities helped develop a critical mass of institutions
such as schools, churches, and libraries that were designed to foster a Victorian American culture. On the other hand, as we have
seen, myriad social problems accompanied the saloons, gambling

halls, and houses of prostitution that also came from urbanization. In addition, the Pacific Northwest experienced significant
economic depressions triggered by the financial crises of 1893 and
1907, and the region became known at the turn of the century for
its deep labor unrest. Many residents of the Northwest struggled
with inadequate health care, poor housing, and a lack of child care
for working mothers. Young men struggled with unemployment
and underemployment in poor working conditions. Throughout
the Northwest, cities were plagued by massive corruption and an
inadequate infrastructure of public services.

This was the context that motivated pastors, priests, and rabbis
across the country and in the Pacific Northwest to become engaged
in political activity and social reform. At root was the ongoing concern that adolescent and adult males were vulnerable to corrupting
social influences in the city. There was the perception, along with
empirically verifiable facts, that crime, alcohol abuse, and other
forms of deviant behavior mushroomed in these urban environments.
Throughout the United States, "moral reformers" developed strategies for mitigating the worst behaviors. On one hand, they fought
for legislation that prohibited the consumption of alcohol and the
existence of dance halls. On the other hand, they also fought to
establish a public and private school system that would help nurture
moral values as well as equip students increasingly for the middle
class. For most religious activists, small-town America provided a
framework for their belief about what community life should be in
the city. According to historian Paul Boyer, "Common to almost
all the reformers . . . the city, although obviously different from the
village in its external, physical aspects, should nevertheless replicate
the moral order of the village. City dwellers, they believed, must
somehow be brought to perceive themselves as members of cohesive
communities knit together by shared moral and social values."[2]

Across the country, religious reformers and organizations threw
themselves into a variety of causes. None was more visible or well
known than New York City Presbyterian minister Charles Parkhurst.
Most famous for his work in the 1890s in New York City, where he
denounced the city's moral climate, he worked tirelessly on behalf
of reforms he believed would end corruption and improve the city.
Likewise, Charles Sheldon, a Congregational minister, wrote an enormously influential book in 1896 entitled *In His Steps*, which asked the

question "What would Jesus do?" if he lived in America today. Would he not be about the business of trying to banish vice, intemperance, and social injustice from the city? Hundreds of pastors took Sheldon's question seriously and became engaged in social reform.[3]

Intertwined with this effort to generate a moral awakening in many American cities was what came to be known as the Social Gospel movement. Largely centered in the industrial Northeast and Midwest, Social Gospel ministers addressed issues associated with the massive numbers of immigrants who had come to the United States in the late nineteenth century. Protestant clergy from a variety of denominations—most notably Presbyterians, Congregationalists, Unitarians, Episcopalians, and Methodists, along with Catholic priests and Jewish rabbis—engaged issues related to public health, legal aid, employment assistance, and other social services. They tackled alcohol, child labor, public hygiene, and municipal corruption.[4] Central to the belief of many who considered themselves advocates of the Social Gospel was the emphasis to try to realize the Kingdom of God on Earth. As one scholar wrote, the Social Gospel was an "indictment of the complacency of a Protestantism that had become too comfortable, individualistic, and otherworldly."[5]

Many religious leaders who arrived in the Northwest during the late nineteenth and early twentieth centuries were influenced by these reform impulses associated with moral awakening and the Social Gospel. Virtually all of the issues dealt with by socially inclined clergy in other parts of the country were found in the Pacific Northwest and addressed there by individuals who had directly encountered the Social Gospel in the Midwest, East, and even the South. The concerns for women and children, the desire to improve working conditions and mitigate unemployment, and the need to create better health care all found expression among religiously inclined people in the Northwest. According to historian Ferenc Szasz, the fact that so few social institutions existed in the Pacific Northwest in the last quarter of the nineteenth century seemed to encourage newly arrived pastors, priests, and rabbis to become particularly active in the establishment of such institutions.[6]

In Oregon, Thomas Lamb Eliot surfaced as an early proponent of the Social Gospel. Born in 1841, Eliot grew up in St. Louis, graduated from Washington University, and attended Harvard Divinity School. In 1867, Eliot received an invitation to become the first pastor of Portland's First Unitarian Church. Married two years earlier to Henrietta Mack, Eliot decided to come west and begin his ministry, though Portland was still not much more than a frontier village.[7] He served as pastor until 1893, but something must have captivated Eliot about the region, because he worked and lived in the Portland area until his death in 1936. He became one of the most prominent civic leaders in the city. One historian notes that Eliot was widely regarded as "the conscience of the community."[8] He threw himself into multiple causes, but he paid special attention to child labor, education, and women's issues.

Portland's Thomas Lamb Eliot was once referred to as the "conscience of the community." Courtesy Reed College Eric V. Hauser Memorial Library Special Collections and Archives, Portland, Oregon

Eliot encouraged his parishioners to consider the possibility of a Portland that truly reflected their moral values. In "A Sermon on the Times," he spoke about his hopes for the city he had come to love. Portland, he predicted, could easily deteriorate into "an accident, a railroad station, a crossroads, a tavern or emigrant barracks—a stock yard of gold heaps, a corral of struggling humanity, grown huge by time or luck." Or under wise and principled leadership, it could become "a city set on a hill that cannot be hid, a community with the glory of a mountain and sky and emerald forest and shining streams and oceans rolling to its feet, worthy to lead in commerce and useful arts."[9] Eliot passionately believed that the church should engage the most important social issues of the day. His ministry included the establishment of unemployment bureaus for the poor, advocacy for penal reform, juvenile justice, and tireless efforts to end political corruption. He fought for the prohibition of alcohol, found homes for orphans, and committed himself to the expansion of educational opportunities in both the public and private spheres.[10]

Eliot was far from alone; Protestants, Catholics, and to a lesser extent Jews had migrated to the Pacific Northwest in significant numbers after the 1870s with hopes of transplanting Victorian culture into this remote region of North America.

Another religious figure who engaged social issues in Portland was Rabbi Stephen Wise. A close friend and colleague of Eliot's, Wise exercised a remarkable influence on Portland in only six years before returning to New York City to become one of the leading rabbis in the country. According to historian Steven Lowenstein, "in that short time [Wise] had a profound impact. His passion for justice and social reform involved him deeply with the problems of living and working conditions in South Portland and throughout the city."[11]

Born in Budapest, Hungary, in 1874, Wise was the grandson of the chief rabbi of Hungary, known for his Orthodox piety and political liberalism. Wise grew up in New York City, where his father was a rabbi as well. In 1899, he came to Portland on a fund-raising tour for the Zionist movement. Officials from Temple Beth Israel in Portland asked him to serve in the Pacific Northwest, and he agreed to a five-year contract. He married Louise Waterman and subsequently threw himself into Portland social and civic issues. At his installation, Wise reportedly stated that he had but one condition: "I ask it as my right. You will and must allow it. This pulpit must be free. This pulpit must be free," referring to his desire to engage any issue without any prior restraint from the Jewish establishment.[12] Wise supported the Council of Jewish Women as well as the Consumer League in their fight for women's suffrage; he also opposed gambling, prostitution, and child labor.[13] The Portland rabbi helped elect reform mayor Harry Lane in 1905 and was asked to be a part of his cabinet. He refused that position but did accept appointment by the governor to the state's new Child Labor Commission in 1903. As we will see, Wise took a particular interest not only in the plight of Jewish immigrants in the Portland area but also in the larger social needs of all Oregonians.[14]

Perhaps the most influential Catholic priest from this era in Oregon was Father Edwin Vincent O'Hara. Born on a farm in southern Minnesota in 1881, Edwin was the youngest of eight children.[15] O'Hara attended St. Thomas College in St. Paul, Minnesota, where his interest in politics was inspired by hearing the speeches of Ignatius Donnelly, William Jennings Bryan, and Theodore Roosevelt. The larger social, economic, and religious questions of the day stirred in him, and in the fall of 1900 he entered seminary in preparation for the priesthood.[16]

O'Hara was ordained in 1905 by Archbishop John Ireland and assigned to the archdiocese in Oregon City. He assumed the duties of assistant pastor at the cathedral and almost immediately became editor of the *Catholic Sentinel*. In this capacity, O'Hara found himself in the midst of struggles over labor problems, unemployment, and unjust wages. In 1907, he organized the Catholic Education Association of Portland and spoke frequently on issues related to education and social reform. O'Hara served as chair of the Consumer's League of Portland in order to investigate the wages, hours, and conditions of work of female employees in the state. Eventually appointed to be the head of the Oregon Industrial Welfare Commission, O'Hara played a vital role in the passage of the country's first minimum-wage law for women.[17]

Seattle had several Protestants and Catholics who could be considered practitioners of the Social Gospel. The Reverend Sydney Strong, pastor of the Queen Anne Congregational Church from 1908 to 1922, typified the liberal Protestant minister. Strong believed that Christ's compelling message was one of social activism. He was convinced that Christianity had to be taken to the streets and into the union hall if it ever expected to survive the onslaught of industrial capitalism and modern philosophy. Christianity had to reach people where they lived and worked.

Born in 1860 in Seville, Ohio, Sydney Strong had been raised by Methodist parents who believed in temperance and abolition—the two great social reform movements of the mid-nineteenth century. Strong attended Oberlin College, where he studied under Washington Gladden, one of the leading proponents of the Social Gospel. Gladden's influence led Strong to believe that every individual was sacred and that one was obligated to live out Christ's great commandment to love one's neighbor.[18]

In 1908, Strong moved to Seattle to accept the pastorate at Queen Anne Congregational Church. Strong worked tirelessly on issues related to child welfare and women's suffrage. He became an ardent pacifist and a staunch supporter of the unionization of labor. His son Tracey became a central figure in the YMCA in Seattle, and more famously, his daughter, Anna Louise Strong, emerged as one of the leading social critics and an advocate of the Seattle General Strike in 1919. Overall, Sydney Strong was one of Seattle's most recognizable advocates of the Social Gospel.[19]

One of the most influential rabbis in Seattle during the first few decades of the twentieth century was Samuel Koch. Born in 1874 in Denver, Koch came under the influence of Rabbi William Friedman. Koch graduated from Hebrew Union College in 1896 or 1897; he first served a synagogue in Pensacola, beginning in 1902, where he exhibited interest in social justice issues. Coming to Seattle in 1906, he served as the principal rabbi at Temple De Hirsch until his death in 1944. During those years, Koch collaborated frequently with Sydney Strong.[20] For a number of years the two of them shared interest in the social and political issues of the city, in particular the coordination of citywide charity activities, including the Central Council of Social Agencies, municipal ownership, and child welfare. One historian wrote, "Rabbi Koch would establish himself both locally and nationally as a spiritual leader, teacher, innovator, and committed reformer. He devoted a significant part of his time to education, particularly toward the religious education of the temple's young people."[21]

If one Catholic priest in Seattle is noteworthy for his commitment to social Christianity, it is Father Edward O'Dea. Born in Boston on November 23, 1856, Edward O'Dea was the eldest son of a tailor who had immigrated to America as a youth from his home in County Limerick, Ireland. By 1866, the family had settled in the Portland area. O'Dea attended college in San Francisco but graduated from St. Michael's College in Portland in 1876. He went to seminary in Montreal and was ordained to the priesthood in 1882; he returned to Portland the following year. In 1896, he was named the third bishop of Nesqually and enthroned in St. James Cathedral in Vancouver, Washington. In 1907, O'Dea moved to Seattle when St. James Cathedral was constructed. One writer described the bishop as being "everywhere, organizing new parishes, approving and encouraging plans for new churches, hospitals and schools, stimulating development of spiritual life through activities of pastors in planning missions and multiplying devotions."[22] In 1932, Archbishop Edward Howard, preaching in St. James Cathedral, declared, "To Bishop O'Dea, more than any other man, is due the development of the Church in the Northwest."[23] O'Dea led the way in developing an array of institutions that addressed the needs primarily of the large number of Catholic immigrants who arrived in the city during the early twentieth century.

Without question, the one Protestant figure looming over the Northwest who more fully embodied the Social Gospel than anyone else was Seattle minister Mark Matthews. Serving Seattle's First Presbyterian Church from 1902 to 1940, Matthews built his congregation into the denomination's largest, with nearly ten thousand members at its height—a remarkable accomplishment. It was the first great megachurch in the Northwest. Matthews's saying, "The church is my force and the city my field," guided his congregation's commitment to social problems.[24] Matthews led First Presbyterian to develop a wide array of social services, from day nurseries and kindergartens for working mothers to support for unemployment bureaus, antituberculosis tents, city parks, hospitals, and changes in the criminal justice system.

The roots of Matthews's evangelical religion and social involvement can be found surprisingly in his native Georgia. Born in Calhoun on September 24, 1867, he was the son of a carriage maker who experienced great hardships after the Civil War. Matthews's childhood poverty encouraged an ethical outlook that emphasized hard work and traditional moral values. His moral orientation and piety were further influenced by the environment of Southern revivalism with its standard fare of itinerant preachers, tent meetings, and fiery sermons. In addition, he was exposed to radical agrarian politics of the post-Reconstruction period.

Matthews never went to seminary, receiving his theological education largely through the efforts of a local pastor. By 1886, when he was nineteen years old, he began to preach in his hometown and surrounding communities. First in Calhoun and subsequently in Dalton, Georgia, and Jackson, Tennessee, Matthews established a pattern that he would bring to Seattle in 1902. He attracted new members to his church, developed social ministries

Mark Matthews challenged Seattle's political leadership and embodied many elements of the Social Gospel. Courtesy University of Washington Libraries, Portraits Collection, UW 3354, Seattle, Washington

around unemployment and health care, and took on local politicians whom he believed were corrupt.

When first asked to consider moving from Tennessee to Seattle, Matthews resisted. But gradually he changed his mind as he began to see Seattle as a strategic city. He believed that Seattle was perfectly positioned to send missionaries to Asia as part of an effort to bring Christianity to the world. As did Thomas Lamb Eliot about Portland, Matthews came to refer to Seattle as "truly a city set upon a hill. . . . We should not try to hide nor should we conceal our resources nor withhold the fact of our future glory from others."[25] He believed that the force of history positioned the Northwest strategically for God's purposes. "We are the descendants of Japheth who moved northward and westward from Babylon through Asia, Europe and America and on westward until we have arrived at Seattle, and our feet have touched the shores of the Pacific in our tramp of the ages back to Asia from Babylon to Seattle."[26] He once told his congregation at First Presbyterian, "This town is destined by Almighty God to be the center of world events. It will be the ground of arbitration between great nations. It will be the gate for the golden commerce of the world. It will be the hospital for the world's discouraged and sick. It will be the world's school and college for the ignorant and uninstructed. . . . From this church's pulpit the gospel will be preached to Asia, and Asia will come to Christ and be saved."[27] It was this convergence of religious imagery and the conviction that the Pacific Northwest was vital to the fulfillment of God's promises that informed his work.

An imposing figure at six-feet-five-inches tall, with flowing hair and a Southern-style frock coat, Matthews combined evangelical religion that sometimes bordered on fundamentalism with social concerns. These twin commitments made him the most influential and controversial Protestant minister in the Pacific Northwest until he died in February 1940.

As suggested, most religious activists and reformers agreed that the moral environment of most cities had been compromised and that industrial capitalism had produced an unjust distribution of wealth and political corruption. While many ministers flirted with more radical ideas such as Christian Socialism, for the most part they hoped to achieve their ends by simply moderating the excesses of capitalism, extending a social safety net, and ending municipal corruption.[28] While an increasing number of advocates of Social Gospel tenets began focusing on the role that the social environment played in creating problems that afflicted urban and industrial America, most religious activists, as products of the Victorian age, still focused on the moral failure of too many American males. Moral corruption was thought to have infected most every level of society. Businessmen and politicians were just as vulnerable to moral decay as was an uneducated immigrant population. Religious activists frequently asserted that if more men accepted Christianity and committed themselves to the development of personal character and moral virtue, the vast majority of social problems facing America would significantly diminish, if not entirely disappear.

In many ways, this was not unexpected; most of these activists were preachers who were steeped in the language of moral redemption. Given the amount of attention paid by activist women to the problems of male behavior and the commitment of Victorian men and women to moral education in public and private schools, one should not be surprised at the number of sermons that addressed the problem of moral decay on the part of men.

Yet the issue of male identity and behavior proved to be increasingly complicated in the late nineteenth and early twentieth centuries, and this made simple prescriptions for moral improvement more difficult. Historian Gail Bederman noted that as men moved from the farm to the city, the traditional definition of manliness began to be replaced by more middle-class characteristics.[29] New cultural tensions emerged around the virtue of sexual restraint versus male sexuality; the tension between compassion versus strength and a powerful will; and the tension between humility and aggressiveness.

Indeed, clergy found themselves walking a fine line between offering a steady stream of criticism regarding male behavior, particularly male aggression toward women, and a need to make Christianity compatible with a robust view of manhood with hopes that more men would be attracted to the Christian faith. As we have seen, ministers felt compelled to warn their male and female parishioners of the dire consequences that came from overly aggressive male behavior. Christians should embody kindness, compassion, love, and humility. They should avoid alcohol, work hard, and protect their women and children from harm. On the other hand, ministers did not want men to feel alienated from the church and Christianity. They often tried to convince men that a Christian man could cultivate traditional male virtues of strength, determination, and even power.

Seattle's Mark Matthews tried to walk this fine line. He believed that men needed to be convinced that religion was indeed compatible with masculine values. He exemplified what historians of American religion have described as "muscular Christianity." He attacked any notion that Christianity consisted of unmanly virtues. Matthews believed that men could be convinced of the importance of infusing Christianity into the great social and political problems of their day. He believed that the cultivation of a "manly" Christianity in its own way led to a Social Gospel in urban America. Far from being passive and sentimental, Christianity fostered for Matthews strength and even virility. "A man should pass from the child state of Christian life to the strong, robust, muscular period of Christian manhood," preached Matthews in a sermon titled "Wanted: More Man in Men." He further stressed that the "physical powers of man should be trained to express truth, to embody cleanliness and to manifest a purpose and design for God's glory, and the elevation of the human race." Matthews believed that the true Christian man embodied the virtue of empathy for others while being bold and courageous. "The greatest evil this country has to combat is the lack of boldness born of righteousness. Therefore, we want in men a righteous, masculine boldness."[30] This approach to manliness, he believed, would be the antidote to alcohol abuse, sexual exploitation, and gambling addiction, as well as to municipal corruption and capitalist greed.

In 1909, Matthews preached a fairly typical series of sermons focused on vices to eliminate and virtues to develop. In the first sermon, "Homeless Man," Matthews preached, "Idleness is a crime. If it is a voluntary idleness, the idle man is the criminal. If it is forced idleness, those who are responsible for the condition of idleness, are criminals."[31] In the second sermon, titled "Friendless Man," he urged each man to take up some great task or cause: "The man who represents, stands for and is the embodiment of a great cause, a controlling principle and an all-absorbing idea, makes friends who would die for him though they never saw him." In "Penniless Man," a week later, Matthews excoriated verbosity, laziness, prodigality, extravagance, sin, and stinginess. He then moved on to behavioral and social responsibility. In "Heartless Man," he berated any man who mistreated women and children but focused in particular on horse beaters and those who were otherwise cruel to animals.[32] In "Conscienceless Man," he attacked greed and exploitation: "Do you suppose landlords who are systematically and persistently raising rents on office buildings, stores, restaurants, bakeries, barber shops, hotels, flats and residences are controlled by the dictates of a righteous conscience? No." The next to last sermon, "Childless Man," emphasized the importance of family and stressed Matthews's belief that every man ought to produce a family. And, finally, the series culminated with an emphasis on conversion to Christianity in the "Christless Man."[33]

These deep-seated concerns about male behavior underlaid much of the effort by religious activists to shape the public life and culture of the region. Pastors, priests, and rabbis believed that if they could address social problems related to male behavior, they would do much to bring in the Kingdom of God to the Pacific Northwest. They believed that a Social Gospel largely depended on a combination of legislative action and moral reform if the society were to be redeemed in any significant way.

As suggested, one of their central concerns was protecting the vulnerable from aggressive male behavior, and one of the first clergymen to take leadership in this cause in Oregon was the aforementioned Thomas Lamb Eliot. The Unitarian pastor helped organize the state's first Humane Society in 1868, devoted to protecting animals as well as women and children. Eliot's memory had been seared with the image of a horse being beaten, and he vowed to try to prevent that from happening as much as possible. Four years later, he organized the Society for the Prevention of Cruelty to Animals. Eliot, along with others, lobbied the state legislature so relentlessly that by 1885 the state outlawed specific instances of cruelty to animals and children. In that same year, members of the Humane Society elected Eliot to the presidency, a position he held for the next twenty years.[34]

Eliot's concern for children who were victims of physical violence or neglect led him to work with Oregon's growing number of orphans. He supported a major orphanage called "The Home" by fund-raising in Portland's business community.[35] Eliot recognized that a cycle of neglect and violence had to be broken. He helped organize the Boys and Girls Aid Society. In essence a reform school, the Aid Society grew out of Eliot's belief that Portland needed an effective response to the problem of juvenile delinquency. Established in 1885, after

Eliot convinced several of Portland's leading citizens to lend their financial support, the Boys and Girls Aid Society served the homeless and embraced neglected and abused children throughout the state. For six years, from 1885 to 1891, Eliot served as superintendent of the society.[36]

The Social Gospel ministers and rabbis in Oregon and Washington focused not only on children's safety but also on issues related to child labor. In Oregon, Rabbi Stephen Wise worked with Eliot on issues connected to the exploitation of child labor in fish canneries in Astoria and at other Columbia River fisheries.[37] Their effort helped produce a child labor law and create the State Child Labor Commission. Wise served as a member of the commission until he left for New York in 1906.[38]

This interest in the welfare of children and concern for the struggles of working mothers were central features of the Social Gospel era. Both Sydney Strong and Rabbi Samuel Koch took particular interest in these issues. Seattle mayor George Cotterill appointed Strong, who had served Seattle's Queen Anne First Congregational Church since 1908, to oversee the new Central Council of Social Agencies, which was designed to coordinate the work of more than one hundred city charities.[39]

By 1914, Strong, along with Koch, worked closely with Strong's daughter Anna Louise to bring the national Child Welfare Exhibit to Seattle as part of the exhibit's national tour. Koch believed that the Child Welfare program would awaken the conscience of the city. In the April 1914 issue of *Temple Tidings*, he noted that the upcoming exhibit "promises to be the most significant social event that has ever taken place in the city." [40] The event raised new levels of awareness regarding child labor legislation, hygiene, recreation, education, and other factors bearing on child development. The exhibit also identified social welfare agencies in Seattle that were addressing the social needs of children. Amazingly popular, the exhibit drew roughly six thousand people each day, with an estimated forty thousand attending on the final day, May 31.[41]

If the Child Welfare Exhibit underscored the desire of religious figures to draw attention to mistreatment of children, an equally significant concern lay with the plight of adolescent males. For example, Thomas Lamb Eliot worked tirelessly on behalf of young men jailed in Portland. Eliot's interest in the ways criminals were treated stemmed from the influence of Dorothea Dix. In 1869, Dix, one of the nation's leading advocates for prison reform, visited Portland for the purpose of evaluating the conditions for prisoners in the Multnomah County jail. Eliot escorted Dix while she was in Portland, and as a consequence he caught her vision. He lobbied municipalities and legislatures to upgrade their prison facilities and urged a heightened sense of justice. Eliot helped establish a reform school in Portland.[42] He convened the State Conference of Charities and Corrections in 1889 and became its president in 1902, remaining in the position for over a decade.[43]

Mark Matthews also preached on the need for reform in the criminal justice system, with an eye toward redeeming the young men who were incarcerated. "The first change should be the substitution of psychological and physiological treatment for penal punishment," he believed. "It is a false theory to think you can punish a criminal and reform him or benefit society." He argued that the concept of a prison should be based on ideas gleaned from the field of health care. Principally, he believed that this meant the creation of a healthy environment for the prisoner or "patient." On one occasion he suggested that the city purchase twenty to twenty-five acres close to the city and build cottages, erect workshops, and establish forges, shoe shops, and small manufacturing plants. "To this farm every vagrant, every petit criminal and worthless, indolent person in the community should be forced to go."[44] Asked in 1903 about what Seattle needed the most, Matthews stressed the "poverty of public facilities." He believed that "it is cheaper to establish schools, parks, amusement halls, art galleries, libraries, and places of refinement, culture and morality, than it is to support a standing army of hundreds of policemen, jails, penitentiaries, and asylums for inebriates."[45] Matthews pushed for legislation that established the juvenile court in 1905.[46]

The Protestant-led institution most associated with improving the welfare of young boys and early adolescents was the Young Men's Christian Association. Initially established in London, England, in 1844 by George Williams, the YMCA sought to take young men off the streets by substituting Bible study and prayer for a life of vice or crime.[47] By 1851, the YMCA had formed a branch in Boston and soon began to spread across the United States. Portland, Oregon, residents could join the YMCA as early as 1868 and Seattleites by 1876. Northwest communities embraced the Y; by 1886, YMCAs had been established in Portland, Seattle, Tacoma, Spokane, Astoria,

Ashland, Salem, Hillsboro, The Dalles, Forest Grove, East Portland, Albina, and many other regional locations.

Until the 1890s, most of the YMCAs in the Northwest were small-scale operations that moved from building to building. But in that decade, the associations in the larger cities such as Portland, Spokane, and Seattle developed boardinghouses in downtown areas, providing inexpensive lodging to young men looking for work. YMCA staff offered assistance finding employment, low-cost food, Bible study, reading rooms, and recreation. Basketball, volleyball, gymnastics, and other physical activity all were presented as healthy alternatives to life in the city. The purpose was to develop young men of character.[48]

Decidedly evangelical in the late nineteenth and early twentieth centuries, YMCA leaders aimed to convert young men to Christianity by persuading them that they could be "manly" by developing physical fitness as well as spiritual well-being.[49] But the Y also believed that it could win converts by providing practical vocational and technical education that equipped young men, who had relatively few skills, to live and work in an urban world. Classes included arithmetic, bookkeeping, penmanship, shorthand and typewriting, mechanical drawing, and vocal music. Of these, the penmanship class was among the most popular, as the typewriter was still something of a novelty and a legible hand was essential in business. Because many of the young men came directly from the farm, they were singularly ill equipped to compete in the emerging professional world of the middle class; the Y served a distinct need.[50]

In addition to the YMCA, urban revivalism also reflected the commitment to win male converts to Christ and apply Christianity to the social problems of the region. In 1905, the two largest revivals in the Pacific Northwest were led by Presbyterian evangelist J. Wilbur Chapman and his team. Chapman was the nation's foremost advocate of a specialized team approach to revivalism; these evangelists focused on groups ranging from children and middle-class businessmen to skid row inhabitants and blue-collar workers. The Chapman team attempted to proselytize entire cities by employing more than one approach. Chapman helped orchestrate tent revivals, large cathedral gatherings, marches through red-light districts, small rallies among the working class, and public lectures for the middle class.[51]

The Chapman team made it a point in both Portland and Seattle to reveal the underbelly of male culture that embraced alcohol, illicit sex, and gambling. In both cities, evangelists took reporters into red-light districts in order to expose the lurid conditions that existed. In Seattle, the Chapman team organized a large public demonstration against prostitution. On April 17, 1905, a crowd estimated at more than fifteen thousand took to the streets. The Salvation Army furnished a marching band, and newspapers reported that this was the most remarkable demonstration in the city's history. Evangelists marched up and down the streets, hoping to draw attention to the seamier side of Seattle's night life.[52]

If evangelists pushed hard on Seattle's and Portland's underside and vigorously opposed traditional vices, Charles Stelzle, another member of Chapman's team, had a different message for the blue-collar laborers of the two cities. An advocate for organized labor, Stelzle, a former machinist turned minister, had taken a position in the national Presbyterian Church in the Workingmen's Department. Stelzle's task was to break down barriers between the church, working men, and the unions.[53] During Chapman's revivals, Stelzle would go down to local labor halls or onto the docks and find a place to preach.[54] His principal message was one of reconciliation between labor and management. He pushed the Presbyterian Church as well as other denominations to support labor unions. Stelzle expressed great concern that blue-collar workers were turning away from Christianity and toward socialism because the church was not responding to their needs. He believed, as did many others, that evangelism and social reform could work together. "I have a conviction that the right kind of evangelist," he wrote, "who has a message which is broad and deep and thoroughly evangelistic, but with a social spirit backed by knowledge of social conditions and principles, could win his way in every community in this country."[55] This was the hope of Social Gospel advocates throughout the United States. If the Gospel could be contextualized to the problems of the city as well as the problems facing the working class, God's Kingdom could be brought into fruition.

Chapman's revivals in Portland and Seattle occurred at a critical time. Labor unrest in the Pacific Northwest continued to grow, and tension between the laboring class and the rising middle class was increasing. In December 1905, the former governor of Idaho, Frank Steunenberg, was murdered outside of his home in Caldwell,

Idaho, for his role in labor disputes in the Coeur d'Alene mining district several years earlier. In February of the following year, the leader of the Western Federation of Miners, Bill Haywood, was arrested for conspiring to murder Steunenberg. As Haywood's trial unfolded over the next year, much of the Northwest as well as the nation closely followed Clarence Darrow's spirited defense of the president of the Western Federation of Miners; the trial ended in his acquittal—a decision that did not sit well with Spokane's middle class. In 1909, the growing professional class was further unsettled by the free speech fight in Spokane. Members of the more radical Industrial Workers of the World (IWW) took to the street corners and were arrested, but jails were soon filled to overflowing as more IWW demonstrators flooded Spokane, and city officials were forced to relent and let the dissidents go. From the standpoint of the middle class, a war was being waged for control of the streets. As the next decade wore on, labor's drive for recognition as well as better working conditions was deeply unsettling.[56]

Mark Matthews and Sydney Strong attempted to weave something of a middle path in their effort to secure justice for working men while trying to temper more radical elements of the labor movement. Matthews frequently preached on the tension between labor and capital, and his sermons were often carried in the *Seattle Times*. "Capital," he argued, "has no right to accumulate wealth until it crushes to death those who seek the right to live and the right to toil."[57] In another sermon he stated, "I do not know that there is anywhere a promised reward for the man who sits down and takes advantage of the labor of others to fill his coffers. The man who has grown wealthy by the unearned increments is nothing more or less than a parasite."[58]

Matthews believed that laborers needed protection from the acquisitive ethic that seemed to pervade the capitalistic system. Although he opposed strikes as the best means of securing these safeguards, he acknowledged their necessity as the only recourse available to workers. "We deplore the existence of strikes. They injure everybody concerned," he preached. "Capital is injured, labor is hurt and the general public suffers, but, the strike is the only weapon in the hands of defenseless labor."[59] Matthews challenged the church as well as the broader society to offer help and protection for an unprotected laboring class. In one of his frequent sermons on the plight of labor, he asserted, "Everyone knows that the laborer is being forced to the wall. Show me the church that is demanding an increase in wages for the poor. Show me the church that is trying before its courts those infamous kings thus grinding to powder our poor."[60] He fully believed that Christians should assume moral and political leadership in this area of public policy. Entirely confident that applied Christianity could solve any social problem, he frequently exhorted the larger church to become proactive in societal matters. "The great sociological problems properly belong to the church. The differences between capital and labor will never be removed without the church's influence," wrote Matthews. "The next step is for the church . . . to go forth with a determination to destroy the agencies of evil."[61]

If issues related to labor occupied Matthews and other ministers of this era, one other issue demanded even more attention: municipal corruption. Many activists believed that corrupt municipalities led to moral corruption of men in all walks of life. Beginning in the late nineteenth century, questions related to the nature of city government surfaced across the country. Investigative journalists (commonly known as muckrakers) exposed ways in which political machines, such as Tammany Hall in New York City, controlled city governments. In response, increasing numbers of reformers attempted to change the system.[62] And perhaps the best known religious reformer in the Northwest who sought to expose municipal corruption was, once again, Mark Matthews.

The fight in Seattle centered on the person of Hiram Gill, who believed that Seattle needed to be an open town—one that catered to the working-class male with cheap amusements and recreation. Gill and Matthews had first drawn public attention in 1905. At that time, Hiram Gill was president of the city council when the Seattle minister first lodged a general accusation that the council was afflicted with graft. Called to account by the council, Matthews made more charges that fanned the fire. When the feisty Gill had heard enough, he accused Matthews of consorting with prostitutes himself back in Tennessee. The press had a field day, but there apparently was more smoke than fire and things seemed to calm down. However, the lines in the sand had been drawn.[63]

When Gill decided to run for mayor in 1910, Matthews and a number of other Seattle ministers grew alarmed. None of them believed that Gill was good for the city. Challenging Gill for the Republican nomination was A. V. Bouillon, and Matthews soon publicly committed to Bouillon by asserting that a Gill administration would lead directly to "the gospel of corrupt politicians and infamous political bodies."[64] Matthews claimed that First Presbyterian Church would cast its votes for Bouillon, and the Reverend George Cairns of the Temple Baptist Church reportedly urged his congregation to do the same.[65]

Election tactics, as usual, were questionable: Gill was accused of "colonizing" the once-empty hotels and lodging houses of the First Ward with hundreds of men and transporting them for voter registration, a charge he vigorously denied. On the Sunday before the election, Matthews delivered a vitriolic attack on Gill and any Christian who failed to vote against him: "The infamous cowards, slothful sluggards and stupid Christians who have refused to register and who are now taking no part in politics, are the greatest enemies to good government and the most formidable impediments in the way of the establishment of righteousness we have in the community."[66] Despite Matthews's efforts, Gill won the general election.[67]

Yet the election results did not end the public debate over vice. Matthews, along with other clergy and social reformers, kept a sharp eye on Gill's activities. Almost immediately, the mayor raised concerns by appointing as his police chief Charles Wappenstein, a man who openly argued that vice could not be effectively regulated.

Wappenstein came to Seattle after working for the Pinkerton Detective Agency and serving as a police chief in the Midwest. But from his early days on the police force, rumors circulated regarding his tolerance of scam artists, kickbacks, and protection rackets.[68] A biographical description of Wappenstein in a local publication about Seattle police and fire personnel raised the hackles of Matthews and other middle-class Seattle residents: "Chief Wappenstein has the widest acquaintance with crooks of any peace officer in the West. He has also a very wide circle of friends and acquaintances among the business and professional men of Seattle."[69] One of those friends was Colonel Alden Blethen, publisher of the *Seattle Times*, who defended Wappenstein against any and all charges.

As historians Sharon Boswell and Lorraine McConaghy assert in their biography of Blethen, "Wappy was back and so was the Tenderloin. The saloons and dance halls, gambling dens and hurdy-gurdy joints all swept away the dust and unboarded the windows as the 'lords of vice' once more opened for business."[70] In fact, Wappenstein relaxed the boundaries of the restricted district and attracted many new arrivals from outside the city, who, according to Boswell and McConaghy, "engaged in every form of debauchery imaginable."[71]

Gill's troubles began when he left town for a few days in September 1910. Acting mayor Max Wardall, outraged by the developments in the city, decided to exercise his power and remove Wappenstein for alleged improprieties. Gill quickly returned and reinstated Wappenstein, much to the general disgruntlement of the city. Beginning in October, the Public Welfare League started to circulate petitions for a recall election. Charging that Gill was "a menace to the business enterprises and moral welfare of said city," the Public Welfare League by December had gained the required signatures to force an election in February 1911.[72]

The recall movement involved a great many of the city's clergymen. In early October, the *Post-Intelligencer* noted how many Methodists and Baptists were behind the petition drive.[73] One minister, Dr. Adna Wright Leonard, was so outspoken in his attacks on Gill and Wappenstein that he was reportedly threatened with bodily harm. Matthews asked Gill to resign prior to the election, and, when the mayor refused, Matthews urged voters to elect George Dilling. "Every ballot cast will be either for or against righteousness, civic purity, and law enforcement," he wrote. "There isn't the slightest doubt in the minds of the general public of the fact of police graft, chicanery, double crossing and the infraction of the law at the investigation of the authorities."[74] In the meantime, Matthews decided to take more covert action. Borrowing money on his insurance policies, the preacher hired one of the most famous detective agencies of the day, the William Burns Agency, to search for specific evidence of Wappenstein's illicit activities, because Matthews did not want to be caught unprepared if it became necessary to oppose the mayor publicly, as he had done in 1905.

In mid-November 1910, Burns operatives began supplying Matthews with daily reports.[75] The Seattle minister pored over the details, hoping to find evidence that would be damaging to Gill and Wappenstein. Matthews made certain that his role was kept entirely secret, although when the editor of the *Seattle Post-Intelligencer*, Erastus Brainerd, accused Matthews of not doing his fair share to recall Gill, Matthews almost revealed his private efforts. "I hope what I am doing will be successful and if it is," he replied to Brainerd, "you will find that I have done more in the last four months than all the Welfare Leagues in this city have done to rid this city of the infernal corruption."[76] The preacher must have realized that secrecy had its continued advantages. If the investigation proved unsuccessful, he would not have to be associated with its failure. Matthews might also have believed that the information gathered could be used to make Gill more pliable, even if the recall failed.

Matthews must have faced election day with anxiety; he had invested money and emotional energy in his effort to influence the future of Seattle politics. And as the results came in, he must have felt great personal satisfaction in Gill's defeat. Women in Seattle had just gained the right to vote the previous November, and they went to the polls with banners that read "Dilling for Decency"; this was enough to counteract a reported five hundred "ladies of the night" who had been brought by limousine to vote for Gill. The election produced an obvious irony in that Matthews, who had fought vigorously against women's suffrage, now obviously reaped the benefits of women being able to participate in the electoral process.[77]

But the success of the recall did force Matthews to make a decision regarding the Burns investigation of Gill and Wappenstein. Although there is no direct evidence of any extended discussion between Burns and Matthews, the two probably reasoned that criminals should be prosecuted and Wappenstein brought to justice.[78] Consequently, one week after the election, Burns went to the prosecuting attorney, John Murphy, with the evidence collected. After reviewing it, Murphy said he believed that he should seek an indictment of Wappenstein before a grand jury.[79] At the time, Burns boldly stated to the press that the conviction of Wappenstein would be a "cinch." While holding Gill blameless, the famous detective confidently claimed, "We've got the goods on Wappy."[80] On February 25, the grand jury indicted the former police chief on the charge of accepting a $2,500 bribe for the protection of illegal gambling establishments and houses of prostitution.[81]

From the day of the indictment, rumors circulated regarding who might have been responsible for bringing Burns to Seattle. A number of prominent businessmen were mentioned as possibilities, but Matthews's secret was extremely well kept.[82] In May it was finally revealed that Matthews had funded the investigation. Wappenstein was charged with bribery. However, enough questions were raised about the legitimacy of the testimony that the trial ended in a hung jury. A second trial was held, and this time the jury returned a guilty verdict; Charles Wappenstein was sentenced to three to ten years at the state penitentiary in Walla Walla.

Not everyone was happy with Matthews's covert approach. To many Seattleites, he was meddling too much in politics. But there were also many who supported him, including the editor of the *Post-Intelligencer*, Erastus Brainerd, who said in 1910, "The best single individual influence at present exerted in Seattle, is probably that of Mark A. Matthews."[83]

Father O'Hara spearheaded the effort to pass the first minimum-wage legislation for women in the country.

If Matthews best reflected the combination of Social Gospel and Progressive impulses in Seattle, it was Father Edwin Vincent O'Hara in Portland in 1913 who took the lead in passage of the first minimum-wage legislation for women—not only in the Northwest but in the country. In this instance, O'Hara and his supporters believed that a living wage was central to the issue of social justice. As mentioned above, O'Hara had grown up in Minnesota and absorbed the Populist/Socialist vision of late nineteenth-century social thinkers. For O'Hara, the commitment to a just wage was also influenced by the teachings of Pope Leo XIII, who had made this a major emphasis in his 1891 encyclical, *Rerum Novarum*.

But a living wage was only part of the solution for O'Hara. Arriving in Portland in 1905, O'Hara soon encountered the city's growing slums. He was appalled by housing conditions in Portland. On more than one occasion, O'Hara stated, "Bad housing breeds poverty, for poverty grows under the same conditions that tuberculosis does—either will thrive in sordid, dark, filthy surroundings."[84] He cited three reasons for such pathetic living conditions: "Neglect, ignorance, and greed. Neglect on the part of the public to provide adequate code and inspection; ignorance on the part of the architects and builders as to what is really necessary for proper sanitation and housing; and lastly, the greed of the landlord, who desires to get as much out of his building in rentals as possible, with minimum of expense."[85] O'Hara publicly advocated for a new code that would ensure sufficient space, light, air, and sanitation in all municipal housing. Shortly thereafter, Portland adopted a code and appointed O'Hara to be on the board of inspection for a three-year term.

But the issue for which O'Hara was best known is labor justice. One story recounts how on Thanksgiving Day, 1912, as O'Hara walked down Washington Street in downtown Portland, he stopped to listen to a street corner orator vehemently claiming that "religion [was] the enemy of the working man" and challenging any clergyman to prove him wrong.[86] Father O'Hara could not resist and soon found himself engaged in debate. Apparently this went on for several days and soon drew the attention of reporters for the *Oregonian*. In one letter to the newspaper, Tom Burns, the socialist orator with whom O'Hara debated, exhorted workers to pay more attention to Karl Marx's vision; Marx, he claimed, proposed a socialist vision in which all individuals would be dignified in their work and receive from others according to their need. Burns charged that workers should be suspicious of the likes of Father O'Hara and other Social Gospel ministers because they have "never suffered as we proletarians have."[87]

Burns's direct attack on O'Hara helped provide the priest with a defense against members of his church and the broader community who considered him too liberal. The press coverage also proved helpful in another way. O'Hara's debate with Burns helped raise awareness of issues facing the working poor in Portland.[88] O'Hara became convinced that the establishment of a minimum wage would provide some relief.

Rooted in Progressive-era reforms of the early twentieth century, the minimum-wage concept appealed to O'Hara as a reasonable way to improve the lives of the working poor. O'Hara's thinking was clearly influenced by one of the nation's leading female labor leaders, Florence Kelley. In 1912, Kelley, in her capacity as secretary of the National Consumers' League, appointed a special committee in Oregon to develop legislation in support of a minimum wage, and she asked Father O'Hara to chair what became known as the Oregon Consumers' League.

One of the key individuals who assisted the committee was Caroline Gleason, who later entered a convent and assumed the name of Sister Miriam Theresa of the Sisters of the Holy Names. Having lived and worked at the Chicago Commons, a famous settlement house, Gleason was appointed by O'Hara to be field secretary for the Portland Catholic Women's League and was responsible for organizing night classes and the employment bureau. She worked to gather data through interviews that would be used to draft the state law.[89] O'Hara's committee studied wage, hour, and working conditions for women and minors in Oregon. Utilizing additional help from Massachusetts attorney and future Supreme Court justice Louis Brandeis and Harvard Law faculty member and likewise future Supreme Court jurist Felix Frankfurter, O'Hara's committee crafted legislation that was passed by the Oregon legislature and signed into law on June 3, 1913, making it the first mandatory minimum-wage law in the country for women.[90]

O'Hara campaigned up and down the West Coast for this law. "It is far more to the point to show," he reportedly said to a Seattle audience, "that underpaid girls are not only preserving their virtue but are living on two meals a day and are forced to practice other pitiable economies which undermine their health and unfit them for the duties of wife and mother and thus sap the foundations of society."[91] The impact of O'Hara's work was immediate. The Oregon Minimum Wage Act, unchanged, was passed in the states of Washington and California in 1913 as well.[92]

Not everyone was pleased with the minimum-wage law. Several employers continued to express outrage over the fact that they would not have total control of an employee's wages. The more radical elements of the labor movement in the Pacific Northwest also objected because they felt that this would likely diminish worker demands on their capitalist employers. Oregon's law was challenged, and eventually the case made its way to the US Supreme Court. In April 1917, the court ruled in favor of the constitutionality of the law. Clearly Father O'Hara had a huge influence on one of the most significant issues of the early twentieth century.

CONCLUSION

Throughout this era, these men saw themselves, as did their female activist counterparts, as battling against a culture that was often unsympathetic at best and hostile at worst to their vision of society, which reflected more fully their religious values. As outsiders, they seldom expressed confidence in moral persuasion alone. Instead they organized new social institutions and voluntary organizations. They often strategized around political goals and sought allies in the larger political world. And for the most part, they continued to focus on protecting women and children while trying to shape the behaviors of men, whether they were mayors and police chiefs or itinerant workers looking for jobs.

The Social Gospel made a substantial impact on the social landscape of the Pacific Northwest. It is not an exaggeration to claim that, combined with the work of women's organizations, religiously motivated people dramatically improved conditions for women, children, and many working men. Did they establish the socially just communities for which they hoped? No, but if their reach exceeded their grasp, they had reason to be optimistic. Thomas Lamb Eliot had exerted considerable influence in Portland, along with Rabbi Stephen Wise. The largest Presbyterian Church in the country was situated in downtown Seattle, with a Southern-born minister who believed that the church should have something to do or say about most every issue in the public square. A Catholic priest had successfully led the fight for the nation's first minimum-wage law for women. The Social Gospel had brought Protestants, Catholics, and Jews together around common concerns for the working poor, immigrants, women, and children in the Pacific Northwest. These common concerns took many forms and expressed themselves on many issues, but this drive to shape the cultural ethos of the Northwest translated itself most profoundly into the most significant reform movement of the era: Prohibition. And once again, these religious activists would see themselves as the ultimate outsiders.

CHAPTER 4

GRAND CRUSADES

On February 11, 1909, four days after the end of the six-week revival led by evangelist Billy Sunday in downtown Spokane, the *Spokesman-Review* ran the headline, "BEER SALES FALL; BIBLES in DEMAND." If the newspaper writers were a bit optimistic, they had good reason to be. An earlier editorial exclaimed, "'Billy' Sunday bears from Spokane the respect and admiration of thousands, and in this host are hundreds of the able, upright business men of the city, who feel deeply that Spokane is better for his coming and has higher standards of life and duty in the home, the counting room and the public office."[1]

Without question, religiously motivated people had made a significant imprint on the culture and social life of the Pacific Northwest by the early twentieth century. From schools and hospitals to libraries and orphanages, the landscape of communities throughout the region reflected the work of Victorian Christians, Catholics, and Jews on behalf of their fellow human beings. They had developed a remarkable consensus around the idea that together they could change the culture by focusing primarily on the ill effects of male behavior. But two issues more than any other vexed significant numbers of Christians, particularly Protestants, and moved them to become politically engaged: Prohibition and prostitution. Prohibition dominated political discussions in the region for more than forty years, thanks to the relentless grassroots effort on the part of thousands of Christians. Although comparatively less important than Prohibition, the struggle over the legalization and regulation of prostitution also revealed how important religious impulses were in the region during the late nineteenth and early twentieth centuries.

Today, it is generally accepted that Prohibition was both a mistake and a failure. Yet most Americans today can hardly imagine the scale of alcohol abuse that existed in the nineteenth and early twentieth centuries. Americans consumed a staggering amount of alcohol compared with today, and the social effects were observable everywhere. As one historian put it, "Public drunkards were a pathetic, everyday spectacle in villages and cities throughout America. Drink really did kill men and ruin families, and millions of citizens felt that the best way to meet the crisis would be to eliminate alcoholic beverages."[2]

The effort of religious communities to prohibit the consumption of alcohol has a long and complicated history. Not all faith traditions treated the issue in the same way. Many Catholics and Lutherans, for example, had integrated moderate consumption of alcohol into their customs and traditions. But most Methodists, Presbyterians, and Baptists opposed alcohol in any form. The majority of southern and eastern Europeans (most of whom were Catholic or Jewish) accepted alcohol as a part of their culture, while significant numbers of Pacific Northwest residents descended from northern Europeans did not. But despite this variance, the effort to pass alcohol-related legislation reflected strong religious influence.

From the beginning, liquor in vast quantities had been a staple of frontier life. But it also had been a point of contention. Temperance and Prohibition were among the very first issues of public debate in the Pacific Northwest. As early as the 1830s, John McGloughlin, chief factor for the Hudson's Bay Company at Fort Vancouver, worked diligently to limit the distribution of liquor to Native Americans after observing its devastating effect on Indian populations.[3] Most of the early Methodist missionaries to the Willamette Valley believed in total abstinence, and in 1836, within two years of their arrival, they established the Oregon Temperance Society.

These efforts in the Pacific Northwest coincided with the national movement for temperance spearheaded largely by religious activists. Ten years earlier, in 1826, Protestants had organized the American Society for the Promotion of Temperance in Boston. By the mid-1830s, more than five thousand groups with a total membership of well over a million existed for the purpose of limiting the consumption of alcohol.[4]

In the Northwest, missionaries Marcus Whitman and Henry Spalding followed suit, establishing a temperance society in 1838. By 1849, the Oregon Territorial legislature passed a licensing act in order to regulate the manufacture and sale of "ardent spirits." The law prohibited the sale or the gift of alcohol to Native Americans, but the legislature allowed anyone else with $200 to establish a saloon. Shortly thereafter, the passage of Prohibition in the state of Maine in 1851 encouraged an increasing number of settlers in the Oregon Territory to take up the cause of temperance and/or Prohibition. In 1852, territorial residents gathered in Salem for a temperance convention to devise strategies for implementing the Maine law out West.[5] In the following year, another temperance convention met in Salem's Methodist Church, and attendees dedicated themselves "to use all practicable means to prevent by law the traffic in intoxicating liquors."[6] Four of the seven original officers of the state organization were ministers.

Beginning in the 1850s, more settlers traveled west on the Oregon Trail. As we have previously seen, one of the most influential was George Whitworth. In 1853, the same year in which Washington was organized into a territory, Whitworth arrived in Oregon and moved north, taking up residence in the Olympia area. He hoped to establish a Presbyterian colony but surmised that he could make an immediate impact by organizing a temperance society. In 1854, Whitworth presented a petition to prohibit the consumption of alcohol in the new territory. Whitworth's petition moved the legislature to call for a public vote in 1855. In this first vote, Prohibition was defeated 650 to 564.[7] Similar efforts in Oregon to pass specific legislation were also defeated. However, religious figures leading the effort did not give up.[8]

While there is evidence that this first vote was initiated because of ongoing fear of the effect of alcohol on Native Americans (settlers believing that alcohol promoted violence), people like Whitworth also worried about the effect of alcohol on white males. Whitworth became involved in the International Order of Good Templars. The order believed, according to historian Norman Clark, in making "a masculine appeal through an emphasis on companionship, ritual, 'wholesome' entertainment, and 'clean manhood,' on pool tables, reading rooms, and good talk."[9] Members committed themselves, in principle, to complete abstinence from alcoholic drinks. The Order of Good Templars also found its way into Oregon politics in the decade after the Civil War. The Reverend George B. Taylor established sixteen divisions of the order in Oregon in 1865, with the Portland lodge boasting nearly 150 members.[10]

By 1874, the newly formed Washington Territorial Temperance Alliance elected Whitworth as its first president. He, like others, hoped that the budding churches of Washington Territory would lobby the legislature for a Prohibition law. But the real action that year came as a part of the Woman's Crusade that blossomed in Portland, Oregon. Originating in New York and Ohio, the crusade was a grassroots effort involving thousands of women that quickly spread across the country. Deciding to confront saloon owners with song, prayer, and protest, Portland women now felt the time was ripe to bring attention to their desire to see the elimination of the saloon. They canvassed the city, seeking individuals who would commit to abstinence, and in an open letter they pleaded with the liquor manufacturers and dealers of the city to quit selling alcohol:

> That our husbands, brothers, and especially our sons, be no longer exposed to this terrible temptation, and that we may no longer see them led into these paths which go down to sin, and bring both soul and body to destruction. We appeal to the better instincts of your hearts; in the name of desolated homes, blasted hopes, ruined lives and widowed hearts; for the honor of our community; for our prosperity; for our happiness; for our good name as a town.[11]

Succeeding days found ever-increasing numbers of women setting out from the Taylor Street Methodist Church and marching to various saloons in order to sing and pray. At the end of the first week, on April 1, 1874, crowds of onlookers reached such a size in front of one of Portland's most prominent saloons that police asked protesting women to withdraw. On April 7, the police arrested several female crusaders. Over the next ten days, more women were arrested, and several were convicted and sentenced to a few hours in jail. But their protests proved effective; within the next several days an estimated two thousand Portlanders signed a pledge of abstinence. Clearly, the impetus behind this effort at reform came from the Presbyterians, Baptists, Unitarians, Congregationalists, and Methodists who were present at the initial rally. According to one historian, "a religious fervor had seized the women and carried them on."[12]

The Woman's Crusade singled out the saloon as the problem, and despite early efforts, as the pace of settlement increased, the problem of alcohol increased as well. The frenzy of railroad building in the Pacific Northwest in the 1880s brought the unintended consequence of readily available beer. Until the completion of the transcontinental railroad, the saloon had been almost exclusively an urban phenomenon. The lack of refrigeration and pasteurization presented considerable problems for the aspiring saloon owner outside of the burgeoning cities of the Northwest. But with the completion of the Northern Pacific, these problems disappeared. "Brewers saw the opening of a great world and began, with unseemly haste, to encourage the cultivation of saloons in the small communities that were sprouting along the Northern Pacific right-of-way," according to historian Norman Clark. As the number of saloons grew in small communities, resentment among more rural folk increased as well.[13]

On the heels of the Woman's Crusade came the Woman's Christian Temperance Union (WCTU). As noted earlier, the WCTU was led by the remarkable Frances Willard. Willard energized women wherever she went and proved to be just the impetus necessary to establish chapters of the WCTU in the Northwest. The *Oregonian* reported that thousands had to be turned away when Willard spoke in Portland. On June 15, 1883, Willard presided over the initial meeting of the first chapter in Oregon at the First Methodist Episcopal Church. Six days later, she spoke in Olympia before making stops in Tacoma and Seattle.[14]

While in Seattle, residents, probably out of both conviction and curiosity, came to hear this woman pronounce on the state of moral affairs in the city. According to one account,

> Yesler's hall was packed—it was jammed, until every door and window had to be opened, and people climbed up the sides of the house, hung on by the windows, and scaled the sides of neighboring piles of lumber, to see and hear a small part of what passed within. Dozens came and went away, unable to get within sound of the voices, and there were constant appeals for the speakers to speak louder. Two such buildings could not have held the people who came.[15]

In addition to several of Seattle's clergymen, other luminaries came to hear Willard. Judge Thomas Burke, one of the most influential business leaders in early Seattle history, welcomed the WCTU president and commented that "women have fearfully suffered because of the ravages of intemperance, and it is proper that they lead in this reformation." Chief Justice Roger Greene of the Washington Territorial Supreme Court, himself a Baptist minister, followed with several

The WCTU lobbied for decades on behalf of Prohibition and for the protection of women and children.
Courtesy Washington State Historical Society, Tacoma, Washington

minutes of remarks that underscored the importance of the temperance movement in the Pacific Northwest.[16] And L. J. Powell, president of the University of Washington, addressed the throng in Yesler's Hall by saying that this was the proudest moment of his life to welcome such a champion as Frances Willard, who "comes to help us throttle the monster who is doing such a terrible work of destruction here.... Open your eyes and you will see the harvest of destruction and death being constantly reaped. Our sons and our daughters are going down to dishonored graves."[17] Clearly, members of the burgeoning middle class in Seattle believed that alcohol was at the center of numerous related cultural issues at stake in the late nineteenth century. Throughout the Northwest, Francis Willard spoke before large crowds and succeeded in organizing local chapters of the WCTU.

Most importantly, the WCTU provided hope for women across the country, as it did for women in the Pacific Northwest. According to one historian, "Women saw in temperance salvation from poverty, domestic violence and abandonment."[18] Thousands of women measured social progress in terms of the Prohibition of alcohol; along with the suffrage movement, Prohibition efforts motivated significant numbers to enter into the public square for the first time.

The most notable early accomplishment of the WCTU in the Pacific Northwest was the legislative approval of temperance education. Led at the national level by Mary Hunt, the WCTU's national superintendent for the Department of Scientific Temperance Instruction, the curriculum movement swept the country in the mid-1880s. In the Pacific Northwest, legislation mandating temperance instruction passed first in Oregon in 1885, and then in the following year in Washington and Idaho, after WCTU women had circulated hundreds of petitions, sponsored lectures, and kept the issue alive in the press with letters to newspaper editors. Advocates developed curricular materials that, in retrospect, exaggerated to some extent the health risks as well as the social impact of alcohol. Instruction centered on the addictive character of alcohol, even in limited quantities. Lessons stressed the likelihood of a life of crime as the most common result of overconsumption. The intent was to scare young children about the evils of alcohol.[19]

If the passage of Scientific Temperance legislation in the 1880s buoyed the spirits of Prohibition forces, final victory was still nearly three decades away. Opposition to Prohibition remained strong, particularly within sectors of the business community worried about the economic cost of diminished alcohol consumption. And "dry" forces did not always present a united front. They frequently disagreed over what strategy would prove most effective. For example, in the 1880s, Methodist street evangelist Edward Sutton arrived in Seattle and began a prodigious effort on behalf of total Prohibition. Relentless in his preaching about the evils of alcohol, Sutton made hundreds of speeches. On more than one occasion, he exhorted his listeners to consider, "If your liberty to take a glass of beer when you want it means the subjugation of a nation to the worst enemy man ever had, then, I would dash your beerglass into a thousand pieces. When the liberty of one man means the subjugation of a hundred, let his liberty cease then and there."[20] However, Sutton often alienated moderate reformers who sought some kind of middle ground.[21]

During the following year, Sutton and others patched up their differences sufficiently to get statewide Prohibition on the ballot in 1889, along with statehood for Washington and women's suffrage.

Nevertheless, despite receiving more votes than the suffrage petition, Prohibition went down to defeat. Dry forces remained undeterred. From the late 1890s through the first decade of the twentieth century, Christians kept the temperance issue alive. Methodists, Presbyterians, Baptists, and Congregationalists led the way. Activists received a boost with the establishment of the national Anti-Saloon League (ASL) in Ohio in 1893. Proudly referring to itself as "the church in action against the saloon," the organization was designed to be an all-male counterpart to the WCTU. In 1898, the ASL was established in Washington and in Oregon as well. Tactically, the ASL relied on the individual congregation as its basic organizational unit, with the local minister serving as a sort of precinct whip.[22]

As a consequence, momentum continued to build toward Prohibition in the region. The initial strategy focused on passing the possibility of local option (the ability for a municipality to control or limit the access to alcohol) and then moving toward complete statewide Prohibition. In every case, religious individuals and organizations provided the major impetus behind the movement. Protestant churches, the Anti-Saloon League, and the Woman's Christian Temperance Union battled side by side against distillers, hotel keepers, saloon owners, brewers, and hop growers.

In 1904, the local option passed in Oregon—the first of the Northwest states to do so. Just how many establishments shut their doors is a matter of debate, but one report identified 128 saloons that closed as a result of the 1904 election.[23] A measure for statewide Prohibition was defeated in 1910 but subsequently passed in 1914. According to historian John Casswell, "The organized strength of the movement was in the Protestant churches, to which the Anti-Saloon League and the Woman's Christian Temperance Union were closely allied."[24]

In Washington by 1907, both the *Seattle Post-Intelligencer* and the *Seattle Times* endorsed local option as a reasonable solution, but it was still defeated in the House of Representatives in Olympia by one vote. The Anti-Saloon League publicized the names of those legislators who had voted against the measure, and in the 1908 election, of the forty-four who had opposed local option, only fifteen won reelection.[25]

In retrospect, one of the most important religious figures to arrive in the Pacific Northwest and actively campaign for Prohibition was the revivalist Billy Sunday. Born in Iowa and orphaned in the Civil War, Sunday had gained notice as a professional baseball player. But a conversion experience had led him to give up the game and begin work as an evangelist with J. Wilbur Chapman of the Presbyterian Church. In 1896, Sunday began to conduct revival campaigns in the Midwest. By the time his reputation reached the Pacific Northwest, Sunday had emerged as a preacher who could speak directly and passionately to working-class men. He once was quoted as saying that only after he "loaded my Gospel gun with rough-on-rats, ipecac, dynamite, and barbed wire" did he succeed. By the time his career ended in 1935, it was estimated that he had preached to more than a hundred million people. Without question, he was the most widely known preacher of his era.[26]

However, long before he achieved his greatest national fame, Sunday came to the Pacific Northwest, and he subsequently returned several times before buying a small ranch near Hood River, Oregon. But Sunday first made his mark in Spokane. In 1907, Dr. H. I. Rasmus, pastor of Spokane's First Methodist Episcopal Church, and Dr. E. L. House, pastor of the city's Westminster Congregational Church, began to entreat Sunday to come to the Inland Northwest to hold a revival, knowing that his focus would be on the working-class men who took up residence in the city during the winter months, when work in the mines and forests was scarce. Finally, after several rejections, Sunday agreed to come to Spokane during Christmas 1908 to hold a revival for approximately six weeks. Promoters printed placard cards for saloons—ten thousand prayer cards and twelve thousand convert cards—as well as four hundred streetcar signs. One Spokane pastor expressed his hope for the results of Sunday's campaign on the behavior of working-class males: "Drunkards will be reformed, hearts will be reclaimed, the whole atmosphere will be purified and Spokane will be in every way a cleaner, better city in which to live. Every good citizen, whether he be a Christian or not, ought to fall in line and help to boost for Billy Sunday and his revival."[27]

Approximately eight thousand folk gathered for the opening of the revival in a wooden tabernacle, a short walk from the train station. After introductions and the singing of the "Battle Hymn of the Republic" and "Blest Be the Tie that Binds," Sunday appeared for the beginning of a remarkable religious event. The packed house stood and began to wave handkerchiefs and hymn books. "Off his mark like a sprinter, at full speed from the start, Billy Sunday told the people how he loved God and hated the devil," reported the *Spokesman-Review*. "His collar

Billy Sunday made several trips to the Northwest to rally thousands behind Prohibition. Courtesy Bain Collection, Library of Congress

[is] wilted and limp, his voice hoarse and his hair matted to his brow with sweat. . . . He hits the pulpit tremendous blows with his fists and performs feats of balance on that piece of furniture that would lay the ordinary preacher by the heels with general breakdown." It was the age of vaudeville, and Sunday certainly understood the medium; he impersonated the "worldly deacon and the college 'rah rah' boy . . . with equal fidelity."[28] He never paused from beginning to end; between exhorting his listeners to commitment and pleading with them to change their ways, he performed college yells that brought his audience to its feet screaming and shouting.

For six weeks Sunday railed against saloons, dance halls, and the theater. Thousands responded; on January 17, some thirty-five thousand people attended services at the tabernacle. Two days later, the *Spokesman-Review* published a list of legislators from Spokane and their probable votes on the local option bill then pending in the state legislature in Olympia. Sunday led a special train filled with Spokane businessmen to Olympia to help in the lobbying efforts. Once in Olympia, Sunday preached to women in the afternoon, and in the evening he delivered what was known as his "booze sermon" at the opera house to senators, representatives, and the general public. That two-hour exhortation against liquor elicited enthusiastic applause from listeners, who repeatedly rose, cheered, "waved their hands and shouted at the unique climaxes and expressions made by the noted speaker." Marion Hay, the acting governor, hosted a banquet for the Sunday party. The Spokane group met with its state representatives and presented a petition with more than eight thousand signatures urging passage of the local option bill. The US senator from Spokane,

Miles Poindexter, along with select members of the Sunday party, spoke in favor of the measure.[29]

A large crowd met the party on its return to Spokane and escorted Sunday and his entourage from the train station to the tabernacle for another sermon. The immediate result of the lobbying effort was failure, for opponents amended the local option bill to death, but a compromise bill finally passed both houses later that year.

Sunday's ultimate impact on church attendance in Spokane is undetermined, but what is clear is that civic leaders hoping to build more momentum toward Prohibition in the Northwest believed Sunday was an effective spokesperson. Shortly after his stint in Spokane, the former baseball player received an invitation to come to Bellingham, Washington, which in 1910 had just under twenty-five thousand residents and an estimated sixty saloons. As he had done in Spokane, Sunday led a six-week revival. While it was not universally endorsed by the Christian community, the vast majority of churches supported Sunday's efforts. An estimated twenty-six churches joined the campaign and closed down their pulpits during the six weeks of the revival.[30] A large wooden tabernacle was constructed, slightly smaller in size than the one in Spokane, although it still held approximately fifty-six hundred people. Sunday preached two sermons a day for the next six weeks. His message was clear: young men should give up alcohol, devote themselves to hard work, and take care of their families. He told his largely male audience that there was nothing unmanly about being a Christian. Later that fall, Bellingham did in fact vote to go dry.

Billy Sunday next turned to Everett, Washington. Local prohibitionists hoped that the evangelist might provide the tipping point in the November 1910 local option election. Sunday arrived in Everett a week before the election and worked diligently to assist the Everett Local Option League (which included a number of evangelical ministers) organize the anti-saloon forces. In addition to Sunday's sermons, prayer meetings were held throughout the city. Saloon supporters brought noted defense attorney Clarence Darrow to town to persuade voters to keep the city wet. But on this occasion the dry forces, sensing victory, continued to push hard. Two days prior to the election, twenty-five hundred children, four abreast and seven blocks long, marched against the saloon. On the day of the election, Everett voted dry, 2,208 to 1,933, and church bells tolled hourly for the death of the saloon.[31]

Sunday had been asked to make his appeal for a dry vote in Oregon only a few weeks before returning to Everett. Voters had approved the local option in 1904, and county after county debated the issue. In March 1909, leaders from the WCTU, the Anti-Saloon League, and the Prohibition Party strategized for the 1910 campaign and decided to bring Billy Sunday to the state.[32] Even though total statewide Prohibition in Oregon failed once again in 1910, Billy Sunday's efforts, along with the WCTU and Anti-Saloon League, had made significant inroads in both Washington and Oregon.[33]

In retrospect, the passage of statewide legislation in both Oregon and Washington depended on women, which meant that suffrage was indispensable to this movement. With some notable exceptions, such as Seattle Presbyterian pastor Mark Matthews, many Christians and Jews in both Washington and Oregon worked diligently to pass legislation ensuring women the right to vote. In 1909, Seattle's Plymouth Congregational Church was selected to host the National Woman's Suffrage Convention, largely because Plymouth's pastor, the Reverend F. J. Van Horn, had developed a national reputation for his support for women's suffrage, and more than a dozen other Seattle clergy were involved. Meanwhile, in both Oregon and Washington, members of the WCTU actively promoted the right to vote, often in partnership with pastors and parishes. Scores of suffrage speeches were given in local churches throughout both states. A typical event occurred in Portland in 1912, when the WCTU sponsored an institute at the Woodstock Methodist Church. The overall theme was, "The hand that rocks the cradle should mark the ballot." Speaker after speaker hammered on the importance of gaining the right to vote.[34] In that same year, Quakers formed an equal suffrage society in Portland, and various other Portland churches participated in "Equal Suffrage Sunday."[35] As a consequence of these efforts, as well as countless others, women's suffrage was achieved first in Washington in 1910 and subsequently in Oregon in 1912.

As predicted, the vast majority of women were inclined to vote for Prohibition, and this culminated in Washington and Oregon in the election of 1914. A Prohibition amendment was placed on the ballot by initiative petition in both states. Resources from the national Prohibition agencies poured into the Pacific Coast states in order to win them for the "dry" column. Oregon, Washington, and Idaho were considered the best prospects, and the national organizations of the Presbyterian and the Methodist Churches assisted the effort. From the national Presbyterian headquarters came the announcement of a $50,000 fund to put 250 workers in the Pacific states during the year for the purpose of organizing support for Prohibition. The Methodists committed to have seven hundred ministers work at the grassroots level in Oregon, Washington, and California.[36]

Before the general election, a group called the "Flying Squadron of America" toured the state. The squadron included some twenty men and women, including the heads of temperance work for the Methodists and Presbyterians respectively.[37] The Anti-Saloon League organized activity in both Oregon and Washington into "precincts" averaging 120 families each. The Flying Squadron brought speakers, singers, automobile parades, brass brands, and hundreds of young people who staged marches in support of the Prohibition initiative.[38]

Momentum toward Prohibition was building even within some circles of the Catholic Church. In 1914, Augustine Francis Schinner from Wisconsin was appointed to be the first bishop in Spokane. Schinner arrived with a reputation for the promotion of abstinence from alcoholic beverages. Schinner was once described by Catholic historian Wilfred Schoenberg as "no Methodist, but in a gentle, heart-warming manner constantly urged sobriety." It was known that several years earlier, he had promoted the use of something called "Neal's Three-Day Drink Habit Cure." Schinner claimed that he had convinced an alcoholic man to employ the remedy and supposedly he "was perfectly cured in three days."[39]

Nevertheless, Seattle proved to be the central battleground in the state of Washington. Major newspapers, from the *Seattle Times* and *Seattle Post-Intelligencer* to the *Argus* and *Town Crier*, opposed Initiative 3—the Prohibition initiative, as did much of the business community. Historian Norman Clark asserted that it "became the most anguished conflict between the evangelical churches and the business community in the city's history."[40] While anti-saloon forces did not have any newspapers at their disposal, they did have on their side Mark Matthews, pastor of Seattle's First Presbyterian Church, the largest Presbyterian Church in the country, with close to ten thousand members. Matthews, an inveterate opponent of the saloon, loved to

■ ──

use his invective against the evils of alcohol. Matthews once called the saloon the most

> fiendish, corrupt and hell-soaked institution that ever crawled out of the slime of the eternal pit. . . . It takes the kind, loving husband and father, smothers every spark of love in his bosom, and transforms him into a heartless wretch, and makes him steal the shoes from his starving babe's feet to find the price for a glass of liquor. . . . But perhaps you, like thousands of foolish co-conspirators, will say that the saloon is a necessary institution. You never uttered a more blasphemous lie on earth. . . . The open saloon as an institution has its origin in hell, and it is manufacturing subjects to be sent back to hell.[41]

Matthews was a publicist's dream, and he was not alone in his sentiments. Scores of ministers, as well as the vast majority of newly enfranchised women throughout the Northwest, believed as he did, and they rode a wave of reform against the saloon in community after community in the Northwest.

Matthews and other ministers encouraged parishioners to vote for any measure that might lead to greater regulation or outright prohibition of alcohol. In October, prior to the November election in 1914, Matthews led a daily revival at his church and preached incessantly on the evil of the liquor conspiracy. He finished with a sermon titled "Satan at the Polls" and joined a throng of ministers throughout the city who hoped that their congregants would turn out in record numbers to vote for the most transformative social change of their generation. On election day, the women of the WCTU placed signs in every precinct and then attended prayer services.[42]

When it came time to go to the polls, more people voted on this issue than on any other in Washington state history. Nearly 95 percent of the total electorate participated, with 189,840 for passage of Initiative 3 and 171,208 against. Incredibly, it was an off-year election.

In Oregon, the same forces were at work. Churches took charge of getting out the vote. Tremendous effort was made to register new voters, particularly women. Final figures showed 136,842 for Prohibition and 100,362 against. Approximately nine hundred saloons and eighteen breweries soon closed in an estimated ninety-eight Oregon towns.[43]

Clearly, several factors contributed to the victory for Prohibition forces. Rural voters throughout the Northwest seized upon the initiative as an opportunity to battle against "immoral" urban interests. Women saw Prohibition as an important strategy for decreasing domestic violence and voted by a two-to-one margin for the measure against saloons.[44] And clearly, evangelical Christianity played a major role. Temperance education, a result of relentless WCTU effort, had been a part of the public school system in the Northwest since the 1880s, and as Norman Clark observed, "when the people of Washington voted for anti-drink measures in 1914, 1916, and 1918, they had been exposed to over three decades of formalized, official anti-drink instruction" by religious organizations.[45]

The Anti-Saloon League, the Woman's Christian Temperance Union, and countless pastors like Mark Matthews played a major role in organizing the vote. Unnumbered sermons were accompanied by parades, rallies, and songs. An almost apocalyptic rhetoric charged the troops and ultimately carried the day. Certainly some voters longed for the return to a more moral agrarian world, but many more were motivated by the hope that eliminating alcohol would make life better for women and children. It was one thing for a man to make a choice about the consumption of alcohol, but it was another to let that choice ruin the lives of others. Improving lives of the vulnerable was certainly the great hope of a majority of voters.

But the story did not end in 1914, or even in 1916, when the law went into effect. From the first day, enforcement proved difficult, and "wet" goods crossed the Canadian border with ease. Dry forces continued to lobby for more enforcement, while anti-Prohibition forces in Oregon and Washington continued their fight to restore the sale of alcohol. Nevertheless, momentum toward national Prohibition continued to gain strength; the onset of World War I triggered concern for the well-being of US military troops, and dry advocates seized on the argument that prohibition of alcohol would help ensure a more able fighting force. To this end, they successfully pushed for an amendment to the US Constitution.[46]

It was only a few years after the end of World War I, however, that the elements that had combined to bring about Prohibition, first at the state level and then at the national level, began to fall apart. Farmers, members of the urban middle class, elements of the trade unions, and, of course, churches and organizations such as the ASL and the WCTU began to divide among themselves regarding policies of enforcement. [47]

As the momentum for repeal of Prohibition grew, traditional supporters of the law also reemerged. Mark Matthews and other ministers, as well as leaders from the WCTU, all jumped back into the fray. Numerous speeches, sermons, and leaflets were spread across Washington. The same was true in Oregon in 1925 and 1931. Initially, dry forces prevailed in the Oregon State legislature, and they refused to pass bills that would have put the Prohibition question back before the voters. But in November 1932, building upon the momentum of wet forces across the nation, Oregon voters used the initiative to effectively eliminate the state's ability to enforce Prohibition laws.

In Washington, similar events unfolded as voters, in November 1932, repealed Prohibition. Mark Matthews and others believed that voters would surely come to their senses and never fully repeal the Volstead Act, but the handwriting was on the wall.[48] As it turned out, the middle class throughout the United States did not accept total abstinence. The vast majority of Americans came to see Prohibition as too extreme.

In retrospect, the drinking culture in America did change in significant ways. While organized crime around alcohol increased and enforcement proved problematic, the saloon essentially disappeared as a disreputable drinking place. Some scholars estimate that the amount of per capita consumption of alcohol declined by over 50 percent compared with 1910.[49] Historian Catherine Gilbert Murdock persuasively argues that the habits of alcohol consumption among millions of men moderated after the 1920s. In her words, males accepted more "domesticated" practices of drinking. Murdock credits groups such as the WCTU—in some ways the ultimate outsiders to the prevailing alcohol-abundant culture of the Northwest—for bringing attention to the overconsumption of alcohol by men. Domestic violence, loss of employment, and political corruption associated with the saloon all gained attention in public consciousness through the arguments of religious activists who favored Prohibition.[50] At the same time, Murdock also argues that the drive toward total abstinence on the part of religious activists alienated millions of men and women in the middle class. "Radical drys never recognized that alcohol control as entailed in federal prohibition was not the only solution to the problem of alcoholism. Prohibition failed because of this dry extremism."[51] Those within the Christian community who believed in abstinence did not anticipate the acceptance within the middle class and, particularly within a younger generation of women in the middle class, of moderate consumption of alcohol. If the public drunkard did not entirely disappear, the saloon as a male-only experience did, for the most part. In its place emerged the barroom that welcomed respectable women, and with women's inclusion, male drinking habits changed. Men's behavior came under greater scrutiny. Fewer and fewer men were willing to get publicly drunk in the company of women.

Religious forces, while generally failing in this effort to change radically the social culture of the Pacific Northwest, had nevertheless exerted a significant influence. Alcohol reform was the most visible evidence to date that they could impact the world in which they lived. Meanwhile, commitment to the protection of women and children remained steadfast and was manifested in the desire to eliminate another form of female exploitation: prostitution.

PROSTITUTION

If the saloon symbolized one of the two key concerns for the Christian community, the brothel reflected the other. In the late nineteenth century, virtually every city in America had its red-light district. Journalists and clergymen all over the country attempted to expose the vagaries of prostitution, which was often referred to as "white slavery," and the Pacific Northwest was no exception. As one Portland pastor put it in 1886:

> We have in our midst and all over our city a vice not hidden— shameless, horrible, unblushing, which sweeps like a roaring river of death past our business houses, through our busy streets, alongside our pure homes and under the very shadow of God's temples, bearing its regiments of corrupted, lustful and lost humanity on to a death more dreadful and hopeless than all the plagues, pestilences, dire calamites that have ever blackened our sin-cursed earth.[52]

Concern over prostitution had been growing since the 1880s, with the explosion of population following completion of transcontinental railroads. From the outset, religious individuals and organizations attempted to eliminate or at least regulate "the world's oldest profession." The goal was to "rescue" fallen women, arrest prostitutes, and eliminate political influence on regional police forces that might impede enforcement.[53]

Ministers in Portland and Seattle led investigative crusades into red-light districts to determine the identities of prostitutes, owners of unsavory businesses, and patrons. Religious reformers also linked prostitution and corrupt city government. They made municipal reform a central goal, given that extralegal "licensing fees" and other means of illicit regulation were the rule rather than the exception, and the police rarely enforced laws against prostitutes or brothels.[54]

In Portland, one of the early figures to advocate for legal reform and improvement of moral standards was Reverend Ezra Haskell. Arriving in Portland in 1886, Haskell was shocked to discover that prostitution was rampant. He concluded that the problem was fundamentally one of enforcement.[55] Like many other social purity reformers, Haskell accused police officers of accepting hush money to look the other way, and he openly attacked Portland's police chief, S. B. Parrish, for his cavalier approach to enforcement. For Haskell and other reformers, prostitution was integrally tied to the saloon. Haskell's investigation revealed that of the 164 saloons in the city, 140 were owned by people of nonnative birth. He expressed outrage that most of these saloons were open on Sunday in direct violation of the Sabbath closure law. Haskell frequently berated city officials for being too tolerant and the business community for its double standards. But in spite of Haskell's public condemnation, little changed over the next several years. Moral suasion seemed to have had little effect.[56]

By the fall of 1893, the Portland Ministerial Association decided to take another run at reform. It appointed a committee to compile a list of property owners who ostensibly were conducting business for immoral purposes. Led by the Reverend H. V. Rominger of the Hassalo Street Congregational Church and the Reverend Hugh F. Wallace of the First United Presbyterian Church, the committee found a surprising number of brothels, saloons, and gambling dens that were owned by some of Portland's most prominent businessmen, including brewer Henry Weinhard, wealthy investor Van B. DeLashmutt, former mayor R. R. Thompson, and Northern Pacific Lumber Company president Lauritz Therkelson.[57] Throughout the fall of 1894, Portland ministers fed the *Oregonian* a series of articles that focused on the rampant vice and corruption in the city.[58]

Portland's religious community openly debated their strategy for reform. Should law enforcement officials be pressured to arrest offending women, or should the focus be on identifying the owners of establishments that made prostitution possible? Reverend George R. Wallace, pastor of the First Congregational Church, favored the latter approach. Wallace, who arrived in Portland in the spring of 1894 from East Saginaw, Michigan, decided to preach sermons such as "What Can Respectable Property Owners Do with Property Located in Districts Given Over to Saloons and Houses of Infamy?" and "A Study in Scarlet; or the Fallen Women of Our City and Their Patrons." Wallace proved to be one of Portland's most popular speakers and seemed to care little about whom he might offend.[59] The Portland preacher condemned police for their practice of targeting women instead of men who patronized the women or who owned offensive establishments. He demanded that city officials "stop the supply, . . . [and make] the conditions of support for girls such that they can obtain sustenance and also retain their purity." He further called on people to "ostracize the impure man."[60]

Yet Wallace's approach failed to gain much traction with city officials. His criticisms were not much appreciated by the rich and powerful. As a consequence, he grew increasingly frustrated by what he saw as a double standard and an unwillingness to commit to real reform. In February 1896, he announced his departure. The *Oregonian* printed his parting speech, a clear illustration of the disdain he felt and also of his conviction that what he had tried to do was right:

> The time will come when those men who have done most to thwart me, and who have made me the most trouble, will say, "Wallace was right; he was truthful.". . . I tried to shut up the gambling houses and make our public officials do their duty. I would have been a renegade if I had done otherwise. . . . The great day of judgment comes, and if we believe in judgment, I believe that those who opposed me will then want to hide their faces in shame.[61]

Elsewhere in the Northwest, segments of the religious community continued to try to end prostitution, and in so doing they frequently battled with the business community. In Spokane, an estimated three hundred to five hundred prostitutes worked the downtown area at the turn of the century. While publicly most people decried the existence of prostitution, the business community generally supported the trade as long as city officials regulated it in some fashion. What many businessmen generally opposed was the complete elimination of prostitution. When periodic efforts surfaced to ban prostitution altogether, businessmen often spoke openly against reform: "It must not be lost sight of that we are a growing city. . . . Much of the city's financial success depends in no small measure on the floating population, which in the winter is unusually large. This class of population demands cheap amusement, and is entitled to it," according to O. L. Rankin, president of the Whitehouse Company.[62] Adolph Levy, secretary for Baum and Company, was quoted as saying that the "reforms proposed by the [city] council would greatly injure the general business interests of the city."[63]

In the end, Spokane City Council members failed to enact ordinances that would end prostitution in the city. Predictably, the clergy condemned the inability of politicians to address the situation to the satisfaction of the reformers. Bishop Lemuel H. Wells of the Episcopal diocese of Spokane, in an open letter to the *Spokesman Review* in 1899, asked, "Do you realize what this means? It is a bold bare-faced avowal that they are utterly without principle in this matter; that they are unblushingly sordid; that money is their God; that a few dollars are more important than purity, honesty, temperance, and virtue."[64]

Members of the religious community, as well as public health officials, kept up lobbying pressure. On six separate occasions, reformers attempted to pass ordinances in Spokane that would have significantly restricted prostitution. But unlike the case with temperance, the business community successfully fought the reformers and defeated them every time.[65]

Portland proved to be a different story. The city still had a reputation as an "open town" well into the twentieth century. One reporter for the *Oregonian* described the city in the following terms in 1911: "The trains are loaded with gamblers, macquereaux, touts, pimps, confidence men, common women . . . who have heard that the town is wide open, the pastures are green, and the feeding good."[66] And once again the spirit of reform or enforcement or both filled the air. On August 23, 1911, the Portland City Council passed an ordinance that authorized the mayor to appoint a committee to conduct a full-scale investigation of Portland's moral conditions. Shortly thereafter, a fifteen-person vice commission was appointed with four ministers, including the Reverend Henry Talbott, pastor of St. David's Episcopal Church. Fully authorized with badges of authority, the commission walked block to block gathering evidence of the existence of illegal gambling, alcohol, and prostitution.[67]

By January 1912, the commission issued its first report on the extent of venereal disease within the city. By April, the commission recommended that girls not be employed at any of the city's many shooting galleries. By August of that same year, the momentum for reform reached the governor's office. Governor Oswald West, who had styled himself as an antivice reformer, announced that he was "going to clean up Portland next."[68] The vice commission published a second report in August 1912 that revealed the widespread nature of the problem, including the collusion of the business community. As a result, police raided thirteen establishments in the downtown and North End, and the *Oregon Journal* reported that Governor West was committed "to wage relentless war upon vice."[69] The *Journal* informed its readers that the commission had uncovered a "shocking moral status" of the city by proving that "prominent citizens" profited from vice.[70]

All of this public exposure in the Progressive Era continued to generate momentum toward reform. By September, public outrage had increased significantly. On September 4 at the Gypsy Smith Tabernacle, thirty-five hundred people heard Governor West criticize Mayor Rushlight for being too willing to protect the interests of breweries and the "higher-ups." West declared at that rally that "Weinhard's brewery won't rule the state of Oregon. . . . There isn't a brick in the brewery down here that doesn't represent a broken heart."[71] West vowed to keep fighting for legislation that would expose the interests that supported prostitution in the city.

By October, the city council had debated two ordinances that had been recommended by the vice commission. One initiative was the "Tin Plate Law," which would require owners of hotels, rooming and lodging houses, and saloons to display signs indicating the name of the owner and the address. The second ordinance required a business permit and the posting of a $1,000 performance bond for hotels and rooming and lodging houses. Both measures passed in October. During the five weeks prior to the laws' taking effect, owners employed a number of creative tactics designed to protect their reputations and interests. Several name plates went up in Arabic, Hebrew, and French;

some of the properties were now owned by groups. But in the end, over forty indictments for violating the ordinances were handed down, and in general, business owners came into compliance. Some owners remodeled their buildings and forced the occupants to move. The Weinhard Brewery canceled contracts with five of its saloon outlets.[72]

CONCLUSION

In retrospect, the grand crusades against alcohol and prostitution were the culmination of Victorian Christian efforts to change the culture of the Pacific Northwest and specifically to exercise social control, primarily over single males. These efforts clearly mirrored national efforts to change drinking habits and sexual practices. In particular, the crusade against alcohol was the result of several decades of lobbying, preaching, and organizing voters to see more clearly what could be done to better protect women and children. These efforts, however, produced mixed results at best. In neither case did the hopes of reformers match the results. It is easier to see now, in retrospect, that both moral suasion and legislative coercion had limitations. The religious community relied heavily on the former and intermittently advocated for the latter. It would become commonplace to consider these efforts naïve, but more than anything else, the religious community can be credited with relentless effort to expose the vulnerability of women and children to domestic abuse and prostitution. Religion helped motivate tens of thousands of individuals to believe that they could reshape male behavior and eliminate the saloon as a social institution. Over the course of the century, these concerns continued to resonate, not just with the religious community but with other individuals and organizations concerned about the plight of women.

Meanwhile, that same hope in the efficacy of moral suasion and legislative reform motivated the religious community to work on complex issues related to race and ethnicity. In this case, however, religious activists were more divided in terms of strategy and approach. The Northwest would prove to be an important battleground on which conflicting views over how people of color should be treated played themselves out.

CHAPTER 5

TOLERANCE AND INTOLERANCE

In November 1885, a mob of some three hundred white Tacoma residents decided that the "Chinese must go!" Specifically, they wanted all of the Chinese to be expelled from the city. Not everyone agreed, however, including Presbyterian minister Reverend W. D. McFarland. In one sermon, McFarland denounced the actions of self-appointed vigilantes in a message that so offended some of his congregation that several walked out, only to have McFarland yell, "Go! Go! I will preach on till the benches are empty." The *Tacoma Ledger* called him a "pro-Chinese fanatic of the most bigoted sort," who was "utterly unfit to occupy any position of honor."[1]

Tacoma's mayor, R. Jacob Weisbach, led the charge to remove the Chinese. Public sentiment was so hostile to the Chinese and those who supported them that McFarland believed he needed to arm himself for protection. One Tacoma resident observed, "It probably was the only time in the city's history that a minister went about his pastoral duties, visiting business men in their homes and taking tea with his feminine parishioners with a brace of big army revolvers strapped beneath his Prince Albert."[2] McFarland, for all of his efforts, could not save the day, and the Chinese were shamelessly hustled out of town. To this day, Tacoma is one of the only major West Coast cities without a Chinatown.

Exercising a good deal of courage, Reverend McFarland certainly felt like an outsider when he stood up for a group that had become the object of hatred and suspicion. But religion could cut both ways. Nearly forty years later, a Disciples of Christ minister, Reverend Reuben Sawyer, drew the notice of local newspapers when he openly praised the Ku Klux Klan in Portland, Oregon, and attacked virtually anyone who was not Anglo-Saxon Protestant as a threat to the American way of life. For Sawyer, the threat included not only African Americans but, most notably, immigrants from southern and eastern Europe. And Sawyer was not alone. The Ku Klux Klan in Washington and Oregon gained much of its support from Protestants who feared the erosion of what they believed were traditional American values. While not the outsider in the same way that Reverend McFarland must have experienced, Sawyer and others of his generation believed their world was slipping away. If they did not feel immediately to be outsiders to the prevailing culture, they feared that they soon would be. For them, religious activism often took dramatic form in the shape of white robes and burning crosses in an effort to stem the tide of cultural change in the twentieth century.

These two episodes provide a glimpse into the conflicted history of religion and race-related matters in the Pacific Northwest. From the middle of the nineteenth century through the first three decades of the twentieth century, intense conflict over the civil rights of multiple groups considered to be threats to mostly white Anglo-Saxon Protestants erupted constantly. Religious individuals and organizations found themselves frequently in the middle of these disputes—and often on opposite sides, as McFarland and Sawyer reflect. On some occasions, these ministers stirred anxieties and appealed to the fears held by many of their parishioners. At other times, ministers and preachers vigorously fought for a more hospitable Northwest—one that welcomed people of different colors, religions, and ethnicities. This chapter explores a number of episodes in Pacific Northwest history where religious activists attempted to shape the larger cultural response to those who were not defined as white Anglo-Saxon Protestants.

THE "NEGRO QUESTION"

As early as the 1840s, Oregon settlers debated the "Negro Question" as it was framed in the era prior to the Civil War. In 1844, the Oregon territorial legislature passed a bill that stated that anyone who brought slaves into Oregon must remove them within three years, or else the slaves would be freed by the government. The bill also stipulated that any free blacks in the territory would have to leave within two years if they were male or within three years if female. Any African American who remained in Oregon after that time would "suffer a whip lashing, to be repeated after six months if they still refused to leave."[3] After complaints that the law was too harsh, the whipping punishment was removed. Instead, violators would be hired out at a public auction, in other words, temporarily enslaved, and their employers would escort them out of the territory at the end of their period of service. Apparently only one African American was actually expelled, but undoubtedly these laws contributed to the fact that fewer than one hundred African Americans lived in the Oregon Territory by 1855. Nevertheless, the question was more about the future than the present, and people with deep religious convictions entered the fray with strong opinions on both sides of the issues.

The urgency surrounding the "Negro Question" accelerated with the passage of the Kansas-Nebraska Act in 1854, which overturned the Missouri Compromise of 1820 and introduced the concept of "popular sovereignty." Settlers soon had the opportunity to vote on whether slavery should be permitted. Recent arrivals in the upper Willamette Valley brought both abolitionist and proslavery opinions with them. The issue of the extension of slavery focused the energies of Democrats and the new Republican Party on the future of race in the region.

Newspapers throughout the Oregon Territory reflected the division of opinion, and frequently, ministers from various denominations felt compelled to weigh in. The Reverend Milton Starr, Congregational minister in Corvallis, wrote, "The Baptists have recently established a paper in Corvallis ... edited by pro-slavery ministers. Up to this time I have felt that Oregon would come into the union a Free State. There are now many alarming prospects that this curse of all curses will be entailed upon Oregon."[4] Republicans garnered their own religious support for their opposition to slavery. Congregational ministers in Oregon at annual association meetings from 1854 to 1857 passed resolutions opposing the extension of slavery and declaring it to be morally wrong.[5] The Congregational Association committed to work peacefully and legally to abolish slavery.

The debate over Oregon's proposed entry into the union continued to raise concerns over the future status of African Americans. Three ballot issues faced Oregon voters in 1857. The first one centered on approval of the state constitution, which passed by a vote of 7,195 to 3,195. The second issue focused on slavery, and Oregonians voted to prohibit the "peculiar institution" by a vote of 7,727 to 2,645. In contrast, the third ballot issue proposed that African Americans essentially be made illegal aliens without citizenship or legal rights; voters approved this measure by a margin of 8,640 to 1,081, reflecting the intense desire on the part of Oregonians to keep the state free of African Americans.[6] Anyone wanting to lobby for increased civil rights for African Americans or any other nonwhite group faced considerable challenges during the middle decades of the nineteenth century.

One of the nineteenth-century clergymen most outspoken in defense of African Americans was the Reverend Obed Dickinson. In 1852, the American Home Missionary Society sent Dickinson, a Congregational minister, to Salem, Oregon, to serve the First Congregational Church.[7] Once in Salem, Dickinson, a Caucasian, soon found himself embroiled in debate surrounding the extension of slavery into Oregon. Dickinson believed deeply in the dignity of African Americans. He preached often about his belief in racial justice, while other ministers, many of whom were apparently Southern Methodists, opposed the legalization of rights for African Americans and frequently criticized Dickinson.[8] But Dickinson persisted; he exhorted his congregation to understand that discrimination, let alone slavery, was against God's will. Yet it was a struggle. When three African Americans wanted to join Dickinson's First Congregational Church, some parishioners wanted separate services, but Dickinson refused. Other members were furious when he presided over the wedding of two African Americans. In a long letter to the secretaries of the American Home Missionary Society, Dickinson explained how members of his church had tried to turn the congregation against him because of his outspoken view that African Americans should be admitted as full members to their congregation. He explained in a sermon that "there is a wrong public opinion in this town. It has closed the doors of all our schools against the children of these black families dooming them to ignorance in life. I said it was wrong to take away the key of knowledge from any human being. Especially wrong when their property was taxed to support our schools not to let them have some privileges in the schools."[9]

Ultimately, Dickinson succeeded in convincing his congregation to admit African Americans into membership, but the tide of public opinion against African Americans was strong in Oregon. The intensity of feeling was reflected in the fact that the Reverend Milton Starr was

Obed Dickinson (standing right) spoke out frequently against the discrimination suffered by many of Oregon's early African Americans. Courtesy Capi Lynn of *Statesman Journal*

run out of Corvallis and Albany because of his pro–African American preaching.[10]

Dickinson, however, continued to advocate for African Americans, even in the face of considerable resistance from his congregation, which finally forced him to leave in 1867. In retrospect, Dickinson's struggle with his congregation foreshadowed what would be repeated on many occasions over the next century. Many Christian ministers sought an end to discriminatory practices. On the other hand, many other Christian ministers expressed sympathies to more racist notions and certainly did not stand in the way of their parishioners who attempted to make life difficult for persons of color in the Pacific Northwest. Struggles between black and white Oregonians continued to fester for the next century, and religious individuals continued to reflect and contribute to those struggles, sometimes actively promoting equality and the cause of civil rights.

CHINESE

By the 1870s and 1880s, attention turned toward the significant influx of Chinese, who had been employed to build the railroads. Railroad companies utilized Chinese by the thousands to do the most difficult and dangerous jobs. It was estimated that by 1865, 80 percent of the workers who built the Central Pacific Railroad were Chinese, as were the majority of miners in Idaho.[11] By 1880 an estimated three thousand Chinese lived in Washington Territory, and nearly ten thousand lived in the state of Oregon.[12]

While certainly fewer in number than Chinese men, Chinese women faced considerable hardships once in North America, and prostitution became a common occupation. In response, churches from numerous denominations established urban missions in Portland and

Seattle in the 1870s and 1880s. Initially founded to meet the basic needs of Chinese females who had been forced into prostitution, the missions offered English-language courses and employment assistance for a significant number of women. As prostitution continued to be a problem, churches also established "rescue homes" and placed Chinese women in the homes of church members.[13]

More courageously, in the face of broad anti-Chinese sentiment across the region, several clergy in the Northwest spoke out in support of the Chinese. The *Pacific Christian Advocate*, a Methodist-sponsored publication, deplored the 1882 Exclusion Act, which was intended to prohibit future immigration of Chinese to the United States. Editors called it "dishonorable" and a terrible example for a Christian nation. The Puget Sound Association of Congregational Churches condemned the law and labeled it "anti-Christian."[14]

However, just as clergy were split over the slavery of African Americans, they were also divided regarding their attitudes toward the Chinese. Roman Catholic priests expressed frequent anti-Chinese sentiments, as Irish-Catholic workers competed with Chinese for the most menial jobs. The *Catholic Sentinel*, as early as 1870, urged its Irish readers to "agitate" and vote for anti-Chinese candidates in the upcoming election. Protestant ministers also could be found criticizing the Chinese. Reverend J. A. Cruzan from Portland, for example, did not advocate discrimination but did conclude "that the Chinese contributed to the moral decay of Portland and drove down wages."[15] And the Reverend E. Trumbull Lee from Portland's Calvary Presbyterian asserted that Chinese were "unclean heathens" who deprived American workers of jobs and showed no evidence that they ever would be Americanized.[16] At times, Protestant concerns about the challenge of Americanizing the Chinese were even mingled with an anti-Catholic perspective. The *Pacific Christian Advocate* speculated that much of the anti-Chinese agitation in the Pacific Northwest was inspired by Catholics in order to "gratify the Irish by crafty priests and designing demagogues." The Oregon Methodist Conference even declared, "We do not encourage Chinese immigration, but we think it less a source of danger than the papal superstition of Europe."[17]

Whatever positive or negative impact Protestants and Catholics exerted on the public debate over immigration, the climate continued to deteriorate. In 1885, a riot broke out in Rock Springs, Wyoming, which left twenty-eight Chinese dead and fifteen wounded in a railroad camp. The Rock Springs incident seemed to agitate citizens in Washington Territory, and on September 11, 1885, vigilantes raided a Chinese settlement in Coal Creek, just outside of Renton on the east side of Lake Washington, and three Chinese were killed in the community of Issaquah, ten miles east of Seattle. Several vicious incidents occurred throughout Oregon in 1885 and 1886, and several efforts were made to run the Chinese out of Portland, although they failed to succeed.[18]

Meanwhile, as we have seen in Tacoma, a group of individuals appointed themselves to committees for the purpose of expelling the Chinese. As mentioned earlier, Reverend W. D. McFarland, a Presbyterian minister, used his pulpit to condemn the advocates of expulsion, and he was not alone: Reverend E. C. Oakley of the Congregational Church and eight members of the Tacoma Ministerial Alliance went on record condemning the expulsion. Nevertheless, on November 3, 1885, approximately three hundred men drove seven hundred Chinese out of Tacoma on wagons and killed two Chinese.[19]

Seattle was equally unsettled in regard to the Chinese population. As in Tacoma, plans surfaced to expel the Chinese from the city, but local ministers and churches quickly rallied against such notions. The Seattle Methodist Episcopal Ministers' Association passed a resolution denouncing plans for the expulsion of Seattle Chinese as "cruel, brutal, un-American, and un-Christian." Several Seattle ministers called for protection and declared that the churches should be places of refuge. The Reverend Louis Albert Banks of the Battery Street Methodist Episcopal Church compared the Tacoma expulsion to that of the Moors and Huguenots and challenged Seattle Christians not to stand by and "look on in silence."[20] Yet as in Tacoma, clergy who openly resisted anti-Chinese hysteria were frequently chastised in the local press. The editor of the Seattle *Daily Call* criticized what he called "over-zealous pastors [who] lean so heavily toward the heathen horde because of the money made through the Chinese mission school."[21]

In spite of the efforts of several clergy and churches in Seattle, anti-Chinese riots broke out in February 1886. The territorial governor quickly responded by activating local forces into a "Home Guard," for the purpose of protecting the Chinese against vigilante mobs. Several local pastors supported the governor's efforts. According to one account, Reverend Bates of the Plymouth Congregational Church left midway through his own service and, with rifle in hand, joined the local forces in preserving order. Laymen from other denominations also armed themselves and, as part of the Home Guard, formed a line of defense between the Chinese and the mob. Another member of the Seattle clergy, Louis Banks, also stopped short of finishing his sermon and rushed out to join in defense of the Chinese against the rioters.[22]

The precise motive for Seattle pastors, as well as anyone who fought to protect the safety of the Chinese, is not clear. While some explicitly expressed a belief in justice and fairness, Mildred Andrews, who wrote the history of Seattle's Plymouth Congregational Church (Reverend Bates's church), was less charitable: she asserted that some Plymouth members defended the Chinese simply out of self-interest. Parishioners, she claimed, "took advantage of the cheap labor by employing Chinese servants or relying on Chinese businesses to do their laundry."[23]

In other less ambiguous ways, however, Christians supported Chinese immigrants in the Northwest. In spite of considerable public opposition, numerous churches offered Chinese a safe haven. Chinese Baptist churches were established in Seattle and Portland, and the Chinese Presbyterian Church in Portland became a particularly important place of refuge.[24] In addition, Seattle's First Presbyterian Church, under the leadership of Reverend Mark Matthews, sponsored a night school for Chinese immigrants in 1903. The school served the dual purposes of assisting recent arrivals in finding jobs and converting them to Christianity. During the first year, approximately thirty Chinese attended the school; by the second year, a conversation class was organized in which all speaking was done in English, with violators being fined a penny. Typically, sixty to sixty-five people attended.[25] On balance, Protestant ministers and churches played at least a mitigating role in the struggle to develop humane conditions for Chinese in the Pacific Northwest.

AFRICAN AMERICAN CHURCH

The most consistent religious community to express opposition to the social injustice that emerged in the Pacific Northwest in the nineteenth and early twentieth centuries was the African American church. The African American church served as the major social refuge for its

CHAPTER 5: TOLERANCE AND INTOLERANCE

primarily black constituents in the Pacific Northwest. The church functioned as a social hub and allowed African Americans to retain elements of black culture that they brought with them, largely from the South. But the church also helped organize protests against the more egregious forms of segregation and discrimination.

The last thirty years of the nineteenth century were a period of growth for the African American religious community. The first black church in Portland was organized in 1862 and given the name the People's Church. In 1869 the African Methodist Episcopal Zion Church incorporated in Portland. A third black church, the Mt. Olivet Baptist Church, was established in Portland in the 1890s.[26] In Spokane, Calvary Baptist and Bethel African Methodist Episcopal (AME) both organized in 1890. In Seattle, the Jones Street African Methodist Episcopal Church began meeting in 1886 and was incorporated in 1891 (and later became the First African Methodist Episcopal Church); Mount Zion Baptist Church began holding services in 1890 and was incorporated in 1894. These churches served as the social center for the African American community. One early black pastor wrote that the church "remains the one resort in the community where they may develop their latent powers without embarrassment or restraint."[27]

Black churches did more than simply nurture an African American spirituality that was vital to the well-being of its members; churches helped shape a broader social culture for African Americans. They presented lectures, plays, and concerts as well as helped raise money for southern black colleges. Black churches provided critical support for widows and orphans. Members from the Jones Street AME Church in Seattle formed the Frances Ellen Harper branch of the Woman's Christian Temperance Union, and these women spent considerable time in the Seattle jails working with the poor, prostitutes, and drug addicts, both black and white.[28] According to historian Quintard Taylor, churches "formed the nucleus of the self-defined community and were part of a network of African American churches in the Pacific Northwest which provided mutual support and encouragement."[29]

In Spokane, the best-known African American from the period was the Reverend Peter Barrow. An ex-slave from Virginia, Barrow fought with distinction in the Union Army. Elected to the Mississippi House of Representatives, he served two terms as state senator in the Vicksburg area. In 1889, Barrow migrated to the Pacific Northwest, looking for a fresh start after white Southerners put an end to Reconstruction governments. He settled near Deer Lake, forty miles north of Spokane, and in 1890 he and his family moved to Spokane and helped establish Calvary Baptist Church, the first permanent African American Baptist church in the state. But Barrow also maintained his land north of the city and established the Deer Lake Irrigated Orchards Company. Tragically, he died in a streetcar accident in 1905, but his son took over the company, which employed over a hundred African American workers. In 1911 the Barrow family launched the *Citizen*, an African American issues-oriented newspaper, which became a major voice of expression for the African American community in Spokane.[30]

After Barrow's death, however, Calvary Baptist Church and Bethel African Methodist Episcopal Church (AME) continued to provide pastors and laypersons who played significant roles in Spokane's public life. For example in 1919, Emmett Reed, pastor of Calvary Baptist, helped establish the local chapter of the National Association for the Advancement of Colored People (NAACP). Two years later, Reverend T. F. Jones organized a gathering of concerned African Americans at Bethel AME Church when rumors surfaced concerning a possible branch of the Ku Klux Klan in Spokane. Jones was quoted as saying, "We believe we must present a united front if the rights of the colored population are to be protected. . . . The Ku Klux Klan is organized to intimidate colored people and we have had enough of that already. We are trying to head off any such movement before it gains any headway."[31] Six months later, Reverend Jones and others confronted the Klan directly in Spokane for what was believed to be an attempt to intimidate the black population, and this seemed to result in a moderation of Klan activity in the city.[32]

Perhaps the Northwest's most remarkable African American from this era was a woman, Beatrice Cannady, who lived much of her adult life in Portland, Oregon. Born in Littig, Texas, in 1889, she graduated from Wiley College in Texas and then attended the University of Chicago. She left in 1912 for Portland, where she married Edward Cannady, founder and editor of the African American newspaper the *Advocate*. Once in Portland, she considered the First African Methodist Episcopal Zion Church to be her home church, and she became president of the congregation for a short time. But sometime during the 1920s, Cannady was also drawn to the Baha'i faith, with its emphasis on human rights. According to her biographer, Kimberley

Beatrice Cannady helped found Portland's NAACP and spoke out against racism in its many forms. Courtesy Oregon Historical Society

Mangun, Cannady "embraced the Faith's tenets and made the religion part of her life and civil rights work for the next fifty years."[33]

Cannady quickly became involved in the broader Portland community. She lectured frequently to high school and college students; she held interracial and interreligious teas in order to help educate Portland's white community about black history in an effort to diminish stereotypes that she frequently encountered. She earned the distinction of being the first black female to practice law in Oregon after graduating from Portland's Northwestern College of Law in 1922.[34]

Cannady had risen to prominence within Portland's African American community as early as 1914, when she helped found the local chapter of the NAACP. They soon faced their first significant challenge when, in 1915, D. W. Griffith released his epic portrayal of the Civil War era, *Birth of a Nation*, in which he glorified the role of the Ku Klux Klan. The film enthralled as well as inflamed audiences around the country, and in several cities, race riots broke out. Cannady worked to have the film banned in Portland, but her efforts failed. Much to her dismay, Portland audiences generally loved the film. The *Oregonian* reported that Portland audiences "went wild with enthusiasm. They applauded, they cheered, they stood up in the intensity of their emotions as they saw the great army of mounted Ku Klux Klan sweeping down the road, fording streams, dashing to the rescue of either Northerner or Southerner in peril."[35]

Over the next several years, Portland movie theaters repeatedly brought back *Birth of a Nation*, and each time Cannady led the protest. Only in 1931 did she finally succeed in having the movie banned from Portland.[36] And her work expanded throughout the twenties. While still focused on the Griffith film, Cannady helped to repeal many of

Oregon's laws of discrimination against African Americans, including legislation designed many years earlier to prevent the settlement of African Americans in Oregon. At various times she served on the Oregon Prison Association, the Oregon State Federation of Colored Women, and the national board of the Commission on the Church and Race Relations for the Federal Council of Churches. In all these efforts, her impact was profound. In 1929, the Portland Council of Churches nominated Cannady for the Harmon Foundation's annual award for Distinguished Achievement among Negroes in the Field of Race Relations.[37]

KU KLUX KLAN AND ANTI-CATHOLICISM

In spite of efforts such as Cannady's to limit the influence of *Birth of a Nation*, the Ku Klux Klan did, in fact, experience a rebirth in the early twentieth century. The new Klan, led by William Simmons, developed in the aftermath of the film but did not grow particularly fast during the years of World War I. Nevertheless, the war contributed significantly to the mind set that fostered the Klan. As the war turned into a crusade to make the world "safe for democracy," the underlying premise was an enhanced patriotism built around the concept of "100 percent Americanism."

The years following World War I witnessed a heightened sense of anxiety on the part of many Americans, including those in the Pacific Northwest. Many white Anglo-Saxon Protestants, the core of an emerging middle class, feared that their cultural status was in jeopardy. The influx of immigrants from southern and eastern Europe brought Catholics and Jews in greater numbers than ever before. The Russian Revolution and the Seattle General Strike led to the "Red Scare," nationally as well as locally. The Spanish influenza pandemic of 1918–1920 struck hard and disrupted many communities by bringing a silent death and an anxiety about the future that is often unappreciated. From the introduction of ragtime and jazz to the automobile and the flapper, urban America posed challenges to the world that most of the white middle class had never known. Many Americans across the country, including the Pacific Northwest, were susceptible to a growing anxiety about their future.

The Protestant middle class responded in a variety of ways. Some certainly embraced "modern" America and found ways of adapting their moral code and ethical norms to these new social conventions. Other Protestant leaders, such as the Reverend Mark Matthews, railed against "screenitis" (a reference to the newly developed interest in Hollywood movies), while evangelist Billy Sunday harangued those who embraced secular values.

A far more troubling response came in the form of the Ku Klux Klan. Organized by disaffected white Southerners in the turmoil that accompanied the end of the Civil War, the original Klan had used violence to intimidate freed slaves who came to power in the Reconstruction South. However, the organization had languished by the late nineteenth century. But with the help of D. W. Griffith's *Birth of a Nation*, as we have seen, and forces unleashed by urbanization, populism, immigration of Catholics and Jews, and World War I, a nasty mix of elements led to the revival of the Klan in the 1920s. Once again the Klan resorted to violence, including lynching, primarily in the Deep South. It is estimated that approximately 150 African Americans were lynched each year between the 1880s and the mid-1920s. And the Klan, including this culture of violence, soon spread to other parts of the nation, including the Pacific Northwest.

Coming in force to Oregon in 1921, the Ku Klux Klan wielded remarkable influence for the next three years in Oregon politics, most specifically in the Oregon State legislature. The Klan helped elect a Democratic governor and assisted in the passage of a law that prohibited ownership of land by people who were not American citizens. The Klan also helped pass a law prohibiting teachers in public schools from wearing religious garb. They were also the force behind the passage of a law requiring the "teaching of the Constitution of the United States in the public and private schools of the state," as well as legislation requiring all students to attend public schools instead of private schools—a direct attack on Catholic education.[38] While its influence waned significantly by 1925, the Klan left a significant mark on Oregon politics and to a lesser extent on the state of Washington. How did this happen?

In some respects, despite a history of resistance to African Americans and Asian immigration, Oregon seemed to be an unlikely place for the Klan to take root. In 1920, only 13 percent of the state's population was foreign born (half of them naturalized) and only 0.3 percent African American, with most of them clustered in Portland. The state's residents were comparatively well educated. Nearly 95 percent of all children between seven and thirteen were in school, and over 93 percent of those students attended public schools. Only 1.5 percent of the population ten years or older was considered illiterate. And while by 1920 there were still several thousand Chinese Americans, as well as a small percentage of Japanese who lived and worked in the mill towns and in the Hood River Valley, there seemed to be little reason on the surface that might indicate Oregon would be fertile ground for the Ku Klux Klan.[39]

On the other hand, the predominantly white Anglo-Saxon Protestant population, according to historian Eckard Toy, "reinforced a moralistic determinism about the cultural imperatives of a chosen people in a promised land and explained, at least in part, the violence directed at Indians and Chinese Americans in the nineteenth century and the negative attitudes toward Japanese Americans in the twentieth century."[40] In other words, Oregon was indeed ripe for an organized effort that played on the cultural fears of many white Protestants. Oregonians, along with millions of Americans, believed that "traditional" American values were under attack both internally and externally. It is in this environment that the Ku Klux Klan began to flourish in many parts of the country in the 1920s, including the Pacific Northwest.[41]

The first kleagle, or Klan leader, arrived in Oregon in 1921, and while there was some initial resistance on the part of editorial writers in local newspapers, the Ku Klux Klan began to organize rapidly in Portland, Astoria, Salem, Tillamook, Ashland, Medford, and Hood River.[42] Klan membership reached between fourteen thousand and twenty thousand in the state by the mid-1920s, totaling perhaps fifty thousand in the decade. With an active membership between nine thousand and fifteen thousand, Portland became the virtual headquarters of Klan activities west of the Rocky Mountains.[43]

Before long, members of the Klan began to employ some of the tactics commonly associated with it. While no African American appears to have been lynched, several black Oregonians were threatened, roughed up, and forced to leave the state. In one case, hooded Klansmen tracked down an African American who had "made several insulting remarks" to a young woman, and after the confrontation he was apparently not seen in the town again. Governor Ben Olcott condemned the actions of Klan members, and the city council for Oregon City passed a resolution criticizing Klan activities.[44]

The racial and moralistic attitudes of Klansmen, however, were not significantly out of line with those of the majority of state residents. If their methods seemed bizarre and the clandestine nature of the meetings put many people off, their message resonated with many others in the post–World War I world. Many Oregonians, not just Klansmen, wanted to protect the state from alien influences, whether they were Bolshevik or papal. And most importantly, Oregon residents believed that the public school symbolized a commitment to "Americanism" as a foundational belief. Children needed to be protected at all costs from radical ideas.[45]

More recent studies of the Ku Klux Klan nationwide undermine the stereotype of the typical Klansman as uneducated, rural, fundamentalist, and generally backward. Klan members were lawyers, bankers, doctors, dentists, teachers, businessmen, and ministers.[46] For example, in Eugene, home of the University of Oregon, a number of Klansmen owned businesses that catered to students, and several were university alumni. A few Klansmen were faculty members, and a half-dozen were students.[47] In fact, the head of the University of Oregon's Latin Department, Frederick Dunn, was the exalted cyclops of Klan No. 3 during its early years. Born in Eugene in 1872, educated in its public schools, and graduated from the University of Oregon in 1892, Dunn went to Harvard and earned a master's degree in classical languages. He returned to Oregon in 1896 and began teaching at Willamette University. The University of Oregon hired him in 1898, and he took an active role in the Methodist Episcopal Church, the Republican Party, all branches of masonry, and the Elks Club. On campus, he served for many years as faculty sponsor of the YMCA chapter.[48] But when the Klan arrived in Oregon, he quickly found himself resonating with their articulated fears of what was happening to American society, and so he joined the klavern. Without question, Dunn's religious values and worldview were a significant part of his attraction to the Klan.

The relationship between Protestantism and the rise of the Klan in the Northwest is complicated. Historian Kelly Baker has done much to unpack the complex ways in which religious motivation permeated the order. He strongly asserts that "Klansmen and Klanswomen avidly promoted their affiliations within Protestantism. The second revival of the order continually articulated its allegiance to Protestantism, nationalism, and white supremacy. Christianity played an essential part in the collective identity of the order, and neglecting religious commitment ignores a crucial self-identification."[49]

The Klan required church membership, and the most common affiliations were Baptists, Methodists, Church of Christ, Disciples of Christ, Quakers, and United Brethren. But they could be found in almost every Protestant denomination. According to Baker, they were more likely to be evangelical than fundamentalist.[50]

On an absolute level, only a small percentage of Protestants joined the Klan. Nevertheless, religious affiliation seems to have played an important part in determining voting patterns, and more importantly, several Protestant ministers provided influential leadership for the Klan in Oregon. None was more visible than the Reverend Reuben Sawyer. On January 7, 1922, Klansmen set a cross on fire just outside of Eugene. On the next day an advertisement in the *Eugene Morning Register* announced a lecture, "The Truth about the Ku Klux Klan," by "Dr. R. H. Sawyer, formerly pastor of the Christian Church of Portland, and for several years Masonic lecturer in England, Canada, and the United States." For fifty cents admission to the Eugene Theatre, anyone interested could hear Sawyer's lecture and watch an accompanying motion picture double feature, *The Face at Your Window* and *The Ku Klux Klan Rides Again*, described as "Eight Reels of Thrilling

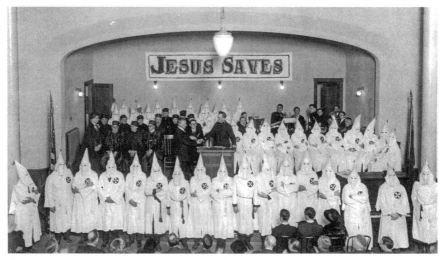

The Ku Klux Klan in Oregon drew heavy support from white Protestants. Courtesy Oregon Historical Society

Pictures with a Message of Warning to American Manhood and Womanhood."[51]

When Reverend Sawyer spoke, his stage was generally decorated with a sword, a Bible, an American flag, and a replica of a burning cross. He claimed that the Klan "is not 'Anti-Catholic' or 'Anti-Jewish,' ... but is simply non-Catholic and non-Jewish." Typically, Sawyer ran though a litany of issues that underscored perceived dangers associated with allowing too many aliens or noncitizens to come into the country. He spoke of a "rising tide of color" throughout the world. "We control madmen, mad dogs, and other mad beasts," he exclaimed. "The negro [sic] in whose blood flows the mad desire for race amalgamation is more dangerous than a maddened wild beast and he *must* and *will* be controlled."[52]

The Ku Klux Klan sought to form alliances with Protestant ministers, particularly from the more conservative Baptist, Methodist, Christian, and United Brethren denominations.[53] Klan organizers waived the fee for any Protestant minister wishing to join the Klan. In addition to Sawyer, the Methodist minister O. W. Jones was particularly active in the Oregon Klan, as was Reverend Harold Fosner.[54] Fosner liked to refer to the Christian Church as the "Klan Church." One of the most popular Protestant ministers to extol the virtues of the Klan was the Reverend V. K. "Bearcat" Allison, a pastor from Lebanon, Oregon. He could pound away for up to three hours at a time on the theme of "pure Americanism." In one sermon, he confidently proclaimed, "The white race is supreme and the Anglo-Saxons are ordained by God to be the leaders of the world and to assist inferior races."[55]

The heart of the Klan appeal to Protestants in Oregon was its vitriolic attack on Catholics and Catholicism.[56] Tapping into a long history of anti-Catholic sentiment across America, Klan publications railed against the Pope and the threat of hordes of immigrants from non-Protestant lands. Fearful of a lack of loyalty to America, Klan spokesmen associated Catholics with aliens and foreigners. Whenever possible, the Klan took advantage of any Catholic who left the church. In October 1922, the La Grande klavern sponsored a speech by "Sister La Precia" (Lucretia) at the city's Star Theater. A former nun and floor supervisor at Portland's St. Vincent's Hospital for seventeen years, Sister Lucretia hurled such invective at the church that the local klavern adjourned its weekly meeting so that members could attend the much-heralded lecture.[57] Another former pastor in the Christian

Church, James R. Johnson, Portland's exalted cyclops, liked to excite audiences by claiming sexual misconduct on the part of priests and an unrelenting number of papal conspiracies. Without fail, his lectures would find some way of portraying Catholic immigrants as illiterate, criminal, and not truly American.

Anti-Catholic rhetoric knew few boundaries. "We must ever consider ourselves engaged in battle until we . . . behold the downfall of Catholicism buried in the ruins of its own iniquity," declared one Klan officer in eastern Oregon.[58] George Estes, an attorney of Methodist background, authored the 1923 pamphlet entitled *The Roman Katholic Kingdom and the Ku Klux Klan*. In this pamphlet, Estes "described the manner in which the confessional provided priests with information more exhaustive than that compiled by any political party in the world. This material, he alleged, allowed the church to control and direct national legislation, court policy, and executive affairs in its own interest. The church's wealth flowed to Rome, he proclaimed, where it was used to acquire world supremacy."[59] In a similar vein, an issue of the *Klamath Falls Herald* asserted that a gun and ammunition were hidden underneath the church to prepare for the day that the government will be overthrown on behalf of the Pope.[60]

While not quite as active as in Oregon, the Ku Klux Klan surfaced in Washington state as well. It was estimated that as many as fifty thousand Washington residents joined the Klan in the early 1920s. On January 12, 1923, the *Auburn Globe-Republican* reported that "Silently, but none the less certainly, the sinister form of the hooded Klan is casting its shadow over the entire White River Valley. . . . The initiation will occur in a wooded place not far from Auburn . . . and a large number of the class has been recruited in this city. It is a known fact that Auburn has been flooded with application blanks for the Klan for the past week."[61] It was estimated that there were two thousand members in Seattle, with smaller groups in Walla Walla, Tacoma, Spokane, and the White River Valley. Although it is always difficult to track with certainty those who belonged to the Klan, it is clear that Protestant ministers played an important role. For example, in March 1923 the same Auburn newspaper reported that the Reverend C. C. Curtis from Vancouver, Washington, had delivered a speech titled, "Why the Ku Klux Klan?" Curtis articulated the typical Klan fears against the Catholic Church and argued that "the Klan stands for pure Americanism and its vows are only what red-blooded, Christian Americans stand for."[62]

Klan activity reached a high point in Washington on July 14, 1923, when organizers held a "Konvention" near Renton, just southeast of Seattle. Somewhere between five hundred and one thousand new members were initiated. There were multiple cross burnings, fireworks, and a crowd estimated at between ten thousand and twenty thousand.[63] The following year, a similar rally in Issaquah, ten miles east of Seattle, drew an estimated thirteen thousand people. According to the *Issaquah Press*, those attending the rally were "entertained" by "stirring, patriotic music" from a thirty-two-piece band, a play by schoolchildren, and speeches "on Americanism." As part of the event, a "fiery" electric cross—forty feet high and twenty-seven feet wide— was illuminated. Deputy sheriffs worked with hooded Klansmen to direct traffic "which clogged roads for two hours following the rally." The newspaper reported that a Catholic storeowner in Issaquah was harassed, and that Klansmen made midnight visits to Catholic families. "Catholic dairy farmers experienced difficulties in having their milk picked up, and instead it was allowed to spoil."[64]

In August, evangelist and faith healer May Turner came to Auburn, Washington, and "instructed the Klan to 'get wise' and attend her revival."[65] Fifty robed but unmasked Klansmen attended, where Turner "complimented them highly as a noble body of 100 percent Americans" and "exhorted them to be 100 percent Christians as well."[66]

The hatred expressed by the Ku Klux Klan against Catholics culminated in efforts in both Oregon and Washington to destroy the Catholic school system through the Compulsory Education Law. According to historian Kelly Baker, "In the order's thinking, the parochial schools were breeding grounds for un-American ideas and foreign allegiances, and those schools created youth and children versed in an alien religious system."[67] Simply stated, the proposed legislation would require all students to attend public schools. Supporters of the school initiative portrayed themselves as antielitists and advocates of popular democracy.[68] But at heart, it was a thinly veiled effort to undermine the Catholic Church in the Pacific Northwest.

The issue of public and private education had surfaced earlier during the First World War. The theme of "100 percent Americanism" had come to dominate discussions around what curriculum should be taught in Northwest public schools. Many communities banned foreign language instruction in elementary schools, and increasing doubts had surfaced about the patriotism of students instructed in Catholic parochial and German Lutheran schools.[69] As a consequence, following the war, Klan organizers had seized on the issue of public education and brought it to a head.

These efforts of the Klan did not go unanswered. Opponents of the Klan and the Compulsory School Bill, as it came to be known, were a varied lot. Labor leadership, ministers of mainline churches, and conservative politicians joined Catholics, Jews, and other minorities in resisting the Klan. Episcopalians and Lutherans, along with Presbyterians and Seventh-day Adventists, supported private education and opposed the initiative.[70]

Most observers believed that the initiative would fail. The editors of the *Oregonian*, the state's biggest newspaper, gave ten to seven odds against it. They were wrong. On November 7, 1922, 115,506 citizens of Oregon went to the polls and voted for the initiative; 103,685 voted against it. In addition, voters elected Walter Pierce, a Democrat from LaGrande who was openly supported by the Klan, and he in turn supported the Klan—as well as the Compulsory School Bill.

But opponents of the legislation were undaunted. On December 22, 1923, lawyers working for the archbishop of Portland asked for an injunction against the Compulsory School Law on behalf of the Society of the Sisters of the Holy Names of Jesus and Mary, which ran several schools in Oregon. They did not argue for the injunction on the basis of the First Amendment, the right to freedom of religion. Rather, they argued on the basis of the Fourteenth Amendment, that the Compulsory School Law would force private schools to close and thus deprive their owners, like the Sisters of the Holy Names, of their property without due process. Presbyterians, Episcopalians, Lutherans, Seventh-day Adventists, and the American Jewish Committee, in addition to the Catholics, all filed briefs with the courts in opposition to the law.[71]

Judges heard the case and on March 31, 1924, granted an injunction against the state of Oregon, ordering it not to implement the law. However, supporters of the Compulsory Education Law were not finished. The state, under Governor Pierce's direction, appealed the case to the US Supreme Court. Following the precedent it set in 1923, when it had struck down a Nebraska law prohibiting private elementary schools from teaching foreign language, the Supreme

Court overturned the Oregon school law for good on June 1, 1925. While gatherings of the Klan persisted through the decade, its influence waned rapidly in the second half of the twenties.

In the meantime, Washington state voters deliberated over Initiative 49, which was modeled on the Oregon Compulsory School Bill. The same arguments pro and con were bandied back and forth prior to the November 1924 election. The *Catholic Northwest Progress* bitterly opposed the bill, as did several other newspapers in the state. As in Oregon, the initiative generated a coalition of varied opponents ranging from the business community to prominent members of Protestant denominations. Klan members and supporters of the bill were probably disappointed when Mark Matthews, Southern-born leader of Seattle's First Presbyterian, the denomination's largest church in the country, openly opposed the initiative.[72] In the end, the measure was defeated by more than fifty-nine thousand votes.[73]

CONCLUSION

The rise and fall of the Ku Klux Klan in the Northwest highlighted the volatile nature of issues related to race, ethnicity, and culture that had been part of the region's history from the beginning. In almost every case, activists saw themselves as outsiders to the prevailing culture and wanted to change some aspect of it. Many religiously motivated individuals advocated vigorously for better treatment and protection for frequently marginalized individuals and groups who themselves were outsiders to the dominant white culture. Other religious activists argued just as vigorously for exclusion of those individuals who failed to meet cultural, religious, or racial tests as defined by white Anglo-Saxon Protestants. At least by the end of the 1920s, the balance seemed to be shifting toward more inclusion rather than less, but this resolution remained unsettled. For much of the rest of the twentieth century, conflict over racial issues would continue to percolate.

At another level, the rise and fall of the Ku Klux Klan in the Northwest marked the transition from one set of cultural conflicts to another. As we have seen, so much of what galvanized religious activists—men and women, Catholic and Protestant, evangelical and mainline—was the desire to moderate male behavior and create a safer environment for women and children. The great desire was to recast the discussion of male character and focus on the importance of blending a new sense of masculinity with conventional Christian values of love, compassion, and humility.

In an odd way, the Klan reflected nearly the apotheosis of this definition of manhood. The Klan provided purpose, traditional values, and the blending of patriotism and Protestant Christianity with an exaggerated sense of being vital to the protection of pure womanhood and the home. In the struggle to define masculinity, the Klan had what it thought was an answer. But ultimately the Klan's vision for manhood foundered on its racism, nativism, and religious bigotry. It became an embarrassment and source of shame for the mainstream of Protestant Christians.

While many forms of bigotry and racism would continue to emerge in the Northwest, the impulses that produced the Klan lay dormant for several decades until the Christian Identity Movement and Aryan Nations reemerged (more in Idaho than in Washington and Oregon) in the 1980s. Once again these groups tied manhood, Christianity, and a radical form of patriotism together in a volatile mix.

In the decades between the Klan activity of the 1920s and the reemergence of the radical Christian Right, a noticeable shift began to emerge in the ways religious activists engaged the public square. Increasingly, the issue was tension not so much between present and desired forms of male behavior but between two competing visions for American society. One vision emphasized religious toleration, cultural pluralism, and social justice. In other words, a broadly liberal social ethic informed many religious communities. The other vision emphasized conservative social values and grew resistant to forces for liberalism, humanism, and secularism in the culture. As a consequence, the foundation of a new culture war was taking root in the 1930s and 1940s in the middle class. And it is this culture war that shapes the dynamic of religious activism for the next three-quarters of a century. What is interesting is that both emerging liberals and conservatives continued to view themselves as outsiders to what they believed was the prevailing culture. Liberal activists, for the most part, believed that the Northwest still lacked the fundamental commitments to racial equality and economic justice. To these activists, these values seemed lacking in a society still dominated by a resource-based economy, business entrepreneurs, and various expressions of racism and discrimination. For conservatives, the Northwest still seemed far too vulnerable to radical social and political ideas, far too vulnerable to influences that felt threatening to traditional family values and American capitalism. The Northwest, in other words, felt uncertain; its cultural foundations were still undefined, in a way that promoted religious activism on both sides of the equation.

CHAPTER 6

JUSTICE ON THE RISE

In 1929, Portland's long-time attorney, Roscoe Nelson Sr., addressed the Union of American Hebrew Congregations in San Francisco. In a stirring speech, Nelson, himself a Jew, exclaimed that

> Justice, not charity, is the end of religion. . . . If we thought of charity, therefore, as the culmination of religion, it would mean that we contemplate with equanimity that throughout all eternity there must be boundless luxury for some, while others suffer for the barest necessities; . . . that some shall be bred in palaces, and others exist in slums; that one group shall be pampered, and another continue so undernourished as to invite the ravages of disease and death.[1]

While most people sitting in the San Francisco audience might not have recognized it, Nelson's impassioned appeal for justice over charity reflected a shift in the way religious activists were engaging the culture of the Northwest. To be sure, Victorian Christian emphasis on managing the behaviors of young men, protecting women and children, and regulating vice would continue. But beginning in the late twenties and early thirties, religious activists focused attention as well on economic and social justice and the protection of civil liberties and civil rights. There was growing appreciation for the pluralistic character of American culture.

Several factors contributed to this shift. In the minds of many religious activists in the late 1920s, Prohibition had failed to produce the anticipated change in American culture. The great effort to regulate male drinking habits had raised awareness of domestic violence and helped shift patterns of social behavior around alcohol, but the idea that you could prevent the vast majority of middle-class Americans from consuming even moderate amounts of alcohol was naïve. Likewise, the spasm of hyperpatriotism associated with World War I as well as the nativism and racism embodied in the Ku Klux Klan were increasingly viewed as troublesome. The Scopes Monkey Trial in 1925 had highlighted the debate over the teaching of evolution, linking fundamentalist religious forces with resistance to modernism and changing social values. The Victorian dream that homogeneous and conservative cultural values would prevail throughout the country seemed increasingly narrow and parochial.

As a consequence, liberal activists mobilized in their critique of the United States' economic system; activists asserted themselves on behalf of international cooperation, the alleviation of human suffering, and world peace. And perhaps most significantly, Northwest religious activists developed a stronger commitment to the civil rights of marginalized groups than had been the case in the earlier period. In this way, liberal activists liked to identify themselves with the outsider—individuals and groups who were the victims of discrimination.

The Great Depression of the 1930s and the onset of World War II accelerated this change. Social trauma associated with those two seminal midcentury events forced religious people to reexamine some of their most foundational assumptions. As was the case around the country, many Northwest leaders in established Protestant denominations, from Presbyterian and Congregationalist to Methodist and Episcopalian, followed the direction of the liberal National Council of Churches and engaged social and political issues. These issues ranged from concerns for economic justice and civil rights to American foreign policy. The Catholic Church was similarly mobilized, as were activists such as the aforementioned Jewish attorney Roscoe Nelson, who lived out deep commitments to fairness and equality. These social justice efforts proved daunting but would establish a foundation for liberal engagement with culture in the Northwest that would persist to the present.[2]

With the stock market crash in October 1929 and the onset of the greatest economic disaster in American history, individuals and organizations throughout the Pacific Northwest faced an unprecedented set of challenges. Never before had so many Americans been in trouble. Never before had the need for food, shelter, and clothing been so dire. Jobs dried up, mortgages went unpaid, and soup lines grew. Seattle and Portland were known for their "Hooverville" shanty towns, but all communities were touched by the Depression.

In some ways, the response of Catholics, Protestants, and Jews to the calamity of the 1930s was predictable. Churches and synagogues had for decades provided the first line of defense for the poor against hunger, joblessness, and despair. American society depended heavily on the resources of millions of individuals who voluntarily gave through charities and religious organizations. And so, in this most difficult of economic crises, countless people called again on ministers and churches to help them survive this devastating economic and social period.

Within the Catholic Church, bishops responded to the increasing needs of the public with particularly direct forms of assistance. Extending back to work of the Sisters of Providence, the Catholic Church had a long record of meeting the needs of the poor. In 1918, Bishop O'Dea had established the Seattle Council of Catholic Women to tend to the needs of orphaned children. In 1923, the Catholic Welfare Bureau had been organized in Tacoma to assist single mothers as well as homeless children.

But the swelling unemployment in the early thirties dictated an expanded response. In Oregon, Archbishop Edward Howard authorized the establishment of a Catholic Charities office in 1933. Three years later, Bishop Gerald Shaughnessy established an office of Catholic Charities of the Diocese of Seattle. In that same year, the National Conference of Catholic Charities met in Seattle. The city's mayor, Fred Dore, along with Washington's governor, Clarence Martin, addressed the gathering that included archbishops, bishops, and more than ten thousand priests and lay members. Participants discussed the dire economic circumstances facing people across the country and what the Catholic Church might do in response.[3] For the rest of the decade, Catholic Charities opened offices in most of the cities throughout the state, and the same pattern unfolded in Oregon.

Protestant churches, the Salvation Army, and YMCAs and YWCAs all stepped up their relief efforts. The 1931 minutes of the Greater Portland Council of Churches offer a glimpse into their efforts to serve the poor, hungry, and unemployed. The council lobbied local organizations to provide relief and employ people whenever possible. It urged the city to create a permanent committee to prevent unemployment and even argued that firemen should be granted a day's rest.[4] Members met with leaders of the Portland YWCA to discuss ways in which church women might aid unemployed women. By the end of 1931, the Portland Council, in a joint statement with the Catholic Church and Jewish rabbis, issued a report that urged President Hoover and Congress as well as the state governments to become more active in addressing unemployment through the use of public works:

> We believe that immediate and adequate appropriations should be made available by national as well as local governments for much needed and useful public works such as road construction, development of parks, elimination of grade crossings, flood control projects, reforestation, and the clearing of slum areas in our society. . . . Society's responsibility for the preservation of human values in industrial life makes the principle of social insurance, particularly insurance against unemployment and want in old age, an indispensable part of sound social policy and the most self-respecting form of relief. We protest against the misleading use of the word "dole" to describe systems of unemployment insurance.[5]

Franklin Roosevelt employed public works more vigorously than Hoover, but religious groups continued to offer important sources of relief to an increasingly desperate public. In 1937, Reed College students in Portland conducted a survey of Protestant social service agencies and concluded that Protestantism was responsible for far more social services than commonly realized. Their study revealed that twenty-three agencies of welfare, relief, and character-building were defined as Protestant.[6]

The Jewish community in both Oregon and Washington also responded resolutely to the economic and social crisis. In Washington, the Jewish Welfare Society (formerly known as the Hebrew Benevolent Society) stepped in to provide emergency relief to homeless men.[7] A 1931 society document reported that "all our transients are sent to the Central Registry for men . . . and single men and unemployed family men are registered for what public works are available, but so many men are out of work, and so few jobs listed that the agencies are taxed to their limit."[8] As the relief programs of the New Deal came on line in the mid-1930s, the Jewish Welfare Society supplemented the basic resources available to Jewish families in the Seattle area.

The same general pattern of response was seen in Portland, as well as in other major cities of the Northwest. In the fall of 1932, Portland women organized a sewing unit in the Jewish Neighborhood House. The Red Cross provided cloth, and approximately four hundred women worked two days a week for two years to make over four thousand garments to be distributed to the poor.[9] In 1934, the Portland Jewish Council collaborated with the B'nai B'rith and the Women's Auxiliary to establish the Opportunity Bake Shop to employ women needing work to support their families. The shop produced noodles and caramels, as well as pickles, herring, chicken fat, bagels, strudel, and cookies.[10]

As the Depression worsened, however, religious organizations and individuals pursued more radical alternatives. In 1933, the Social Committee of the Columbia River Conference of the Methodist Episcopal Church suggested that common ownership of natural resources and the means of production might be a solution to the worsening economic conditions.[11]

This hint of radicalism on the part of the Methodists was not isolated. One of the more publicized efforts to inject socialism into the political mix occurred when Fred Shorter organized the "Church of the People" in Seattle's university district in 1934. Shorter had been the pastor of Pilgrim Congregational Church since 1925. But as the Depression wore on, he became convinced that socialism was the only answer. Eventually, controversial statements and sermons led to his dismissal by the Pilgrim Church, but for Shorter this simply provided an opportunity to start a new congregation. He continued to state strongly that "Christianity and Capitalism as they now exist are not compatible"; he also formed a consumers' cooperative and joined the Socialist Party.[12] As pastor, Shorter brought socialist leader Norman Thomas to his church, along with British Labor leader Harold Laski and local radical Anna Louise Strong. Shorter developed a weekly newspaper, the *New Religious Frontier*, which focused on racial discrimination, abuse of the poor, and the suppression of free speech. And in one of his most controversial moves, a standard for which he had already set a high bar, his People's Church housed the only birth control clinic in the state of Washington.[13]

Another radical expression of commitment to economic justice was the development of the Catholic Worker movement in both Seattle and Portland. Founded by Peter Maurin and Dorothy Day, the Catholic Worker movement attempted to organize roundtable discussions with workers, establish houses of hospitality in the urban environment where workers lived, and ultimately form rural farming communes to bring urban workers out to reclaim the land. Maurin and Day hoped that the houses of hospitality would be staffed by volunteers and dedicated to poverty, pacifism, and the fourteen corporal and spiritual works of mercy. They believed that voluntary poverty was central to the foundation for the Catholic Worker's commitment to freedom, dignity, and love.[14] Dorothy Day was quoted as saying, "I do not know how to love God except by loving the poor. I do not know how to serve God except by serving the poor."[15] Rejecting capitalism for its embrace of usury and dehumanization of people through mechanization, the Catholic Worker movement also rejected socialism for its commitment to an impersonal state. The agrarian vision seemed to offer a third way, where all individuals could "work according to [their] ability and receive according to [their] need." Dorothy Day, Maurin, and others believed that this could be a foretaste of heaven, a return to the early Christian communities of the first disciples.

In Seattle, Catholic seminarian James Deady began discussion with Dorothy Day about the possibility of establishing a St. Francis House of Hospitality. For a year, concerns delayed its start, until finally two stoves were received from St. Vincent de Paul, and St. Francis House opened in March 1940. Immediately the kitchen began serving from six hundred to eight hundred meals a day, including to machinists who recently had gone on strike.[16]

The biggest challenge to the movement came, however, when disagreement erupted over pacifism. Dorothy Day fully believed that to be part of the Catholic Worker movement meant being a pacifist, but apparently many of the workers at St. Francis did not accept that premise; instead they maintained belief in the centuries-old Roman Catholic doctrine of the "just war." With the onset of World War II, pacifism became a more difficult position to hold. Meanwhile, poverty began to abate (as a result of the war). St. Francis House closed in 1946, though it remained a symbol of commitment to economic justice among Northwest Catholics.[17]

In retrospect, the resources of religious organizations simply were inadequate to address the overwhelming human needs of the era. Nevertheless, it is clear that religious agencies provided a major source of assistance both materially and spiritually for vast numbers of people who were simply trying to survive the Depression. Perhaps motivated by commitments to alleviating poverty, religious leadership increasingly supported the Roosevelt administration's liberal initiatives and, in some cases, even more radical solutions to the country's economic woes.

As religious leaders undertook Herculean efforts to address poverty and took interest in national economic programs, they likewise expressed increasing interest in American foreign policy. In many respects, this was an outgrowth of reaction to the First World War. Many Northwest clergy had responded to President Woodrow Wilson's call to support a "war to end all wars" and a war "to make the world safe for democracy." More than one pastor framed the war in apocalyptic terms, believing that God's hand was firmly behind US involvement.[18] Mark Matthews of Seattle's First Presbyterian Church was one such pastor. He advocated that the United States join the League of Nations and spoke out against the Harding-sponsored Washington Disarmament Conference in 1921. Matthews also argued that the United States needed a more realistic foreign policy in regard to Germany. He urged Congress to assist the defeated nation in finding ways to pay its reparations or risk being responsible for more serious economic complications.[19] Other pastors, including Seattle's Sydney Strong, an ardent pacifist, led in a more isolationist direction. Although they leaned in different directions, Matthews and other clergy took a keen interest in American foreign policy and attempted both to persuade their congregations to get involved in politics and, more broadly, to sway public opinion.

By the 1930s, the Seattle Council of Churches began weighing in regularly on issues of American foreign policy and advocated that the United States avoid war at nearly all costs. This shift in focus was led primarily by a remarkable woman, Gertrude Apel. Licensed in 1920 by the Methodist Church to preach, she was one of the first two women ordained in the church in 1926. After serving several parishes in eastern Washington, Apel came to the Seattle area, where shortly she was named the first general secretary of the Seattle Council of Churches.[20] It was clear that she wanted to move the council toward addressing larger social issues. For example, in 1931 she helped push the council to identify three major goals for American foreign policy: ending the Sino-Japanese controversy over Manchuria; supporting the World Disarmament Conference in Geneva; and advocating for American membership in the World Court. The next year, following her lead, the council encouraged President Herbert Hoover to consider the following: "We urge the government to use its full influence in conjunction with the other powers and preferably with the cooperation of the League of Nations to the end that the conflict between China and Japan may cease. We urge use of diplomatic and economic sanctions against any government refusing to arbitrate differences."[21] The council organized a letter-writing campaign to the president urging disarmament. In 1932, the Peace Committee of the Council of Churches appeared before the Seattle School Board to protest high school pupils being recruited into summer military training camps.[22] An additional report from the Seattle Council of Churches Committee on National Defense, dated October 12, 1933, requested substantial reduction in existing armaments, no rearmaments, and abolition of aggressive weapons. The council urged an immediate elimination of all bombing from the air and the elimination of poison gas.[23]

Seattle's Mark Matthews did not share the pacifist leanings of the council but did raise concerns about the plight of European Jews. He criticized the German persecution of the Jewish people. In an article in 1938 for the *Presbyterian*, a national journal, Matthews wrote, "America should never tolerate racial prejudice or religious prejudice." He attacked Hitler and predicted that "the persecution of Jews and Christians is only the beginning of greater atrocities. It is impossible for the Jews to fight this battle alone. It is a battle that must be fought by the Christian Church."[24]

In retrospect, virtually all of these pronouncements and recommendations to the nation's political leaders seem a bit naïve. But clergy and ecumenical religious groups, such as the Seattle and Portland Councils of Churches, believed that they had a moral responsibility to comment on American foreign policy. In doing so, they shifted their focus away from the behavioral issues (gambling, alcohol, and prostitution) that had dominated their attention during the previous two decades. More interested in the political realm, the Council of Churches espoused polices that favored isolationism and pacifism. They felt no inhibition about criticizing American presidents or American policy.

CIVIL LIBERTIES AND CIVIL RIGHTS

Perhaps the most dramatic shift in emphasis during the 1930s among mainline Protestants, Catholics, and Jews surfaced in the area of civil liberties and civil rights. In this area in particular, liberal activists took up the cause of outsiders. They sought to identify various forms of discrimination and worked to raise consciousness about both the reality and the solution.

Jewish activists clearly saw themselves as outsiders. Nevertheless, Jewish influence on public life in the Pacific Northwest surfaced in many forms. One of the most important was the role that Jewish attorneys played in taking up the cause of civil liberties. According to one historian, "The civil rights activism that emerged in response to anti-Semitism became a central aspect of Jewish concern. Community service and the defense of civil liberties became core modern components in fulfilling the traditional requirement of

Roscoe Nelson Sr. and other Jewish attorneys emerged as some of Portland's most important spokespersons for social justice. Courtesy Roz Babener

Jewish heritage, the injunction to act righteously. Jewish lawyers led the way."[25] In addition to the previously mentioned Roscoe Nelson, another Jewish attorney who played a prominent role in Oregon public life was Harry Kennin. A graduate of Reed College in Portland, Kennin served ten years on the Portland School Board and was elected to the state senate from 1938 through 1942. He was among the first to introduce civil rights legislation in Oregon and was acknowledged at the time of his death in 1954 for his devotion to social justice.[26]

Perhaps the two individuals who shaped public life most directly in this era were Gus Solomon and Irvin Goodman. Born in Portland in 1906, Solomon returned to Portland after graduating from Stanford Law School to help establish legal aid for the poor and set up a branch of the American Civil Liberties Union (ACLU). Solomon was widely known for assisting Jews in securing jobs, as well as breaking down social barriers throughout the city. Solomon's biographer called him a "centrist liberal." He was appalled by the disparity in income between the rich and poor. He railed against the middle class's materialist values and overdeveloped individualism.[27] According to historian Steven Lowenstein, Solomon helped "institutionalize the ideals of social justice."[28]

One of Solomon's major cases involved Dirk DeJonge, who had been convicted under Oregon's criminal syndicalism law for having participated in a meeting sponsored by the Communist Party. *DeJonge v. Oregon* was one of the most celebrated cases to arise in the state before or since. Solomon argued the case before the US Supreme Court, where Chief Justice Charles Evans Hughes declared that Oregon's criminal syndicalism law was unconstitutional as applied to DeJonge. Instead, the court upheld the right to hold a public meeting regardless of the unpopularity of the cause espoused.[29] Frequently criticized by conservatives for his support of civil liberties, Solomon eventually was named by Harry Truman in 1949 to be a federal district court judge and served until his death in 1987, making him the longest-serving federal judge in Oregon history.[30]

Another Jewish lawyer from Portland, Irvin Goodman, also gained significant attention during this era. Known for his willingness to defend "the downtrodden whomever they might be,"[31] Goodman took on a wide range of cases, including that of a communist news vendor who had been sentenced to five years in prison for distributing leftist literature to labor organizers and striking mine workers. He also defended African American clients and was counsel to Portland's NAACP. Historian Albert Gunns acknowledged that Goodman was in the "forefront of Portland's civil liberties lawyers" and the "person most instrumental in the creation and maintenance of a civil liberties movement in Portland."[32]

Jewish activists certainly identified themselves as outsiders to the mainstream of Pacific Northwest culture in the 1930s and 1940s. Firm in their convictions and often effective in their politics, these civil libertarians helped establish a stronger commitment to the region's marginalized individuals and groups. However, this commitment to the marginalized would be severely tested when Japanese Americans throughout the Northwest experienced the trauma of World War II.

DISCRIMINATION AGAINST JAPANESE AMERICANS

Racial discrimination against Asians had been common in the Pacific Northwest since the 1870s, when Japanese- and Chinese-born immigrants were prohibited from becoming citizens or owning property. Religious communities in the Northwest had often expressed criticism of this discrimination. Seattle's Mark Matthews had spoken out in 1921, asserting that the percentage of Japanese on the West Coast, let alone in the country, was not sufficient to warrant concern. "Racial and national prejudice and suspicion are un-American," he wrote.[33]

By the late 1930s, an increasing number of Seattle ministers, most of whom had personal contacts with Japanese Americans, began speaking out against discrimination. Most visible was Harold Jensen, pastor of the First Baptist Church in Seattle. He urged his parishioners in the months before Pearl Harbor to adopt a spirit of "neighborliness" toward those of different racial or ethnic backgrounds and to avoid speaking in derogatory stereotypes.[34] Jensen asked his parishioners to accept the fact that "we must see in the Japanese . . . neighbors, who need our understanding and co-operation, rather than our scrap iron and our most un-neighborly exclusion act."[35]

But the attack on Pearl Harbor on December 7, 1941, changed everything overnight. By December 9, the FBI had apprehended 1,212 Japanese in the continental United States and Hawai'i, including 116 Seattleites, and incarcerated them in Montana. In the days following Pearl Harbor, the Catholic bishop of Seattle, Gerald Shaughnessy, wrote a pastoral letter urging caution regarding one's reaction to persons of Japanese descent. He reminded his readers that Christians must stand up against violence, hatred, and racial prejudice. "Our Catholic heritage inculcates upon us . . . that we embrace our fellow American citizens of Japanese extraction in a special bond of charity, for they are no less loyal than others, and no less claimants of true American citizenship . . . innocent victims, as in many cases they will be, of antipathies and unreasoning prejudices."[36]

In January 1942, a delegation from the Seattle Council of Churches Emergency Committee traveled to Missoula to support the local Issei (first-generation Japanese immigrants) who had asked the Enemy Alien Hearing Board to recommend their release. The Seattle delegation agreed and asked the government to free any Japanese alien who met at least one of three criteria: had a son in the army, engaged in essential activities such as farming, or had an American citizen willing to sponsor him. The committee believed that, based on these criteria alone, the government could free half of all incarcerated Japanese; their argument, however, fell on deaf ears.[37]

General public opinion continued to turn against a lenient policy toward Japanese Americans. On February 19, 1942, Franklin

Roosevelt issued Executive Order 9066, which would affect more than a hundred thousand individuals of Japanese descent. Meanwhile, the Seattle Council of Churches continued to demand that the government explain why it was a military necessity to expel and relocate Nikkei (American citizens of Japanese descent). Even as Governor Langlie and Mayor Earl Millikin supported relocation, the Council of Churches insisted that the city treat its Nikkei community fairly.[38]

Among the most outspoken advocates for fairness was Floyd Schmoe. A Quaker, Schmoe coordinated the American Friends Service Committee activities in Seattle and warned that internment of Japanese Americans would have long-term consequences for an entire generation.[39] At a series of hearings, Schmoe spoke eloquently regarding the loyalty of the Nisei (born in the United States—and therefore an American citizen—as opposed to an individual of Japanese descent who had emigrated to the United States):

> They are American citizens by virtue of birth and training. They are the product of our own schools. They have grown up with our children. As with each of the immigrant groups that have made America what it is today, they have contributed their share to America's prosperity and well being. . . . Those of us who have known them well have confidence in them. We have come to value them as neighbors, as friends, and as business associates. We agree that anyone, whether Japanese, German, or American, who is proven dangerous to the community should be removed, but justice cannot be done by branding all men, who by accident of their birth come from countries now at war with America, as enemy aliens.[40]

Another important voice in this advocacy movement was the Reverend U. G. Murphy, superintendent of the Methodist Church in Seattle, who submitted a statement on behalf of the Northwest Oriental Evangelization Society. Murphy urged the Tolan Committee (the authorized federal body charged with overseeing possible evacuation) to permit Japanese Americans to be supervised by their white friends. "We here on the coast must live with the Japanese after this war is over, and we are anxious that nothing be done that would make us ashamed of the manner in which they are treated now. . . . The manner in which minority groups are handled is a final criterion of the standard of national civilization."[41] Murphy, as well as the pastor of the Japanese Methodist Church in Seattle, E. W. Thompson, adamantly asserted that the overwhelming majority of alien Japanese were only of that status because American laws had prohibited naturalization.[42]

Thompson later wrote, "We would be repeating the deed that Hitler perpetrated against the Jews, though our policy would be gentler than Hitler's in many ways would, the basic injustice would be the same. Thus we should be conquered by Hitler's spirit and methods even though not by his military machine. We cannot fight for democracy by such methods."[43] Another Seattle minister, the Reverend Thomas Gill, representing the Puget Sound Chapter of the American Association of Social Workers, also challenged the need for "indiscriminate evacuation" based entirely on "nationality or race."[44]

But on March 23, 1942, any hope of avoiding evacuation came to an end. Orders were given to remove all residents of Japanese descent from Bainbridge Island. Three days later, Arthur Barnett, a Quaker, who was serving as the attorney of the Emergency Committee of the Seattle Council of Churches, wrote, "Since late January, all the Christian forces which have been attempting to find out information from the government have been shunted from official to official, all of whom had no authoritative information."[45]

As evacuation notices were posted, several pastors of predominantly Caucasian churches joined with ministers from Japanese churches to help the Nikkei community. Frequently, clergymen were present when officials investigated Nikkei in their homes. Pastors visited Japanese families to reassure them that they were blameless and should not feel disgrace. Clergy served as conduits for relief supplies and foodstuffs donated by Christians to needy families. Churches also arranged to store furniture and household goods for the Nikkei. On April 30, when authorities began transporting the Nikkei to the assembly center at the fairgrounds in Puyallup, east of Tacoma, white parishioners accompanied and, in some cases, drove families to the makeshift compound known as Camp Harmony.[46]

In Oregon, the religious opposition to internment of Japanese Americans was not as strong or as well organized as resistance in Seattle. Representatives from the Portland Council of Churches did not testify before the Tolan Committee, although the council did submit a list of nine resolutions. The Portland Council of Churches asked the federal government to bear the "cost of . . . moving and resettlement," as well as to provide protection for public health and medical costs. The council also tried to ensure that the children of evacuees received schooling at the "reception centers."[47] But overall, the response of the council was more tepid than that of its counterpart in Seattle. As historian Ellen Eisenberg observed, "The Portland Council focused its statement on recommendations about the process and logistics and made no comment on the appropriateness of relocation and mass internment."[48]

One of Oregon's most vocal individuals (religious or otherwise) to express moral opposition publicly to internment was Azalia Emma Peet of Gresham, Oregon. A Methodist missionary to Japan, Peet spoke on February 26, 1942, before the Tolan Committee and said, "These are law-abiding, upright people of our community. What is it that makes it necessary for them to evacuate? Have they done anything? Is there anything in their history in this area to justify such a fear of them developing overnight?"[49] But she was alone, as the Portland City Council and overwhelming public support for internment carried the day with the Tolan Committee. Frustrated and disappointed, Peet chose to protest the decision by choosing to live among the Japanese Americans in relocation camps, first in Gresham and later in Nyssa, Oregon, in order to do what she could to help people whom she believed had been treated unjustly.[50] In Eisenberg's opinion, the weaker level of support was largely attributable to the fact that Portland clergy had far less interaction with Nikkei before the war than had been the case in Seattle.[51]

In just one area, religious leaders had more visible success in shaping the response to Japanese Americans. From early in the war, momentum began to develop around facilitating the transfer of Japanese American students who were attending schools such as the Universities of Washington and Oregon, where they faced internment, to other colleges and universities outside of the restricted zone. While several Christian organizations, including the YMCA and the YWCA, became involved, the Quakers, through their American Friends Service Committee, took the lead during the relocation process.

Many colleges and universities throughout the country received Japanese American students who had been attending West Coast schools. But federal officials determined that major research universities were off-limits for security purposes; small liberal arts colleges were thought to be the safest places for relocation.

In Washington State, one of the most accepting colleges for Japanese Americans turned out to be the Presbyterian-affiliated Whitworth College in Spokane. The college president, Frank Warren, had been a missionary to Japan in the 1920s; informed and motivated by this experience, he was particularly interested in offering refuge to Japanese American students. Roughly twenty Japanese American students (about 10 percent of the student body) were enrolled by 1944, with several coming directly out of the internment camps. Half of the 1944 Whitworth basketball team was made up of Japanese Americans. One student and basketball player, Tom Haji, who had been interned at Tule Lake, was drafted into the all–Japanese American 442nd Battalion and killed in Italy just weeks before the end of the war.

In another effort to offer ministry and advocacy, a few church leaders moved near the Minidoka camp in southeastern Idaho near Twin Falls, where most of Seattle's Japanese Americans were interned. Reverend Emery E. Andrews, of the Japanese Baptist Church, rented an oversized house in Twin Falls so that he could provide a stopping-off place for Nikkei moving in and out of the camps for such things as work-release programs, university study, and military service. An average of 167 Nikkei visited Andrews's home every month. From 1942 to 1945, he made an estimated fifty-six trips between Minidoka and Seattle. He brought goods and supplies to the Nikkei in camps.[52] Floyd Schmoe provided a similar courier service during the war years. Father Leopold Tibesar from Seattle also made the move to Minidoka to be with his flock. Tibesar had ministered largely to Japanese and Filipino Catholics at Our Lady of Martyrs Church on Seattle's First Hill. Tibesar, who spoke fluent Japanese,

A Quaker, Floyd Schmoe played a significant role in supporting Japanese Americans during the period of internment. Courtesy Densho, the Mamiya Collection, Seattle, Washington

had been a missionary to Japan and Manchuria before the war. He lived in the barracks in Minidoka and set up a chapel near his quarters for weekday Mass. He baptized newborns and performed weddings and even a few funerals. When the building was not being used for Mass, Tibesar turned it into a library and clubroom for adults and children. Throughout the war, Tibesar worked to relocate Japanese families in the Midwest and East.[53]

Margaret Peppers and Gennosuke Shoji also exemplified the extent to which some individuals would go to assist Japanese Americans during the war. Before coming to the Episcopal diocese in Olympia in 1928, Peppers had served for ten years in the Philippines among the Igorot people of Northern Luzon. During the 1930s, as a deaconess in the church, she was assigned to the Japanese missions of St. Peter's in Seattle and St. Paul's in the rural White River Valley southeast of the city. Shoji had emigrated from Japan in the late 1800s and had worked closely with Herbert Henry Gowen, who was rector of Seattle's oldest Episcopal parish and also a noted Asian scholar at the University of Washington. Shoji served as St. Peter's priest-in-charge until he retired in 1940.[54]

Once evacuation of all persons of Japanese descent took place, Margaret Peppers found herself first at Camp Harmony in Puyallup where she was among just a handful of Protestants who were ministering to the seven thousand residents. She attempted to continue her work in Christian education and youth ministry, but she soon found herself helping evacuees with issues related to business, banking, and financial matters. When the government moved evacuees to Minidoka, Peppers received permission to move to Idaho. Required to live outside of the camp, she daily made the forty-mile round trip from her home in Jerome, Idaho, to the camp.[55]

As a matter of conscience Gordon Hirabayashi refused to obey the exclusion order against Japanese Americans during World War II. Courtesy University of Washington Libraries, Special Collections, UW 36485

Father Shoji came out of retirement and also moved to Minidoka, along with Reverend Kenneth Nakajo from Portland and Father Joseph Kitigawa.

Between them they ministered to both Issei and Nisei at Minidoka. Deaconess Peppers worked closely with all of them as they attempted to ease the burden of internment.[56]

In addition to supporting Japanese Americans undergoing internment, other Christians worked on behalf of the country's most famous war resister, Gordon Hirabayashi. An undergraduate at the University of Washington, Hirabayashi refused to obey the exclusion order. On May 16, 1942, he turned himself in to the FBI. Hirabayashi was a Quaker, employed by the American Friends Service Committee. In his opposition to war and injustice, he received significant support from the religious community, most notably from lawyer Arthur Barnett.

Barnett, born in Scotland in 1907, moved to Seattle with his family when he was twelve years old. After high school, he earned undergraduate as well as law degrees from the University of Washington. He then joined the military, but after five years of service he became a Quaker out of deep commitment to its religious tenets, including pacifism. During World War II, he served as chair of the American Friends Service Committee in Seattle, as well as chair of the Seattle Church Council's Japanese Emergency Committee. In 1943, Barnett stood with Hirabayashi before the US Supreme Court when the justices unanimously ruled against Hirabayashi for defying curfews and refusing to register for internment. Despite this setback, Barnett continued to fight for compensation for Japanese Americans who had been interned. Barnett later would help lay the groundwork for the fair employment practices legislation for the state of Washington, the Public Accommodations Act of 1953, and the Omnibus Civil Rights Bill of 1957.[57]

As defeat of the Japanese became more inevitable, members of the religious communities of Seattle and Portland turned their attention to the resettlement of Japanese Americans back on the West Coast. Their first and primary task was to counter the considerable public resistance to Japanese Americans who wanted to return home. In Kent, a small community south of Seattle, for example, signs were posted that called for permanent exclusion. The Reverend Howard Slocum, chair of the Race Relations Committee of the Seattle Council of Churches, issued a press release condemning the anti-Japanese expressions of Kent's mayor and business community, as well as similar discriminatory expressions in West Seattle.[58]

On February 21, 1944, a year before the government lifted the ban on Nikkei on the West Coast, the Seattle Council of Churches officially announced, "We recommend that loyal Americans of Japanese ancestry be permitted to return to their homes as soon as the military situation permits." The council exhorted all Christians "to prevent violence being done to interned Japanese when they return to their homes."[59] In Portland, in the same year, the National Conference of Christians and Jews and the Portland Council of Churches created the Committee to Aid Relocation in order to assist Japanese Americans returning to Oregon.[60]

But opposition to the resettlement of Japanese Americans to the West Coast had powerful spokespersons. US congressman from Everett Henry Jackson was an enthusiast for internment and expressed serious reservations about whether Japanese Americans should be allowed to return to their homes.[61] Warren Magnuson, US senator from Washington and a well-known liberal on most issues, also expressed opposition, as did labor leader Dave Beck.[62] Notably, the governor of the state of Washington, Mon Wallgren, openly resisted the return of any Japanese Americans to the Pacific Coast. In response, the Seattle Council of Churches roundly criticized Wallgren for his position.[63] The pastor of Seattle's First Baptist Church, Harold Jensen, along with Arthur Barnett and the Reverend James Wilbourn, a Disciples of Christ minister and chair of the Race Relations Committee, issued a news release chastising the governor for his inflammatory remarks and for confusing Japanese Americans with the enemy. Japanese Americans were serving their nation as soldiers; moreover, "Not a single [Nikkei] person has been charged with an overt act against the government." Barnett then wrote a personal letter to Wallgren expressing his concern that the governor's comments would "result in raising hysteria" among the citizenry. But Wallgren refused to change his anti-Japanese position.[64]

In spite of public opposition, the Seattle Council of Churches recruited church members throughout the city to sponsor returnees and provide temporary or permanent quarters, noting that the use of a spare room for even a few days would help families make the transition. As the need continued to exceed the availability, the council launched its most ambitious effort on behalf of the Nikkei in April 1945 when it created the United Church Ministry to Returning Japanese (UCMRJ). E'Lois Shook was hired to direct the organization, which handled services as diverse as meeting returnees at train stations, providing private counseling, securing medical care, translating for older Issei, and helping Nikkei reestablish their positions in the community. The UCMRJ served as a liaison between individuals and government welfare agencies. It set up bank accounts, arranged for legal services, and gave valuable assistance to those searching for employment. Finally, it ministered to people's social, recreational, and spiritual needs by sponsoring social gatherings and developing special religious services. The UCMRJ created an interdenominational Japanese-language worship service for the Issei.[65]

In July, the United Church Ministry to Returning Japanese was informed by the War Relocation Authority that the Minidoka internment camp would be closed on November 1. An estimated eighteen hundred people, once released, would want to return to Seattle, creating a significant housing shortage.[66] In response, the UCMRJ established hostels in the Japanese Methodist Church and Saint Peter's Episcopal mission. In one six-month period, the UCMRJ investigated eighty-nine cases of racial discrimination, ranging from personal insults and housing discrimination to physical assault. It secured employment for 402 Nikkei. Finally, it established an interdenominational church program for the Issei and energetically promoted the integration of Nisei youth and young adults into white churches through special interracial programs and social events.[67]

The council's efforts to draw Nikkei—particularly Nisei—to white churches highlighted the ecumenical body's belief in a causal connection between the isolation of the prewar Japanese community and the evacuation process. Advocates believed that prewar separation of Caucasian and Japanese American populations made the latter more vulnerable to racial discrimination. By discouraging the reestablishment of distinctly Japanese churches and encouraging integrated ones, the UCMRJ hoped to prevent a repetition of targeted discrimination against a particular ethnic and racial group.

The Seattle Council of Churches, through the UCMRJ, pursued a variety of strategies to develop more integrated churches, but generally these efforts failed. Integrated churches held little appeal for returnees. Issei, in particular, actively resisted. Clearly, three years of forced exile made the goal of immediate integration into the white community unrealistic.[68]

In Portland, considerable resistance to the resettlement of interned Japanese Americans emerged. In 1945, the Oregon legislature tightened laws prohibiting the ownership of land by "aliens" and prevented

Japanese Americans from living on land owned by American-born relatives. However, in 1945 the local chapter of the National Conference of Christians and Jews met with the Portland Council of Churches to try to aid potential returnees. Compared with their minimal efforts before internment, Portland's religious community responded more proactively on behalf of the Japanese American community after the war. Religious leaders such as the Reverend I. George Nace, president of the Portland Council of Churches, Isabel Gates of the Baptist Mission Board, Father Thomas Tobin, and Jewish lawyer Gus Solomon participated in the Portland Committee to Aid Relocation. As a group, they helped internees find jobs and secure temporary housing. Solomon assisted many Japanese Americans in negotiating settlements for property that had been seized during internment.[69]

As mentioned earlier, in Hood River, sixty miles to the west of Portland, resistance and assistance to Japanese Americans took a different form. Of the county's approximately 11,500 citizens, just over 460 were of Japanese descent. Nevertheless, this still made it the largest population of Nikkei outside of Portland. All of them were relocated, and most of them were interned in southern Idaho at Minidoka, Tule Lake, California, or Heart Mountain, Wyoming. Although incarcerated with no charges, several Japanese Americans from Hood River ended up volunteering or were drafted into the US Army and served with distinction in the all–Japanese American 442nd Battalion. Back in Hood River, officials erected a billboard near the county courthouse with the names of all the community's residents, including sixteen Japanese Americans who were serving in the war. However, the hatred toward persons of Japanese descent was so strong that in December 1944, the local chapter of the American Legion decided to remove the sixteen Japanese American names. At that point, Reverend William Sherman Burgoyne, who had come to Hood River in 1942 to serve the Asbury Methodist Church, formally complained in the *Hood River News* about the Legion's actions. He stated that "every person in Hood River County . . . is disgraced." He urged them to replace the names immediately. In response, the city's former chamber of commerce president took out six large ads in the local paper in the form of "an open letter to W. Sherman Burgoyne." The first ad began, "So Sorry Please, Japs Are Not Wanted in Hood River." Burgoyne and his wife Doris were appalled. To work against such discrimination, the Methodist minister cofounded the League for Liberty and Justice, which aimed toward supporting Japanese Americans as well as countering propaganda and bigotry. In the end, Burgoyne succeeded in getting the names restored.[70]

But resistance to Japanese returning remained unabated. Hood River mayor Joe Meyer set the tone with a visceral comment: "We trusted them so completely while they were here among us, while all the time they were plotting our defeat and downfall. They were just waiting to stab us in the back. . . . We must let the Japanese know they're not welcome here." Nevertheless, Japanese Americans slowly trickled back to Hood River to try to recover their homes, their property, and their lives. Reverend Burgoyne's League for Liberty and Justice comprised over fifty members. They wrote a letter to Japanese Americans in camps in which they offered sympathy and support. Individual members of the league offered to meet returning internees at the train depot, shopped for local Japanese Americans, urged chain stores to accept Japanese business, and drove trucks to warehouses when produce and fruit were denied by local vendors. Burgoyne served as their spiritual leader. In a letter to those who volunteered to help, Burgoyne wrote, "The battle for American decency happened to be here this year. We fought it and won. Next year it may be in your part of America and I'm counting on you to stand true."[71]

Reverend Burgoyne's efforts did not go unnoticed. In 1947, the Methodist minister was selected in a national poll of a thousand civil liberties and service organizations and over five hundred editors to receive the Thomas Jefferson Award for promoting democracy by the Council Against Intolerance in America, along with Frank Sinatra, former Georgia governor Ellis Arnall, and Eleanor Roosevelt. Labeled the "fighting minister from Hood River" by the press, Burgoyne received his Jefferson prize in New York City.[72]

Back home in Hood River, Burgoyne was hardly treated as a hero. More than once, Burgoyne and his wife, Doris, were referred to publicly as "Jap lovers." They were frequently shunned. A rock was thrown through their window, and the Rotary Club, as well as other civic clubs, refused him. Initially the Methodist Board of Missions supported Burgoyne, but pressure continued to mount. In the same year that he received the Jefferson Award, Burgoyne was reassigned—or in some people's minds, exiled—first to a congregation in Shedd, Oregon, with fewer than ninety members, and shortly thereafter to a Methodist church in Spokane.

Burgoyne's story is both uplifting and tragic. When asked why he did what he did, he simply said, "I've done nothing unusual, I'm just an ordinary Methodist minister trying to be a Christian. The Redeemer put love in my heart, and I want to use it."[73] But Burgoyne knew he was an outsider to the Hood River community. He seemed to find courage in his identity as one who challenged the prevailing powers, whether that was in the form of members of the chamber of commerce or the local chapter of the American Legion.

Historian Roger Daniels observed that the most important element in helping evacuees reenter life on the West Coast "was the existence of a well-organized and active minority of whites who for one reason or another wanted what they considered justice for the Japanese Americans."[74] An unusual number of those individuals who worked for justice were members of the religious community, prompted to act by the injustice they had seen.

In hindsight, while Christians had failed to stop the internment of Japanese Americans during World War II, significant numbers of Catholics, Protestants, and Jews acted on behalf of Japanese Americans during and following the war. Without the likes of Harold Jensen, Emery Andrews, and Frank Warren, as well Father Tibesar, Arthur Barnett, Gus Solomon, the Seattle Council of Churches, and the United Church Ministry to Returning Japanese, as well as the Portland Committee to Aid Relocation, the situation could have been even worse for Japanese Americans in the Pacific Northwest.

CIVIL RIGHTS AFTER THE WAR

While the plight of Japanese Americans gained the attention of many Christians and Jews during the war, a sudden influx of African Americans into the region also exposed underlying patterns of racism and discrimination throughout the Northwest. In Seattle, lucrative defense contracts to Boeing, as well as the Seattle and Portland Kaiser shipyards, lured an unprecedented number of African Americans to those cities. Seattle's black population jumped from 3,800 in 1940 to 15,700 in 1950, while Portland's grew from 1,900 to 9,500. Almost immediately, racial tension increased in Seattle and Portland over the issue of housing.

Likewise, in Spokane racial issues began to percolate to the surface of public consciousness. On November 14, 1944, a group of nearly a hundred people, representing several religious and civic organizations, gathered at the YWCA to form a permanent race relations committee. The group, including Rabbi A. H. Fink and Father Ernest Mason, articulated several ambitious goals, including better interracial relations, equal economic opportunity, and increased access to public education and recreational facilities.[75] In 1945, the committee formally changed its name to the Spokane Committee on Racial Relations (SCRR). Throughout the remainder of the 1940s, the SCRR organized interracial clinics at churches and hotels. These clinics were cosponsored by the Spokane Council of Churches, Council of Church Women, Spokane Parent and Teacher Association, Spokane and Northwest Regional NAACP, the YMCA, and the YWCA.[76]

During the next several years in Spokane, the SCRR and the NAACP took responsibility for monitoring and reporting incidents of racial discrimination. In addition, African American Reverend Emmett Reed, pastor of Calvary Baptist Church since 1919 and active in the NAACP, had become increasingly active in denouncing segregation both in Spokane and in Pasco. In 1950, Reed gained attention when he forced some Pasco businesses to remove window signs that read, "No Dogs or Negroes Allowed" and "Whites Only."[77] James M. Sims, who later would become pastor of New Hope Baptist Church in Spokane, became the new president of the NAACP in 1956, and he too would play an important role during this period in exposing discriminatory employment practices in the city.[78]

In Seattle, one of the key groups to emerge in the struggle for civil rights was the Christian Friends for Racial Equality. In May 1942, seventeen people representing Christian and Jewish groups met to discuss how best to fight discrimination and foster better race relations in Seattle. Members of this new organization included representatives from the YMCA, the American Friends Service Committee, the Race Relations Department of the Seattle Council of Churches, and the Anti-Defamation League, along with the National Association for the Advancement of Colored People, the Japanese American Citizens League, and the Seattle Urban League. Out of that meeting, the Christian Friends for Race Equality (CFRE) was born (identified as Christian by title, despite the fact that many of its members and supporters were Jewish). The CFRE developed into Seattle's largest local interracial civil rights organization in the city's history.[79]

The tactical emphasis of the CFRE was conservative. From the beginning, the leadership eschewed direct confrontation in the form of sit-ins or rallies. Consensus emerged around the belief that moral suasion, investigation, and publicizing injustice would be more effective strategies. Women, notably, made up approximately two-thirds of the membership and almost three-quarters of the officers.

One of the more remarkable members of CFRE was Bertha Pitts Campbell. Born in 1889, she moved from Topeka, Kansas, to Seattle in 1923. Thirteen years later, Bertha Campbell became the first African American woman to exercise the right to vote on the local YWCA board and served four terms as chairperson of the East Cherry Branch. When the chance arose to join a group committed to racial justice and the expansion of housing possibilities for African Americans, she leaped at the opportunity.[80] Other key figures in the CFRE included the Reverend Fountain W. Penick, from Mount Zion Baptist, and attorney Charles Stokes. Stokes became Seattle's first black legislator, and both men helped form organizations such as the Association for Tolerance (1943) and Fellowship Committee of Black Churches (1944), created to support integration.[81]

In the 1940s, the Christian Friends for Racial Equality began to fight against restrictive neighborhood covenants that banned home owners from selling property to African Americans. In the 1950s, the CFRE began asking ministers to encourage property owners to rent or sell to minorities.[82]

Committed to reliance on moral persuasion and consciousness-raising, the CFRE organized theater outings, small teas and luncheons, picnics, nature walks, folk dances, and art classes as strategies for developing cross-cultural understanding. They published the *Racial Equality Bulletin* from 1946 through 1968. The *Bulletin* had extensive reach; at one point, the mailing list included individuals and organizations from sixteen states as well as Canada. The publication provided updates of the organization's board meetings, suggested-reading lists, and inspirational passages regarding Christian faith and the CFRE's goals of racial brotherhood.[83]

Members wrote regularly—many at least once each week—to legislators and government officials, condemning discrimination; they sent letters supporting business leaders who fought for justice. The CFRE collectively campaigned against racially discriminatory practices, including higher automobile insurance rates for nonwhite drivers and the exclusion of African Americans from the city's cemeteries. In addition, the group compiled a list of sixty-four housing covenants that prohibited a home owner from selling to a person of color.[84] In 1959, a survey indicated that the CFRE was the third most influential civil rights group, behind the Urban League and the NAACP.[85]

Formation of the Christian Friends for Racial Equality reflected the changing nature of religious engagement with the public square in the Northwest. The group's focus on civil rights helped bring Christians and Jews together from all over the city. In its stance and effectiveness, it represented the best of religious idealism in the region. If Seattle (or the Northwest) was to be a "city on a hill," racial hatred needed to end. For those who gave countless hours to the CFRE, action grew out of belief that moral commitment to justice and equality would carry the day. And while it failed to achieve its most global objectives, the group certainly prepared the way for even more significant ecumenical activity on behalf of civil rights that would emerge in the 1960s and 1970s.

In Oregon, the war years found the Portland Council of Churches beginning to take up the issue of civil rights with new vigor. In 1942, the council urged the Federal Housing Authority to make adequate provision to house Negro defense workers in Portland. The most important voice in the city at this time was that of Reverend Jesse James Clow, pastor of Portland's Mt. Olivet Baptist Church. Clow was critical in raising consciousness concerning the plight of African Americans in the city.

Born in Texas, Clow graduated from the Tuskegee Institute. He served churches in Virginia and Georgia before coming to Oregon in the middle of the Great Depression. By 1942, he was asserting that racial tension in Portland could be avoided only if realtors and landlords adopted a "no segregation policy."[86]

Clow built Mt. Olivet into the largest African American church in the state and was elected president of Portland's NAACP during World War II. Shortly after assuming the presidency, he went to Washington, DC, to demand that the Fair Employment Practices Commission (FEPC) investigate discriminatory hiring against African Americans in Portland. As a result, the FEPC identified numerous discriminatory practices, in particular citing the Kaiser Company and union hiring practices.[87]

Clow, other black pastors, and the leadership within the Portland Council of Churches were committed to racial integration. They formed a coalition of like-minded activists who advocated for changes in areas of employment, housing, and education. Clow pleaded for an open housing policy in the city. He warned that tensions between blacks and whites in Albina, the neighborhood where most African Americans lived, were approaching a dangerous level and might result in serious consequences if not relieved.

Meanwhile, the Portland Council of Churches (PCC), energized by the coalition, led the way in promoting education about black history and the black experience. The PCC, cooperating with the NAACP and the Library Association of Portland, encouraged dissemination of books such as W. E. B. DuBois's *Color and Democracy*, Richard Wright's *Black Boy*, and Rayford Logan's *What the Negro Wants*.[88] According to historian Stuart McElderry, the Oregon Conference of Congregational Churches and the Oregon Council of Church Women likewise worked to raise consciousness concerning racial discrimination in the state of Oregon in the years following the war.[89] While by most accounts these efforts were moderately successful and conditions improved incrementally after the war, de facto segregation as well as outright discrimination against African Americans in restaurants, hotels, and other business establishments continued to occur with frequency. In the public accommodations struggle that surfaced after the war, the Portland Council of Churches urged its members to boycott businesses that refused to serve African Americans. However, despite these initiatives, the civil rights bill of 1945 was defeated by the Oregon legislature.[90]

In the years immediately following the end of World War II, the pace of civil rights progress could be measured in fits and starts. For every one or two steps forward, there seemed to be one step backward. It was clear that this was going to be a tough slog. But religious activists persisted in bringing issues of discrimination before city officials.

By 1950, the Portland City Council was still struggling to pass a civil rights ordinance after taking a full year to study it. As debate intensified, with heavy opposition still coming from the Portland Hotel Association, ministers of the mainline downtown Protestant churches (Christian, Congregational, Methodist, Presbyterian, and Unitarian) went on record and enthusiastically endorsed the ordinance. Just days before the city council vote, the National Conference of Christians and Jews awarded to the city of Portland its human relations award for 1949 as the city with the most improved race relations and civil rights. The conference noted the work of the Urban League, the League of Women Voters, the United Committee for Civil Rights, the NAACP, the Portland Council of Churches, and the AAUW Interracial Fellowship group, "all of whom had changed the city's general racial climate," according to historian McElderry.[91] However, in spite of the growing support for civil rights, the ordinance failed to win approval—the opposition from the business community was too strong. Nevertheless, support for an open-housing ordinance continued to grow throughout the state with the aid of mainline Protestant church leadership. Finally, in 1953, a state law passed.

CONCLUSION

From the late 1920s to the early 1950s, the role of religion in public life shifted in the Pacific Northwest. Many Protestants, Catholics, and Jews engaged social and political issues in the middle decades of the twentieth century, but with a different agenda than had the previous generation. Less focused on Victorian cultural issues, these religiously motivated individuals committed themselves to expressions of social justice. From economic deprivation during the Depression to the plight of Japanese Americans, African Americans, and other minority groups, significant effort and thought were directed at moving toward a more just society. It would be hard to overestimate the degree to which these efforts laid a foundation for renewed and even more effective efforts to achieve social justice during the 1960s and 1970s. In virtually every case, these activists saw themselves as outsiders to a culture dominated by white economic, political, or racial privilege. And yet they persisted in articulating a vision of society that should be marked by justice for all.

However, at the same time that forces of social justice and racial liberalism were shifting the nature of religious influence on public life, other Christians in the Northwest were organizing themselves around issues of a more conservative nature. Fears over Communism, liberalism, and secularism all translated into concerns about the traditional family and the understanding of the United States in God's greater plan. These religiously motivated conservatives also saw themselves increasingly as outsiders to a culture that, in this case, had become increasingly secular and nonreligious. And that was cause for action.

CHAPTER 7

THE RIGHT GATHERS ITSELF

In the middle of the 1930s, Postmaster James A. Farley, on a visit to Seattle, reportedly offered a simple toast: "To the forty-seven states and the soviet of Washington." As historian Charles LeWarne noted, "No one in the audience could have missed the point."[1] By then, the Pacific Northwest had earned a national reputation for reform and radicalism. The free speech fights in Spokane, the Everett and Centralia massacres, and the Seattle General Strike all underscored the progressive and often radical character of the region politically and socially. Early adoption of women's suffrage, along with early requirements for minimum wages, helped Farley's audience resonate with his point about the liberal character of the region.

As we have seen, many religious activists supported these larger efforts to achieve social justice for marginalized groups. Many progressive activists spent countless hours lobbying, organizing, and testifying to the many ways in which injustice, discrimination, and poverty demanded a more vigorous political response from the region's citizenry. But there was also another set of responses from religious activists who considered themselves more conservative and at the same time outsiders to this culture of liberalism, progressivism, and even radicalism that had formed the national reputation of the region. As outsiders to this emerging culture, they organized new associations, established private schools, built coalitions among themselves, and created something of a counterculture to the progressive Pacific Northwest.

Rather than continuing to focus on the issues of a previous generation—alcohol abuse, prostitution, and gambling—this new generation of religious conservatives framed their critique of American and specifically Pacific Northwest culture around what they described as leftist, liberal, and radical ideas. Ever since the Scopes Trial in the mid-1920s, conservative Christians had begun to distance themselves from the public school system. Politically, conservatives feared that the Roosevelt years were destroying American capitalism's core beliefs, and most notably, conservatives feared that liberals were too soft on the communist threat both internally and externally. As a consequence, conservative evangelicals and Catholics gathered themselves around a new set of issues and found some common ground as outsiders in their opposition to the prevailing secularism of the region.[2]

It was during the Great Depression of the 1930s that new individuals and organizations dedicated to the resurgence of conservative principles emerged in the Pacific Northwest, as they did across the nation. Many evangelicals expressed deep anxieties regarding Franklin Roosevelt and his New Deal, fearing that the country was being led down a path toward socialism. Apprehension about the decline of traditional religious and moral values percolated throughout the country and in the region.[3]

Two especially influential individuals in the national effort to promote conservative religious and political values were Joseph Newton Pew Jr. and his brother, J. Howard Pew. The Pew brothers controlled Sun Oil and grew to hate Roosevelt and the New Deal. During the height of the Depression, the Pews directed millions of dollars into the Republican Party and millions more toward the cultivation of conservative Christian leadership. Howard Pew supported conservative business associations, religious organizations, newspapers, books, films, and conferences. He became chairman of the board of Grove City College, which became a model for teaching a Christian worldview, including an emphasis on free market capitalism. In the 1930s, Pew was also an active supporter of the Liberty League, which organized opposition against the New Deal. In addition, he contributed substantial financial support to a group called Spiritual Mobilization, which merged Christian piety and conservative politics, and he directed the United Presbyterian Foundation, known for opposing religious modernism.[4]

The Pacific Northwest, while somewhat removed from the center of these efforts, nevertheless saw its fair share of conservative grassroots activity combining religion and politics. For example, a group of Seattle women united by strong religious convictions formed a political group in 1932 named Pro-America. The women, originally members of a garden club, drew together around their common concern about the Roosevelt election. According to historian June Benowitz, the women "were worried that the government would not lead the country in a manner that would uphold values like patriotism, religious devotion, and sexual purity."[5] These women built support for the Republican Party in all forty-eight states by casting Franklin Roosevelt and Democrats in general as serious threats to the traditional values (patriotism, religious devotion, capitalism, etc.) that they espoused. Their greatest support came in Oregon. Establishing a chapter in 1935, Pro-America in Oregon secured 509 members in the greater Portland area in its first year. Eventually an estimated twelve hundred Oregon women joined the organization, and the group ranked among the top ten independent contributors to the Republican presidential campaign by 1940.[6]

Perhaps the most unusual expression of conservative religious influence to come out of the Pacific Northwest emerged from the ministry of Seattle pastor Abraham (Abram) Vereide. Born in 1886 in Norway, Vereide emigrated to the United States in 1905. After graduating from Northwestern College in Chicago, Vereide received his theological education at the Methodist Garrett Theological Seminary, also in Chicago. After serving churches in Spokane and Portland for a brief period, he moved to Seattle in 1916 and served as the pastor of a Norwegian Danish Methodist church. Vereide's ministry focused on the alleviation of poverty among Seattle's Scandinavian immigrants and promoted their Americanization. He established an employment bureau and organized courses in English for recent arrivals. In 1918, Vereide launched the Beulah Retreat Center and Farm on Vashon Island in Puget Sound near Seattle in order to provide vocational training for unwed mothers, unskilled men, and homeless children. All of this activity brought him to the attention of city leaders, who asked him to explore expanded social services for the region. Eventually, he recommended that Seattle adopt a model that had been pioneered in Boston—Goodwill Industries. In 1923, Vereide helped establish Seattle's version of Goodwill Industries, and he served until 1931 as its superintendent. In that year, he left for Boston to become associate general superintendent of Goodwill Industries of America, as well as pastor of the English department of the Church of All Nations. He held the All Nations position for three years, until he returned to the West Coast to head evangelistic efforts for the Methodist Church in San Francisco.[7]

While in San Francisco, Vereide's vision for ministry began to change. In May 1934, San Francisco's longshoremen went on strike,

and shortly thereafter, fellow dock workers up and down the Pacific Coast, including two thousand from Seattle, struck in sympathy. Lasting eighty-three days, the sometimes violent strike achieved gains for longshoremen, but it also divided the labor movement between the craft unions of the American Federation of Labor (AFL) and the less-skilled trades of the Congress of Industrial Organization (CIO).

Reverend Abram Vereide, left, attempted to organize the business community in Seattle against Communism. (Eisenhower in center.) Courtesy Archives of Billy Graham Center, Wheaton, Illinois

For Vereide, the specter of labor violence and industrial chaos caused a change of heart and turned him toward the political and religious Right. No longer would his focus be on addressing poverty. Instead, Vereide turned to Seattle's power brokers (businessmen and politicians) with hope that influential leaders would be amenable to conservative religious and political values. According to writer Jeff Sharlet, "The strike of 1934 scared Abram [Vereide] into launching the movement that would become the vanguard of elite fundamentalism, and elite fundamentalism took as its first challenge the destruction of militant labor."[8] Toward this end, Vereide allied himself with community leaders. As his biographer put it, Vereide believed that the "greater the sphere of influence in government or industry, the more responsible they are to make it plain by their personal living, by their conduct of affairs, and by their verbal witness, that Jesus Christ as Savior and Lord is the only answer to the human problem, and that He must be given in our era and in our tangled affairs all the lordship we His servants can give Him."[9]

However, gaining the ear of Seattle's political and business leaders posed certain challenges. Vereide often recounted his meeting with Seattle developer Walter Douglass, and how he told Douglass of his desire to reach business executives by preaching a manly Christ instead of a Christ who exhibited compassion for the poor.[10] According to Sharlet, Vereide believed that his message must be a "rejection of the 'Social Gospel' of good works for the poor in favor of an unhindered Christ defined by his muscles, a laissez-faire Jesus proclaimed not by spindly necked clergymen bleating from seminary, but by men like Major Douglass, officers who commanded troops who brought order to cities."[11] With Douglass's help, Vereide began meeting with top business executives of the city, including William St. Clair, president of Frederick and Nelson, Seattle's major department store. St. Clair embraced Vereide's idea and identified others who were mostly non-churchgoers but also rallied to Vereide's message. These allies included James Pollard, president of the Seattle Gas Company; Jess Kennedy, president of the Kennedy Lumber Company; William Devin, attorney; Fred Ernst, president of Ernst Hardware Company; and future governor Arthur E. Langlie, then of the city council.

By 1935, Vereide had organized this group of local Seattle businessmen to pray in hope of mitigating the impact of socialism on the country, as well as the influence of the Industrial Workers of the World, better known as the Wobblies, on organized labor in the Northwest. The group, including labor and government leaders, met regularly for breakfast with the goal of cooperating in order to avoid more labor conflict.[12]

By 1937, over two hundred similar prayer breakfast groups had been organized throughout Seattle. Vereide found the idea of bringing businessmen together to pray for common conservative concerns exhilarating. He traveled throughout the Northwest and eventually throughout the country organizing groups. In 1940, on the occasion of Langlie's election as governor, over three hundred men, including elected officials, gathered for a prayer breakfast with the newly elected Republican. For Vereide, this gathering epitomized the possibilities of the prayer breakfast.[13] In that same year, Vereide became the executive director of City Chapel, an organization that served as the national center for the prayer breakfast movement, focusing on Bible study, fellowship, and the promotion of Christian principles.[14]

In 1942, Vereide and his supporters established an organization called The Fellowship in Chicago, and this became Vereide's center for national outreach to businessmen and civic and clergy leadership. In that same year, The Fellowship also established itself in the nation's capital and began sponsoring weekly congressional prayer breakfasts, as well as prayer groups organized by governors, mayors, and state legislators across America. Vereide's Fellowship program became one of the country's most influential Christian conservative groups during the Eisenhower years. Interestingly, despite its move east and subsequent national presence, the organization held its national convention in Seattle in 1955.[15]

Just as people like Vereide were moving to the right during the Depression, other conservative religious impulses were also taking root in the Pacific Northwest. Beginning in the 1930s, a new wave of migrants from the South flocked to the region, as they had done in the late nineteenth century. The Depression forced thousands of individuals from Texas, Oklahoma, Arkansas, and Missouri to move to Washington and Oregon with hope of finding a better life. Most of these transplants to the Northwest brought more conservative religion with them. Southern Baptist, the Assemblies of God, and the Church of God in Christ denominations grew rapidly in this period throughout the Pacific Northwest. And with them came a change in religious culture, as pastors from these churches preached a message that emphasized "profound salvation experiences, believed in the power to heal and an impending millennium, abhorred worldliness, and loathed Catholicism and Communism," according to historian David Jepson.[16]

In fact, not only conservative groups but nearly all Christian denominations increased their numbers in the Pacific Northwest during the years between 1940 and 1960. However, the Baptists and the Assemblies of God communities grew more than most and much faster than the population as a whole.[17]

The influx of evangelicals in the Pacific Northwest created a spirit of receptivity toward national conservative movements. By the 1940s, Carl McIntire had developed a significant following. One of the nation's leading fundamentalists, McIntire had organized a group of Bible-believing Christians, the American Council of Churches, who objected to the liberalism of the Federal Council of Churches. McIntire's group emphasized the importance of understanding the Bible as the infallible word of God. Claiming that the United States was a Protestant country, McIntire vigorously opposed what he believed was the heretical "ecumenical unity of Christendom" associated with the Federal Council of Churches.[18] He further criticized the social doctrines of the Federal Council that were "hardly to be distinguished from Communism." In contrast, he asserted, the American Council of Churches affirmed that the Bible offers clear support for the underlying presuppositions of capitalism.[19]

In 1942, a broader, more inclusive group of white evangelicals formed the National Association of Evangelicals (NAE), which also had a growing following in the Pacific Northwest. Led by Harold John Ockenga, pastor of Boston's Park Street Church, and J. Elwin Wright, head of a New England association of evangelicals, the National Association also proclaimed itself to be opposed to the Federal Council of Churches. Clearly the NAE, like McIntire's group, wanted to move American politics to the right. But the NAE wanted to be less contentious and to reach a broader cross section of Americans. Unlike McIntire's council, the NAE welcomed members of Holiness or Pentecostal churches and evangelical Protestants from mainstream denominations. The NAE's initial membership of about 300,000 surged to 1.3 million by 1950.[20]

By midcentury, the NAE had gained financial backing from conservative businessmen. The NAE's 1950 convention called for "participation by Christians in political affairs and training of Christian young people for government." As was the case with McIntire's group, the NAE made a specific point of opposing Communism and embracing free-enterprise capitalism. The NAE opposed national health insurance, civil rights laws, and federal aid to education, and objected to all forms of advertising for alcohol. School textbooks that reflected secular humanism also drew the group's attention and ire.[21]

But in addition to attacking what they perceived to be the Godless elements of American culture, the American Council and the National Association of Evangelicals assailed the Catholic Church for both its theology and its politics. The traditional quarrel over Catholic belief in papal authority, priestly powers, worship of saints and relics, and opposition to capital punishment moved into additional criticism of Catholic teaching on economics. Both the American Council and the NAE denounced Catholic support for organized labor.[22] And speaking at the NAE's 1945 convention, Ockenga berated the Catholic Church as presenting an even broader threat, "a greater menace than Communism itself, [which was] now reaching for control of the government." Ockenga asserted that Catholics wanted to "transform a fundamentally Protestant culture to a fundamentally Roman Catholic culture in the United States," replete with the "autocracy, monopoly, and undemocracy [that] now prevails by Roman Catholic dominion in South America."[23] Without question, the American Council and the National Association of Evangelicals set a tone that would influence a generation of evangelicals in the Pacific Northwest.

The National Association of Evangelicals hoped to exercise its most important influence on the burgeoning youth culture of the mid-twentieth century. Many middle-class Americans believed that young people were in a state of spiritual crisis. From the vantage point of the twenty-first century, the 1950s appear remarkably homogeneous and conservative. The countercultural movements as well as the gap between generations that followed in the sixties and seventies make the fifties look tame by comparison. But from the vantage point of the late forties and early fifties, significant numbers of individuals believed that the youth of America were in trouble already. A large number of middle-class parents came to believe that the economic catastrophe of the Great Depression and the threats first of Nazism and then of Communism made it incumbent to inculcate values of religion, capitalism, and patriotism in their youth. In the minds of many, the absence of a strong belief in orthodox Christianity, of a strong belief in private enterprise, and of a strong belief in America as God's favored nation made the country vulnerable to both internal and external enemies. And while there were many manifestations of these fears for the hearts and minds of young people, one of the most interesting occurred in the form of Christian youth groups outside of the traditional church.[24]

One of the most influential efforts to reach America's youth was Youth for Christ (YFC), which typified a conservative evangelical approach. In 1946—inspired in part by the work of Jack Wyrtzen, evangelist and founder of Word of Life Ministries—Torrey Johnson, a Baptist minister who pastored the Midwest Bible Church in Chicago, along with Charles Templeton from Toronto, Canada, founded Youth for Christ, International. Johnson was the first president. They believed that young people would be attracted to Christian music and movies, Bible games, discussion groups, and personal testimonies. "Rallies featured sports stars, repentant hoodlums, and even a pious horse that kneeled at the cross and stomped its foot three times to worship the Trinity," according to historian Allan Lichtman. "Teens could join the legion of the saved, redeem their country, and have good clean fun."[25] A young Billy Graham emerged as the group's first full-time evangelist and came to Tacoma, Portland, and Seattle to help start YFC chapters. In the early days, Youth for Christ in the Northwest sprang up in lots of places, with Saturday-night rallies led largely by local pastors. Jack Hamilton established a group in Seattle and became the national director. Other Seattle leaders included a close friend of Abraham Vereide, Bob Pierce, who went on to found World Vision, one of the largest relief organizations in the world.[26] Paul "Tex" Yearout began a YFC chapter in Bellingham, Washington. Yearout organized rallies and Bible quizzing before moving on to work with the Seattle YFC in the 1950s. Doug Ross directed the Seattle chapter from 1956 to 1962. As many as thirty-five high school chapters were established in the area, attracting several thousand teenagers.[27]

YFC leaders around the country, as well as in the Pacific Northwest, emphasized the importance of avoiding worldly temptations such as smoking, drinking, and the movies. Encouraged to "win" their friends for Christ, youth were told they would play a key role in restoring Christian America to its former greatness with the defeat of Communism. Young people were also attracted to YFC not only because of the spiritual benefits, but also because it promised to be fun and aimed to attract "popular" kids.[28]

For YFC leaders, conversion of youth was more important than social action. Leaders believed that by their bringing people to Christ, juvenile delinquency and the potential appeal of Communism would be blunted. "YFC leaders warned that American civilization," according to historian Thomas Bergler, "would be swamped by crime, immorality, juvenile delinquency, and Communism."[29] In starting youth groups, YFC leaders facilitated the transition from Fundamentalism to Evangelicalism and solidified an important expression of Christianity in the years following World War II. The organization reinforced core commitments to orthodox Christianity and American patriotism that would be critical to the establishment of conservative social values for the next several decades.

Young Life was another evangelical organization that took root in the years immediately following World War II. Founded by Jim Rayburn from Texas, the organization moved to Colorado Springs in 1946 and shortly thereafter began to establish chapters in cities throughout the Northwest. Famous for saying that "it's a sin to bore a kid," Rayburn utilized students primarily from Christian colleges such as Seattle Pacific and Whitworth in Spokane. Young Life leaders aimed to reach high school-aged students and convert them or "win" them to Christianity.[30] Stressing the importance of establishing a personal relationship with Christ, and therefore evangelical in character, Young Life, like Youth for Christ, attempted to build strong mentoring relationships between students and their leaders. Having a fun experience was paramount. In 1953, Young Life purchased a camp at Malibu on British Columbia's Sunshine Coast. "The Malibu Experience" became a hallmark of the Young Life program. Not overtly political in its message, Young Life reinforced traditional family values, a belief in the authority of Scripture, and a sense that elements of secular culture should be resisted.

The surge of evangelicalism in the Northwest after World War II also manifested itself in the establishment of Protestant private schools. In only twenty years, many evangelicals had generally lost faith in the public school system. Whereas in the 1920s, evangelicals had supported initiatives that would have eliminated private schools and forced everyone to attend a public school, now they found themselves wanting to provide an alternative education system to public education.

By 1945, only three years after it was formed, the National Association of Evangelicals established a network of private Christian schools across the country. In the Northwest, between 1945 and 1951, several schools sprang up in and around Salem, Spokane, Portland, and Seattle. In 1949, for example, as part of the local chapter of the NAE, pastors and parents formed Northwest Christian Schools in Spokane. One spokesman who came to the city was quoted as saying,

> I feel the philosophy underlying the public school system has been influenced by John Dewey [secular philosopher and educational theorist] and his followers. The question of separation of church and state, which we believe in, has been carried to the point in many schools where there can be no Christian influence. Schools must steer a neutral course so religion is left out. This does not suit many Christian parents who want their children to receive their education in Christian schools, so private schools are filling this need.

According to Clate Risley, president of the Inland Empire Association of Evangelicals, "There are literally hundreds of Christian parents and boys and girls in the Inland Empire, ranging all the way from old-line Methodists, Baptists, and Presbyterians to the Pentecostals,

Brethren, and Alliance congregations who are far from satisfied with the evolution, the 'isms' and the non-Christian activities of the public schools."[31]

A similar tale could be told of Christian schools in Salem, Oregon. In 1936, the Beacon Bible School began as a Mennonite-sponsored school, but in 1945 it combined with the Salem Bible Institute to form the Salem Academy. In Seattle, during the same period, conservative Lutherans established the Lutheran Bible Institute. Other evangelicals organized the Seattle Christian School, the first interdenominational Christian day school in western Washington in 1946. Conservative Christians founded King's Garden schools in 1950 in North Seattle. These schools provided a biblically centered education and a set of cultural and political values that were much more conservative than founders believed were being taught in the public schools.

While attracting proportionally a very small number of students, these alternative schools and institutes represented growing dissatisfaction with the public school system, discontent that would only grow over the next several decades. Using the Bible as a teaching text, teachers attempted to connect scriptural teachings with values that centered on the family, the flag, and capitalism.

The rise of private Christian schools in the Northwest coincided with increasing anxiety over the spread of Communism at home and abroad. In Washington, DC, the House Committee on Un-American Activities raised concerns about the possibility of subversive activities, particularly in Hollywood, after the war. Whittaker Chambers's assertion that Alger Hiss was a communist while working for the State Department added further fuel to the fire. The arrest and eventual execution of Julius and Ethel Rosenberg for espionage related to the atomic bomb also helped create an atmosphere of suspicion throughout the country. And Senator Joe McCarthy's claims that communists posed a major threat to the internal security of the United States further increased anxiety on the part of citizens across the country.

In the Pacific Northwest, concerns about communist influence manifested themselves in a number of ways and certainly cast a chill over public education. In 1948, Albert Canwell, Washington state senator from Spokane, held hearings that centered on the loyalty of faculty at the University of Washington. Eventually three professors were fired for what were deemed subversive teachings.

Conservative Protestants quickly embraced the anticommunist cause for a number of reasons. Communism's rejection of God and the Bible made it an easy target for all Christians but particularly for more conservative Christians. The United States represented for conservative Christians a country that had been founded not just on a principle of religious freedom, but one in which the Founding Fathers had privileged the expression of Christianity.

In 1950, Billy Graham arrived in the Northwest to begin crusades in this least-churched region of the country. In Portland, Graham attracted more than 45,000 for a three-day event. In Seattle, he stayed for five weeks, and more than 440,000 heard him speak. Perhaps because of the size of the crowds, the young revivalist made little note of the region's reputation for being irreligious, focusing instead on the dire circumstances in which the entire country found itself as a result of the Cold War. In fact, Graham spoke to his Portland audience only a month after North Korean armies had poured over the border and sent South Koreans and a handful of US troops into retreat. "Communism is a form of religion: a supernaturally-empowered religion," preached Graham. "There is no other way to account for the successes the communists have had. The devil is directing their maneuvers."[32] With the memory of Pearl Harbor still seared in his audience's minds, Graham contended that "Portland and Seattle would be the No. 1 targets in any sneak attack because they are only 8 1/2 hours away from secret Russian air bases."[33]

In Seattle a year later, Graham preached much the same message. He told an audience of nearly nine thousand that "Tonight, this is one of the most dangerous nights in our history. I don't think we are prepared to meet Russia on the battlefield. But I want to tell you, if you got on your knees to God, He could defeat the Russians without firing a shot." Graham further claimed, "I believe that all blessings that America enjoys come from God. But this generation of Americans has betrayed God, and His judgment will be upon us unless we repent."[34] When Graham's time ended in Seattle, he reported that the crusade had produced the greatest number of converts of any campaign that he had run to that point.[35]

Evangelicals found common ground with the Catholic Church in its concern about Communism. In a June 1950 editorial in the *Catholic Northwest Progress*, the writer proclaimed that "conversion of Russia through prayer and reparation offered to God is the only sure way to bring lasting peace to the world."[36] The Cardinal Mindzenty Foundation, based in St. Louis, emerged as one of the most conservative expressions of the Catholic Church, and several chapters took root in the Northwest. According to observers in the secular press, the foundation was occasionally compared with the John Birch Society, an organization that vehemently opposed Communism. The Mindzenty Foundation sponsored a radio program entitled *Dangers of Apathy* and organized between three and four thousand parish-level study groups.[37] Relentless in its efforts, the Mindzenty Foundation painted a picture of an America under attack from intellectuals, leftists, and entertainers, as well as from communists and atheists. As did Youth for Christ, the Mindzenty Foundation believed that American youth were the target of a concerted communist effort to brainwash teenagers with pornography, morally offensive paperbacks, procommunist lecturers, and, in general, secular education. The foundation frequently sponsored showings of two provocative films: *Communism on the Map* and *Operation Abolition*. Shown on a regular basis throughout the Seattle Archdiocese in 1961, the films reinforced the message that a good Catholic resisted Communism at home and abroad.[38]

Among Protestants, an Australian physician, Fred Schwarz, became a prominent figure in response to Communism in the Northwest. Originally invited to the United States in 1953 by fundamentalist Carl McIntire, Schwarz became a lay preacher and self-proclaimed authority on Communism in America. Soon he began to organize what he labeled Christian schools of anticommunism. Schwarz traveled around the country, asserting that a strong link existed between liberal theology, modernism, and Communism. He urged his audiences to commit themselves to Christianity and to speak out against the forces of Communism wherever they existed. At times, he enlisted the support of well-known figures such as counterspy Herbert Philbrick, an advertising executive who had infiltrated the Communist Party in the 1940s, and Edward Teller, father of the hydrogen bomb, as well as retired admiral Chester Ward. In 1961, Schwarz attracted twelve thousand people to the Hollywood Bowl for a rally with well-known actors Ronald Reagan, John Wayne, and Jimmy Stewart.[39]

Schwarz first came to the Northwest in 1957, when the newly formed First Baptist Church in Bellevue offered him an invitation to speak on the "ever-threatening power of world communism."[40] In 1959, he came to Spokane as well, in response to Whitworth College's invitation to speak to students about the threat of Communism.[41]

Schwarz's major effort in the Northwest occurred in February 1962, when he arrived in Seattle for the purpose of establishing one of his Christian schools for anticommunism; he quickly became a vocal and active presence. More than five hundred people heard Schwarz describe his intention to establish the Christian Puget Sound School of Anti-Communism at one daytime presentation. That night, more than a thousand heard Schwarz warn his audience of the spread of Communism.[42] This was followed by a free youth rally for children and parents at the Civic Ice Arena, where Schwarz was joined by John Drakeford from Southwestern Baptist Theological Seminary. Drakeford lamented what he called "the conformity of non-conformity" on college campuses.[43] Schwarz called on mothers and fathers to be vigilant: "This tyranny is sweeping the earth. Home and children and country stand in mortal danger. Each of us must decide where we stand, and what we will do. Rise up, O men of God!"[44] During the rest of the week, additional speakers recruited to Schwarz's cause asserted that Marxist-Leninist ideas had crept into history textbooks, teaching that morals and religion were merely crutches to support the ruling class.[45] By the end of the week, approximately five thousand were attending Schwarz's school in Seattle.[46] Classes included "Philosophy of Communism," "Communism and Youth," "How to Debate with Communists and Fellow Travelers," and "Communism and Education."

Response to Schwarz and his efforts was generally favorable. The Bellevue School Board publicly supported his efforts.[47] The *Catholic Northwest Progress* offered extensive and admiring coverage of the quasi-political workshops that were part of Schwarz's efforts, and the *Boeing News* echoed its approval of Schwarz's school.[48] Clearly, Schwarz's outspoken connection between Christianity and anticommunism resonated with a good segment of the greater Seattle area.

Historian Lisa McGirr makes the case that Schwarz appealed to pervasive fears of the centralization of the federal government and, more importantly, to "apprehensions over the penetration of liberal ideas into the nation's schools, churches, and communities—under an overarching discourse of 'communist subversion.'" For middle-class men and women, Schwarz touched a nerve. He affirmed their belief that their own individual success had been the result of hard work, as well as their belief in God. All of those values seemed threatened in the modern world; consequently, Schwarz addressed their deep concerns when he stressed the importance of a "return to 'traditional' values, local control, strict morality, and strong authority."[49]

In the Northwest, middle-class fears about the erosion of traditional values found fertile soil in the growing suburbs of Seattle, Portland, Tacoma, and Spokane. Lake Hills, a Bellevue suburb on the east side of Lake Washington, was one such community enmeshed in concerns over communist influence. This was an area that had consisted largely of a few blueberry farms and a small number of houses until the 1950s. With the GI Bill stimulating housing, Seattle's nearby suburbs exploded with new homes and developments, including Lake Hills. Churches also boomed, and by 1960 Lake Hills featured a wide array of congregations. The First Baptist Church formed in 1957; Episcopalians met at the Lake Hills Community Club; the Lake Hills Church of the Nazarene, the Lake Hills Church of Christ, the Free Methodist Church, and St. Andrew's Lutheran Church were all organized in the late 1950s.[50]

Lake Hills grew rapidly into a strong Catholic residential suburb. Sacred Heart Parish offered four masses each Sunday at the local high school gymnasium.[51] The local newspaper, the *Bellevue-American*, reported that eight hundred Catholic families lived in the St. Louise Parish in 1960, making it one of the fastest growing in the Seattle area. In every sense, the community reflected national conservative forces of the 1950s and early sixties. Many members of this Catholic parish joined the Blue Army of Our Lady of Fatima, dedicated "to the Blessed Virgin and anti-Communism," as well as the anticommunist Cardinal Mindszenty Foundation.[52]

Lake Hills' residents considered religious and ethical training of prime importance in their children's education and placed high value on their own spiritual lives.[53] Just as was true in southern California, the Lake Hills suburb provided fertile ground for right-wing political organizations founded on conservative religious values. Of the estimated two thousand grassroots radical rights organizations in the United States in 1961, several were prevalent in Bellevue; the Minute Men, Circuit Riders, We the People, the Cardinal Mindszenty Foundation, and the John Birch Society all had chapters or representatives in the community. These groups shared a common appeal to new suburban families around the issue of protecting their children from liberal, secular forces, particularly in the public schools.[54]

The John Birch Society proved to be one of the most active groups in Lake Hills. Founded by Robert Welch in 1958, the society had made a name for itself nationally by advocating that the chief justice of the US Supreme Court, Earl Warren, be impeached. Welch and others had also asserted that the United States should get out of the United Nations. While not specifically religious in its identity, the John Birch Society, according to historian Lorraine McConaghy, aimed to recruit "a million good patriots" to purify churches and schools, to disrupt and confront, to write letters, to form fronts, and to infiltrate and capture local organizations for the sake of conservative causes.[55]

The John Birch Society appealed to suburbanites by emphasizing that Communism posed an immediate threat to American families. The society "believed that suburban people needed to be jolted out of their comfortable materialism and smug complacency to restore the genuine American community of home, chapel, and schoolroom."[56] The society brought the global battle between forces of good and evil onto home ground and fought the suburban Armageddon as a cultural war. Once radicalized, suburban American patriots would stand against timid conformity and root out dissidents and communist sympathizers from their neighborhoods. What else could a patriot do, asked one Lake Hills man, "when we had people turning garden clubs into front organizations for the Communist Party?"[57] The overwhelming fear was that a significant number of public school teachers were, if not card-carrying communists, at the very least steeped in socialist values and intent on directing students' political and social values to the Left. The battle centered on the hearts and minds of the next generation, and that battle occurred on a daily basis in the classrooms of the public schools.[58]

A culture war had taken hold. Conservative religious values had helped support conservative political values. While it would be an overstatement to suggest that conservative religious activism was the root cause of the anxieties associated with secularism, liberalism, and Communism, it would not be an overstatement to suggest that conservative religious impulses helped foster an environment of concern for what might be going on in the public schools.[59]

Although ultimately subsiding, the situation in Lake Hills was likely repeated in suburban communities throughout the Northwest in the late 1950s and early 1960s. And if conservatives needed one more reason to suspect that liberal forces were on the verge of taking control of the culture, it was the fact that in 1963, prayer in public schools was ruled unconstitutional. In Oregon, the Oregon Conference of Methodist Churches gave its public support for the decision, asserting that prayer should be "reserved for private conscience, homes and the church."[60] However, conservatives and evangelicals were aghast. The Evangelical United Brethren Churches (representing two hundred congregations) expressed dismay. Dr. Wilmer Brown indicated that it is "a sad departure from this nation's heritage under God." He cited Richard A. Cook, president of the National Association of Evangelicals, who had issued a statement saying that "far from putting the government in a position of neutrality toward religion, this ruling is another step in creating an atmosphere of hostility toward religion."[61] Cook had gone on to say:

> Rather than serving to protect against the establishment of religion, it opens the door for the full establishment of secularism as a negative form of religion. The fact that America has become a multi-faith culture does not necessarily prove that it should not, as a nation, continue to acknowledge our dependence as a nation upon Almighty God even in the classroom. If this interpretation of the First Amendment is allowed to stand, it will make it far more difficult for the home and the church to put fiber and character into the lives of our children in this time of national peril, and this will have great consequences.[62]

For many conservative Christians in Oregon and Washington, this was the crux of the matter: liberals were intent on purging religious values from the culture, instead substituting secularism, humanism, pluralism, and—worse yet—Communism. These ideas threatened the very core of their beliefs about what was at the heart of American values.

CONCLUSION

In the middle decades of the twentieth century, a significant number of conservative evangelicals as well as Catholics shifted the focus of their efforts to shape the public life of the Pacific Northwest. Less concerned about issues related to the behavior of single males, conservatives tended to point directly to what they believed were serious threats to the fabric of American life. Most specifically, they identified liberalism, humanism, Communism, and secularism in general as fundamentally opposed to their interpretation of both Christianity and Americanism. The social teachings of the New Deal, labor movements in the 1930s, and, most notably, the Cold War between the United States and the Soviet Union provided the occasion for raising concerns publicly and privately about the direction of the country. Fearful that liberal or leftist teachers could persuade their sons and daughters to abandon more traditional values, conservatives attempted to form new groups, from prayer breakfasts and private schools to neighborhood associations charged with enforcing particular ideas. With the help of Billy Graham, the National Association of Evangelicals, Youth for Christ, Young Life, Catholic groups, and a host of other individuals both nationally and regionally, conservatives in the Pacific Northwest gathered themselves for a more vigorous battle against what they believed was the prevailing liberal culture of the region. Issues of abortion and homosexuality had yet to surface, but the root of those later concerns found early expression in the belief that America's traditional values were under siege.

Out of these concerns, and buoyed by urgency, conservative Christians increasingly reentered the public square with vigor. Over the next several decades, conservatives and liberals would battle each other for influence in the broader middle-class culture. Each perceived the other as insider and themselves as the outsider. During the 1960s, however, liberal forces continued to hold the upper hand, and the emerging Civil Rights Movement would come to embody the influence that liberal religious activists could wield in the Pacific Northwest.

CHAPTER 8

TRYING TO END SEGREGATION

Martin Luther King Jr. made his one and only trip to the Pacific Northwest in the fall of 1961. Arriving in Portland on November 8, he spoke to students at Lewis and Clark College, and on the following day he traveled to Seattle and addressed more than two thousand people on the campus of the University of Washington. Later that evening he spoke to another large audience at the Jewish Temple De Hirsch, where he called on President Kennedy to make all segregation unconstitutional.[1] On his last day in the Northwest, King delivered an electric speech to students at Seattle's Garfield High School in the heart of the city's African American community. But King's evening speech was couched in controversy. Originally scheduled for the First Presbyterian Church, King had to move to the Eagles Auditorium. Church leaders had reneged on their agreement to let him speak after receiving intense criticism from those in and outside the congregation who opposed the black civil rights leader.

King had been briefed on Seattle's situation by his host and former classmate at Morehouse College, the Reverend Samuel McKinney, senior pastor at Mount Zion Baptist Church. As McKinney would remember more than forty years later, fear and anxiety bubbled up throughout the Seattle community over King's visit. A number of citizens petitioned the Seattle School Board to prohibit King from speaking at Garfield because he was thought to be too "controversial."[2]

King's visit revealed much about race relations in the Pacific Northwest in the early 1960s. Most white Portland and Seattle residents did not want to think that race was a problem, but they also did not want any outsiders, particularly someone like King, coming to stir up controversy. Nevertheless, things had changed in just a few years. World War II had transformed the racial demographics in the larger cities of the Northwest. In Seattle alone, the number of African Americans had grown from fewer than 4,000 before the war to 15,666 in 1950 and 26,901 by 1960, which was just under 5 percent of the total population. The African American population in Tacoma had increased from 650 in 1940 to just under 6,000 (4.0 percent) in 1960. Portland's black population had grown from approximately 2,000 in 1940 to approximately 15,500 (4.5 percent) in 1960.

The rapid growth in the black population exposed more directly the problem of racism in the Northwest. While in the minds of most white people in the region, whites and Negroes seemed to "get along" with one another, many African Americans saw it differently. More subtly expressed than in the South, discriminatory patterns existed in employment and housing. Patterns of school enrollment in Seattle, Portland, Tacoma, and Spokane revealed general patterns of segregation. By the time of King's visit in 1961, social forces that had led to the Civil Rights Movement in the South were beginning to be felt throughout the Northwest.

Not surprisingly, religious activists played a critical role in the Civil Rights Movement in the far Northwest. African American pastors and laypeople challenged the status quo on a number of fronts. They organized protests, risked losing their jobs, encountered personal threats to themselves and their families, and faced considerable opposition to their efforts to end racial discrimination. Once again, most of these activists perceived themselves as outsiders to a culture that largely desired to maintain the status quo of race relations. Calling for significant social change, religious activists positioned themselves largely as critics of long-standing social norms that had privileged white people and marginalized African Americans. Few activists were unaware that the consequences of many of their demands would alter the understanding of race throughout the region.

In the early sixties, African American pastors often inspired their white counterparts to become more active in the movement. Many mainline Protestant, Catholic, and Jewish individuals and organizations played a significant role. These organizations included the Church Council of Greater Seattle, the Greater Portland Council of Churches, the American Friends Service Committee (Quakers), the Tacoma Ministerial Alliance, and the Archdiocese of Seattle and Portland, as well as Temple De Hirsch in Seattle and Temple Beth Israel in Portland.

More subtly, religious leadership and, in particular, African American leadership provided the rhetoric and vision for participating in the movement that proved essential to its overall success. Black pastors made this a moral struggle and one that was deeply intertwined with the history of black liberation. Messages often exhibited a prophetic character that emphasized struggle, persistence, and liberation that differentiated the movement from other liberal reform efforts. Seattle's experience underscored what historian David Chapell found at the national level when he asserted that the "the black movement's non-violent soldiers were driven not by modern liberal faith in human reason, but by older, seemingly more durable prejudices and superstitions that were rooted in Christian and Jewish myth."[3] Drawing on such figures as David and Isaiah in the Old Testament, as well as the theologians Augustine of Hippo, Martin Luther, and Reinhold Niebuhr, black pastors believed the natural tendency of institutions and individuals was toward corruption. They relied less on a liberal belief in inevitable progress and more on the conviction that white society must be confronted by prophets who openly named the "sin of segregation." For Chapell, it was this prophetic character that gave the movement its vibrancy during the decade of the 1960s.

By the end of the decade, however, the world of race relations had suddenly become more complicated. Largely within the African American community, the goal of inclusion drew increasing criticism from a younger generation of African Americans committed to black identity, black power, and in some cases separatism. Religious leaders often found themselves caught in the middle. On one hand, most black and white religious activists continued to believe in the goal of inclusion. On the other hand, many of the criticisms of the more traditional and conventional approach to civil rights had found their mark. Navigating that tension between the two approaches proved to be particularly challenging for both black and white religious activists in the Pacific Northwest.

KEY AFRICAN AMERICAN RELIGIOUS LEADERS IN THE NORTHWEST

1961 proved to be an important year for civil rights in the Pacific Northwest. Not only did Martin Luther King come to Seattle and Portland, but Reverend Mance Jackson moved to Seattle to serve as pastor of the Bethel Christian Methodist Episcopal Church. Jackson had earned a bachelor's degree from Los Angeles State College and had done graduate work at the University of Southern California.[4] Almost immediately, he formed a bond with the Reverend Samuel McKinney, pastor of Mount Zion Baptist Church. Born in Flint, Michigan, McKinney had grown up in Cleveland, Ohio, where his father, Wade Hampton McKinney II, served as pastor to one of the most prominent African American churches in the city—Antioch Baptist Church. From a membership of close to seven hundred when he arrived, the church grew to over three thousand members. Young McKinney watched his father emerge as one of the most active black leaders in the city. He grew up hearing the likes of Thurgood Marshall, Walter White, and A. Phillip Randolph, all of whom spoke in his father's church. Originally planning on going to law school, McKinney matriculated at Morehouse College in Atlanta and became friends with a classmate, Martin Luther King Jr. Graduating in 1949, McKinney felt called by God into the ministry and subsequently enrolled at New York's Colgate Rochester Divinity School. Completing his master of divinity degree in 1952, McKinney took the call to become pastor of Olney Street Baptist Church in Providence, Rhode Island, and subsequently accepted the invitation to Seattle's Mount Zion Baptist Church in 1958.[5]

Jackson and McKinney were soon joined in 1962 by the Reverend John Hurst Adams, who came to be the senior minister at Seattle's First African Methodist Episcopal (AME) Church. He had grown up in South Carolina where his father, Eugene Avery Adams, was an African Methodist Episcopal minister who had been active in the struggle for civil rights prior to the 1950s. John Adams earned his undergraduate degree at Johnson C. Smith University in Charlotte, North Carolina, and later earned his master of sacred theology degree from Boston University, where he too was a classmate of Martin Luther King Jr. Beginning in 1956, Adams served as president of the all-black Paul Quinn College in Waco, Texas, until 1962, when he and his family moved to Seattle.[6] Together, Jackson, McKinney, and Adams proved to be a powerful group of African American leaders within Seattle at just the moment when the national Civil Rights Movement was beginning to take hold.

In Portland, African American pastors also played a strong leadership role. As previously noted, Reverend J. J. Clow, pastor of Mt. Olivet Baptist Church, was one of the most effective leaders through the early

1960s. Something of a senior statesman by the time that King had come to the Northwest, Clow had helped pass a 1953 civil rights bill in the Oregon legislature and was still an active member of the NAACP until he retired in 1963. Portland's black pastors were important members of the NAACP and the Urban League, as well as the Portland Council of Churches and the Albina Ministerial Association.[7]

By 1964, Reverend John H. Jackson had emerged as one of the key African American leaders in Portland. Born in 1912, Jackson was influenced strongly by his maternal grandfather, who was a minister. After attending Duquesne University, Jackson graduated from the University of Pittsburgh in 1940. Subsequently, he received a bachelor of divinity degree from Union Theological Seminary in 1945. From 1949 to 1959, Jackson served as pastor at the Second Baptist Church in Rochester, Pennsylvania. Increasingly involved in the Civil Rights Movement, he marched with Martin Luther King in 1957. Two years later, he moved to Seattle and served as a missionary for the Baptist Church. In 1964, Jackson succeeded J. J. Clow at Portland's Mt. Olivet Baptist Church and would be a force in Portland for civil rights for the next two decades.[8]

One other African American minister would leave his mark on Portland over the 1960s: the Reverend Tecumseh Graham. Born in Washington, DC, Graham grew up in Brooklyn. He entered the ministry in the African Methodist Episcopal Church Zion and subsequently graduated from Livingstone College and Hood Theological Seminary, both in Salisbury, North Carolina. He served a church in Shelby, North Carolina, from 1957 until 1960, when he and his wife moved to Portland.[9]

In the early sixties, fair employment for African Americans emerged as a critical issue across the country. In city after city, civil rights activists began pressing business and governmental agencies to employ more black Americans. Seattle and Portland were no exceptions. The Seattle chapter of the Congress of Racial Equality (CORE) proved to be instrumental in raising the issue of fair employment.[10] Established in 1961, CORE drew support from several black pastors, including Mance Jackson, Samuel McKinney, and Reverend Henry Hall, pastor of the Washington Park Baptist Church. As activists, they challenged Seattle employers to abandon their discriminatory hiring practices.[11]

In the summer of 1961, CORE volunteers began handing out leaflets to residents of the Central Area that read, "Don't Shop Where

You Can't Work! You are one of the thousands of non-whites who, each week, spend the largest part of their earnings in grocery stores, where, because of your color, you cannot work. You have been doing this year after year, even when you have been unemployed. Quit buying discrimination."[12] First targeting Safeway and then other grocery stores, CORE volunteers orchestrated a "selective buying campaign," which eventually resulted in a limited number of African Americans being hired. Reverend McKinney and Reverend Hall played key roles in the negotiations with grocery store management. Throughout 1962, businesses in both Seattle and Tacoma gradually relented and began to hire a handful of African American employees, but progress was slow.[13] Eventually Seattle's department stores—J. C. Penney, the Bon Marche, and Nordstrom—agreed not only to hire but also to recruit and train African Americans at all staff levels. These early successes brought national attention to Seattle's chapter of CORE.[14]

Other strategies for improving employment for African Americans also emerged. African American pastors played a major role in two of the decade's most significant employment programs. Reverend John Adams was one of the cofounders, with former minister Walt Hundley, of the Central Area Motivation Program (CAMP).[15] Established in 1964, just as the Johnson administration was gearing up its "War on Poverty," CAMP was the first community-inspired program in the country to receive funding from the Office of Economic Opportunity. The program focused on job counseling and training, family support services, university recruitment, and housing rehabilitation. Hundreds of unemployed workers were trained to work on dilapidated homes in the Central Area. In 2015, CAMP (now called Centerstone) had the distinction of being the oldest surviving independent agency in the country that had originated during the "War on Poverty" era.[16]

The most energetic and successful effort to address the lack of employment for African Americans took form in the basement of Mount Zion Baptist Church—McKinney's congregation. It was there that the Seattle Opportunities Industrialization Center (SOIC) was started in 1966. Modeled after a program initiated by Reverend Leon Sullivan in Philadelphia two years earlier, the Seattle program took shape under McKinney's guidance. The intent of the program was to provide prevocational and vocational training. By 1970, the school had trained and placed into employment more than nine hundred economically disadvantaged students.[17] McKinney was quoted as saying,

"We are telling people that integration without preparation equals frustration."[18] Through the 1970s, SOIC provided a major source of training for the African American community, while McKinney served as chairman of the board of directors throughout the decade.

In Portland, the NAACP took the lead in the battle for fair employment. African American minister J. J. Clow had played a key role in the NAACP in the 1940s and 1950s, but in the 1960s another African American, Reverend Tecumseh Graham, assumed a much more prominent role. In December 1961, Graham, vice president of the Portland Labor and Industry Committee of the NAACP, stated publicly that "if we cannot end racial discrimination in employment by sitting down and calmly negotiating with management, we will resort to picketing and boycotting."[19] Graham pointed out that there were no African Americans in Portland's fire department, mayor's office, highway patrol, trucking industry, or printing industry; "There might be some broom and mop men employed—what I mean is that Negroes do not get into skilled jobs in these fields."[20] As progress continued to languish, the NAACP, with endorsement from the Albina Ministerial Alliance, a group of black preachers organized by Graham, initiated a boycott of Portland-area Fred Meyer stores beginning in the spring of 1962.[21] The boycott lasted until June 27, when Fred Meyer finally hired two African American women as "food demonstrators."

In addition to African American clergy, Rabbi Emmanuel Rose, who had come to Portland to serve at Temple Beth Israel in 1960, began a twenty-plus-year commitment to social justice. In 1963, Rabbi Rose served as cochair of the Metropolitan Interfaith Commission on Race, along with Robert Bonthius, pastor of the Westminster Presbyterian Church in Portland. Rose and Bonthius conducted an extensive survey of Portland employers to determine how many African Americans were employed and in what types of positions. Confirming the overall results to be extremely meager, Bonthius and Rose exerted more public pressure to improve the employment situation for blacks in Portland.[22]

But it was Reverend Tecumseh Graham who took the most public role in the effort to pressure Portland's employers. He told the press that "we are by no means satisfied with the present overall picture of employment with Fred Meyer. We are waiting to see Negroes hired as checkers and in numerous other positions with the chain." Graham asserted that Fred Meyer still employed only four African Americans out of eighteen hundred people in its workforce. Graham's committee for the NAACP continued to pressure Fred Meyer during the next year, as well as the longshoreman's union, which had never allowed a black worker into its ranks.[23] As a consequence, forty-six African Americans were finally admitted into the Portland Longshoreman's Union in 1964.[24] Overall, employment patterns improved gradually over the decade, but it would not be until the 1970s that conditions changed significantly.[25]

In addition to employment, access to housing in the major cities of the Northwest for African Americans had become a major issue by the early 1960s. Restrictive covenants had been common practice in Seattle and Portland, and while they technically did not have the force of law, according to historian Quintard Taylor, "tradition, income, geography, changing land use patterns, and discrimination proved equally effective in limiting black residence to the Central District."[26] Consequently, by 1960 some 78 percent of all African Americans lived in four census tracts in the Central Area in Seattle.

Much the same story could be told about Portland. Early in Portland's history, African Americans lived in most parts of the city. But between 1910 and 1940, it became increasingly "unethical" for a real estate agent to sell property to nonwhites in a white neighborhood.[27] By 1940, approximately 60 percent of the city's 1,931 African Americans lived in an area along Williams Avenue in the Albina District. With World War II came an influx of fifteen to twenty thousand African Americans, with the vast majority working in the shipyards for Henry J. Kaiser and living in Oregon's second largest city, Vanport, which had been created largely with federally appropriated housing dollars. In 1948, a disastrous flood occurred on the Columbia River and all but destroyed Vanport, leaving eighteen thousand people homeless. Most of the African Americans ended up in Albina, contributing to the overcrowding of the neighborhood. By 1960, 73 percent of all African Americans in Portland lived in the Albina neighborhood.

As was the case with employment, religious activists played a major role in confronting the problem of segregated housing. In Seattle, Unitarian Christians were among the first to organize active resistance. Beginning in June 1962, members of the University Unitarian Church in Seattle created a Fair Listing Service that identified individuals in Seattle who would be willing to sell their homes to any qualified buyer regardless of color. The idea quickly gained traction in some of

Seattle's suburbs. In Bellevue and Kirkland, the East Shore Unitarian Church also developed a fair listing service by going door-to-door to sign up willing participants.[28]

In that same summer of 1962, civil rights groups along with the black religious community convinced Mayor Gordon Clinton to appoint an advisory committee on housing. Clinton's committee concluded that the city needed a more enforceable open housing ordinance that would prohibit discrimination on the basis of race for both home buyers and renters. However, the mayor was reluctant. Encountering significant resistance from the real estate and business communities, Clinton refused to endorse the housing ordinance.

However, events nationally made white resistance look increasingly out of step. The violent entry of James Meredith into the University of Mississippi took place in the fall of 1962, and the following spring found Bull Connor unleashing his police dogs on civil rights marchers. In April 1963, King was arrested and placed in jail in Birmingham, Alabama. When eight white clergymen criticized King for breaking the law, he responded with his famous "Letter from a Birmingham Jail." In it King expressed a phrase that would later come to inspire generations of activists: "Injustice anywhere is a threat to justice everywhere." King challenged the white Christian community to step forward and support the movement with greater commitment and vigor. While not formally published until June, parts of the letter were made public in the May 19 issue of the *New York Post Sunday Magazine.*

All of this seemed to affect both black and white religious leaders in the Northwest. On May 31, 1963, Seattle's Roman Catholic archbishop Thomas Connolly issued a letter to all priests in the diocese: "The racial question is undoubtedly our nation's most critical domestic problem.... The Church leadership in the City of Seattle must come out on the side of justice and equality for the Negro. It is most imperative that we as priests take a definite role of leadership in this most crucial field."[29] Archbishop Connolly wanted Catholics to be more aware of the problems of race and urged that priests in all parishes announce a major effort to raise public consciousness about racism in the Pacific Northwest by encouraging attendance at the Conference on Race and Religion scheduled for June 1963 at Seattle University in the heart of the Central District. The conference itself hoped to bring attention to several problems as well as to mobilize grassroots activists. Approximately four hundred pastors, priests, Jewish rabbis, and laypeople participated in various workshops that focused on the problems of housing, employment, and education. Speakers implored the mayor and city council to pass the proposed open-housing ordinance and establish a Human Rights Commission.[30]

Over the course of the summer of 1963, national events, including the murder of civil rights leader Medgar Evers, continued to motivate religious activists in Seattle and Portland. McKinney, Adams, and Jackson mobilized both black and white allies to march on several occasions from their churches on Capitol Hill to downtown Seattle. Frequently quoted in Seattle newspapers, the three pastors helped raise the consciousness of the larger population regarding the challenges of race relations in the city. Jackson, for example, stated that they were declaring "war on one of America's greatest enemies—discrimination, segregation and racial bigotry."[31] They aimed their criticism directly at the mayor's office and tried to walk that fine line between intimidation and persuasion.

As the summer wore on, more religious leaders in the Northwest felt compelled to speak out on the issue of public housing. On June 30, eighty-four clergymen, including Archbishop Connolly and Rabbi Raphael Levine, issued the following statement: "We call on all citizens to consider the seriousness of the hour in which we live—to examine our souls and practices in human relations—to repent of the blindness and callousness (yes, even the sin) of our past attitudes, failures, and oppression—and to become directly involved in one of the most significant moral and social crises in our nation's history."[32]

Archbishop Thomas Connolly (left center) worked closely with other civil rights leaders in Seattle. Courtesy Archives of Roman Catholic Diocese of Spokane

Nevertheless, the business community in general—and real estate representatives in particular—continued to resist. One real estate agent was so irritated at the clergy that he told the *Times*, "It is disheartening for us to see clergymen jumping on the bandwagon for forced housing. If the clergymen fail to achieve a change of hearts in their own congregations, how can they expect to bring it about by law?"[33]

Civil rights marches continued, and in July, thirty-five young people of the Central District Youth Club staged a sit-in of the mayor's office and occupied it for nearly twenty-four hours.[34] By August, however, Mance Jackson had had enough, particularly after his house had been twice firebombed.[35] He announced that he was leaving the Northwest for Atlanta to attend seminary. His final comments excoriated both the black and white communities for their failure to show courage:

> Too many Negroes who are long-time residents are afraid of rocking the boat, or disturbing the relationships they think they had. I am not sure attitudes are changing much. . . . I don't know how long it will take for the transformation of the Negro, for him to attain a better way of life. I do know that even if doors are opened and opportunities become more equal, we still have the job of getting the Negroes ready. They aren't ready now. They have psychological barriers of racism that date back to the beginning of this country. . . . When you constantly are relegated to the low end of the economic scale; when you constantly are told that you are fit only for menial jobs; when you picture yourself as inferior, then you are inferior.[36]

Mance Jackson spoke poignantly of "job barriers" that existed in Seattle in the various trades and "even in truck driving, where Negroes aren't considered good enough to take the wheel."[37] As discouraged as Jackson sounded, he never gave up. He spent the next forty-four years working for civil rights causes in the state of Georgia, and upon his death in 2007, the Georgia State Senate honored him for his lifetime of work on behalf of racial justice.[38]

Jackson's departure, however, did not lessen the fervor of that summer of 1963. Both John Adams and Samuel McKinney traveled back to the nation's capital to participate in the famous march on Washington, DC, and were present when Martin Luther King delivered his riveting "I Have a Dream" speech.[39] Both returned to Seattle with renewed energy for continuing the fight.

By the fall, the council had decided to put the issue of the housing ordinance on the ballot. However, this disappointed civil rights leaders because they feared, for good reason, that the vast majority of white citizens would vote against the measure. Black leaders had been arguing that the issue of housing was so dire that it fell under the umbrella of an emergency. The city charter provided the possibility of the council simply enacting a change if they deemed the problem to be an emergency.[40]

Religious activists, however, worked to get out the vote. For example, an umbrella organization titled Churches United for Racial Equality (CURE) included Baptist, Episcopal, Lutheran, Methodist, United Church of Christ, Presbyterian, and other congregations. In the months prior to the vote for open housing, CURE activists helped host over a thousand coffee hours at homes and churches throughout the city, where they encouraged people to vote for the ordinance.[41]

Three days before the election, Samuel McKinney and John Adams, along with Reverend Paree Porter and Father John Lynch, led an estimated fifteen hundred people in a march of support for open housing. The day before the election, supporters picked up pamphlets endorsing the ordinance from the Plymouth Congregational Church and fanned out across the city to hand them to people leaving work. On that same day, the Catholic journal *Northwest Progress* dedicated most of its issue to open housing and highlighted Archbishop Connolly's call for a total commitment to racial justice. Connolly had spoken to some seven hundred priests and laypeople under the auspices of the Catholic Interracial Council of Seattle:

> We wish it distinctly understood that we are totally involved in this proposal, that we are totally committed to the obligation of securing racial justice in the fields of housing, employment, education and recreation for all our fellow citizens, irrespective of race, creed, color or national origin.... We believe that the conscience of this great city of ours is on trial before the entire country in connection with the successful passage of the Open Housing Ordinance at the election on next Tuesday, March 10th. Remember that the most crucial test of the love of God is the love of neighbor.[42]

But the real estate board also was well organized. They ran newspaper ads and produced leaflets that said a YES vote would mean "Forced Housing, and the loss of your rights."[43] Real estate representatives issued a constant threat of a decline in property values if this should go through. The results were devastating: voters defeated the open housing legislation by a more than two-to-one margin—115,627 to 54,448.

In Portland, similar struggles for better access to housing also marked the decade. The murder of Medgar Evers in 1963 led over four hundred black and white citizens to march in protest, and speakers denounced what was described as a string of broken promises from Portland city officials regarding housing and jobs.[44] Civil rights leaders in the Rose City focused their attention less on an open housing ordinance and more on decisions related to the location of proposed public housing projects in Portland. In a simple sense, the argument focused on whether housing should be built primarily within the Albina neighborhood (the one predominantly black neighborhood in Portland), on the border between Albina and a neighboring white community, or entirely within a predominantly white part of the city. In December 1961, the housing authority decided that a project should be built totally within the Albina District, and they named it the Daisy Williams Apartment Court in honor of the deceased wife of longtime NAACP member Edgar Williams. However, if housing officials expected to deflect criticism from the black community, they were sadly mistaken.

A bitter struggle broke out within Portland's African American community and within other civil rights groups. Many Albina residents did in fact want the project to be built within the Albina neighborhood. Many homes were in a dilapidated condition, and better stock was definitely needed. The *Northwest Defender*, Portland's black newspaper, supported the project. However, in June 1963, the *Oregonian* published an article with the headline, "Religious, Negro Leaders Oppose 135 Unit Albina Project." Representatives from Jewish, Baptist, Quaker, Methodist, Presbyterian, and Catholic churches, along with Young Democrats, the ACLU, the Urban League, and the NAACP, all opposed the project out of belief that it would perpetuate racial segregation in Portland.[45] As a result of such protests, the zoning decisions necessary for the project to go forward were tabled.[46]

The stalled Daisy Williams project was soon followed by another controversial project called the Northwest Towers. This project again divided Portland's civil rights coalition because it turned out that all of the residents would be white. The NAACP was furious and vigorously protested. President John Kennedy, who originally agreed to come to Portland to dedicate the project, canceled his trip. The NAACP, with support from the Portland Council of Churches, forced federal officials to examine the selection process of the Housing Authority of Portland (HAP). Although eventually cleared of charges of racial discrimination, HAP did form a committee with members of the Greater Portland Council of Churches to review all of its practices. Shortly thereafter, the first black resident was admitted to Northwest Towers.[47]

Over the next several years, various religious groups continued to criticize HAP. For example, in January 1964, the Greater Portland Council of Churches (GPCC) issued a thirteen-page document that criticized HAP for its facilitation of an ongoing pattern of segregation in the city: "HAP has made every effort to construct projects that could be nothing but all Negro eventually, in an area of our city which comes as close to being a slum as any we have in Portland."[48] Later that spring, Presbyterian minister Robert Bonthius, representing the GPCC, contacted Oregon's US senator Wayne Morse and persuaded him to read a statement into the Congressional Record indicating that the housing authority was tainted with racial bias.[49]

In retrospect, the fight to end segregation in both Seattle and Portland mirrored the struggles that were going on nationally. Seattle civil rights leaders seemed more unified than Portland when it came to strategizing how to effect change; Seattle's goal was to pass an open housing ordinance that would require residents to rent or sell to persons of color. Religious leaders played a key role in advancing that agenda throughout the decade of the sixties. In Portland, there was more division within the coalition of groups, many of which were religious, that took up the issue of housing. While integration remained a specific goal for many activists, increasing numbers of African Americans opposed the notion that African Americans should be dispersed throughout the city, and this emerged most painfully when it came to the issue of how best to desegregate public schools.

School desegregation was the third and most complicated issue for civil rights leaders. Early in the decade, most activists believed that African Americans should be integrated into predominantly white schools. The images of black students attending Central High School in Little Rock, Arkansas, in 1957 and James Meredith gaining entrance into the University of Mississippi in 1962 were still fresh in people's minds. In both Seattle and Portland, schools within the Central District and the Albina neighborhood were underresourced and poorly maintained compared with most white schools. Few activists who believed in integration envisioned that a significant number of white students would agree to come to school in largely black neighborhoods. Therefore the task seemed clear: work to make possible the voluntary transfer of African American students into better schools in other parts of the city. And once again, black and white clergy played a crucial role in these efforts. Protestants, Catholics, and Jews all collaborated in an effort to effect what might be the most significant social change in their lifetime.

In Portland, several religious leaders took prominent roles in the discussions surrounding the desegregation of public schools. In addition to black pastors Tecumseh Graham and John H. Jackson, the most prominent white pastor to get involved in Portland's civil rights struggles was the Reverend Paul Wright, pastor of the First Presbyterian Church. Born in Iran to missionary parents in 1895, Wright had come to Portland in 1941 after serving as the pastor of the First Presbyterian Church in Oklahoma City. Under Wright, his Portland congregation grew significantly to more than three thousand in 1950 and became Oregon's largest Protestant congregation. From the outset, Wright encouraged his congregation to be engaged in the social problems of the world. After World War II, First Presbyterian made a major effort to sponsor and relocate European refugees.[50]

In 1963, Reverend Wright decided to become more directly involved with civil rights issues and helped form a new group called the Portland Citizens Committee on Racial Imbalance in the Public Schools. Wright hoped that this 125-member group could "advance the NAACP's desegregation campaign in a less confrontational manner."[51] Wright's group did not demand immediate change on the issue of racial imbalance but wanted the school board to commit to studying the effects of racial imbalance on black children. At that time, 70 percent of African American children attended only five Portland schools. Wright, as did others, wanted integration.[52]

Initially, the school board balked when Wright's group suggested that a study be done to determine the impact of segregation on African American students.[53] Under considerable pressure, however, the school board agreed to appoint a committee to study the situation, and in June 1963 it formed the Committee on Race and Education (CRE).[54] After a year of study, the CRE produced a 249-page report that did not recommend forced integration but instead urged that more resources be put into predominantly black schools in a manner that was labeled "compensatory education." Specific changes were recommended to the curriculum, which would include more attention to black history.[55]

The report, unfortunately, divided various civil rights groups in Portland. Many constituencies supported the recommendations as a good first step, including Reverend Wright's group and the board of directors for the Greater Portland Council of Churches.[56] But the NAACP did not support the report because in its opinion, the recommendations fell short of requiring integration of Portland public schools. Reverend John Jackson, vice president of the NAACP, said that any funds appropriated by the state for disadvantaged children should carry a mandate that they be used for integrated education.[57] In the same year, the Albina Ministerial Association came out with a strong statement objecting to state and federal funds being used to support the model school program:

> It is our sincere hope [that] our State of Oregon and our Federal Government will not become a party to segregated education. It would also be a waste of taxpayer's money to invest it in these schools. Compensatory education in these schools cannot be successful without the cooperation of the citizens involved. Such cooperation is not foreseeable in the Negro community so long as the program is carried out in segregated institutions. Thus, in the present setting, the Compensatory Education program is doomed to failure.[58]

The coalition of various civil rights groups, including the various religious groups, was seriously divided over the tactics of integration.

That division centered primarily on whether integration of the black and white populations was a good thing, particularly if it only went one way. The African American community had grown increasingly uncomfortable with busing as a solution. More and more people, particularly in the Albina neighborhood, believed that busing children into largely all-white schools would simply stigmatize black students on the basis of race and that there would be few opportunities to develop any sense of black identity. In spite of those concerns, most racial liberals, both black and white, continued to advocate for mandatory integration. According to historian Stuart McElderry, "The NAACP's claim, that segregation of any kind—*de jure* or *de facto*—resulted in black educational inequality, complicated this struggle and drove a wedge between and among different members of Portland's postwar civil rights coalition."[59]

In Seattle, the story was similar but had several different twists to it. One of the most important groups to advocate for school desegregation was the Central Area Civil Rights Committee (CACRC). Formed in 1962, the committee was initially led by Mance Jackson and subsequently by John Adams. The CACRC included Samuel McKinney, Walt Hundley, Charles Johnson, and E. June Smith, who represented the NAACP.[60] Later, Reverend Mineo Katagiri, a United Church of Christ minister and the only Japanese member, joined the CACRC. They met weekly in order to coordinate both philosophy and strategy. Historian Quintard Taylor noted that "this self-appointed leadership cadre reached a remarkable consensus on strategy and tactics which eluded their national counterparts throughout the 1960s. It provided a single voice on civil rights issues and, through 1968, determined the local civil rights agenda."[61] That agenda focused on jobs, housing, and the integration of public schools. By May 1963, the CACRC and various civil rights groups threatened to file a lawsuit against the Seattle School Board if more significant steps were not taken to desegregate Seattle schools.[62]

Of the religious activists, Adams continued to apply the most pressure on the school board. Beginning in 1963, he persistently lobbied the board on behalf of racial integration. Until then, most Seattle School Board members did not think that *Brown v. Board of Education* had any relevance to Seattle. Frances Owen, president of the school board in 1954 and still on the board in 1965, remembered that Adams

Reverends Samuel McKinney (bullhorn) and Mance Jackson (below) were on the front lines of protest against Seattle's discriminatory housing and employment practices. Courtesy Museum of History & Industry [MOHAI], *Seattle Post-Intelligencer* Collection, 1986.5.5923.4

"used to come to every School Board meeting. . . . I think he began to wear us down more than anything else. I don't think he changed our thinking so much—except that he must have—because something, and I don't remember what it was, brought us to this feeling that we must open things up, and allow students to go to other schools if they wanted to."[63]

In addition to Adams, Samuel McKinney, along with Edwin Pratt of the Urban League and leaders in CORE and the NAACP, also took a strong position in favor of integration. By May of 1963, various civil rights groups threatened to file a lawsuit against the Seattle School Board if more significant steps were not taken to desegregate Seattle schools.[64]

In the meantime, Reverend Adams, along with other clergy and civil rights activists, kept the pressure on. They warned that direct action needed to be taken by the school board or citizens would resort to more confrontational tactics such as "study-ins" at predominantly white high schools. They continued to organize meetings and marches as well to distribute leaflets with the message, "All Seattle children need quality integrated education."[65]

By late 1965 and early 1966, the slow pace of change encouraged a number of activists to consider the possibility of a school boycott. CORE, the NAACP, the CACRC, African American pastors, and the Church Council of Greater Seattle all ended up supporting the idea, but it was CORE—and in particular Reverend Adams—that provided the key leadership and frequently addressed the press. Scheduled for March 31 and April 1, 1966, the boycott was intended to provide an alternative educational experience. The plan involved organizing eight "freedom schools" that would hold class for two days, largely on African American history and culture. These were modeled broadly on the freedom schools that were created during the summer of 1964 in Mississippi. Boycott leaders hoped that a substantial number of white students would participate in the two-day experiment.[66]

In the weeks leading up to the boycott, more support came from Seattle's religious leadership. The Reverend Peter Raible from the University Unitarian Church was particularly outspoken in favor of the boycott.[67] His congregation ended up passing a resolution urging the Seattle School Board to take necessary steps to end racial imbalance within the school district. The Catholic Interracial Council affirmed the boycott and raised $200 for the purchase of milk for the children. Archbishop Connolly issued his own statement, as did the Unitarians for Social Justice and the Presbytery of Seattle, with sixty-three member churches, favoring the freedom schools without technically endorsing the boycott.[68]

But on March 16, the Church Council of Greater Seattle triggered a backlash among more conservative churches when it sent a letter directed in large part to white churches in both the city and the suburbs. For all intents and purposes, the letter endorsed the boycott as "the only form of protest which will bring this issue sharply" to public attention. In response, fifteen ministers from downtown churches, serving some of the city's most influential congregations, publicly disavowed support for the boycott and disassociated themselves from the council's pronouncement. Among the churches represented were First Presbyterian, Trinity Episcopal, Gethsemane Lutheran, First Covenant, First Methodist, First Baptist, and Plymouth Congregational. The ministers offered their own assertions:

1. In this instance we do not accept the technique of boycott because it calls for illegal action.
2. It is a deliberate attempt and treacherous use of undiscerning young people as the tools and victims of the motives and objectives of adults.
3. It fosters disrespect for law, and condones insubordination thinly veiled by the problem of civil rights.
4. The resultant ferment is destructive of the educational process and is a perversion of the strength most needed in an evolving integrated society.

This group of fifteen asserted that the issue of segregated schools in the Central Area reflected "the deeper problem of our restrictive housing and employment opportunities for minority groups."[69]

The Seattle Association of Evangelicals, representing 150 churches, also opposed the boycott.[70] The Reverend Dr. Robert B. Munger of University Presbyterian Church argued that "dramatic steps" must be taken to awaken the community to growing segregation, but he disagreed that "the ends justified the means." One other clergyman stated, "I support the cause wholeheartedly, but not the method."[71] A number of other white clergy, including the Very Reverend John C. Leffler of St. Mark's Episcopal Cathedral were "wholeheartedly in support of integration in schools" but objected to truancy as a tactic.[72]

Twenty black ministers held their own news conference, and John Adams did most of the talking. He shot back at his fellow clergy and asserted that their opposition "to the proposed boycott is another example of clerical cowardice in the face of the need for justice and social change." Adams angrily asserted that

> these ministers of a diluted Gospel say that the boycott is illegal and disruptive. I would remind these custodians of the status quo that these segregated schools against which we boycott have been illegal for 12 years and they never have said a mumbling word. I would remind them that this same segregated school system has been immoral for the lifetime of their congregations in the city. As soon as we propose action which disturbs their comfortable pews and ask them to put their commitment on the line they sell out the Gospel to preserve their big comfortable and irrelevant churches.[73]

Rabbi Raphael Levine, assuming the role of peacemaker, called for a conference of concerned citizens and leaders, and in a final attempt to negotiate differences, a meeting was held on March 29 in the mayor's office. The theme of that meeting appears to have been that "the Negro should be assured that the white community does have his interests at heart," but the effort failed to impress the black leaders who were present. A *Seattle Times* reporter described Seattle as "a city of tortured consciences and divided churches."[74]

Seattle ministers, from both the Right and the Left, were remarkably engaged on the issue of the boycott and underscored the importance of this public issue. Seattle's two daily newspapers sided with the more conservative ministers. The *Post-Intelligencer* opined on the eve of the boycott that civil rights leaders would gain a much greater degree of community respect if they called off the boycott.[75]

But the boycott went ahead, and quietly, the NAACP filed suit against the school district, requiring the district to submit a desegregation plan. On March 31, the boycott came off without a serious hitch. Freedom schools opened with approximately one hundred teachers and two principals at each site. Elementary schools opened at First AME Church, Madrona Presbyterian Church, East Madison YMCA, Goodwill Baptist Church, St. Peter Claver Center, and

Cherry Hill Baptist Church. Sites for junior high schools opened at Mount Zion Baptist Church and the Tabernacle Baptist Church. And senior high schools held classes at the Prince Hall Masonic Temple, the East Side YMCA, and Woodland Park Presbyterian Church. The religious community was very involved in supporting the boycott. An estimated three thousand students participated, and the rates of absence in the Central Area schools were as high as 50 percent. Approximately 30 percent of the students were white. Classes focused primarily on African American history and race relations. Children wrote moving statements about what the experience had meant to them. Several white teachers risked their own jobs in support of the boycott.[76] Organizers declared the boycott an unqualified success.

In spite of the success of the boycott, the fundamental problem of segregation still remained. Nevertheless, just prior to the boycott, the school board restated its position on racial discrimination: "We believe that an integrated education provides better racial understanding among all people. We will work to bring this about by whatever just, reasonable and educationally sound means are available to us."[77] But at that point, the voluntary transfer program was still the only live option.

By the mid-1960s, the Black Power Movement and the idea of black separatism began influencing the struggle for civil rights in the Pacific Northwest. Malcolm X had been the most outspoken black critic of racial liberalism and the strategy of integration. After his assassination in 1965, more African Americans began to express their belief that white society would always be racist at its core and that the most important statement that a black person could make was one of black pride, black identity, and black power. Separatism rather than integration should be the goal. Stokely Carmichael became chairman of the Student Nonviolent Coordinating Committee (SNCC) in 1966, and in the following year he cowrote a book with Charles V. Hamilton titled *Black Power: The Politics of Power of Liberation in America*. Carmichael helped transform SNCC from a multiracial organization into an all-black organization. In the meantime, Huey Newton and Bobby Seale organized the Black Panther Party in October 1966.

The concept of Black Power began to gain traction in the Pacific Northwest almost immediately. Several Portland churches organized a conference in October titled "Black Power and the Exploding City!" Chaired by John Jackson, pastor of Mt. Olivet Baptist Church, the conference included speakers from the University of Oregon, members of the Urban League in Portland, and Samuel McKinney from Seattle.[78]

In Seattle the most dramatic moment around black power occurred on April 19, 1967, when Stokely Carmichael came to Seattle and first spoke to roughly thirty-five hundred students at the University of Washington and talked about a "new day" for Negroes. Later he addressed an audience estimated at nearly four thousand at Garfield High School, where his theme was racial pride. "You have tried so hard to be white. You have gone to Tarzan movies and applauded as Tarzan beat up your black brothers. We have identified with white people. We have been brainwashed." He urged black students to throw off the shackles that had been placed on them by white "honkies." Carmichael took aim at the civil rights moderates, many of whom were black clergy. He asserted that "integration is meaningful only to a small chosen class. The fight is against white supremacy and that's where the fight has always been."[79] Those in attendance reported that middle-aged blacks as well as youths enthusiastically cheered Carmichael's riveting speech.

The net effect of Carmichael's speech was to put the moderate integrationists on the defensive. Carmichael had stated bluntly that

Pastor of the First African Methodist Episcopal Church in Seattle, John Adams (center), repeatedly pushed for the integration of public schools. Courtesy John Hurst Adams

integration and busing should be rejected. He had urged Seattle blacks to demand their own teachers, their own curriculum, and their own schools. Garfield should never be closed.

Just two weeks after Carmichael had spoken, the Greater Seattle Council of Churches, with McKinney now president, organized a forum on May 4 at Mount Zion Baptist on the subject of black power. The overall tone was moderate, at moments acknowledging the critique that Carmichael and others were leveling against traditional strategies for integration. John Adams gave the keynote address. He declared sympathetically that black power "is one of the many youthful expressions of judgment upon the phoniness and emptiness of our commitment to the values we claim. . . . life for the American Negro has become worse, not better in the last few years. . . . [Black Power] was a revolt against the whiteness of American cultural values . . . a result of the failure of the white community to respond to the civil rights efforts of the last several years."[80]

But Adams walked a fine line between affirming the central message of black power and at the same time warning of the "dangers inherent in the Black Power Stance":

> There is a real danger of excesses by Negroes in this new found sense of manhood and strength. . . . There is the ever-present danger because Human Perversity Knows No Color. . . . There is the danger that this new racial definition and its unsettling overtones will cause too many whites to use it as a rationalization to withdraw and escape duty on a tense and unpopular front. I plea that the Church not take this course. . . . There is the continuing danger that in the emergence of Black Power the white community and situations will be neglected and further alienated. . . . There is the danger that the Black Power Position will not work.[81]

Adams said that the dialogue between black power and American culture had just begun. "I admit that I am perplexed in regard to where this meeting is going and how it will finally come out. But I do know that the anguished cry of long endured pain and his hopeful offer of unused possibilities have been unheeded by the church. Manhood and inclusion denied, he looks inward for identity and the strength he needs to be fully human in a world of powers and principalities, primarily white."[82]

All of this contributed to the growing tension in Seattle's black community during the summer of 1967. Adams and McKinney, along with other African American pastors, worked with CORE and NAACP leadership to keep Seattle from imploding. Just weeks after Carmichael had raised the consciousness of young blacks, race riots had broken out in several northern cities and made front-page news across the country. Seattle seemed ripe for some kind of riot itself. Several anonymous threats against the annual Torchlight Parade, a featured part of the city's summer Seafair Festival, set city officials on edge. Many citizens argued that the mayor should cancel at least the parade if not the whole event. However, Mayor James "Dorm" Braman resisted and a month later spoke to the press and thanked the black leadership of the city for their efforts in preventing a riot. Specifically, Mayor Braman made mention of Reverend John Adams for his helpful suggestions, including the installation of a street pool, the use of sprinklers and fire hydrants to keep things cool, and transportation of kids at city expense to a neighborhood pool. But the main thrust of Adams's exhortation was jobs. He had urged the mayor to find three hundred part-time jobs for inner-city youth. As a result, the mayor noted, "The big thing that happened to these summer kids was that they found there was someone that would hire them and give them an opportunity to do something. And this breaks down, at least to a degree, the biggest wall and barrier which they have told themselves. The Negro people have over the years convinced themselves that nobody will have them."[83]

The summer of 1967 provided a difficult context for the school board elections that fall. Several new board members were elected, and in February 1968 the board approved a proposal to provide a Continuous Progress Center in the southeast part of the city. No more than 25 percent of the student body was to be African American, but that decision was received well enough in the black community that the NAACP dropped the lawsuit that it had filed in 1966. Still, the debate over whether Garfield should be closed persisted. Early in 1968 the school district presented the Central Area Civil Rights Committee with a proposal for integration that would have retained Garfield as a high school. However, the CACRC objected, believing that Garfield would soon be 90 percent black. CORE wanted to retain Garfield as a high school, and thus the stage was set for another confrontation within the black community.[84]

On March 6, 1968, at the East Madison YMCA, John Adams and his CACRC colleagues decided that the community should decide whether integration or separatism should be the overall objective. Adams clearly wanted to challenge the idea of black separatism and make it a "watershed evening."[85] On that evening, members of the CACRC read to the school board an eleven-point proposal, which included the closure of five Central Area schools, including Garfield. Adams and the CACRC hoped that this would force the hand of the district to send neighborhood students to better-funded, predominantly white schools, although he wanted both white and black students bused. However, the newly formed Seattle Association of Black Student Unions, comprising mostly students from the University of Washington and Seattle University, had quietly gathered eleven hundred signatures before the meeting in opposition to the CACRC's proposal. An estimated crowd of four hundred assembled that night.[86] While several individuals spoke in support of the CACRC proposal, as the discussion wore on, younger, more militant African Americans vigorously objected to Adams and the CACRC.[87] Historian Doris Pieroth interviewed Roberta Byrd Barr, who was a black administrator in the school district at the time and soon would be the first woman secondary school principal in Seattle, and Ed Banks, a highly respected grassroots black leader. Both attended the meeting and believed that Adams lost some influence that night. Banks had warned Adams not to call the meeting, because clearly the tide was turning against Adams and other more moderate integrationists.[88]

The school board decided not to close Garfield. Instead, the focus shifted toward middle schools and the idea that both white and black students would be bused. That decision provoked ongoing resistance that ultimately delayed mandatory busing until 1977.

In 1968, however, the future of desegregation remained unclear. And if Adams and the CACRC had lost some standing within the black community, the assassination of Martin Luther King Jr. on April 4 thrust both McKinney and Adams back into positions of leadership. Days of rioting around the country followed the shooting in Memphis. Seattle and Portland, as well as the rest of the Northwest, were spared most of the overt violence, but there was collective grief on an unprecedented level within the African American community and certain elements of the white community. Because of their close connection with King, Reverend Adams and Reverend McKinney received the lion's share of the press coverage. Adams was quoted as saying, "I feel like a lot of me died tonight. You don't follow a man's leadership for 12 or 13 years, or know a man of his kind of personality without his death having a traumatic effect." He hoped that King's death would "turn on" all those "who are indifferent or unconcerned about their fellow man not only in the white community but in the black."[89] McKinney said that "Dr. King was an apostle of love. While the mood of America today has been one of hate and anger, he brought to it a dimension of love."[90]

On April 8, an estimated ten thousand marchers made their way from East Madison Street to the Seattle Arena near the Space Needle for a memorial service for Dr. King. So many people joined the march that the event had to be moved to the adjacent outdoor high school stadium that could accommodate up to fourteen thousand individuals. Singing "We Shall Overcome," the crowd assembled to hear a litany of speakers. It was Adams who delivered the main eulogy, which was a version of King's own eulogy of John F. Kennedy at the time of his assassination in 1963:

> This cannot be dismissed as the isolated act of a madman. Martin King was assassinated by a morally inclement climate. It is a climate filled with heavy torrents of false accusation, jostling winds of hatred and raging storms of violence. . . . The death of Martin King challenges each one of us to set aside our grief and go forward with more determination to rid this city, this state, and this nation of every vestige of prejudice, every evidence of discrimination and every kind of injustice practiced here.[91]

Adams received a standing ovation when he called for passage of the open housing bill. Five thousand petitions were passed out at the memorial service. Just a few days after King's assassination, President Lyndon Johnson signed the Civil Rights Act of 1968 with a provision that guaranteed "fair housing." Perhaps out of guilt, or perhaps out of fear, on April 19 the Seattle City Council unanimously passed its own fair housing ordinance that had been the object of such controversy earlier in the decade. This time it was passed with the emergency clause that made it impossible to appeal by referendum.[92]

If the Civil Rights Movement in the 1960s in the Northwest was marked at the outset by Martin Luther King's visit in 1961 and in some respects ended with his death in 1968, the decade closed with one more tragedy in 1969. On a snowy January evening, Edwin Pratt, head of the Seattle Urban League, was home with his family in South Seattle when he heard something hit a window. He went to the door, and as he opened it his wife yelled to him that someone with a gun was outside. It was too late, and Ed Pratt was shot in the face and died almost immediately. Pratt's killer was never identified, although the case is still considered open by the Seattle Police Department. Pratt's death sent shock waves through Seattle's African American community.

It would be easy to look at 1969 and feel nothing but discouragement if you were a religious activist who had advocated for civil rights during the prior two decades. But in hindsight, it is easier to see that not all had been lost. According to historian Doris Pieroth, Seattle had experienced comparatively less rancor and less polarization than many other northern cities. She gave much credit to the religious leadership in the movement:

> The black clergy was a driving force for school desegregation, [and] strong backing [came] from white colleagues both Catholic and Protestant. A determined, though small, group of white citizens, many of whom had participated in the early boundary controversies of the fifties, remained committed to integration. They supported the public schools, worked to integrate them and to improve their education climate, and by 1968 had gained considerable support.[93]

CONCLUSION

Religious individuals and organizations played an extremely important role in the Civil Rights Movement in both Seattle and Portland. For much of the decade, the vision of a more integrated city motivated thousands of people to challenge the discrimination that African Americans faced in employment, housing, and education. At no other time in the history of both cities did more cooperation and collaboration exist between the white and black communities. In Seattle this was a function of people such as Samuel McKinney and John Adams working together with Archbishop Connolly, Raphael Levine, and Lemuel Peterson on a shared vision of racial integration. Likewise in Portland, Tecumseh Graham and John Jackson worked closely with Paul Wright, Emmanuel Rose, and Robert Bonthius. They shared a vision of social justice that grew largely out of their belief that the Bible provided a mandate to work for the end of discrimination and for social justice. By the end of the decade, however, that shared commitment to racial liberalism and integration was increasingly challenged by primarily younger African Americans who had grown frustrated with the slow pace of change but also more conscious of their own identity and desire to say that race does matter. The desire to achieve a stronger sense of black identity, black culture, and black power all made the vision of a more just society increasingly complex.

Nevertheless, the Civil Rights Movement had changed the social dynamics of the Pacific Northwest in significant ways. To be certain, not all civil rights leaders were religiously motivated. A good many activists simply recognized that racism undermined the present and future of communities throughout the region, and that African Americans deserved better from their country. But it is also clear that a significant percentage of civil rights leaders and activists engaged these issues out of deep religious convictions and values. Whether the sense of urgency came from a prophetic tradition in the black church or whether it came from Jesus's command to love thy neighbor or from the many biblical passages exhorting one to work for justice in the face of hate and fear, Protestants, Catholics, and Jews rallied around these issues.

It is also clear, whether one was black or white, Protestant, Catholic, or Jew, that these activists understood themselves to be outsiders to the mainstream of a culture that resisted a change in the status quo. They sought to change the way hundreds of thousands of people viewed the practice of race relations; they sought through both legislative action and moral persuasion to convince a largely white world that they enjoyed privilege and preference that discriminated against persons of color.

As the twentieth century wore on, however, it became clear that social change would come in fits and starts. If the Civil Rights Movement reflected an important element in a more liberal set of social values, conservative religious activists in the Northwest would soon organize themselves more vigorously in opposition not so much against civil rights as it pertained to race relations, but against civil rights as it related to issues of feminism and sexual orientation.

CHAPTER 9

THE CHRISTIAN RIGHT STRIKES BACK

In July 1977, the battle over the proposed Equal Rights Amendment (ERA) to the United States Constitution erupted in Ellensburg, Washington, of all places. It was there that over four thousand women gathered for a three-day conference to discuss a range of issues and elect delegates to a national conference later that year in Houston, Texas, as part of the International Women's Year. Organizers hoped to generate support for the ERA and to build momentum at the state level for women's issues ranging from more day-care support to an appreciation for the plight of women from minority racial and ethnic groups. All, however, did not go according to plan. Conference organizers expected close to two thousand attendees who would most likely be pro-ERA, but in the few days prior to the conference conservative opponents of the proposed amendment rallied an additional two thousand Washington women to drop everything and come to Ellensburg to do their best to oppose the ERA. Although no formal tally was made of the religious affiliations of the women who attended the conference, reporters and attendees seemed in agreement that the vast majority of conservative opponents were members of the Mormon Church.

According to the *Ellensburg Daily Record*, "When registrars . . . looked out the window at the waiting horde of women on Friday, many shook their heads in apprehension. Others murmured, 'What a madhouse!'"[1] When asked what these unexpected women hoped to accomplish, one spokesperson, Susan Roylance from Kennewick, member of the Mormon Church, indicated that the purpose was to block the ERA and represent the needs of "motherhood, anti-abortion, and anti-child care."[2] With the skill of seasoned organizers, these opponents of the ERA identified themselves with blue and white ribbons, and for the next two days they offered what they considered to be pro-life and pro-family proposals while vigorously resisting every resolution that they deemed at odds with their conservative perspective. At the climax on Sunday, liberal conference delegates put forward a resolution affirming the need to support racial minority women. However, attached to this resolution was support for the ERA. While a handful of conservative women rose to speak in favor of the resolution (and they were heartily cheered by supporters of the ERA),

Susan Roylance, a member of the Church of Latter Day Saints, organized opposition to the Equal Rights Amendment in 1977. Courtesy Susan Roylance

most conservative women voted against the resolution and succeeded in defeating the motion. When the dust settled, advocates of the ERA could be found at one end of the hall singing, "We Shall Overcome," while conservatives left feeling a measure of triumph for what they had accomplished.[3]

Unbeknownst to many, however, were the results of balloting for delegates to be sent to Houston. Both the pro- and the anti-ERA sides had put forward a slate of delegates. Conference registrants could vote throughout the two days, and when it became evident that conservative forces had been successful in registering close to two thousand anti-ERA women, pro-ERA organizers got on the phone and called hundreds of additional supporters to come, register, and vote for the liberal slate of delegates before the conference ended. In the end, after ballots were challenged and recounted, liberals succeeded in electing twenty-three of a possible twenty-four delegates to Houston, much to the chagrin of conservatives.[4]

The Ellensburg convention revealed how deeply split women had become over issues related to gender and gender roles in American society. A number of key organizers on the liberal or progressive side had come out of mainline Protestant churches, but the vast majority of individuals who identified themselves religiously were affiliated with Mormonism, conservative evangelicalism, or Catholicism. By

1977, the Christian Right, as it came to be known, was no longer content to sit quietly on the sideline and let liberal or progressive voices dominate the agenda for women's issues in American culture. And for the first time, significant numbers of Washington Mormons were willing to become actively involved in the public square.

Clearly these women saw themselves as outsiders to a culture that, from their perspective, had become increasingly liberal in the last quarter of the twentieth century. They anticipated correctly that it would be a bitter fight to maintain "traditional" roles for women in a society that had embraced new forms of gender equality and opportunity in their lifetime. As outsiders, they found themselves engaged in a range of issues for the first time and often found themselves the object of criticism in the press. Nevertheless, their efforts help explain the passion that each side exhibited in the Northwest's version of a culture war that permeated the nation.

If the Civil Rights Movement had energized liberal Protestants, Catholics, and Jews in the Northwest, the other side of the 1960s— the sexual revolution and feminism—exacerbated the worst fears of conservative evangelicals. As a decade that promoted more acceptance of recreational drugs, more rejection of institutional authority in all forms, and more abandonment of traditional moral values, the 1960s represented for conservatives the worst of American culture and politics. Conservatives objected to the protest against the war in Vietnam as a betrayal of the nation's highest values. They cringed at a youth counterculture and its penchant for sex outside of marriage. They despised the women's movement for its challenge to existing social norms, and they saw the growth of the federal government as a threat to their personal freedom. Conservatives believed that the US Supreme Court under Earl Warren contributed to radical social change in America, and the court's decision to deny prayer in school in 1962 symbolized the secularization of American culture. All of these events and movements underscored the conservative perception that liberals did not believe in patriotism, capitalism, traditional moral values, orthodox Christianity, or a conventional view of marriage.

As the 1970s unfolded, things went from bad to worse from a conservative point of view, particularly in the Pacific Northwest, where liberal cultural values seemed to surface everywhere. In 1969, Oregon became one of the first states to legalize abortion. Washington state followed suit in 1970. In Washington, a state equal rights amendment, HJR61, was narrowly approved by voters in November 1972. In 1973, Oregon was an early state to ratify the national Equal Rights Amendment.

The US Supreme Court's affirmation of the right of women to seek an abortion in *Roe v. Wade* in 1973 created something of a crucible moment for many evangelical Christians. Until then, evangelicals had not paid much attention to the abortion issue and largely considered it a Catholic concern. But *Roe v. Wade* changed that. Legalized abortion was understood as one more part of a liberal agenda that included efforts to pass the Equal Rights Amendment, to approve a gay and lesbian lifestyle, and a relentless criticism of US foreign policy. Conservatives of all stripes increasingly believed that the republic was on a path to self-destruction. These events galvanized conservative religious individuals and groups throughout Washington and Oregon.

Conservative activism in the region began to coalesce in what became known nationally as the Christian Right in the early 1970s. Beginning in 1972, conservative activist Phyllis Schlafly played a major role in reviving grassroots conservatism and halting the momentum of the Equal Rights Amendment just three states short of ratification. Schlafly's claim that the ERA would require women to serve in the military, undermine men's obligation to support their wives and children, relegate children to being raised in day-care centers, and force women into the workplace resonated across the nation among conservative groups. Fear of shared bathrooms and the assertion that women might lose alimony and child support all played to the anxieties of millions of men and women who considered themselves believers in traditional role models. Joining Schlafly in this conservative backlash was former Miss America Anita Bryant, who grabbed national attention in 1977 with her opposition to Florida's Dade County gay rights ordinance. She charged that supporters of the ordinance were making a "disguised attack on God" and were "recruiting children" to a life of immorality.[5]

Family values had always been a major component of what conservative evangelicals supported. But during the late 1960s and early 1970s, a new urgency surfaced. According to historian Allan Lichtman, "conservatives used their family values agenda to seize the moral high ground from liberals who were slow to respond."[6] While liberals eventually fought back with assertions that family planning, along with a social safety net, adequate housing, and affordable child care all contributed to the health and well-being of the family, conservatives continued to claim the mantle of being more pro-family.

In the Northwest, this urgency about the plight of the American family and the declining state of American culture once again received a boost from evangelist Billy Graham. In the spring of 1968, he returned to Portland and held a ten-day crusade in the Rose City. Graham possessed a special knack for capturing the tenor of the times, particularly from a conservative evangelical point of view. In 1950, he had focused on the threat that Communism posed to the United States and to Christianity. But in 1968, he turned his attention to the counterculture of the 1960s. Preaching only weeks after Martin Luther King's assassination, Graham stayed away from the volatile racial issues of the day. Instead he focused primarily on the danger of a youth culture that seemed inexorably headed in a liberal direction. In one sermon directed specifically at those under the age of twenty-five, he said that their most important decision was to say "no" to "this day of permissiveness."[7] He listed four things that young people must resist: "dishonesty, lawlessness, psychedelic drugs and all others not prescribed by a doctor, and premarital sex."[8] Graham noted that 41 percent of Americans were under the age of twenty-five: "Unless our young people begin marching to another drum, under another flag and for another cause," democracy is on its way out.[9] Graham, then forty-nine years old and nearly twenty years into his career as America's foremost evangelist, seemed almost apoplectic when talking about the way in which "hippy songs, poetry and literature" were all driving youth in a "desperate search for pleasure, purpose, a moral code, hope, security and a 'meaningful experience.'" And then he reminded his audience that all of these things are obtainable only through an "experience with God."[10]

Five days later, a little over twenty-five thousand Portland residents heard Graham speak on "Youth, Sex, and the Bible." Graham returned to his concern that America had become a "permissive society. . . . Even some of our clergy say it is all right to indulge in sex if it is meaningful. . . . But what does the Bible say about it?" he asked. He warned that a "sex license" is destroying love relationships between male and female and "sending love out the window." "We have taken something wonderful and beautiful and pulled it down into the mud," Graham said. Sex is a gift from God, he added. "There is nothing dirty about sex according to the Bible" if it was used in the context of marriage. Hearkening back to his Victorian forefathers and mothers, Graham stated that "the mark of a Christian is self-control and self-discipline."[11] Graham knew his audience. In 1968 there were many Northwest Christians who were looking for an alternative to the liberal social culture of the decade.

In 1976, Graham once again returned to the Northwest, and this time it was to participate in the inaugural event of Seattle's new domed stadium—the Kingdome. Graham stayed in the Emerald City for nine days and drew an estimated 434,000 people, which made it the most heavily attended Graham crusade in North America during the previous five years. Surely some attended just to experience the Kingdome, and many came to hear African American singer Ethel Waters and country superstar Johnny Cash, but most came to hear Graham. By the 1970s Graham, like other evangelicals, had turned his attention to family values and specifically to marriage. On May 13 in front of 57,600 persons, Graham declared that marriage was an institution worth saving. "Marriage has lost its status. . . . Divorce has lost its stigma. . . . The weakening of marriage is part of the general weakening of our institutions."[12] Graham further preached, "We're losing confidence in ourselves; we're losing confidence in our institutions we have cherished. Emancipation of women has encouraged young women to stay out of marriage and older women to get out of it." He warned of the social disorder that would result if the present American trend toward nonmarriage continued.[13]

A year later, in 1977, James Dobson created Focus on the Family, with its headquarters in Colorado Springs, Colorado. Dobson's stated objective was to preserve traditional values and the institution of the family. He provided advice on all sorts of topics, from love and marriage to child rearing and adoption.[14] Dobson's organization wielded significant influence in the Northwest, and one other organization, Concerned Women for America (CWA), also influenced conservative evangelicals in the region. Founded in 1979 by Beverly LaHaye, the wife of Tim LaHaye, who would later develop an international audience with the best-selling *Left Behind* series, CWA focused on white evangelical Protestant women for the purpose of lobbying lawmakers at all levels on behalf of a conservative political agenda.[15]

In that same year, evangelical Southern Baptist Jerry Falwell established an organization that gained considerable national attention—the

Moral Majority. Falwell wanted to unite "the vast majority of Americans against humanism." Pastor of the Thomas Road Baptist Church in Lynchburg, Virginia, Falwell founded Lynchburg Baptist College, which later became Liberty University. He hosted a television ministry, the *Old Time Gospel Hour*, and joined Jimmy Swaggart, James Robison, Rex Humbard, Oral Roberts, Jim Bakker, Pat Robertson, and a host of other white evangelical males who preached to millions of Americans as televangelists. Many of these individuals blended revivalism with conservative messages on various topics ranging from the evils of Communism and liberalism to abortion, homosexuality, and feminism. Falwell was particularly assertive in pushing ministers to register voters and get them to the polls.[16]

In the Northwest, the number of conservative evangelicals grew significantly after the 1960s. While more difficult to track during the 1970s and 1980s, the numbers get clearer beginning in the 1990s. For example, between 1990 and 2000, those considering themselves evangelical grew 32 percent in Washington and 25 percent in Oregon. The Catholic Church grew at the rate of 35 percent in Washington and 25 percent in Oregon, with the influx of significant numbers of Hispanic individuals. Mainline Protestants declined by 5 percent in Washington and 9 percent in Oregon.[17]

According to sociologist James Wellman, at least four major factors contributed to the growth of conservative evangelical religion in the Pacific Northwest since the 1970s. First was the fact that the Northwest, as we have already seen, is among the most open religious environments in the country. Without a dominant religious faith tradition such as Baptist or Catholic, ample opportunity existed for all sorts of religious groups to establish a foothold. That openness fostered a strong entrepreneurial spirit among conservative evangelical pastors. Evangelism and the conversion of souls emerged as much stronger priorities for conservatives than was the case for most mainline Protestant congregations during the late twentieth century. Second, entrepreneurial conservatives have been particularly adept at using media and contemporary music in the context of worship to recruit and retain new and younger members. That entrepreneurial spirit has played well in burgeoning suburbs outside of Portland and Seattle. Much less tied to denominational polity or policies regarding the appointment of pastors, evangelicals have simply put more effort into planting or establishing new churches compared with their mainline counterparts. Third, Wellman observes that evangelical churches frequently develop their own sports groups, family activities, and an assortment of other services intended to meet the need for community in contemporary America.[18] The fourth and perhaps most critical element, according to Wellman, is the fact that overall, evangelical and independent churches have placed more emphasis, comparatively speaking, on the importance of holding on to the youth in their respective congregations. The vast majority of liberal and mainline churches, according to Wellman, are much more comfortable allowing their youth to leave the church and "make up their own mind about their religious faith" and then hope that they return to church once they are married and begin to raise a family. Evangelicals, on the other hand, direct much more of their resources into programming that is intended to keep their youth attached to the church from childhood to early adulthood. All of this has seemingly made a difference in the relative growth of conservative evangelical churches and the decline of membership in the mainline Protestant churches.[19] Perhaps one more factor has come into play, although it is difficult to provide hard data, and that is that conservative evangelical churches generally reinforce values that have been more consistent with the overall worldview of a significant segment of the upper middle class. More comfortable with capitalism and the acquisition of wealth, along with general affirmation of America's role in the world and a commitment to traditional family values, evangelical churches appealed to the growing suburban populations of Seattle, Bellevue, and the greater Portland area.

The growth of large churches in the Northwest during the 1990s and early twenty-first century underscored Wellman's observations concerning the appeal of conservative evangelicals. A 2010 survey conducted by the Hartford Institute for Religion indicated that in Oregon, twenty-two churches were classified as megachurches with more than eighteen hundred members (the largest claimed six thousand members). None of those twenty-two fell into the category of mainline Protestant or Catholic. All of them were independent, nondenominational, Foursquare Gospel, Southern Baptist, or Assemblies of God. Likewise in Washington state, thirty-seven churches fell into the megachurch category. Only First Presbyterian in Bellevue and University Presbyterian in Seattle could be classified as mainline, and in each of these cases there was a strong evangelical ethos. Otherwise, the other thirty-five were classified as nondenominational, independent, Baptist, Foursquare Gospel, or Assemblies of God.[20]

Many of these churches have remarkable stories of growth at a time in which the culture of the Northwest seemed to be becoming increasingly secular. For example, in the mid-1970s, twenty-five-year-old Roy Hicks became the pastor of a small Foursquare Gospel Church in Eugene, Oregon, which at the time had only fifty members. Over the years, Hicks's church grew to approximately five thousand members before he died in a plane crash in 1994. During the course of his ministry, Hicks developed an ability to start other churches as well. From Hicks's original church, more than fifty other churches in the West were spawned.[21]

Casey Treat provides another remarkable story with the development of the unusually successful nondenominational church, the Christian Faith Center in Federal Way, Washington. Growing up in Seattle, Treat became heavily involved in drugs by the early 1970s. While attending a drug rehabilitation center, he became a Christian. By 1980, he and his wife, Wendy, along with thirty other people, had established the Faith Center. Over the next three decades, Treat emerged as one of the most successful televangelists in the country. He became known for his "possibility thinking" theology and was often compared to Robert Schuller of the Crystal Cathedral in Southern California. In recent years, Treat has been linked with "Possibility Thinking" and the "Prosperity Gospel," which connected the power of prayer with material blessing. In 2010, the church claimed that an estimated eighty-two thousand individuals attended weekly services on two separate campuses (Federal Way and Mill Creek), making it the second largest church in Washington. Treat built his ministry around specific groups, including infants, teens, and parents. Faith Center developed hundreds of small groups in the greater Puget Sound area.[22]

Kevin Gerald is another individual who developed a huge church in the Northwest. In 1986, Gerald became the pastor of Meridian Christian Ministries in Puyallup, Washington, just southeast of Tacoma. In five years, Gerald grew the church from one hundred active worshippers to eight hundred members. In 1993 a merger took place, and it became the Covenant Celebration Church, with more than five thousand people attending weekly services. As part of the church, Gerald developed the Champions Centre organization, which focused on the development of Christian leadership in a variety of contexts.

Other megachurches in the Northwest fit Wellman's general picture, as well as his formula for growth. These included Portland's Beaverton Foursquare Church, which was originally founded in 1961 and still had only seventy-five members by 1968. However, by 2000, the church was considered the largest in Oregon, with six thousand members.

In Seattle, Marc Driscoll established the Mars Hill Church in 1996, which over the course of the next decade emerged as the most successful in terms of followers and the most controversial in the Pacific Northwest. By 2006, Mars Hill had grown into a multicampus church and continued to grow at a significant rate over the next five years. However, in 2014, with Mars Hill at the height of its influence, with as many as thirteen thousand people attending services at its fifteen locations, Driscoll became embroiled in several controversies and resigned as pastor. More will be said about his ministry later in this chapter.[23]

These young conservative evangelical pastors and their churches were not carbon copies of one another. They did not agree on every political issue or how one should view aspects of American culture or foreign policy (which they rarely spoke about). But they did generally agree on their opposition to homosexuality and abortion. And they did speak frequently about the importance of traditional marriage, as well as the role of gender in the church and larger society. In many respects, this emphasis on gender roles underscored historian Daniel Rodgers's observations that since the 1970s, "of all the certainties whose cracking seemed to culturally conservative Americans most threatening, the destabilization of gender roles and gender certainties set off the sharpest tremors."[24]

While there were some exceptions, these churches took issue with the egalitarian commitments to gender espoused by most progressive mainline Protestant churches, which largely approved of the ordination of women to be pastors beginning in the 1970s. Conservative churches held fast to variations of what came to be known as complementarianism. This particular view asserts that men and women are inherently different in nature and as a consequence have different roles in families, churches, and society. The complementarian view holds that women are not to exercise spiritual authority over men and that their roles must be limited within the church. In most of these churches, women were prohibited not only from being pastors but also from serving as elders or deacons, serving communion, teaching men, leading worship, or speaking in a church service. Women could participate only in ministries for other women and children.[25]

This attention to the role that women played in the church reflected larger concerns about gender roles outside the church. Certainly the idea of the "traditional family" predominated in most conservative evangelical churches. Although there was not complete unanimity, a broad consensus existed that it was preferable for women to be married, to stay at home, to largely oversee the moral upbringing of the children, and to support their husbands. A man, on the other hand, should be the spiritual head of the household, be a "Godly Christian," be the principal breadwinner, and exercise leadership in the broader community. Conservatives reacted with alarm to the fact that six million mothers of infants and school-age children were absorbed into the labor force during the decade of the 1970s. In addition, the divorce rate had increased by two and one-half times from the mid-fifties to the end of the 1970s before stabilizing. Perhaps most alarming to conservatives were the number of feminist writers and critics who denounced a patriarchal culture in America that had exploited women's unpaid family labor and had contributed to a systematic discrimination in the work world. Feminists increasingly decried what they believed was male domination over their reproductive choices. Still others spoke of physical domination in the form of rape and sexual violence. Traditional gender roles came under attack from a number of quarters. All of these social forces resulted in a strong reaction on the part of many religious conservatives across the country and in the Pacific Northwest.

In the Northwest, the Promise Keepers movement generated considerable energy in regard to gender roles in and outside the church. Organized originally in 1990 by Bill McCartney, head football coach at the University of Colorado, Promise Keepers aimed to develop "Godly Men." By 1993, fifty thousand men filled the University of Colorado football stadium, and three thousand pastors were in attendance at a national conference. Men were encouraged to "take back" leadership in their churches, in their homes, and in their communities. Large rallies emphasized the importance of being "men of integrity" and committed to their roles as husband, father, church member, and American. Speakers frequently addressed what was described as the feminization of the church and the feminization of the American male. Within the context of the Promise Keeper movement, feminization meant an abandonment of leadership to women within the church, home, and society.

Beginning in Portland in 1994, Promise Keepers held several large gatherings in the Northwest. For two successive years beginning in 1995, over sixty thousand men gathered in the Kingdome in Seattle. Those events also placed special emphasis on racial reconciliation, in addition to the standard commitments to male leadership.[26] Other Promise Keeper gatherings were held over the next ten years in Seattle, Portland, Tacoma, and Spokane.

A backlash against the women's movement and specifically feminism erupted among other influential conservative religious voices in the Northwest. Among the most vocal and controversial critics of feminist impulses before his downfall in 2014 was Mark Driscoll, pastor of the Mars Hill Church in Seattle. By any standard, his story is remarkable. Born in 1970, Driscoll, by his own description, grew up in a rough neighborhood in South Seattle with its own sense of dislocation, poverty, and dysfunction. "Without a local police force, it resembled the Wild West," noted Driscoll. "There were multiple strip clubs, seedy massage parlors, and hourly rate motels down the street from my home. The prostitutes walked the streets openly and were brazen enough to even walk up and knock on my car window."[27] Driscoll, although raised Catholic, describes himself as uninterested in church by the time he attended high school. It was during high school, however, that he met Grace, his future wife. After dating in high school, they initially attended different universities. While at Washington State University (WSU) in Pullman, Driscoll found fraternity life wanting, and he reports turning to the Bible that Grace had given him years earlier. Driscoll reported that God told him to "marry Grace, preach the Bible, train men and plant churches."[28] He did in fact marry Grace, graduate from WSU, and begin work as a college outreach pastor for the Antioch Bible Church in Kirkland on the east side of Lake Washington. He later earned a master's degree in theology from Western Theological Seminary in Portland, where he gravitated toward Calvinist theology, although according to Driscoll, one of his major influences has been Charles Spurgeon, the late-nineteenth-century Reformed Baptist preacher who challenged the liberal theological tendencies of his day.

By 1996, Driscoll felt called to start a church in his Seattle home in the Wallingford neighborhood. From the beginning, he wanted a church that attracted young, creative urban people who had not only given up on the church but had generally opted out of the conventional middle-class dream of living in the suburbs. Immersed in popular culture and in particular in the grunge culture of Seattle, Driscoll found himself thinking more about how to engage the body-pierced, punk rock generation—those young men who literally thought of themselves as outsiders to the mainstream culture. He later remembered that at the time, "I envisioned a large church that hosted concerts for non-Christian bands . . . embraced the arts, trained young men to be godly husbands and fathers, planted other churches, and led people to work with Jesus Christ as missionaries to our city."[29] For the most part, Driscoll stayed true to his vision. He presented himself as an out-of-the-box thinker and an iconoclast—an outsider to the prevailing culture of the Pacific Northwest. Famous for his blue jeans and untucked shirt, Driscoll was more comfortable with the style of stand-up comedy. He attracted attention on more than one occasion for his frankness about sexual behavior in and out of marriage.[30]

By 2003, Mars Hill Church moved into a renovated NAPA Auto Parts store in the Ballard neighborhood in Seattle. Additional campuses were established in West Seattle, Downtown Seattle, Bellevue, Olympia, the U-District, Federal Way, and Albuquerque, New Mexico. In 2012, Mars Hill was ranked by Kent Shaffer and his national organization, Church Relevance, as the third most innovative church and the seventh most important church in the United States based on a combination of factors.

Driscoll described himself as an adherent to many of the ideas associated with sixteenth-century Protestant reformer John Calvin. Like Calvin, Driscoll's emphasis was on God's sovereignty in the world, and the Seattle pastor stated that the purpose of church was to be missional in the sense that the church's "primary task is sending Christians out of the church and into the culture to serve as missionaries through relationships, rather than bringing lost people into the church to be served by programming."[31] For Driscoll, that meant engaging and even embracing Seattle's youth culture. Writing in the *New York Times*, reporter Molly Worthen noted that "new members can keep their taste in music, their retro T-shirts and their intimidating facial hair, but they had better abandon their feminism, premarital sex and any 'modern' interpretations of the Bible."[32]

Apart from Driscoll's unconventional approach, it was his attitude toward gender roles that attracted the most comment and was among his most controversial positions. Early on in his ministry, Driscoll became convinced that the vast majority of evangelical preachers and churches were portraying an image of Jesus that was far too effeminate. As one writer observed, "Driscoll is adamantly not the 'weepy worship dude' he associates with liberal and mainstream evangelical churches, singing prom songs to Jesus, who is presented as a wuss who took a beating and spent a lot of time putting product in his long hair."[33] Driscoll presented Christ in much more manly terms and frequently objected to what he believed was the predominant image of Christ—an effeminate man who embraces children and cuddles lambs. Driscoll has written that the mainstream church has made Jesus into "a Richard Simmons, hippie, queer Christ," a "neutered and limp-wristed popular Sky Fairy of pop culture that . . . would never talk about sin or send anyone to hell."[34]

On the foundation of this more "manly" Jesus and what he believed Scripture says, Driscoll advocated for a patriarchal view of the church and society. He wrote that "as an intense biblical literalist, [I believe] that the man is the head of the home, that the man should provide for his family, that children are a blessing, and that we would not have so many deceived feminists running around if men were better husbands and fathers because the natural reaction of godly women to godly men is trust and respect."[35] In another sermon, Driscoll stated that the divine task of the Mars Hill Church is to become "a man factory, they come in boys, they go out men."[36] At his height, Driscoll was known for his "boot camps" for young men, where they were challenged to embrace their masculinity and to hear presentations about marriage, sex, money, and fatherhood. Participants heard lectures on how to get a wife, have sex with that wife, get a job, budget money, buy a house, father a child, study the Bible, "stop looking at porn, and brew decent beer."[37]

It would be hard to overstate the importance of the issue of gender for these younger, more conservative evangelical males. For Driscoll and most other conservative evangelicals, the dominant culture of American society and in particular the Pacific Northwest is liberal in its embrace of feminism and egalitarianism. As critics, these mostly young male pastors understand those values to be directly at odds with what they believe the Bible is saying about the ways in which men and women should function, both in and out of the church.

Most of these young pastors work hard to cultivate in their attendees and members a sense that they are outsiders to a mainstream culture and need to live lives that distinguish them from the "norm." These evangelical ministers foster a sense of conviction among many of their parishioners that Northwest culture needs to return to what they imagine to be the traditional role models for men and women in the past. They see themselves as part of a broader movement to change the culture of the Pacific Northwest. As sociologist James Wellman has observed, "They want to expand and create larger circles of influence on the moral, cultural, and eventually the political life of the region."[38]

This emerging conservative evangelical voice in the culture of the Northwest manifested itself in a number of different ways in the late twentieth and early twenty-first centuries. And while it would be inaccurate to say that everyone who self-identified as a conservative evangelical or who attended a megachurch was conservative politically or supported the Christian Right, there is no doubt that a strong base of support for the political Christian Right came from conservative evangelicals.

In retrospect, conservative religious voices in both Oregon and Washington during the 1960s and 1970s were less active when compared with those more liberal or progressive activists who mainly came out of the mainline Protestant and Catholic communities. Nevertheless, even in those decades, conservative activists were beginning to make their presence felt in the Northwest's public square, particularly on issues related to gender, homosexuality, and abortion. The most visible Christian conservative in Oregon politics prior to the 1980s was a fundamentalist minister, Walter Huss. Huss had started his own newspaper and developed a reputation for being both anti-Semitic and opposed to the Civil Rights Movement.[39] In 1966, he decided to enter politics and run against Oregon US senator Mark Hatfield. While unsuccessful, Huss's campaign brought many Christian conservatives to the polls. In the aftermath, Huss persuaded other conservative Christians to begin running for precinct committee and state party offices. This grassroots effort paid off, and in the late 1970s Huss was briefly elected to be the statewide chair of the Republican Party.[40] In 1982, he ran unsuccessfully for governor against Vic Atiyeh, but again he brought many conservative Christians to the polls.

The 1980s witnessed the emergence of the most influential and controversial grassroots organization with conservative Christian roots—the Oregon Citizens Alliance (OCA). Organized initially as a political action committee by Don Baird, who ran conservative Baptist minister Joe Lutz's unsuccessful campaign to unseat US senator Bob Packwood, the OCA grew significantly under the leadership of Lon Mabon.[41] A Vietnam veteran who became a fundamentalist Christian, Mabon organized support in 1988 for a ballot measure that would overturn Governor Neil Goldschmidt's executive order banning discrimination based on sexual orientation in the executive branch of the state government. The measure, which also prohibited any job protection for gay people in state government, passed with 53 percent of the vote. Eventually, the state supreme court overturned the measure, but it certainly underscored the potential influence of the OCA.

In 1990, the Oregon Citizens Alliance focused on abortion, with a ballot initiative that would have required parental notification for a minor's abortion, but that measure failed to pass.[42] Two years later, the OCA returned to homosexuality and proposed an amendment to the Oregon Constitution that would prevent "special rights" for homosexuals and bisexuals. Opposed by mainline clergy and other groups, the measure failed 56 to 44 percent, but it drew national attention to Oregon.

Lon Mabon attracted statewide attention for his attack on gay rights. Courtesy Toots Crackin, Ballot Measure 9, a Toots Crackin Productions film, https://vimeo.com/ondemand/10619

The defeat of the statewide initiative forced Mabon to recenter his efforts on local antigay/lesbian ordinances in various communities across the state. Beginning in May 1992 and extending through November 1994, fifteen out of sixteen communities in both eastern and western Oregon passed ordinances that would have prevented gays and lesbians from achieving "special rights," as the OCA framed the issue. In the following year, however, the state legislature, with the eventual approval of the state supreme court, overturned all of the local ordinances. Hoping that opinion had changed statewide, the OCA sponsored a statewide antigay ballot measure in 1994, and although the outcome was closer than the 1992 election, voters defeated the measure by a 52 to 48 percent margin.[43] If ultimately unsuccessful in its bid to pass statewide measures, the OCA had certainly shaped a large part of the political discourse in Oregon during the 1990s.

Another group that reflected the rise of the Christian Right in the Pacific Northwest was the Oregon Christian Coalition. Linked to the Reverend Pat Robertson's national Christian Coalition, it attracted conservatives who were not always sympathetic to the OCA. The Oregon Christian Coalition, along with the Oregon Association of Evangelicals and other politically active conservative churches (most notably Portland's Bible Temple, a Foursquare Gospel Church), lobbied the state legislature on issues ranging from antipornography to homeschooling.[44]

Despite some tension within conservative Christian organizations in Oregon, the OCA continued to keep Oregon voters engaged with issues related to homosexuality and abortion. In 2000, the OCA, with the help of the Christian Coalition, secured enough petitions to put forward another anti–gay rights initiative. This version proposed to prohibit public schools, including colleges and universities, from "encouraging or promoting" homosexuality. But the measure was defeated by almost exactly the same result as in 1994, 52 to 48 percent.[45]

Conservative Christians, however, would not let the debate over homosexuality end. In 2004, a variety of Christian groups secured enough signatures to place Initiative 36, which proposed to ban same-sex marriages, on the ballot. This initiative also gained the support of the Oregon Catholic Conference and Oregon's Mormon Church. A large number of Oregon's evangelical churches actively campaigned for the initiative, and this one did pass, thus becoming one of the few legislative victories for conservative Christians.

The one issue outside of abortion and homosexuality that attracted the attention of conservative Christians in both Oregon and Washington was the fight over physician-assisted suicide and the "Death with Dignity Act." In 1994, Oregonians approved Measure 16 by a 51 to 49 percent margin. By doing so, Oregon became the first state in the union to pass an act that established a process by which a competent adult Oregon resident, diagnosed by a physician with a terminal illness that would kill the patient within six months, may request in writing from his or her physician a prescription for a lethal dose of medication for the purpose of ending the patient's life. The law stipulates that the option is voluntary and the patient must initiate the request. Any physician, pharmacist, or health-care provider who has moral objections may refuse to participate.

Passage of the law did not ensure its existence. A number of appeals delayed implementation until the Ninth Circuit Court of Appeals dismissed objections to the law. However, the Oregon legislature decided that it would return the law to the voters in November 1997 under the title "Ballot Measure 51." With another opportunity to defeat the measure, opponents, including the National Catholic Conference, Mormons, several Baptist organizations, and other conservative religious groups, poured money into the campaign. Supporters of the "Death with Dignity Act" ranged from those who organized the "Don't Let 'Em Shove Their Religion Down Your Throat Committee" to several but not all moderate and mainline religious groups, which stipulated that individuals should have their own choice in the matter. When the dust settled, Ballot Measure 51 failed in thirty-three of Oregon's thirty-six counties, with an overall vote of 60 to 40 percent, and physician-assisted suicide continued to be an option for Oregon residents.[46]

In spite of losing at the polls on the issue of physician-assisted suicide, conservative religious organizations continued to be active in Oregon. The Oregon Family Council, established in 1980, developed a *Christian Voter's Guide,* which was distributed through a network of Portland-area churches and eventually became popular statewide. In 2009, the Oregon Family Council endorsed the "Manhattan Declaration," which was a document signed by approximately 150 leading Christian voices throughout the country. This effort attempted to organize a movement of conservative Christians to take a public stand on "marriage, life and religious liberties." In many respects, the Oregon Family Council's support for the Manhattan Declaration reflected the ongoing battle over American and, for that matter, Northwest culture. As the website indicated, "The Manhattan Declaration is one excellent way for Christians to take a stand against this cultural assault and begin redirecting our nation back toward the spiritual and moral roots that allowed for the unprecedented peace, prosperity and goodness we've enjoyed for nearly 250 years."[47]

Antiabortion efforts continued to attract significant numbers of Oregon's conservative Christians in the 1990s and the first decade of the twenty-first century. Oregon Right to Life was a local chapter of the National Right to Life organization. Even though it was not officially Christian in designation, its membership and financial support came primarily from evangelical as well as Catholic individuals. The Right to Life group not only lobbied against abortion but also opposed laws that would permit "death with dignity," mercy killing, infanticide, cloning, and stem cell research.[48]

By 2005, however, frustration with the lack of progress against abortion led to criticism of the Oregon Right to Life organization. Conservative Christians formed three other groups in Oregon. One was Oregonians for Life, led by Amy Rabon of McMinnville and Mary Starrett, a former television and radio personality who ran unsuccessfully for governor as the Constitution Party's candidate in 2006. Another Christian group, Life Support Oregon, also organized around abortion, as did Believers against Child Killing, led by Paul deParrie. The coalition of these groups continued to target pro-choice legislators, as well as try to see that all abortion funding was eliminated from the Oregon state budget. [49] While their efforts failed to effect significant change in Oregon's abortion laws, the issue did not disappear. In 2009, an estimated seven thousand people in Portland rallied against abortion, the largest gathering to date.[50]

By the first decade of the twenty-first century, it was clear that conservative evangelicals were a force to be reckoned with in Oregon political circles. The actual results were meager, but clearly conservative Christians had shaped many of the key debates over public policy issues in Oregon. And at the very least, conservative evangelicals continued to make the case that Oregon's middle class should adopt more conservative social values in the face of a secular culture.

In the state of Washington, as was the case in Oregon, the Christian Right made its presence felt on a number of social and political issues in the late twentieth and early twenty-first centuries. Conservative evangelicals played a key role in the surprising victory of Pat

Robertson in the Republican Caucus for president of the United States in 1988. It was the only primary victory for Robertson in his run for the presidency. In the following year, Robertson established the Christian Coalition, and four years later the Washington state chapter was formally launched. Robertson wanted "to mobilize and train Christians for effective political action" and encouraged activists to run for school boards and city councils as well as for positions within the local Republican Party. The coalition developed its own voter's pamphlet for the 1994 Washington state elections and listed candidate positions on abortion, gay rights, outcome-based education, and gun control. Coalition-supported candidates had moderate success in that election.[51]

Other conservative organizations emerged in Washington state, such as the Washington Family Council (WFC), which like the Oregon Family Council was an arm of Jim Dobson's Focus on the Family. Former Seattle Seahawk quarterback and son of conservative political leader Jack Kemp, Jeff Kemp served as the director and stated often that the WFC was focused on marriage and reversing the culture of divorce. For Kemp, the decline of the traditional family was the result of the secularization of America and the misreading of the Constitution that led to the mainstreaming of the sexual revolution. Frequently the WFC objected to the teaching of sex education in public schools.

Conservative Christians formed numerous groups in the 1980s for the purpose of organizing support for a social agenda. Among the most active was the Concerned Women for America (CWA), founded by Beverly LaHaye in 1979 in order to "protect and promote Biblical values among all citizens—first through prayer, then education, and finally by influencing our society—thereby reversing the decline in moral values in our nation."[52] LaHaye once said that CWA opposes everything the National Organization for Women (NOW) stands for—primarily abortion rights and the Equal Rights Amendment. Still active in Washington state in 2015, the CWA continued to advocate for traditional family issues, including opposition to gay marriage.[53]

Successes, however, have been limited for conservative Christians in the Northwest. For example, in 1998, an initiative intended to ban most late-term abortions, Initiative 694, was widely rejected. However, Initiative 200, designed to ban state affirmative action programs, garnered support from the Christian Right and passed rather easily. The difference was that I-200 drew support not just from the Christian Right but also from business conservatives and libertarians. The Christian Right also had a rare success in 1998 when the state legislature voted, over Washington governor Gary Locke's veto, to ban gay and lesbian marriages.[54]

Overall, Washington state, like Oregon, continued to lean in a liberal direction when it came to social issues. Washington became the second state in the union (after Oregon) to approve of a "Death with Dignity Act." Modeled very closely on the Oregon law, Washington's Initiative 1000 in 2008 received strong support from former governor Booth Gardner, who was suffering from Parkinson's disease. Once again, the Catholic Church came out firmly in opposition, as did the Mormons and other conservative groups. And once again, mainline and moderate religious groups were either silent or advocates of personal choice. Most visible in support were the United Church of Christ and the Unitarian Universalist Association of Congregations. Voters approved of the initiative by a 58 to 42 percent margin.[55]

Lack of overall success, however, did not deter the Christian Right from continuing to attempt to influence the public debate over a number of issues. Washington Evangelicals for Responsible Government (WERG) was organized in 1993 under former Republican legislator Skeeter Ellis. WERG developed what was known as the Capitol Project, which tracked bills and state regulations from an office in Olympia. WERG was once described by the King County chapter of Pat Robertson's Christian Coalition as "the first-ever professional lobbying organization for Bible believing churches and Christian organizations." Members of the Washington Association of Churches and the Lutheran Public Policy Office, along with the Catholic Church, would probably take exception to the assertion that it was the first professional lobbying group for Christian organizations in the state, but nevertheless it underscored how separate the evangelical voice was from the mainline. WERG opposed gay civil rights, diversity training, and inclusion of sexual orientation equity in education.

But the influence of conservative Christianity in the Northwest in the late twentieth and early twenty-first centuries was more commonly found at the grassroots level. One of the outspoken pastors on the issue of homosexuality was Ken Hutcherson. After playing several years in the National Football League, including one season with the Seattle Seahawks, Hutcherson, an African American, felt called to the ministry and helped organize Antioch Bible Church. Ordained in 1986, Hutcherson by 2004 was beginning to make a name for himself as an opponent of homosexual rights, asserting that gay rights should not be compared with civil rights.[56] In that year, Hutcherson led efforts to organize a rally at Safeco Field, home of the Seattle Mariners, for those who opposed gay marriage. Called the Mayday for Marriage, the event featured the chairman of Focus on the Family, James Dobson, and drew more than twenty thousand individuals, as well as several hundred advocates of gay marriage who stood outside Safeco and let their voices be heard.[57]

Former Seattle Seahawk turned pastor, Ken Hutcherson was an outspoken opponent of homosexuality. Courtesy Pat Hutcherson

Hutcherson continued to find other ways to express his resistance to gay rights. In 2005, he objected to Microsoft's support for an antidiscrimination bill that would have made it illegal to fire an employee due to sexual orientation. Hutcherson met with Microsoft executives and reportedly told them that seven hundred of their employees attended his church, and if they did not withdraw support of the bill, he would organize a national boycott of the company. Shortly thereafter, Microsoft changed its position to neutral on the proposed legislation. That decision spurred protest from within Microsoft by its gay employees, and the company reversed itself again and decided to support the bill. Once the antidiscrimination law received legislative approval in January 2006, Hutcherson again threatened a boycott, but nothing came of it.[58]

In addition to Hutcherson, one of the most influential religiously conservative individuals in Washington has been Joe Fuiten. He was raised in rural Oregon, where his parents were both ministers in the Assemblies of God denomination. Originally headed for a career in law, Fuiten attended Willamette University. However, while at Willamette he decided to go into the ministry. He actively organized Christian groups on campus and preached regularly to his peers, who identified with the "Jesus Movement." In 1972, he entered into the formal church ministry as a youth evangelist and served churches first in Aloha, Oregon, and later in Tacoma. By 1979 he was elected director of Christian Education for the Northwest District of the Assemblies of God. Two years later, he became the senior pastor at Cedar Park Assembly of God in Bothell, Washington.

Over the next several years, Fuiten established eight branch churches, along with Washington state's largest non-Catholic private school. He founded a Christian television station in Seattle and in 2004 served as the state chairman of Social Conservatives for the Bush-Cheney campaign. Fuiten was named president of the Washington Evangelicals for Responsible Government and founded a political action committee, the Positive Christian Agenda, which sent weekly legislative citizen action alerts to ninety-six thousand people.

Fuiten's counterpart in Oregon was Gary Randall. Beginning in the late 1970s, Randall hosted a half-hour daily talk show on television in Portland until 1990. Randall regularly interviewed the national leaders within the evangelical movement, such as James Dobson, Tim LaHaye, Chuck Swindoll, Phyllis Schlafly, Charles Colson, Pat Robertson, and Bill Bright. He also developed a daily radio program that aired in Portland, Seattle, Spokane, and Eugene for eight years in the 1980s and 1990s. Involved in a variety of humanitarian issues and overseas mission efforts, Randall raised millions of dollars for a number of causes. He served as a pastor in Seattle and Salem, Oregon, for twenty-five years and on the board of the National Association of Evangelicals. In 2004, Randall founded the Faith and Freedom Foundation, a nonprofit organization committed to advancing traditional Judeo-Christian values in America. In 2005, Washington Evangelicals for Responsible Government merged with the Faith and Freedom Foundation. Randall served as president, while Fuiten, who had been the president, assumed the title of chairman of the board and chief executive officer. Together they joined forces to fight same-sex marriage in Washington state.

Over the next few years, Randall and Fuiten worked hard to develop electoral support that would eliminate the civil rights of same-sex partners. Randall developed voters' guides and organized political action committees to support and oppose several candidates. But by 2009, the various campaigns had failed to achieve their objectives. In that year, one longtime observer of religion in Seattle noted that the Christian Right had lost a sense of direction: "Many of the early leaders have stepped back due to health or age, because they feel burned at being called haters or because they're tired of political divisiveness, saying it gets in the way of saving souls."[59] Most prominent among the evangelical leaders who seemed to be withdrawing was Joe Fuiten. Suffering a heart attack in 2004, Fuiten was diagnosed with prostate cancer in 2009. And as one more battle over gay rights ensued in 2009 with Referendum 71, which was intended to confirm the extension of rights of domestic partnership, Fuiten admitted that he did not want "the church to be viewed as oppressive, [and] as opposed to people living their lives and eking out whatever happiness they can." He told one reporter, "God is not coercive. The idea that people ought to be free to live their life and live the way they want . . . I don't object to that."[60]

Nevertheless, Referendum 71 reflected the larger cultural war or divide within the faith communities in Washington state. It was estimated that two hundred clergy and religious organizations across the state (mostly from mainline churches) supported the referendum. Many mainline churches sponsored forums or educational events on behalf of the referendum. "There's this huge fallacy that the debate about gay rights is a debate between gay and lesbian people and secular people on the one side, and people of faith on the other," said Josh Friedes, spokesman for the coalition to approve Referendum 71. "The truth is very, very different."[61] In the end, the referendum did pass, 53 to 47 percent.

CONCLUSION

Overall, the Christian Right could point to few victories on the issues of homosexuality and abortion. Oregon and Washington were still regarded as "liberal" states on the political spectrum. Apart from pockets of conservative resistance on the eastern side of the Cascade Mountains and in some of the suburbs around Seattle and Portland, the dominant cultural tendencies remained on the liberal/progressive side.

But to dismiss too easily the conservative influence on Northwest culture would be a mistake. Sociologist James Wellman makes a compelling case that "entrepreneurial evangelicals" have carved out a foothold in the region and are, according to Wellman, "fast becoming the dominant religious subculture in the PNW."[62] By the first decade of the twenty-first century, conservative evangelicals, conservative Catholics, Mormons, and the Christian Right had established themselves as a force to be reckoned with in the Pacific Northwest and seemed poised for greater influence. In many ways, these churches were becoming the face of established religion in the Pacific Northwest. Megachurches and megapastors were determined to make an impact on the culture, particularly when it came to gender and gender roles. And yet these conservative activists considered themselves outsiders in a Northwest culture that, in their opinion, was dominated by secular and liberal ideas that threatened virtually everything they deemed important.

The sense of being at war over the culture of the region motivated conservatives, but it also motivated liberals. And Oregon and Washington had no shortage of liberal religious activists who also believed that they were fighting an uphill battle to try to change fundamental attitudes and values as well as public policies that affected marginalized populations, which included the economically disadvantaged, homosexuals, racial and ethnic minorities, and women. That ongoing culture war would continue to mark much of the politics of the late twentieth and early twenty-first centuries in the Pacific Northwest.

CHAPTER 10

LIBERAL DREAMS AND ECUMENICAL ACTIVISTS

On the morning of May 9, 1979, more than two hundred religious and lay leaders from across the denominational spectrum came to the King County Courthouse in Seattle to welcome the release of Reverend Jon Nelson, who had just spent the last ninety days in jail. Nelson, the Lutheran campus minister at the University of Washington, had been arrested for repeatedly protesting against the deployment of the Trident nuclear submarine at nearby Bangor, Washington, on Puget Sound. Among those waiting to greet Nelson were Seattle's archbishop of the Catholic Church, Raymond Hunthausen, and the president of the Church Council of Greater Seattle, Bill Cate, who stated that he was there to "honor the prophets in our midst."[1] In solidarity with Nelson, the group marched along Third Avenue and up Columbia Avenue to the First United Methodist Church for a prayer service. Nelson thanked his many supporters and once again spoke about how necessary it was to try to stop the race to build more nuclear arms, because for him the "future of the human race is at stake."[2]

When later asked by a reporter why he risked long-term imprisonment in federal jail, Nelson quoted the Bible: "They shall beat their swords into ploughshares." He then spoke about his love for his children: "What pleasure would there be in life if I was not trying to do whatever I could for them?" Nelson and his wife, Juni, had fourteen children, eleven of whom were adopted. He further noted the statement of the Pacific Northwest Synod of the Lutheran Church in America, which indicated that it was "standing by and upholding those of its members who conscientiously register their opposition to nuclear weapons systems by acts of civil disobedience." Nelson compared his decision to the one that he wished

Lutherans in Germany had made when they first heard that Jews were being herded into boxcars and sent to Auschwitz. To Nelson, the Trident submarine, which carried 408 warheads (each five times more powerful than the Hiroshima bomb) constituted a first strike offensive weapon that violated several international treaties as well as his deepest moral convictions.[3]

Jon Nelson's act of civil disobedience represented one side of a struggle between religious activists on the Left and activists on the Right. For the Left, defying the perceived power of the military and the arms race with the Soviet Union marked the culmination of years of protest that had grown out of the Vietnam War. Thousands of religiously motivated people who thought of themselves as progressive believed that their consciences dictated the necessity of standing against the policies of the American government, which threatened to unravel in thermonuclear war. To many individuals on the religious Right, however, Nelson's act seemed the height of folly and among the most unpatriotic acts imaginable. While few spoke out publicly against the Lutheran minister and his supporters, most conservative evangelicals generally supported the foreign policies of the United States and believed in the necessity of the arms race. They certainly did not believe in civil disobedience, with the exception of the fight against abortion.

This division of opinion ran deep within the religious communities of the Northwest in the decades after the 1960s, as it did in other parts of the country. It still runs deep in the second decade of the twenty-first century. The divide between the Right and the Left has been so strong that it reminds one of the rift between Catholics and Protestants in the nineteenth century and first half of the twentieth, when they often saw each other as the enemy. To understand the role of religion in the public square of the Northwest since the 1960s is to understand the backdrop of conflict between conservatives and liberals over what values and policies should prevail, particularly among the middle class. By the time of Nelson's arrest in 1979, both sides had become very active in the Northwest. Each side had its litmus tests on various issues. Both sides believed that the Bible offered ample support for their respective social and political positions. Both sides sought to influence the broader culture and politics of the region. This chapter examines the liberal or progressive voice in civic life and the public square since the 1960s.

As we have seen, the roots of modern liberal activism in Northwest religious communities can be traced back to the Social Gospel movement during the early twentieth century. The numbing poverty of the 1930s, the Jewish Holocaust of World War II, the internment of Japanese Americans, and struggles among African Americans in the Northwest all helped raise social consciousness among religious activists. Mainline Protestant church bodies and seminaries along with Reform Jewish and Catholic Church officials developed positions on social thought and policy that encouraged an emerging generation of pastors, priests, and rabbis to consider more seriously political and social commitments.[4]

But it was the politics and social movements of the 1950s and 1960s that wielded an even more profound effect on many religiously motivated individuals in the Northwest and across the country. The specter of nuclear holocaust haunted the post–World War II generation and motivated many progressives to join peace movements even before Vietnam. John F. Kennedy's call to serve one's country ignited a younger generation across the country yearning to make a difference. Lyndon Johnson's "War on Poverty" focused national attention on moral responsibility to the marginalized and underclass in American society. Pastors, priests, and rabbis all over the country spoke eloquently of the necessity of addressing the needs of the poor with new zeal. And as previously seen, Martin Luther King's passionate appeal to white and black America to work on behalf of social justice caused tens of thousands of people in faith communities to search their consciences concerning what role they might play in the movement. As the decade wore on, millions of Americans debated the ethics of American foreign policy and specifically the morality of the Vietnam War. Deciding whether to become a conscientious objector, volunteer for the Peace Corps, or go on to seminary or graduate school in order to avoid the draft weighed heavily on the minds of thousands of college-age students. In addition to the war, emerging movements among women and environmentalists captured the attention of a significant number of religiously motivated people and organizations. All of these questions engaged both church leaders and laypeople within the various Protestant denominations as well as within the Catholic and Jewish communities in the Pacific Northwest.

In many ways, Jon Nelson reflected these forces that had been building during the middle decades of the century. Nelson was born in St. Paul, Minnesota, in 1933, and his family was made up mostly of pastors and politicians, including US congressmen and state governors. His mother became an adherent to principles of nonviolence taught by Mahatma Gandhi, and his father, a Lutheran pastor, integrated an all-white congregation in Washington, DC, in the middle 1950s. After being ordained as a Lutheran pastor in 1959, Nelson first served parishes in Minnesota; Olympia, Washington; and Missoula, Montana, before being called to campus ministry. He first served at the University of Montana from 1966 to 1972 and helped develop what is believed to be the nation's first black studies program. In 1972, he assumed the position of Lutheran campus pastor at the University of Washington and immediately became active in the antiwar movement. He served in that position until 1984.[5]

Deeply passionate about a number of causes, Jon Nelson embodied what it meant to be a committed religious activist from the Left. And in the Pacific Northwest he found a fertile environment for his activism. As we have seen, both the black and white church had played critical roles in Seattle's civil rights struggles during the 1960s. The Church Council of Greater Seattle provided an organizational framework for liberal activists from across the denominational spectrum to join together to try to create social change. And Nelson would soon join them and others from different faith traditions in an effort to engage the broader culture on issues of social justice.

Some of this interfaith cooperation may have been inspired by the television show *Challenge*. First aired in 1960, the show was the brainchild of Rabbi Raphael Levine, who had come to Seattle in 1942 to succeed Rabbi Samuel Koch at Temple De Hirsch. Born in Lithuania in 1901, Levine and his family had immigrated to the United States in 1909, and he grew up in Duluth, Minnesota. After becoming a rabbi, Levine served a synagogue in Liverpool, England, in the 1930s, where he began to build bridges with Christians who were open to ecumenical dialogue. Once in Seattle, Levine set about the task of tackling anti-Semitism, which had grown considerably in the Northwest during the decade prior to World War II. He considered it the most pressing problem of his era.[6] Levine broached the idea of an interfaith television show as early as 1956, but there was little interest on the part of the Catholics. In 1960, however, the atmosphere began to change with the preparatory work in the Catholic Church that eventually led to Vatican II and a greater willingness on the part of Catholics to dialogue with other faiths.[7] With Archbishop Thomas Connolly's blessing, the project went forward.

Consequently, Rabbi Levine, Father William Treacy (Connolly's choice to represent the Catholics), and Reverend Martin Goslin, pastor of the Plymouth Congregational Church, the largest Congregational Church in Seattle, opened the show with a debate about whether John Kennedy, as a Catholic, should be president. A few months later, in an effort to examine some of the roots of anti-Semitism, the three discussed who killed Christ. Treacy and Levine stayed with the show for its entire fourteen years. Other Protestant ministers succeeded Goslin, but the essential idea of the program remained the same: provide a lively forum for clergy from the three faith traditions so they could civilly discuss similarities and differences on a variety of issues thought to be important to the public. From birth control and suicide to interracial marriage and religion in politics, the participants spoke to roughly three hundred thousand people each week.[8] Part of the appeal of the program was the genuine respect and friendship that developed among the participants. Treacy and Levine developed a particularly close relationship. They believed that religious values could inform the community in helpful ways and could lead to a more just and compassionate world.[9]

But the show was not without its detractors. According to Levine, "Our severest critics were fundamentalist religious groups who berated us for our religious tolerance of each other. Believing that they had the only way to salvation, they either pitied us for our blindness and prayed for us to see the light, or attacked us, sometimes viciously, for 'perverting Scripture.'"[10] But many others embraced the concept and the direction of the show. In 1962, the National Conference of Christians and Jews presented KOMO-TV with a special national award for the *Challenge* show. Throughout the decade, the three religious spokespersons leaned into a variety of difficult social and political issues. According to one Seattle historian, the show "was able to elevate the three faiths into a position of moral influence in the community that they could not have achieved alone. With a heightened image and enhanced credibility, the churches were able to play an important part in the racial and social turmoil of the 1960s."[11] Another local critic wrote, "It is safe to assume that *Challenge* has been responsible for the development of a greater public spirit of tolerance and understanding than previously existed in the Seattle area."[12]

Overall, *Challenge* represented the effort of progressive religious leaders to shape Seattle's culture in a direction that affirmed pluralism and civic action on behalf of issues of social justice. In 1968, Father Treacy and Rabbi Levine, along with several business persons from the Seattle area, purchased a dairy farm in the Skagit Valley, north of Everett, and founded Camp Brotherhood. Still going strong in 2015, the interfaith camp offers educational, spiritual, and experiential programs designed to facilitate peacemaking and cooperation among different faiths.

Challenge was only one example of a number of cooperative ecumenical efforts designed to influence various social and political issues in the region. Over the next three decades, church bodies banded together to lobby legislatures in Olympia and Salem to change or enact public policy according to a particular agenda. The Washington Association of Churches (WAC) was established in 1975, although its roots extended back to the early 1930s as the Washington Council of Churches. Eventually consisting of ten Christian denominations and twelve ecumenical entities, the WAC remained a key organization in the Pacific Northwest for influencing legislative work and community development. In 2011, the Washington Association of Churches merged with the Lutheran Public Policy Office to form a more effective lobbying organization named the Faith Action Network. Likewise, the Ecumenical Ministries of Oregon (EMO) was organized in 1973 out of the old Portland Council of Churches and the Oregon Council of Churches. In 2011, EMO claimed sixteen Christian denominations and lobbied the Oregon legislature on a number of fronts. The Associated Ministries of Tacoma–Pierce County was created in 1969, with roots going back to 1883. In eastern Washington, the Spokane Council of Ecumenical Ministries reorganized in 1971, with roots in the Spokane Council of Churches extending back at least to 1949. The Church Council of Greater Seattle, organized in 1919, continued to be very active in its efforts to shape public discourse on many issues.

Catholics maintained their own lobbying offices in both Oregon and Washington but frequently worked very closely with other ecumenical organizations. Lutherans also established their own public policy advocacy offices in Salem and Olympia and, like their Catholic counterparts, worked collaboratively with ecumenical organizations on behalf of the poor and the marginalized. In retrospect, in the aftermath of the 1960s, ecumenical organizations generally engaged four major areas of public life, largely from what would be described as a liberal or progressive perspective: civil rights for a variety of marginalized groups, antiwar activity, economic justice, and environmental issues.

CIVIL RIGHTS

Since the 1940s, the Northwest had proven to be a fertile ground for strong interfaith and ecumenical cooperation and activity in the area of civil rights. Most notably during and after World War II, the Church Council of Greater Seattle, the Portland Council of Churches, and organizations such as the Christian Friends for Racial Equality, among others, made civil rights a high priority. The commitment to social justice persisted in the 1970s and drove the Church Council of Greater Seattle to continue to focus on the racial integration of Seattle public schools. Nationwide, the Black Power Movement of the late 1960s had questioned many of the unexamined assumptions of racial liberalism, particularly the assumption that the solution to de facto segregation meant the closing of predomi-nantly black schools and the busing of black students. The followers of Stokely Carmichael and other black militants made compelling arguments that the curriculum in public schools needed to change, that more black history and culture needed to be taught, and that more black teachers needed to be hired. But in the Northwest, most advocates of civil rights remained committed to the goal of creating an integrated community. Two major questions informed the debate in the 1970s: the first centered on whether integration would be voluntary or involuntary, and the second focused on whether the burden of integration should fall primarily on the African American community or should be equally shared among other races and ethnic groups. In other words, would predominantly black schools be closed and black students be bused, or would the burden of integration fall on white students and families as well?

Seattle was part of a larger effort across the country to desegregate public schools. Federal courts were beginning to mandate the integra-tion of schools through court-ordered busing. In 1974, Boston was the first Northern city to experience citywide court-ordered busing, and it went poorly, with significant violence and white resistance. Against this backdrop, Seattle's educational, civic, and religious leaders hoped to develop a plan that would accomplish the goal of integration without being ordered to do so by the courts. The Church Council of Greater Seattle and the Black United Clergy for Action ended up playing key roles in the development of what became known as the Seattle Plan for the desegregation of its public schools.

The first major step toward the creation of the Seattle Plan occurred in 1976, at the encouragement of Don Daughtry, a white pastor of the Beacon Avenue Church of Christ. The Church Council of Greater Seattle formed the Task Force on Racial Justice in Education and named Daughtry as the cochair, along with Peter Jamero, a Roman Catholic layperson. The task force did primarily three things. First, it brought representatives from the white, black, and Asian communities together so that they could reach a consensus on the approach to desegregation. Second, the task force formulated a philosophy of integration that provided a model for integration that was specific to the demographic uniqueness of Seattle. And third, it urged the council to apply pressure to the Seattle School Board by threatening to join in a lawsuit with the NAACP and the American Civil Liberties Union if the board did not accept the plan.[13]

After months of study, the task force concluded that mandatory busing was necessary. But it also firmly believed that the burden of busing should not simply fall on the African American community. The task force asserted that Seattle should be a multicultural city with a pluralistic character. It believed that white-Anglo students needed to come into contact with significant numbers of persons of color, particularly from the African American and Asian communities. In other words, students must learn how to interact with members of other racial and ethnic groups in approximately equal numbers. The Church Council's task force believed that the old model of closing predominantly black schools and dispersing African American students throughout the white communities should be abandoned. For the task force, integration did not necessarily mean assimilation into a majority white culture—members wanted to move the city toward a more multicultural social environment.[14]

The task force presented its findings to the Seattle School Board on December 22, 1976. In order to represent the vision of a multicultural city, the statement was jointly read by Japanese American Edward Iwamoto, pastor of Blaine Memorial Methodist Church; Cecil Murray, pastor of First African Methodist Episcopal Church; William Cate, president/director of the Church Council; and Ann

Siqueland, the director of the Desegregation Project for the Church Council of Greater Seattle.[15]

After several more months of study, the Seattle School Board adopted the Seattle Plan, which reflected much of what the Church Council's task force on Racial Justice in Education had recommended. The plan included all schools in the district and developed a complicated formula that defined segregation in terms of the ratio of white to nonwhite students in the district. The Church Council took an active role in attempting to educate people throughout the city regarding the merits of the plan. Over one hundred churches offered educational programs intended to explain the reasons that busing had become necessary and the expected outcome of the plan. The Church Council issued a statement expressing its commitment to action, as well as its hopes for the city in general: "We intend to be advocates for racial justice in education. . . . If we apply our best energies we may ultimately be moving to the realization, in Seattle, of a truly pluralistic society."[16]

On December 14, 1977, the school board voted to adopt mandatory busing. The plan itself was adopted in January 1978. The action made Seattle the largest city in the United States to undertake voluntarily districtwide desegregation through mandatory busing. The plan went into effect in September 1978 and did not engender the violence or conflict that Boston and other cities had experienced. Across the country, various media took notice of the role that the Church Council of Greater Seattle played in the process.[17] A *Philadelphia Inquirer* headline read, "In Seattle, Church Group Swings a Desegregation Plan." The newspaper acknowledged the influence of key religious leaders on the plan itself and quoted David Colwell, pastor of Seattle's Plymouth Congregational Church, as saying, "We're old battlers from way back, and we insist education for this day be multi-racial and cultural."[18]

Meanwhile, in Portland, civil rights activists also continued to work in the 1970s for an integrated school district and a more integrated community. A broad coalition of individuals and organizations, including the NAACP, the Albina Ministerial Association, and the Portland Council of Churches, ceaselessly advocated for change that would result in the breakdown of segregation in the Rose City. Beginning in 1965, Portland adopted a Model Schools Program that theoretically improved predominantly black schools in the Albina district and would hopefully attract white students. However, after a few years it was clear that the program had not achieved its intended objectives.

As was the case with Seattle, Portland faced the prospect of a plan for integration mandated by the federal government. In 1969, the Portland School Board hired Robert Blanchard as its superintendent. Blanchard soon offered a plan titled "Portland Schools for the Seventies." However, unlike the Seattle Plan, Blanchard's proposal relied heavily on shifting school boundary lines and busing mostly elementary and middle school African American students to predominantly white schools. By the middle of the 1970s, little progress had been made, and there was increasing frustration within the black community that the effort for desegregation was falling largely on the African American community.

As a consequence, several African American leaders decided to form the Black United Front (BUF) in 1979. One of the cofounders, along with African American activist Ron Herndon, was the Reverend John Jackson, African American pastor of Mt. Olivet Baptist Church. Jackson worked closely with Ron Herndon and Herb Cawthorne, who had emerged as two of the leading black activists in Portland.[19]

Almost immediately, the Black United Front called for a boycott of public schools in the fall of 1979, and they rapidly gained a broad spectrum of supporters, including a significant number of white parents.[20] Clearly the goal of the Black United Front was to pressure the school board to change its policies. The overarching goals were to end the busing of students out of the Albina neighborhood and continue improving the quality of the neighborhood school. The BUF plan advocated for pluralism and the importance of retaining a sense of "neighborhoodness." The plan opposed assimilation into the broader white culture. The BUF called for dismissing the school superintendent, which occurred in 1980, demonstrating that the front had become a major influence on education issues in Portland. By 1980, the school board adopted what was known as the Comprehensive Desegregation Plan. The BUF played a significant role in its adoption. After their initial success at ending busing for desegregation in Portland, the BUF effectively kept the largely black Jefferson High School open and continued to advocate for black studies and an expansion of the multicultural curriculum within Portland's public schools. The struggle over the curriculum would persist into the first decade of the new century.[21]

If the effort on the part of religious groups to achieve the desegregation of public schools in both Portland and Seattle was the most noticeable, other social justice issues emerged in the 1970s. In that decade, a number of religious groups rallied on behalf of the protection of Indian fishing rights in Washington state. On May 23, 1973, the Church Council of Greater Seattle convened a meeting at Temple De Hirsch with a group of Native Americans. Out of that meeting, a task force, led by Seattle Lutheran minister Robert Winkel, was established for the purpose of developing a better understanding of key issues affecting native tribes in the region. The task force authorized a subcommittee, which included activist Lutheran minister Jon Nelson, Lutheran layperson Marilyn Bode, and Quaker Joan LaFrance, to write an amicus brief for the purpose of helping inform the judicial decision in *United States v. Washington* in 1974. In the end, US District Court judge George Boldt relied heavily on the brief and handed down a judgment (popularly known as the Boldt decision) that sent shock waves throughout the region. Boldt ruled that the Treaty of 1855, orchestrated by territorial governor Isaac Stevens, promised 50 percent of the harvestable fish to native tribes and 50 percent to the nonnative community. That treaty provision was still in effect, according to Judge Boldt. The white fishing community was outraged, but from the outset the Church Council of Greater Seattle supported the Boldt decision and stood by the Indians.[22] During the next several years following the US Supreme Court's affirmation of the Boldt decision, the council task force served an important mediating role between the Washington State Native American Fishing Commission and the State Department of Fisheries. In the end, the furor over the decision diminished, but the decision of the Council of Churches was not popular.[23]

Throughout the next two decades, the ecumenical community continued to build bridges to Pacific Northwest Indians. In November 1987, the bishops (including Raymond Hunthausen, the archbishop of the Seattle Archdiocese) and the denominational executives of most of the mainline Protestant churches in the Pacific Northwest issued an apology for "long-standing participation in the destruction of traditional Native American spiritual practices." Ten years later, another group of denominational executives once again acknowledged that "our churches have been challenged to act in accordance with this act of contrition." They recommitted themselves to "secure access to protection of sacred sites and public lands for ceremonial purposes; to respect the use of religious symbols for use in traditional ceremonies and rituals; and to participate in the struggles to end political and economic injustice against tribal communities."[24] In 2014, bishops and denominational executives once again offered a letter of support for Native Americans as they issued a joint statement condemning the decision to transport coal and oil by railroad across the Northwest to export terminals near Anacortes.

African Americans and Native Americans were not the only minority groups who drew the attention of religious activists in the Northwest. Throughout this period, the Catholic Church took the lead in offering support to the region's Hispanic population. From the early 1960s through the mid-1970s, nearly forty thousand Hispanics moved into the Puget Sound region as well as into the agricultural communities of Oregon and eastern Washington. Beginning in 1968, the faith communities became more engaged when Cesar Chavez emerged as the principal organizer for the United Farm Workers movement. Chavez frequently came to the Pacific Northwest and sought the support of church leadership for his boycott of table grapes. He wrote Archbishop Connolly of Seattle asking him to become an advocate for the farmworkers. Three weeks after receiving Chavez's letter, Connolly issued an official statement to those priests under his direction calling for support of the boycott:

> The boycott of all Californian table grapes has now reached this area, and we have the opportunity of joining in the boycott in order to give witness to our concern for our Mexican American brothers in Christ who are being denied a living wage and favorable living conditions.... If we can convince our people to make it a "no grape" year, the California land owners' hold-out will surely come to a speedy end.[25]

In addition to migrant farmworkers' rights, Northwest churches rallied on behalf of a variety of refugee groups who resettled in the region. Thousands of Vietnamese, Hmong, and Cambodians came to the Northwest in the years following the end of the Vietnam War. Countless churches assisted in the resettlement efforts.

During the 1980s, several Northwest churches became enmeshed in controversy surrounding efforts to provide sanctuary for Central American refugees who were fleeing political repression and violence. After Ronald Reagan entered the White House in 1981, American foreign policy changed toward Nicaragua and El

Salvador. The American government provided economic and military support for right-wing Contras in Nicaragua and antileftist government forces in El Salvador. To reinforce Reagan's foreign policy, the Immigration and Naturalization Service (INS) began arresting and deporting thousands of Central American refugees. In 1981, however, the Church Council of Greater Seattle asked that congregations offer sanctuary to Central American refugees, and Seattle soon emerged as one of the most active communities in the nation in what became known as the Sanctuary Movement. In response, twelve Christian, Unitarian, and Jewish congregations decided to hide refugees from the INS and provide them food and shelter. In 1985, immigration agents arrested seven Salvadorans accorded sanctuary by the University Baptist Church in Seattle. Ultimately, the United States government chose not to challenge the work of these churches.[26]

More recently, in 2007, the Oregon New Sanctuary Movement (ONSM) emerged from a group of Christians concerned about the plight of undocumented workers. In that year, federal agents conducted a raid on Portland's Fresh Del Monte Produce Company. Officials detained 165 workers and arrested three individuals for lack of documentation. Over the next three years the ONSM held protests, accompanied undocumented workers to court, supported two dozen mothers who were not allowed to work, and advocated for a clear road to citizenship for undocumented workers in the United States. By 2010, twenty-five Christian and Jewish congregations, along with members of Portland's Muslim community, were assisting with jobs and housing programs in the city. The Ecumenical Ministries of Oregon (EMO) lent its support. David Leslie, executive director of EMO, stated to a reporter for the *Oregonian* that "immigration is a topic of concern everywhere in the state. We have a substantial Hispanic community in Oregon. People are thinking about immigration. They are asking themselves, 'What is my faith position? What is my church saying? What has the Bible said over millennia?'"[27]

Since the 1980s, EMO and the Washington Association of Churches have provided services for refugees and worked for their resettlement throughout the Northwest. As just one example, since 1994, EMO has sponsored the Russian School of Social Services. By 2010 an estimated one hundred thousand Russian-speaking refugees and immigrants from the former Soviet Union had settled in the greater Portland area, making Oregon second in the country for the number of Russian-speaking newcomers.

Perhaps most controversially, the decade of the seventies found gay and lesbian individuals becoming more outspoken in regard to their civil rights, as well as their assertion that homosexuality should not be treated as a sin. As early as 1966, Reverend Mineo Katagiri of the United Church of Christ emerged as the first organizer and spokesman for Seattle's gay rights movement. Katagiri had moved to Seattle from Honolulu in 1959 and had initiated a street ministry that had brought him into contact with the gay community. He had also become involved in the Civil Rights Movement and was a member of the Central Area Civil Rights Committee (CACRC) along with several black pastors. The CACRC confined itself to issues concerning African Americans, but Katagiri plowed new ground with his advocacy for the gay community. Katagiri attempted to convince city officials that gay bars should remain open, while encouraging a new group of gay leaders to ensure that sexual activities in the bars would end.[28]

As the decade of the seventies unfolded, the support for gay issues broadened within Seattle's religious community. Once again, the Church Council of Greater Seattle found itself in the midst of controversy. In 1974, the Metropolitan Community Church (MCC), a mostly gay and lesbian denomination, applied for membership to the Church Council. In spite of considerable criticism, a year later the council voted to accept the Metropolitan Community Church.

In 1976, the council set up a task force on the issue of homosexuality. In what was described by some as "a watershed event," Margaret Farley, a Roman Catholic sister and professor of social ethics at Yale Divinity School, spoke at the council's fall assembly on the topic "Changing Times: The Church and Homosexuality." Some 325 delegates discussed openly the theological challenges associated with homosexuality.[29] In 1977, the archbishop of Seattle, Raymond Hunthausen, of whom more will be said later, issued a statement in favor of gay rights: "Homosexuals, like everyone else, should not suffer from prejudice against their basic human rights. They have a right to respect, friendship and justice. They should have an active role in the Christian community."[30] In that same year, Hunthausen endorsed the first-ever Gay Pride Week in Seattle.[31]

By fall 1978, the national campaign against gay rights came to Seattle in the form of local Initiative 13, which would have repealed the City of Seattle ordinances that protected gays from certain forms of discrimination. Supported by Anita Bryant, nationally known singer and former Miss America, the initiative rallied opposition from progressive or liberal Christians throughout the state and helped defeat the proposal by a two-to-one margin.[32] However, the issue continued to prove divisive among Christians for the next three decades. The gay community gained increasing support from mainline Protestant bodies during the last part of the twentieth century.

The United Church of Christ (formerly the Congregational Church) was among the most supportive, and it openly approved gay clergy in 1972. A number of other Seattle Protestant ministers challenged their respective denominations' teaching on homosexuality. Pastors such as Dale Turner at the University Congregational Church were outspoken in their support for homosexuals, and the Reverend Jon Nelson risked being defrocked when he married two gay men at Central Lutheran in 1978. Most visible of all Seattle's Protestants was Pastor Rod Romney at Seattle's First Baptist Church, an American Baptist Church with liberal social values. Romney had come to the Seattle church in 1980 and served until 2000. Committed to a number of liberal social causes, Romney took a particular interest in trying to shape the discourse around homosexuality. His sermons included "Loving One's Neighbor Includes the Homosexual," "AIDS: A Time for Reconciliation," and a passionate address in 1994 entitled "Homosexuality and Human Rights: A Theological and Biblical Perspective."[33]

In Portland, lesbian Jeanne Knepper was ordained in the United Methodist Church in 1982. Her first pastoral appointment was so controversial in Salem in 1992 that it was withdrawn. Since 2003 she has served a North Portland congregation (University Park)—a steadfast presence and voice for gay and lesbian individuals.[34]

In 1997, in Portland, the Coalition against Hate Crimes was started by the American Jewish Committee and supported by the Ecumenical Ministries of Oregon. The primary purpose was to call attention to acts that reflect racist, anti-Semitic, or antigay behavior. For example, the group publicized the fact that a Portland man had been arrested in 2009 for sending a noose to an NAACP leader in Cleveland. And later in the year, the coalition brought attention to a neo-Nazi barbeque in Vancouver, Washington.[35]

In retrospect, the commitment of faith communities, and in particular ecumenical organizations, in Washington and Oregon to the extension of civil rights and social justice to various marginalized groups was significant. Religious leaders and organizations shaped the discourse and rallied thousands of people at the grassroots level around these issues in the Northwest. Often these groups were at the forefront of political activism as well as services for those who for one reason or another were discriminated against. All of these activities tended to reinforce the image that mainline Protestants, Reformed Jews, and frequently Catholics were on the side of liberal social values.

ANTIWAR

If the ongoing struggle for civil rights reinforced the liberal identity of many religious activists within the Northwest's religious communities, so did various antiwar efforts in the decades to follow. Religious communities throughout the Northwest increasingly opposed the Vietnam War during the latter part of the 1960s. A number of churches offered draft counseling services, and in 1971 the Church Council of Greater Seattle worked with the Campus Christian Ministry at the University of Washington to organize a series of antiwar rallies.[36]

But perhaps the most dramatic display of radical protest against US foreign policy and the military-industrial complex occurred after Vietnam and focused on the deployment of the Trident nuclear submarine, which was based in Bangor, Washington, on Hood Canal. With the announcement in 1973 that the US Navy was going to develop a nuclear submarine base in the Northwest, the vast majority of public opinion was overwhelmingly positive. Seattle was in a recession and desperately needed jobs. Defense-related spending had traditionally been an important part of the Puget Sound economy, particularly since World War II. The naval base at Bremerton and Boeing's dependence on defense contracts led most Seattle residents to welcome the Trident project with open arms. The only opposition seemed to come from a few local residents who were worried about the environmental impact on the community.

As the project took shape and more information about the Trident submarine became available, other voices began to object to the newest generation of nuclear submarines. Motivated in part by the end of the Vietnam War, opponents expressed concerns regarding the American government's approach to the Cold War and escalation of the arms race with the Soviet Union. In 1974, a retired United Methodist minister, Robert Shaw, initiated the Action Committee against Trident Submarines (ACATS). Shaw and his followers believed that the Trident, despite government statements to the contrary, was a first-strike offensive weapon. In 1975, Robert and Janet Aldridge formed another group, the Pacific Life Community (PLC), which opposed Trident on the same moral grounds and soon staged a dozen demonstrations at the Bangor complex. Bob Aldridge, who had been a designer on the Trident missile system itself, came to believe that the weapon violated his deepest core beliefs as a Catholic and felt obligated to try to stop its deployment. The PLC comprised a number of people with "radical Christian, Quaker and feminist roots," as well as links to the Catholic Worker movement. Aldridge convinced Canadians Jim and Shelley Douglass, Catholics who were active in the antiwar movement, to join him and others at Bangor.[37]

Over the next few years, the Pacific Life Community repeatedly engaged in a variety of forms of nonviolent action against the Trident project. These actions ranged from members walking onto the base and planting a cross with a global image to cutting portions of the surrounding fence, staging prayers on the base until they were removed, digging a grave for a mock-up of a submarine, and holding memorials on the anniversaries of the Hiroshima and Nagasaki bombings. At one point, Pacific Life Community members created what they called a 550-foot "Trident Monster." Consisting of a long train of people carrying poles connected by black flags meant to symbolize the Trident submarine's 408 nuclear warheads, the Trident Monster was walked onto the naval base in August 1976. In 1977, the Ground Zero Center for Nonviolent Action was created near the Bangor site. Led by the Douglasses, this organization orchestrated ongoing protests against Trident that led to the mass arrests of hundreds over the next several years.[38]

If the early protests against Trident were largely the result of Christian activists with pacifistic commitments, the movement against basing the nuclear submarine in Puget Sound soon expanded to more mainline Catholic and Protestant groups. First and foremost in this next wave was Seattle archbishop Raymond Hunthausen. A native of Anaconda, Montana, Hunthausen received ordination in 1946. Shortly thereafter he was assigned to join the faculty at his alma mater, Carroll College, to teach chemistry and mathematics as well as serve as athletics director and dean of men. In 1957, he was named Carroll College's president. He served for five years before being appointed bishop of Helena in 1962 and in the following year attended Pope John XXIII's Vatican II Council in Rome. He continued to serve as bishop of Montana until being appointed archbishop of Seattle in 1975. Since the dropping of the atomic bombs on Hiroshima and Nagasaki, Hunthausen had wrestled with what the Christian response to nuclear war should be and, as a consequence, he was drawn toward Jim and Shelley Douglass and their arguments against the Trident.[39] Beginning in 1978, he attended his first demonstration at Bangor and by the next year was speaking publicly at the Trident naval base. On that occasion he watched Jim Douglass scale the fence and be arrested, as were the Reverend William Cate, head of the Church Council of Greater Seattle, and his wife, Jan.[40] Soon other denominations and clergy in the Seattle area also began to declare their opposition to Trident.[41] Protests escalated in May 1978. Some thirty-five hundred activists marched outside the base, with several hundred being arrested. During the following year, many of the most committed protesters were jailed, including Lutheran minister Jon Nelson.[42]

On June 12, 1982, Hunthausen spoke to a gathering of mostly Lutheran ministers at Pacific Lutheran University in Tacoma, and in a twenty-five hundred word address brought national attention to Seattle by saying first, "We must take special responsibility for what is in our own backyard. I say with deep consciousness of these words that Trident is the Auschwitz of Puget Sound." He went on to say even more provocatively that Christians and individuals of conscience

Archbishop Hunthausen (third from right) drew national attention for his progressive positions on a number of issues. Here he is with other religious leaders expressing opposition to the Trident nuclear submarine. Courtesy Archives of Catholic Archdiocese of Seattle, VR610.910

should consider refusing to pay half of their income taxes in protest against that percentage of the federal budget that went toward defense.[43] In response, Hunthausen was joined by the director of the Church Council of Greater Seattle, Bill Cate, and his wife, Jan, as well as the head of the Seattle Council's Peace task force staff, Charles Meconis.[44] The Internal Revenue Service garnished the wages of the tax protesters and provided one of the decade's most visible symbols of confrontation between the religious community and the federal government.

But all these efforts failed to stop the project at Bangor. In August 1982, the first Trident submarine, the *Ohio*, slowly made its way down the Strait of Juan de Fuca and into Hood Canal on its way to Bangor. Protesters met the submarine with a large sailboat, the *Pacific Peacemaker*, and a flotilla of small boats that raced back and forth in front of the mammoth submarine in an attempt to stop it. Fortunately no one was injured, but once again the protesters included Jon Nelson and his seventy-eight-year-old mother. And once again he was arrested with several others as the Coast Guard finally impounded the boats.[45]

Lutheran minister Jon Nelson was on board the SS *Plowshares* when it attempted to prevent the Trident submarine, the USS *Ohio*, from coming into port. Courtesy Whitworth University Archives, Spokane, Washington

In spite of not being able to stop deployment of Trident submarines, protests continued. In 1986, efforts turned to stopping the supplying of Trident submarines by what were known as the "white trains," in reference to the color of special railway cars that were carrying weapons. Religious leaders attempted to stop trains from reaching their destination. Bill Cate, Jan Cate (representing the Church Women United), Jon Nelson, Reverend Dick Arnold of the United Church of Christ, and Sister Chauncey Boyle were all arrested, with twenty-four others.[46] In 2009, an eighty-one-year-old Jesuit priest from Tacoma, Father William "Bix" Bichsel, along with four other political activists, continued to keep the danger of Trident's nuclear weapons in the news by using bolt cutters to break into the base. Their intent was to demonstrate how easy it would be for terrorists to set off a chain of events that might threaten the Greater Puget Sound region. Arrested and convicted, Father Bichsel spent three months in prison. Assigned to St. Leo's Parish in Tacoma in 1959, Father "Bix" as he was better known, had been active on many fronts. He frequently advocated for the poor, the marginalized, and the African American community. Arrested an estimated forty-six times for various protests through the years, Father "Bix" was best known for his peace activism and his belief that the Trident base represented a threat to future generations.[47]

Eventually the protests diminished; the government remained steadfast in its commitment to Trident and generally avoided using violence against the protesters themselves. Remarkably, however, the Pacific Life Community and Ground Zero were still going strong in 2015, with periodic protests against nuclear armaments.[48]

The attack on the World Trade Center and the Pentagon on September 11, 2001, posed a different set of challenges to mainline religious activists in the Pacific Northwest than had the Trident submarine. On one hand, most pastors universally condemned the actions of the terrorists and assisted in the national grieving that took place in the immediate aftermath of the tragedy. On the other hand, many mainline religious leaders in the Protestant and Catholic traditions encouraged compassion and protection for Muslims who might be the target of retaliatory acts of violence or discrimination. While generally supportive of the war in Afghanistan against Al Qaeda in pursuit of Osama Bin Laden, religious leaders were much more skeptical of a possible war with Iraq. In the fall of 2002, the Washington Association of Churches (WAC) and the Ecumenical Ministries of Oregon issued statements expressing "grave and profound concerns" about the prospect of initiating war against Saddam Hussein. The WAC opposed the intent to launch a war as "morally indefensible."[49] Churches throughout the region held discussions on the moral implications of war. The Church Council of Greater Seattle called for a protest in October, and a crowd estimated by some to be thirty thousand marched through Seattle. At the time, it was regarded as the largest antiwar demonstration in the country.[50] Seattle's Catholic archbishop, Alex Brunett, gave his assent to the national bishops' decision to oppose instigation of military action by the president, finding that "war with Iraq 'would not meet the strict conditions in Catholic teaching for overriding the strong presumption against the use of military force.'"[51]

In Portland, much the same story could be told. Religious leaders led a protest on November 17, 2002, where between eight and ten thousand individuals took to the streets in opposition to the war.[52] In January 2003, it was reported in the *Portland Tribune* that 125 religious and peace groups joined together in what was one of the largest marches since the Vietnam War.[53]

According to one observer, in the 2004 election, across the country a 24 percent plurality of Americans identified "moral values" as the issue that mattered most in their presidential vote. However, in the Northwest, by far the most important issue (31 percent) was the Iraq war—well above any other region in the country.[54] As the war in Iraq wore on, other religious groups in the Northwest joined in the protest. The Kairos Action Movement was formed in 2006. On November 1, 150 Seattle-area clergy held a press conference and marched to the Jackson Federal Building downtown. They articulated positions on ten areas of public policy, ranging from preemptive war and human rights to threats to democracy, children living in poverty, and environmental challenges.[55]

While most social activists on the liberal or progressive side acknowledged that their protests had little effect on national policy, they did believe that their voices provided a form of moral conscience for the larger community. Whereas in the cases of both Iraq and Afghanistan it was easy for the average citizen to avoid thinking about the war unless a son or a daughter served in the military, the progressive religious community provided a visible reminder to many of their willingness to express their moral opposition to war.

ECONOMIC POVERTY

By far the most visible public impact of ecumenical as well as mainline churches over the past three decades has been through the provision of services for the poor, the homeless, and the traditionally vulnerable—mentally ill, imprisoned, children, and single women. Historically, mainline churches and synagogues have exercised significant influence on public policies toward these groups throughout the Pacific Northwest. Likewise, many evangelical churches and organizations such as the Union Gospel Mission have provided services and support for the homeless and unemployed in communities throughout the Northwest. But since the 1970s, the lion's share of the effort, at least in terms of influence on public policy, has come from ecumenical organizations. The Washington Association of Churches and the Ecumenical Ministries of Oregon, along with the Lutheran Public Policy Offices in both states, have consistently lobbied during the past three decades for causes that would be categorized under the umbrella of economic and social justice. From advocating for increases in minimum wage and the right to organize unions by migrant farmworkers to making the case for more funding for various poverty programs, mainline Protestants and Catholics in both Oregon and Washington have lobbied state legislatures intensively. Over the course of three decades, general consensus emerged among these groups around a set of lobbying principles based on an interpretation of biblical principles: (1) reduce hunger, homelessness, and poverty; (2) increase affordable and accessible housing and health care; (3) reform the criminal justice system and eliminate the death penalty; (4) care for the environment and promote sustainable agriculture; (5) advocate for civil and human rights; (6) advocate for accessible and quality public education; (7) maintain a state-funded safety net; and (8) support comprehensive immigration reform.[56] Over the decades, countless pieces of legislation in these areas have been influenced at the state legislature by ecumenical organizations.

Likewise, major social service agencies ranging from Catholic Charities and Lutheran Social Services (now Lutheran Community Services Northwest) to many other groups have provided significant resources to address social needs in the Pacific Northwest.[57] Catholic Charities expanded significantly after 1975. By 1988, Catholic Community Services of Western Washington (CCSWW) was incorporated as a separate institution, enabling the agency to receive government funding and engage in public-private partnerships. In 2009, CCSWW and Catholic Housing Services employed over three thousand individuals and coordinated the work of more than thirteen thousand volunteers. Its budget exceeded $121 million. Catholic Charities in Spokane, Portland, and Yakima all managed a wide array of housing opportunities for low-income, homeless, and special-needs individuals living in the Pacific Northwest. These organizations provided refugee services, shelters, day-care centers, and transitional and permanent housing, along with a variety of other services necessary for people to live with a certain amount of dignity and respect.

On the Protestant side, scores of churches have attempted to meet the needs of the disadvantaged. As one example among many, Plymouth Congregational United Church of Christ in Seattle put a major effort into low-income housing. Beginning in 1980 under the leadership of Reverend David Colwell, the congregation founded the Plymouth Housing Group (PHG) as an independent, nonprofit organization to develop and operate housing for homeless and very poor people in Seattle. Under Pastor Tony Robinson, the PHG grew into one of the largest providers of low-income housing in downtown Seattle. In 2010, with nearly a thousand apartment units and seventeen retail tenants in eleven buildings, Plymouth Housing Group had an annual operating budget of $11.1 million. The congregation was one of the first to participate in the Walk with Workers project and in 2001 launched its Living Wage Ministry with a focus on low-wage workers in downtown Seattle. In addition, the Seattle congregation developed the Plymouth House, sometimes referred to as the House of Healing, in which mentally ill individuals are treated in conjunction with Harborview Hospital.[58]

Lutherans have been particularly active throughout Oregon and Washington. As early as 1921, an agency called the Lutheran Compass Mission began serving indigent people in Tacoma. Similar efforts spread to Portland and Seattle. In 1944, seven Lutheran synods (from the Seattle/Tacoma area) agreed to organize one Lutheran agency that would offer statewide welfare services. It was incorporated under the name Associated Lutheran Welfare and later became Lutheran Social Services. Over the years, multiple programs included foster care, adoption services, mental health services, alcohol and drug abuse treatment, support for sexual assault victims, and community education. In 2001, Lutheran Social Services of Washington and Idaho joined with Lutheran Family Service of Oregon and Southwest Washington to form Lutheran Community Services Northwest. In 2010, an estimated 120,000 people in Washington, Oregon, and Idaho were served by the Lutheran agency.[59]

In recent years, one of the more dynamic faith-based efforts to meet community needs has been the Emerald City Outreach Ministries (ECOM) in Seattle. Organized in 1987 by an African American, Harvey Drake Jr., Emerald City Ministries engaged thousands of youth and families in the Rainier Valley in programs that include academic mentoring, early childhood education, training in technology, small business development, job preparation, and peer support. ECOM is nondenominational and independent but partners with a number of Christian churches, including Mercer Island Presbyterian Church and Seattle Pacific University, a Free Methodist institution.[60] In 2004, Harvey Drake and Pastor Paul Oliver of Urban Ministries combined forces and created Urban Impact. In 2015, the organization was still going strong.

In 1970, the Church Council of Greater Seattle launched one of its most visible programs in order to feed the hungry—Neighbors in Need. Seattle was entering into its most serious recession in the post–World War II years when Boeing, the city's largest employer, laid off sixty-three thousand workers. By 1972, unemployment reached 12 percent in the city. However, in 1975 the Neighbors in Need program engendered a wave of criticism when it entered into an agreement with William Randolph Hearst Jr. to distribute three million dollars worth of food to the poor in San Francisco as requested by Patty Hearst's kidnappers. In 1976 a legal suit for several million dollars was filed against Neighbors in Need, and the program was forced to disband. After the end of Neighbors in Need a new program, the Emergency Feeding Program, was started by the Church Council, along with the Black United Clergy for Action.[61]

One of the more successful Christian-based housing programs during the late twentieth and early twenty-first centuries was Habitat for Humanity. In Seattle, Portland, Tacoma, Spokane, and a number of other communities throughout the region, Habitat for Humanity mobilized Christians and non-Christians to create affordable housing for low-income individuals. From the 1980s through 2011, the local chapters built between 150 and 200 homes in each city and emerged as one of the most successful interfaith efforts in the Pacific Northwest.

In the mid-1990s, members of Washington's religious communities, labor unions, and other advocates for low-income people joined to form the Washington Living Wage Coalition. Organized by the Washington Association for Churches, the Washington State Labor Council, and Washington Citizen Action, the coalition included local Christian, Jewish, and Unitarian congregations, as well as the Church Council of Greater Seattle. Since forming, the coalition has worked with custodians on the east side and with hospital workers at Northwest Hospital. In 1998 they worked successfully to pass Initiative 688, which raised the state's minimum wage and adjusted it based on inflation. In 2010, Washington's minimum wage was the highest in the nation and Oregon's was second.

During the 1970s, churches and Christian organizations continued to work on issues related to domestic violence. The YWCA, while becoming less explicitly Christian, nevertheless became a significant provider of resources for women who were victims of domestic violence. In 1977, the Reverend Marie Fortune of the United Church of Christ (Congregational) established the Center for the Prevention of Sexual and Domestic Violence in Seattle after coming to the conclusion that religious leaders were not prepared to assist their parishioners with sexual or domestic abuse, and secular service agencies were not prepared to deal with clients' religious questions. By the 1990s the center had grown into an interreligious organization providing education and training to address sexual and domestic violence in communities throughout the world. In 2002, the center was providing resources and counseling for those affected by the sexual abuse scandal within the Catholic Church. By 2015, Marie Fortune was still active; the name of the organization had changed to the Faith Trust Institute, and it attempted to address religious and cultural issues related to abuse.[61] In 1991, the Intercommunity Peace and Justice Center was formed in Seattle. Comprising more than sixteen different religious denominations or organizations, it was making a major effort to combat human trafficking, which gained increasing attention nationally and regionally during the early twenty-first century. The religious community provided an important voice in helping make Washington the first state to make human trafficking illegal in 2003.

If one event typified the response of more liberal Christians to what they believed was the social and economic injustice of the contemporary world, it was the protest around the meetings of the World Trade Organization that occurred in downtown Seattle in December 1999. Seen by many as one more attempt by capitalist nations in the Northern Hemisphere to exploit developing nations in mostly the Southern Hemisphere as well as harm the environment, the World Trade Organization meetings met a firestorm of resistance. Hundreds of delegates met in Seattle from November 29 to December 23. Historian Patricia O'Connell Killen noted, however, that as early as September, a three-day conference on global economic injustice was held at Seattle's St. Mark's Episcopal Cathedral, helping raise consciousness about the upcoming WTO meetings. Many participants in that September conference told reporters from the *Seattle Times* that they planned to be among the protesters. On the first night of the conference, more than three thousand people packed the First United Methodist Church in downtown Seattle as part of "Jubilee 2000,"which featured speakers who advocated the forgiveness of debt owed by developing countries to the industrial countries mostly in the Northern Hemisphere. The interfaith dimension of the gathering was highlighted by "readings of the Koran, the joyful noises of a cappella hymns, a rabbi blowing a ram's horn and Hindu prayers punctuated by a conch shell," according to one reporter. During the course of the week, something called the People's General Assembly, a weeklong counter-WTO meeting, was held at First Methodist. During the protest, the Washington Association of Churches organized a human ring around the Seattle Exhibition Center. For Killen, the protests at the WTO provided something of a microcosm of the Northwest's peculiar blend of ecumenical religious activism and various forms of spirituality mixed with politics.[63]

Unfortunately, the protests in Seattle turned violent. Whatever hopes religious activists harbored of creating a nonviolent expression of resistance against global capitalism deteriorated when on November 30 several hundred protestors, many from outside the region, blocked city intersections and did considerable damage to storefronts and police cars.

ENVIRONMENTAL ISSUES

The most recent area of concern for ecumenical progressive activists has been the environment, and perhaps it will prove to be one of the most critical in the near future. With the first Earth Day being observed on many college campuses in 1970, it was only a matter of time before theological resources and a spiritual concern for the health of the planet became a more important priority. Not only did the physical beauty of the Northwest present an obvious reminder of the importance of the environment, but by the 1970s a whole raft of regional environmental issues had surfaced. An awareness of serious pollution in Puget Sound, Lake Washington, and the Columbia, Willamette, and Spokane Rivers all began to seep into the consciousness of citizens. Fears over the development of nuclear power as well as additional information concerning the radioactive waste produced at Hanford during and after World War II generated considerable concern. The destruction of old-growth forests and the degradation of salmon habitat also led increasing numbers of citizens to express concern. What distinguished religious activism on environmental issues was the wide spectrum of organizations and individuals who became involved. One could find mainline denominations—both Protestant and Catholic—becoming more visible, but one could also find groups and individuals who claimed strong spiritual values but often only a loose religious affiliation.

For example, on the more traditional side, in January 2001 the Catholic Bishops of the Pacific Northwest issued a pastoral letter that encouraged an ethic of stewardship, ecological responsibility, conservation, and pursuit of the common good. And while the letter did not make specific policy recommendations regarding such issues as the breaching of dams along the Columbia and Snake Rivers, it nevertheless established a context for Catholics and other Christians to move toward more regulation of activity within the watershed.[64] In February 2002, thirty-seven leaders from Jewish and Christian traditions in Washington state signed a statement that called on US senators to implement proposals for "energy conservation, fuel efficiency, and alternate energy development to protect God's creation and God's children."[65] Calling on senators to increase vehicle fuel efficiency, to prevent drilling in the Arctic National Wildlife Reserve, and to invest more dollars in renewable energy resources, these religious leaders attempted to leverage their cooperation.

The Ecumenical Ministries of Oregon responded in the early twenty-first century to environmental issues by organizing the Interfaith Network for Earth Concerns. Focusing on care for God's creation, the network assisted congregations with resources for various environmental ministries and sponsored workshops on food, ethics, and the earth. In addition, the network hosted several forums on environmental issues and lobbied the Oregon State legislature on the importance of environmental sustainability.

One of the strongest efforts to raise environmental awareness and move people and legislatures to action was a Seattle organization called Earth Ministry. Established in 1992, Earth Ministry focused

on preaching and teaching at various churches and worked collaboratively with Seattle University's School of Theology and Ministry. As
interest grew, the group organized its first stream cleanup and habitat
restoration project. In 2000, another group of volunteers and ten local
congregations worked to restore habitat along the Duwamish River
near Seattle. In 2006, Earth Ministry became the first faith-based organization to join Priorities for a Healthy Washington, a partnership of
conservation organizations working to pass environmental bills in the
state legislature. Earth Ministry led the religious community's successful efforts to pass I-937, the Clean Energy Initiative, and defeat
I-933, the Irresponsible Developers Initiative. From 2007 through 2010,
Earth Ministry remained exceptionally active. It spun off the Religious
Coalition for the Common Good, which was an ecumenical coalition
of eight statewide faith organizations that endorsed an environmental
legislative platform. In addition, Earth Ministry developed the Washington Interfaith Power and Light, which focused on global warming.
By 2012, this effort encompassed interfaith groups in twenty-eight
states. Jews, Christians, Muslims, Buddhists, and members of other
traditions in Washington state made up this effort and signaled the
ongoing strength of interfaith cooperation in the Pacific Northwest.[66]

In addition to ecumenical efforts to influence public policy, individuals and organizations that identified with various expressions of
Nature religion, a term first utilized by historian Catharine Albanese,
played an increasingly visible role.[67] Less formally religious than spiritual in character and identity, these individuals brought considerable
passion and energy to a number of environmental causes. Sociologist
Mark Shibley observed that while these spiritualities are not unique
to the Northwest, they have greater influence because the religious
environment is so open.[68] Focused on the sacredness of Nature itself,
Earth-based spiritualists increasingly challenged the assumption that
human beings can live in harmony with the natural world. Often
informed by the writings and life of naturalist John Muir, activists
vigorously lobbied governments at all levels for more restrictions on
the utilization of wilderness areas in the Pacific Northwest.[69]

Among the more prominent individuals who drew on spiritual
values to form a belief in the sacredness of Nature was Chant Thomas.
A so-called urban refugee who went "back to the land" in the 1970s,
Thomas was still directing an environmental education program
and spiritual retreat center on his remote southern Oregon ranch in

2015. During the late 1980s and 1990s, Thomas consistently engaged local, state, and federal officials over land use and management policies. Thomas developed a program where educators, activists, and naturalists could come to his ranch in southern Oregon and learn more about how to align their spiritual values with an appreciation for preservation of the natural world.[70]

Chant Thomas and his wife Susan have been engaged in spiritual environmentalism for many years in Oregon. Courtesy Chant and Susan Thomas

Without question, environmental concerns increasingly caught the attention of liberal religious activists in the twenty-first century. The prospect of global warming simply accentuated the long-standing concerns about the decline of old-growth forests, pollution in major rivers, lakes, and Puget Sound, as well as radioactive waste at Hanford. More than any other issue, concerns for the environment brought liberals, evangelicals, and New Age spiritualists together, at least in principle, over the importance of being better stewards of God's creation. Whether that coalition will translate into more effective lobbying for public policies for the protection of the environment remains to be seen. What is clear is that a form of spiritual environmentalism is growing in the Northwest and has brought mainline liberal Protestants and Catholics together with many who identify as spiritual but not religious.[71]

CONCLUSION

In the years following the Vietnam War, liberal and, in some people's minds, radical religious activists were remarkably engaged in political issues in the Pacific Northwest. Inspired by many of the social movements of the 1960s and 1970s, these activists drew energy from their own commitments to social justice on a broad range of issues. Most liberal activists believed in the promise of a more multiracial community. Most liberal Protestants worked to open up roles for women in the larger culture and within the church. They offered support for gay and lesbian rights. They often collaborated in the context of ecumenical organizations to support the poor and unemployed. Liberal activists helped influence legislators in both Oregon and Washington to adopt policies that provided citizens with a higher minimum wage, low-income housing, broader health-care coverage, and a stronger social safety net than in most other regions of the country. Some activists provided sanctuary for political refugees and challenged the federal government's military-industrial complex, whether that was in the form of the Trident submarine or the war in Iraq. And still other activists took up the cause of environmental sustainability with the hope that they could make a difference in the long-term ecological health of the region.

In spite of living in a broadly secular culture that embraced a number of these liberal causes and mildly supported others, most activists still considered themselves largely outsiders in a culture and a society that privileged wealth, consumerism, and, indirectly, white males. They worried about an emerging wave of conservative resistance inside and outside the church. Those anxieties were exacerbated by the reality of a declining mainline Protestant church that affected financial resources as well as the number of people who participated in any particular cause.

But without doubt, liberal religious activists contributed to the Northwest's identity as a progressive region. Their ongoing action in the public square helped raise the consciousness of tens of thousands of citizens in both Washington and Oregon about a number of important social issues. However, by the early twenty-first century, the question seemed to be whether liberal religious activism would survive the ongoing decline of traditional mainline Protestantism. Or would liberal religious activists reinvent themselves and find new sources of support for their vision for the region and America?

CONCLUSION

Mark Matthews, Seattle's often imperious pastor of the early twentieth century, occasionally speculated about the future of religion in Seattle and the Pacific Northwest. He loved to regale his many audiences with his forecast that the "Pacific slope must necessarily take a prominent part in this great work" of redeeming the world. He was fond of saying that "Seattle will be the dominant city of the Pacific . . . [and] if Christianity continues to dominate, grow and prosper, this city will, when it reaches a population of two or three millions, be, from a religious standpoint, the greatest city in the world."[1] A century later it is hard not to smile at either Matthews's naïveté or his sheer boosterism. Surely we would say that he, along with many others, misread some of the critical historical forces that would bear greatest influence on the region.

Nevertheless, he was not entirely wrong. Religious activists, including Matthews, left an important mark on the Pacific Northwest. Most visibly, religious organizations and individuals took very seriously the biblical mandate to feed the hungry, clothe the naked, and care for widows and orphans. Religious activists often stood up for those perceived as vulnerable whether they were women, children, the unborn, persons of color, or immigrants and the poor. Religiously motivated people expended enormous energy in providing health care, protecting essential civil rights, and leveling the economic playing field. Numerous black churches, white churches, and individuals with deep religious convictions put their resources and their time into trying to make life better for the disenfranchised. The Northwest is filled with institutions and nonprofit organizations developed by religiously motivated people for the purpose of serving marginalized people. The multiple social services resulting from religious impulse are not an insignificant accomplishment, and that story should not be lost.

Perhaps less obvious but no less important, religious activists have exercised significant influence on general cultural values. In the latter half of the nineteenth century and into the early twentieth, religious activists viewed themselves as outsiders to a culture that catered primarily to the needs of single males, but outsiders who could influence social norms. Christians and to a lesser extent Jewish citizens imported Victorian culture into the newly formed settlements and budding urban areas of the Pacific Northwest in the second half of the nineteenth century. Committed to building up schools, homes, businesses, libraries, and respectable entertainment, Victorians came to the region and tackled the saloon, the gambling hall, and the house of prostitution. They focused in particular on issues pertaining to the safety and well-being of women and children. The prohibition of alcohol, more than any other single social cause, represented the effort to reform the culture of the region.

If there was general consensus on issues and strategies among religious activists during the late nineteenth and early twentieth centuries, that consensus deteriorated by the beginning of the Great Depression and has been nonexistent ever since. By the mid-twentieth century, religious conservatives and religious liberals had become frequently locked in bitter debate over middle-class cultural values. Some of that had to do with a rightward turn on the part of evangelicals and a leftward turn on the part of mainline Protestants, Catholics, and Reform Jews. Despite their differences, however, activists on both sides were energized by their identity as outsiders with something to say to a culture that was more secular when compared with other parts of the country.

As "outsiders," liberal or progressive religious individuals have worked for more than a half century on behalf of a vision for the Northwest that has been characterized by commitment to civil rights, economic justice, cultural diversity, religious pluralism, and environmental concern. From the ordination of women and homosexuals to the achievement of social justice for racial and ethnic groups, religion has mattered in these cultural debates. The enormous energy directed in the latter half of the twentieth century toward more employment, fair housing, and the integration of schools has been reminiscent of the effort put forth on behalf of Prohibition five decades earlier. Both movements had a moral urgency about them, and both movements depended heavily on religiously motivated people. Most recently, liberal or progressive religious individuals have focused on protection of the natural environment. Conservation of natural resources is now regarded as vital to the future of the Pacific Northwest, and countless religious individuals and organizations have dedicated themselves to that cause.

Likewise, conservative religious individuals have embraced a vision for the Northwest that has seemed to place them largely outside the predominant cultural values of the region. By the 1940s and fifties, concerns about Communism and secularism in the public schools emerged, concerns that contributed to the establishment of private schools. By the 1960s and 1970s, conservative evangelicals argued that American culture had become "too permissive" and that the sexual revolution, along with the women's movement, needed to be resisted. Opposition to homosexuality and abortion has energized thousands of religiously motivated individuals to work in the public realm. Most recently, conservative evangelical churches have expended significant effort combating the effects of what they describe as the feminization of the culture. Clearly, religion has mattered in the Northwest's cultural debates, as it has mattered in other parts of the country.

But culture wars that have pitted religious liberals against conservatives have had unanticipated consequences. The religious divide has, for example, contributed to the polarization of political rhetoric in the public square. Mainline Protestants and conservative evangelicals rarely work together to form alliances on behalf of political or cultural issues. There is a deep schism over issues of sexual orientation. One would have to go back to the middle of the nineteenth century and the religious division over the politics of slavery, or to earlier mutual suspicion between Protestants and Catholics, to find a period marked by such animosity. All of this has made it difficult to unite religious activists around social issues.

As the twenty-first century unfolds, there are developments as well as uncertainties that seem destined to shape the future impact of religious activism in the Northwest. It seems clear that liberal/progressive activists have been more successful in helping shape the liberal identity of Washington and Oregon than have conservative forces. In 2012, Washington became only the fourth state to approve gay marriage. Supported by the Faith Action Network, Washington state's major ecumenical organization, and opposed by conservative Protestant churches and the Catholic Church, the legalization of same-sex marriage provides an example of liberal cultural preference in Washington, particularly on the west side of the state. Likewise, Oregon remains within the "blue" state, or progressive, wing of the political spectrum, as reflected by its support for the right to physician-assisted suicide. In this case as well, churches have been divided. Without doubt, there are other significant cultural forces that influence the liberal social values of the region, but overlooking the role that religious activists have played would be an error.

One particularly compelling example of a recent merging of liberal religious and Northwest cultural voices has been the environmental movement. A few scholars have argued that since the 1970s, the core focus of progressive religious activists has shifted toward "spiritual environmentalism." They make a strong case that mainline Protestants and liberal Catholics have found in the environmental issue a cause that allows them to develop alliances with others who are not formally religious but have great spiritual affinity with the natural environment. Historians Mark Silk and Andrew Walsh argue that this alliance is so strong that together the spiritual environmentalists are creating a critical mass that will establish a new form of civil religion in the region. Effectively, cultural consensus around environmental issues in the Northwest is shaping public policy.[2] There is much to commend in this observation. Without question, environmentalism has become a critical issue in the late twentieth and early twenty-first centuries. It may yet become a galvanizing force in ways that remind one of Prohibition and the Civil Rights Movement.

At the same time, the ecumenical progressive movement remains much more than an environmental religion, and in most respects, including advocacy of justice, retains its identity as an outside, challenging voice. Principal ecumenical agencies (Faith Action Network in Washington state and the Ecumenical Ministries of Oregon) focus on reducing wealth inequality, minimizing violence, and protecting the poor, marginalized, and homeless, in addition to sustaining the environment. Significant effort is being made toward nurturing interfaith dialogue and peacemaking. If those engaged in ecumenical work for progressive causes are sometimes emboldened by legislative initiatives that correspond with their agenda, it is also clear that most liberal activists still feel like outsiders to the corporate and middle-class culture that finds it difficult to pass tax increases to support adequate public services for the poor and marginalized.

Even as progressive religious groups work to influence culture, sometimes successfully and sometimes not, it is evident that mainline Protestantism and perhaps Catholicism are in trouble. Membership in mainline churches continues to shrink. For Methodists, Presbyterians, Lutherans, Quakers, American Baptists, Episcopalians, Congregationalists (United Church of Christ), and Disciples of Christ, long-term prospects appear uncertain at best. Perhaps there will be some consolidation of mainline denominations; these different expressions of Protestantism seem hard pressed to stem the attrition that is taking place. The clergy-abuse scandal within the Catholic Church has taken a significant financial and spiritual toll. Inevitably, the decline in numbers will influence available resources for social ministry and thus threaten mainline religion's impact on the culture. If diminished, the contributions of these Protestant and Catholic organizations and individuals will be hard to replace—they have contributed significantly to the social well-being of the Pacific Northwest.

Meanwhile, despite recently diminished cultural influence in the Northwest, conservative evangelical churches have established a growing regional presence in the twenty-first century. Are conservatives becoming the new religious establishment or are they forming a distinctive counterculture in contrast to the broadly liberal secular culture of the region?[3] The answer appears to be both. As denominationalism continues to atrophy, conservative evangelicals are becoming increasingly the face of institutional religion in the Northwest. Megachurches, comprising mostly socially conservative nondenominational Christians, are growing faster in the early twenty-first century than the region's overall population. Mormons are increasing in significant number. To date, the Mormon Church has been less engaged with public policy issues than its counterparts in mainline Protestantism. But as the church grows, Mormons may be more visible and exert a more socially conservative presence.

So what does the history of religious activism in the Pacific Northwest suggest about how to understand the present and possibly anticipate the future? First, it is quite likely that religious activists will continue to play a role in shaping major social and cultural issues of the region. It is also likely that their greatest influence will emerge out of identity as outsiders to what they perceive as the dominant cultural values. On this note, there may be a word of caution for both those who identify with liberal and those aligned with conservative perspectives. Religious liberals and progressives may rightly believe that a number of their most sacred social values have been adopted by the larger public. They may feel, as has been indicated, that particularly in the area of environmentalism they have found useful allies outside of the church. However, if as some suggest, liberal religion is increasingly indistinguishable from most elements of liberal culture, it may make that religious voice less significant. The history of the Northwest suggests that religious voices are most effective when coming from the outside, with a distinct challenge to offer.

On the other hand, for conservative activists, the opposite caution may be appropriate. Historically, activists have been most effective when the degree of difference between religious and cultural perspectives was moderate. For conservative evangelicals, this has been a challenge during the late twentieth and early twenty-first centuries. Espousal of traditional family values, particularly opposition to homosexuality, feminism, and abortion, have placed conservative religious voices outside of prevailing Northwest cultural norms, especially west of the Cascade Mountains. Although difficult to say with any degree of certainty, it may be that conservative activists are in danger of being too far outside of cultural norms to have relevance. In other words, both liberals and conservatives may be on the verge of lessening their impact, either by being too far inside or too far outside the culture to exercise influence.

Meanwhile, if there are cautionary tales, there are also encouraging signs of promising religious influence. New expressions of religious activism, a hybrid of liberal and conservative impulses, are taking shape; these could significantly influence the role that religious activists play in public life in the Northwest. For instance, there is a comparatively high degree of religious entrepreneurial activity in the region. This is evident in progressive evangelicals' involvement with issues related to the poor, human trafficking, and the environment. One such individual is Ray Bakke, a self-identified evangelical, who cut his teeth on urban ministry in Chicago in the 1970s. Bakke returned to Seattle in the 1990s to establish the Bakke Graduate University, founded to train leaders from all over the world to serve the poor and marginalized in urban settings. A second example of an evangelical church that has continued to evolve in its identity as a hybrid between the evangelical and mainline is Seattle's University Presbyterian Church. One of the largest churches in the city, this congregation is located adjacent to the University of Washington. Its members participate regularly in constructing homes for the poor through Habitat for Humanity, teaching English as a second language to refugees and immigrants, and advocating against human trafficking.

Rick McKinley is another religious entrepreneur who has been enormously successful building the Imago Dei Church in Portland, attended by nearly two thousand people weekly. Part of the emerging church movement, Imago Dei is similar to other large evangelical churches in that it is theologically quite conservative and its leadership is mostly male. Imago Dei, however, is active in serving the homeless, ministering to refugee families, offering food to the poor, and raising consciousness about the environment. And there are other influential churches not easily categorized as conservative or progressive. For example, Eugene Cho at Quest Church in Seattle leads a congregation that is evangelical in character but also is urban, multigenerational, and multiethnic, with a commitment to serve the homeless, promote racial reconciliation, and sponsor refugees. In addition, evangelical parachurch organizations, such as Youth For Christ, increasingly combine evangelistic impulses with urban outreach and social services.

In 2014, EastLake Community Church in Bothell near Seattle and its pastor Ryan Meeks attracted national attention as one of the first mega-evangelical churches in the nation to openly welcome LGBT individuals. The church has started performing gay weddings. At Overlake Christian Church, another large greater-Seattle evangelical church, pastors hold a weekly Bible study for approximately forty LGBT adults. All of these examples clearly hint of the possibility of significant change in the religious landscape in the near future in the Pacific Northwest.[4]

One additional area of emerging religious activity is interfaith dialogue. While it is still too early to see whether this will develop into a more significant voice in public life, it has considerable potential for impact. The Ecumenical Ministries of Oregon is actively promoting interfaith dialogue on a number of fronts. Sheikh Jamal Rahman, founder of Seattle's Interfaith Community Church, Rabbi Ted Falcon of the Bet Alef Synagogue, and Pastor Don Mackenzie from Seattle's University Congregational Church have appeared together often for more than a decade, promoting a vision of reconciliation and justice.[5]

One thing seems certain: despite the complexity of the religious landscape, religious activists will retain influence in the Pacific Northwest. This influence is likely to be strongest on issues where religious persons, whether liberal, conservative, or some mix of the two, can make a compelling moral argument in support of justice and against oppression. Clearly, religious activists will continue to play a role in the environmental movement. But the history of the Northwest tells the story of even broader influence. People like Mother Joseph, Thomas Lamb Eliot, Beatrice Cannady, Mark Matthews, Lola Baldwin, Sherman Burgoyne, Father Edwin Vincent O'Hara, Rabbi Raphael Levine, Samuel McKinney, Jon Nelson, Archbishop Raymond Hunthausen, and many, many others who thought of themselves largely as outsiders stood for a belief in something that needed to change. They became involved in the public square, made clear their religious convictions, and organized others to act on behalf of a moral vision. In some cases, laws, agencies, and institutions were resistant to change. But many times the impact of these religious activists was significant and constituted a compelling force in the social and political history of the Pacific Northwest.

ACKNOWLEDGMENTS

I am deeply indebted to many people for their support, encouragement, and constructive criticism of this project over many years. I am particularly grateful for the role that Tom Edwards has played from beginning to end. He encouraged me in all the right ways; he read the manuscript and offered a number of helpful suggestions and made me believe that this project was worth doing. Ron White has also played a significant role by offering careful criticism and wise counsel as a historian. Patricia O'Connell Killen, herself an astute historian of religion in the Pacific Northwest, read the manuscript and encouraged me to pursue the theme of religious outsiders as an important organizing principle.

This project allowed me to reconnect with the professor who developed my initial curiosity in history at Pacific Lutheran University—David Johnson. He too offered insight and encouragement at important points along the way. I also want to acknowledge the late Lewis O. Saum, my advisor at the University of Washington, who first suggested that I explore topics related to religion in the Pacific Northwest. In addition, James Wellman, Howard Berger, and John Findlay have provided both encouragement and counsel through the years.

Whitworth University has been a wonderful place to work, and my colleagues have supported this endeavor in numerous ways. Arlin Migliazzo and Jerry Sittser read earlier versions of the manuscript and offered helpful comments. Bill Robinson's encouragement through the years has meant a great deal. My other colleagues in the Department of History—Corliss Slack, Jim Hunt, Tony Clark, Janet Hauck, Larry Burnley, and Rafaela Acevedo-Field—have been especially supportive. Many of my students have been helpful along the way, and these include Samantha Keenan, Kyna Herzinger, Jasmine Wilson, and David Perrier.

Over the years I have received much needed assistance from numerous archivists at the University of Washington, the University of Oregon, Whitworth University, Portland Community College, the Oregon Historical Society Research Library, the Washington State Historical Society in Tacoma, the Official Archives of the Catholic Archdiocese of Seattle, the archives at First Presbyterian Church, Portland, the offices of the Ecumenical Ministries of Oregon, and the United Methodist Church Archives in Salem, Oregon. Seth Dalby and Laura Arksey have been particularly helpful. I also benefited from a grant from the Louisville Institute at the Louisville Presbyterian Theological Seminary.

The staff at Oregon State University Press, including Mary Braun, Micki Reaman, and Marty Brown, have been particularly helpful, and Lee Motteler improved the manuscript with his copyediting.

Lora-Ellen McKinney and Juni Nelson provided important assistance, and I also owe a debt of thanks to Reverend Richard Finch and Bishop Martin Wells for their help and steadfast encouragement.

My longtime conversation partners, John Beck, Bruce Bjerke, and Mark Houglum, have offered support and encouragement from beginning to end. My children, Joel and Marta, have always been a source of strength for their father, and lastly my wife Kathy Storm has helped make this a considerably better book, not only with her personal support but also with her careful editing and insightful criticisms.

NOTES

Preface

1. Linda Tamura, *Nisei Soldiers Break Their Silence: Coming Home to Hood River* (Seattle: University of Washington Press, 2012), 148–149.
2. Tamura, *Nisei Soldiers,* 169–170; "Japanese-American," file United Methodist Church, Oregon-Idaho Annual Conference, Salem, Oregon.
3. *Pacific Citizen,* April 19, 1947.
4. The number of works on Native American history and culture in the Pacific Northwest is voluminous; among the most significant works that focus on the encounter between missionaries and Native Americans in the region include Clifford Drury's *Marcus Whitman, M.D.: Pioneer and Martyr* (Caldwell, Idaho: Caxton Printers, 1937) and his *Henry Harmon Spalding* (Caldwell, Idaho: Caxton Printers, 1936); a more sympathetic view of the Indian perspective is Julie Roy Jeffrey's *Converting the West: A Biography of Narcissa Whitman* (Norman: University of Oklahoma Press, 1991); see also Alvin M. Josephy Jr., *The Nez Perce Indians and the Opening of the West* (Boston: Houghton Mifflin, 1997), reprint (New Haven: Yale University Press, 1965); Robert Loewenberg, *Equality on the Oregon Frontier: Jason Lee and the Methodist Mission, 1834–43* (Seattle: University of Washington Press, 1976); Robert H. Ruby and John A. Brown have written numerous books on Indians in the Pacific Northwest, including *Indians of the Pacific Northwest: A History* (Norman: University of Oklahoma Press, 1981); Christopher L. Miller, *Prophetic Worlds: Indians and Whites on the Columbia Plateau* (New Brunswick, NJ: Rutgers University Press, 1985); of the more recent works of importance are Larry Cebula, *Plateau Indians and the Quest for Spiritual Power, 1700–1850* (Lincoln: University of Nebraska Press, 2003); Albert Furtwangler, *Bringing Indians to the Book* (Seattle: University of Washington Press, 2005); Robert Ignatius Burns, S.J., *The Jesuits and the Indian Wars of the Northwest* (New Haven, CT: Yale University Press, 1966); Wilfred P. Schoenberg, *A History of the Catholic Church in the Pacific Northwest 1743–1983* (Washington, DC: Pastoral Press, 1987); Margaret Whitehead, "Christianity a Matter of Choice: The Historic Role of Indian Catechists in Oregon Territory and British Columbia," *Pacific Northwest Quarterly* 72 (July 1981), 98–106; Bonnie Sue Lewis, *Creating Christian Indians: Native Clergy in the Presbyterian Church* (Norman: University of Oklahoma Press, 2003); Francis Paul Prucha, "Two Roads to Conversion: Protestant and Catholic Missionaries in the Pacific Northwest," *Pacific Northwest Quarterly* 79 (1988), 130–137; Robert Carriker, *Father Peter John De Smet: Jesuit in the West* (Norman: University of Oklahoma Press, 1985).

5. Charles Pierce Le Warne, *Utopias on Puget Sound 1885–1915* (Seattle: University of Washington Press, 1975); James J. Kopp, *Eden within Eden: Oregon's Utopian Heritage* (Corvallis: Oregon State University Press, 2009).

6. Carlos Arnaldo Schwantes, *The Pacific Northwest: An Interpretive History* (Lincoln: University of Nebraska Press, 1989,1996), 14.

7. E. J. Klemme, in *The Pacific Northwest Pulpit*, compiled by Paul Little (New York: Methodist Book Concern, 1915), 259.

8. Patricia O'Connell Killen, "Patterns of the Past, Prospects for the Future: Religion in the None Zone," in *Religion and Public Life in the Pacific Northwest: The None Zone*, ed. Patricia O'Connell Killen and Mark Silk (Walnut Creek, CA: Alta Mira Press, 2004), 9–20.

9. R. Laurence Moore, *Religious Outsiders and the Making of Americans* (New York: Oxford University Press, 1986), vii–xv.

10. Patricia Nelson Limerick, *Something in the Soil: Legacies and Reckonings in the New West* (New York: W. W. Norton & Company, 2000), 314–315; Ferenc Szasz, "The Clergy and the Myth of the American West," *Church History* 59 (December 1990), 497–506.

Chapter 1: Here Come the Victorians

1. *Seattle Post-Intelligencer*, July 30, 1899.

2. *Spokesman-Review*, September 27, 1899.

3. Wilfred P. Schoenberg, S. J., *A History of the Catholic Church in the Pacific Northwest* (Washington, DC: Pastoral Press, 1987), 484.

4. Richard White, *"It's Your Misfortune and None of My Own": A History of the American West* (Norman: University of Oklahoma Press, 1991), 304.

5. Julian Rolph, quoted in White, *"It's Your Misfortune,"* 304.

6. Murray Morgan, *Skid Road: An Informal Portrait of Seattle* (New York: Viking Press, 1951), 75.

7. Eugene Clinton Elliott, *A History of Variety-Vaudeville in Seattle: From the Beginning to 1914* (Seattle: University of Washington Press, 1944), 26; see also Kathy Peiss, *Cheap Amusements: Working Women and Leisure in Turn-of the-Century New York* (Philadelphia: Temple University Press, 1986), 16–18.

8. David T. Courtwright, *Violent Land: Single Men and Social Disorder from the Frontier to the Inner City* (Cambridge, MA: Harvard University Press, 1996), 4.

9. *Every Sunday* (Tacoma), November 16, 1889.

10. *Walla Walla Statesman*, January 3, 1893.

11. Elliott, *A History of Variety-Vaudeville in Seattle*, 25.

12. *Spokesman-Review*, March 14, 1895.

13. Louis Stevenson, *The Victorian Homefront: American Thought and Culture 1860–1880* (New York: Twayne Publishers, 1991), xx.

14. In 1909, the Washington legislature passed the "Sabbath Breaking" law (Chapter 249, Section 242, Laws of 1909), which prohibited most businesses from operating on Sunday. The law was commonly called the "Blue Law," and it was a very broad expansion of an 1881 law that only prohibited "fighting or offering to fight, horse-racing or dancing" on Sunday. Religious motivations played a major role in its adoption. However, people also viewed it as being "progressive" legislation that prohibited most employers from requiring their employees to work seven days a

week, in an era before workers had the protection of state labor regulations and labor union collective bargaining agreements.

15. Thomas William Bibb, *History of Early Common School Education* (Seattle: University of Washington Press, 1929), 62.

16. David Tyack, "The Kingdom of God and the Common School: Protestant Ministers and the Educational Awakening in the West," *Harvard Educational Review* 36 (fall 1966), 450; David B. Tyack, "Bureaucracy and the Common School: The Example of Portland, Oregon, 1851–1913," *American Quarterly* 19 (fall 1967), 475–498.

17. Tyack, "Kingdom of God," 451.

18. Frederick E. Bolton and Thomas W. Bibb, *History of Education in Washington*, Bulletin 1934 No. 9 (Washington, DC: US Government Printing Office, 1934), 98.

19. Bolton and Bibb, *History of Education,* 99.

20. Tyack, "Kingdom of God," 461.

21. Tyack, "Kingdom of God,"466.

22. Tyack, "Kingdom of God," 466.

23. Tyack, "Kingdom of God," 465.

24. Donald J. Sevetson, *Atkinson: Pioneer Oregon Educator* (North Charleston, SC: Donald Sevetson, 2011), 13–35.

25. Tyack, "Kingdom of God," 447.

26. Atkinson, quoted in Tyack, "Kingdom of God," 456; Sevetson, *Atkinson: Pioneer Oregon Educator*, 55–72.

27. Donald J. Sevetson, "George Atkinson, Harvey Scott, and the Portland High School Controversy of 1880," *Oregon Historical Quarterly* 108 (fall 2007), 458–473.

28. Tyack, "Kingdom of God," 458.

29. Tyack, "Kingdom of God," 467–468.

30. Tyack, "Kingdom of God," 468.

31. Sevetson, "George Atkinson, Harvey Scott," 458–473; *Oregonian*, February 9, 1880; February 12, 1880; February 24, 1880; February 25, 1880; March 2, 1880.

32. Sevetson, "George Atkinson, Harvey Scott," 464–465.

33. Thomas Lamb Eliot quoted in Sevetson, "George Atkinson, Harvey Scott," 465.

34. Sevetson, "George Atkinson, Harvey Scott," 471; see Sevetson, *Atkinson: Pioneer Oregon Educator,* 201–213.

35. See James Hitchman, *Liberal Arts Colleges in Oregon & Washington, 1842–1980* (Bellingham: Western Washington University, 1981).

36. Alfred O. Gray, *Not by Might: The Story of Whitworth College, 1890–1965* (Spokane: Whitworth Press, 1965), 13.

37. *Whitworth College Catalogue, 1892–1893* (Sumner, WA, Whitworth College, 1892), 26, Whitworth University Library, Spokane, WA.

38. *Whitworth College Catalogue, 1902–03* (Tacoma, WA: Whitworth College, 1902), 12, Whitworth University Library, Spokane, WA.

39. *Whitworth College Catalogue, 1891–92* (Sumner, WA: Whitworth College, 1891), 27, Whitworth University Library, Spokane, WA.

40. James Earley, *The University of Puget Sound 1888–1988: On the Frontier of Leadership* (Tacoma, WA: University of Puget Sound, 1987), 17.

41. Hitchman, *Liberal Arts Colleges,* 80.

42. Earley, *University of Puget Sound,* 17.

43. Philip A. Nordquist, *Educating for Service: Pacific Lutheran University, 1890–1990* (Tacoma, WA: Pacific Lutheran University Press, 1990), 53.

44. Nordquist, *Pacific Lutheran University,* 37.

45. *Catalogue of Gonzaga College for the College Year 1896–7* (Spokane: Pigott & French, 1897), 11, Gonzaga University Archives, Spokane, WA.
46. Philip Gleason, *Contending with Modernity: Catholic Higher Education in the Twentieth Century* (New York: Oxford University Press, 1995), 60.
47. G. Thomas Edwards, *The Triumph of Tradition: The Emergence of Whitman College 1859–1924* (Walla Walla, WA: Whitman College, 1992), 124.
48. Edwards, *Whitman College,* 125–126.
49. Edwards, *Whitman College,* 138.
50. Edwards, *Whitman College,* 164.
51. Edwards, *Whitman College,* 190.
52. Edwards, *Whitman College,* 212.
53. Edwards, *Whitman College,* 234.
54. Enoch Bryan, quoted in George A. Frykman, *Creating the People's University: Washington State University, 1890–1990* (Pullman: Washington State University Press, 1990), 15.
55. Frykman, *Creating the People's University,* 26.
56. Charles M. Gates, *The First Century at the University of Washington 1861–1961* (Seattle: University of Washington Press, 1961), 31.
57. Gates, *University of Washington,* 32.
58. Stevenson, *Victorian Homefront,* xxii.

Chapter 2: Women to the Rescue

1. Valentine Prichard, "1906 Annual Report," People's Institute file, First Presbyterian Church Archives, Portland, OR.
2. Important works on the history of women in the Pacific Northwest include Sandra Haarsager, *Organized Womanhood: Cultural Politics in the Pacific Northwest, 1840–1920* (Norman: University of Oklahoma Press, 1997); Peggy Pascoe, *Relations of Rescue: The Search for Female Moral Authority in the American West, 1874–1939* (New York: Oxford University Press, 1990); and *Women in Pacific Northwest History*, ed. Karen Blair (Seattle: University of Washington Press, 2001, rev. edition).
3. Sister Dorothy Lentz, S. P., *The Way It Was in Providence Schools* (Montreal: Sisters of Providence, 1978), iii; Wilfred P. Schoenberg, *A History of the Catholic Church in the Pacific Northwest, 1743–1983* (Washington, DC: Pastoral Press, 1987), 155–156.
4. Bishop Augustin-Maglioire Blanchet is not to be confused with his older brother, François Norbet Blanchet. François Blanchet was one of the first Catholic priests to arrive in what was then known as Oregon Country. He was the first bishop and archbishop of the Archdiocese of Oregon City, which is now known as the Archdiocese of Portland, Oregon. Two years younger, Augustin-Magloire Blanchet was first appointed to the Diocese of Walla Walla in 1846. In 1850, he was assigned to the newly formed Diocese of Nesqually, which later became the Archdiocese of Seattle. See Patricia O'Connell Killen, *Abundance of Grace: The History of the Archdiocese of Seattle 1850–2000* (Strasbourg, France: Editions du Signe, 2000), 6–11.
5. Lentz, *Providence Schools,* v; Schoenberg, *History of the Catholic Church,* 156.
6. Lentz, *Providence Schools,* 3.
7. Lentz, *Providence Schools,* v.
8. Killen, *Abundance of Grace,* 26; by 1875, the sisters had opened St. Vincent Hospital in Portland, which became the first permanent hospital in Oregon and is now called Providence St. Vincent Medical Center. Two years later, three Sisters of Providence

opened the King County Poor Farm, which became the foundation for Providence Hospital in Seattle. Other hospitals were established in Walla Walla (St. Mary, 1880), Spokane (Sacred Heart, 1886), Yakima (St. Elizabeth, 1891), Colfax (St. Ignatius, 1893—now Whitman County), and Olympia (St. Peter, 1887).

9. John C. Shideler, *A Century of Caring: The Sisters of Providence at Sacred Heart Medical Center* (Spokane: Sacred Heart Medical Center, 1986), 7–17.

10. Nancy Engle, "Benefiting a City: Women, Respectability and Reform in Spokane, Washington, 1886–1910" (unpublished PhD dissertation, University of Florida, 2003), xii.

11. *Pacific Christian Advocate*, December 14, 1904; Priscilla Gilkey, Margaret Crabtree, and Terren Roloff, *The Deaconess Story 1896–1996* (Spokane: Deaconess Medical Center), 5.

12. Norman H. Clark, *The Dry Years: Prohibition and Social Change in Washington* (Seattle: University of Washington Press, 1965), 28–39; Malcolm H. Clark Jr., "The War on the Webfoot Saloon," *Oregon Historical Quarterly* (March 1957), 4–11; Jack S. Blocker Jr., *"Give to the Winds Thy Fears": The Woman's Temperance Crusade, 1873–1874* (Westport, CT: Greenwood Press, 1985), 7–26; Barbara Epstein, *The Politics of Domesticity: Women, Evangelism, and Temperance in Nineteenth-Century America* (Middletown, CT: Wesleyan University Press, 1981), 89–114; Dale E. Soden, "The Woman's Christian Temperance Union in the Pacific Northwest: The Battle for Cultural Control," *Pacific Northwest Quarterly* 94 (fall 2003), 197–207.

13. Ruth Bordin, *Frances Willard: A Biography* (Chapel Hill: University of North Carolina Press, 1986), 155–174; Carolyn De Swarte Gifford, "'The Woman's Cause Is Man's'? Frances Willard and the Social Gospel," in *Gender and the Social Gospel,* ed. Wendy J. Deichmann Edwards and Carolyn De Swarte Gifford (Urbana and Chicago: University of Illinois Press, 2003), 26.

14. Sharon Anne Cook, *"Through Sunshine and Shadow": The Woman's Christian Temperance Union, Evangelicalism, and Reform in Ontario, 1874–1930* (Montreal: McGill-Queen's University Press, 1995), 32; Nancy G. Gardner, "The Woman's Christian Temperance Union: A Woman's Branch of American Protestantism," in *Re-Forming the Center: American Protestantism, 1900 to the Present,* ed. Douglas Jacobsen and William Vance Trollinger Jr. (Grand Rapids, MI: William B. Eerdmans Publishing Co., 1998), 271–283.

15. Gifford, "Frances Willard and the Social Gospel," 26.

16. Haarsager, *Organized Womanhood,* 72.

17. Lucia Additon, *Twenty Eventful Years of the Oregon Woman's Christian Temperance Union, 1880–1900* (Portland: Gotshall Printing Co., 1904), 49.

18. *Spokesman Review,* March, 17, 1909.

19. *White Ribbon Bulletin: Official Organ of the Western Washington W.C.T.U.,* April 1909, Washington State Historical Society, Tacoma, WA.

20. Otto Wilson, *Fifty Years' Work with Girls 1883–1933: A Story of the Florence Crittenton Homes* (Alexandria, VA: National Florence Crittenton Mission, 1933), 415–418, 448.

21. Haarsager, *Organized Womanhood,* 78–79.

22. *White Ribbon Bulletin: Official Organ of the Western Washington W.C.T.U.,* March 1908, Washington State Historical Society, Tacoma, WA.

23. Esther Mumford Hall, *Seattle's Black Victorians 1852–1901* (Seattle: Ananse Press, 1980), 151; Priscilla Pope-Levison, "Emma Ray in Black and White: The Intersection of Race, Region, and Religion," *Pacific Northwest Quarterly* 102 (summer 2011), 107–131; Haarsager, *Organized Womanhood,* 96–97.

■ ──

24. Epstein, *The Politics of Domesticity*, 1–2.
25. *White Ribbon Bulletin*, October 1907.
26. *White Ribbon Bulletin*, November 1902.
27. Haarsager, *Organized Womanhood*,10; for analysis of the WCTU in the broader context of women's issues in the Pacific Northwest, see also Pascoe, *Relations of Rescue*, 17; Ronald C. White Jr. and C. Howard Hopkins, *The Social Gospel: Religion and Reform in Changing America* (Philadelphia: Temple University Press, 1976).
28. Additon, *Twenty Eventful Years*, 42.
29. *White Ribbon Bulletin*, November 1908; for a more extensive discussion of the impact of the WCTU on the efforts to ban cigarettes, see Cassandra Tate, *The Triumph of "The Little White Slaver"* (New York: Oxford University Press, 1999), 30–32, 42–43.
30. Haarsager, *Organized Womanhood*, 81.
31. Epstein, *The Politics of Domesticity*, 1–2.
32. Haarsager, *Organized Womanhood*, 68.
33. Pascoe, *Relations of Rescue*, xvi.
34. Pascoe, *Relations of Rescue*, 10.
35. J. Dudley Weaver Jr., *A Legacy of Faith: First Presbyterian Church Portland, Oregon 1854–2004* (Aloha, OR: Beachwalker Press, 2004), 109.
36. Weaver, *A Legacy of Faith*, 108–110; *Portland Oregonian*, March 25, 1923.
37. Weaver, *A Legacy of Faith*, 110–111.
38. Weaver, *A Legacy of Faith*, 110–111; Valentine Pritchard, "Origin and Development of Settlement Work in Portland Including Free Medical Work," 1939, People's Institute File, First Presbyterian Portland archives.
39. Steven Lowenstein, *The Jews of Oregon 1850–1950* (Portland: Jewish Historical Society of Oregon, 1987), 85.
40. Lowenstein, *Jews of Oregon*, 138; William Toll, *The Making of an Ethnic Middle Class: Portland Jewry over Four Generations* (Albany: State University of New York Press,1982), 61, 103.
41. Lowenstein, *Jews of Oregon*, 141.
42. Molly Cone, Howard Droker, and Jacqueline Williams, *Family of Strangers: Building a Jewish Community in Washington State* (Seattle: University of Washington Press, 2003), 94; Jean Porter Divine, *From Settlement House to Neighborhood House 1906–1976: An Historical Survey of a Pioneering Seattle Social Service Agency* (Seattle: Neighborhood House, 1976).
43. Lowenstein, *Jews of Oregon*, 138–139; Cone, Droker, and Williams, *Family of Strangers*, 92–93, 201–203.
44. Lowenstein, *Jews of Oregon*, 138–139.
45. Lowenstein, *Jews of Oregon*, 145.
46. "History of Portland YWCA," http://womhist.alexanderstreet.com/portywca/intro.htm.
47. "Annual Reports 1904–1906,"YWCA Records, Special Collections and Manuscripts, University of Washington Libraries, Box 1, Folder 16.
48. Mildred Tanner Andrews, *Seattle Women: A Legacy of Community Development* (Seattle: YWCA, 1984), 24–29; Mildred Tanner Andrews, *Washington Women as Path Breakers* (Dubuque, IA: Kendall/Hunt, 1989), 60–66; Mildred Tanner Andrews, *Woman's Place: A Guide to Seattle and King County History* (Seattle: Gemil Press, 1994), 200–203, 253; YWCA Records 1903–1982, Special Collections and Manuscripts, University of Washington Libraries, "Spirit of Seattle YWCA," Box 1, Folder 1.
49. Gary Miranda and Rick Read, *Splendid Audacity: The Story of Pacific University* (Seattle: Documentary Book Publishers, 2000), 17–19.

50. Miranda and Read, *Splendid Audacity*, 22.

51. Doris H. Pieroth, *The Hutton Settlement: A Home for One Man's Family* (Spokane: Hutton Settlement, 2003), 14–15.

52. Patricia Susan Hart, *A Home for Every Child: The Washington Children's Home Society in the Progressive Era* (Seattle: University of Washington Press, 2010), 16–23.

53. Hart, *A Home for Every Child*, 13–14; *A Century of Turning Hope into Reality: A 100-Year Retrospect of Children's Home Society in Washington State* (published by Children's Home Society Washington; Dana Blue, researcher and contributing writer; Patti Harris, contributing writer and project coordinator; Esme Ryan, editor, 1996), 12.

54. *A Century of Turning Hope into Reality*, 14.

55. *A Century of Turning Hope into Reality*, 14.

56. *A Century of Turning Hope into Reality*, 15.

57. Andrews, *Woman's Place*, 137–138; L. E. Bragg, *More Than Petticoats: Remarkable Washington Women* (Helena, MT: Falcon, 1998), 111–119; Cora G. Chase, *Unto the Least: A Biographical Sketch of Mother Ryther* (Seattle: Shorey Book Store, facsimile reproduction, 1972); *Kitsap Herald*, October 5, 1934; *Seattle Times*, June 16, 1946.

58. Emma Ray, *Twice Sold, Twice Ransomed* (Chicago: Free Methodist Publishing House, 2000), 75.

59. Mildred Tanner Andrews, "Rhyther, Mother Olive," HistoryLink.org. Accessed April 10, 2015. http://www.historylink.org/index.cfm?DisplayPage=output.cfm&file_id=546.

60. Andrews, "Rhyther, Mother Olive."

61. Emilie B. Schwabacher, *A Place for Children: A Personal History of Children's Orthopedic Hospital and Medical Center* (Seattle: Children's Orthopedic Hospital and Medical Center, 1977), 3.

62. Walt Crowley, David W. Wilma, and the HistoryLink Staff, *Hope on the Hill: The First Century of Seattle Children's Hospital* (Seattle: University of Washington Press and History Ink/History Link, 2010), 13–15.

63. Gloria E. Myers, *A Municipal Mother: Portland's Lola Greene Baldwin, America's First Policewoman* (Corvallis: Oregon State University Press, 1995), 10.

64. Myers, *Municipal Mother*, 11.

65. Myers, *Municipal Mother*, 9.

66. Myers, *Municipal Mother*, 11.

67. Myers, *Municipal Mother*, 14.

68. Myers, *Municipal Mother*, 14–15.

69. Myers, *Municipal Mother*, 21–22.

70. Myers, *Municipal Mother*, 34.

71. Kathy Peiss, *Cheap Amusements: Working Women and Leisure in Turn-of-the-Century New York* (Philadelphia: Temple University Press, 1986), 88–114.

72. Myers, *Municipal Mother*, 41.

73. Myers, *Municipal Mother*, 54–57.

74. Myers, *Municipal Mother*, 59–61.

75. Myers, *Municipal Mother*, 68.

76. Myers, *Municipal Mother*, 3.

Chapter 3: The Social Gospel

1. *Eleventh Annual Report of the Men's Resort and People's Institute*, March 1907, Men's Resort File, Mission, First Presbyterian Church Portland, archives, Portland, Oregon.
2. Paul Boyer, *Urban Masses and Moral Order in America: 1820–1920* (Cambridge: Harvard University Press, 1978), viii.
3. Boyer, *Urban Masses*, 165–167.
4. The classic account of the Social Gospel is Charles Hopkins, *The Rise of the Social Gospel in American Protestantism, 1865–1915* (New Haven, CT: Yale University Press, 1940); more recent scholarship has centered on groups traditionally ignored by the classic accounts of Hopkins and Robert Handy. See *Gender and the Social Gospel*, ed. Wendy J. Deichmann Edwards and Carolyn De Swarte Gifford (Urbana: University of Illinois Press, 2003); John Patrick McDowell, *The Social Gospel in the South: The Woman's Home Mission Movement in the Methodist Episcopal Church, South, 1886–1939* (Baton Rouge: Louisiana State University, 1982); Janet Forsythe Fishburn, *The Fatherhood of God and the Victorian Family: The Social Gospel in America* (Philadelphia: Fortress, 1981); and Ralph E. Luker, *The Social Gospel in Black and White: American Racial Reform, 1885–1912* (Chapel Hill: University of North Carolina Press, 1991).
5. Robert Handy spelled out the theological emphases of the movement in the introduction to *The Social Gospel in America, 1870–1920*, ed. Robert T. Handy (New York: Oxford University Press, 1966), 10–11.
6. Ferenc Szasz, *Religion in the Modern American West* (Tucson: University of Arizona Press, 2000), 7.
7. John F. Scheck, "Thomas Lamb Eliot and His Vision of an Enlightened Community," in *The Western Shore: Oregon Country Essays Honoring the American Revolution* (Portland: Oregon Historical Society, 1976), 237.
8. E. Kimbarck MacColl, *The Shaping of the City: Business and Politics in Portland, Oregon 1885 to 1915* (Portland: Georgian Press Co., 1976), 178.
9. Thomas Lamb Eliot, "A Sermon on the Times," May 13, 1888, quoted in Scheck, "Thomas Lamb Eliot," 235.
10. John F. Scheck, "Transplanting a Tradition: Thomas Lamb Eliot and the Unitarian Conscience in the Pacific Northwest, 1865–1905" (University of Oregon, PhD dissertation, 1969).
11. Steven Lowenstein, *The Jews of Oregon 1850–1950* (Portland, OR: Jewish Historical Society, 1987), 86.
12. Stephen Wise, quoted in Lowenstein, *The Jews of Oregon*, 86.
13. Lowenstein, *The Jews of Oregon*, 86.
14. William Toll, *Making of the Ethnic Middle Class: Portland Jewry over Four Generations* (Albany: State University of New York 1982), 98.
15. James Gerard Shaw, *Edwin Vincent O'Hara: American Prelate* (New York: Farrar, Straus and Cudahy, 1957), 2.
16. Shaw, *Edwin Vincent O'Hara*, 12–13.
17. Robert D. Johnston, *The Radical Middle Class: Populist Democracy and the Question of Capitalism in Progressive Era, Portland, Oregon* (Princeton, NJ: Princeton University Press, 2003), 24–25; Wilfred P. Schoenberg, S. J., *A History of the Catholic Church in the Pacific Northwest* (Washington, DC: Pastoral Press, 1897), 515–516.
18. Jan C. Dawson, "A Social Gospel Portrait: The Life of Sydney Dix Strong, 1860–1938" (unpublished master's thesis, University of Washington, 1972).
19. Dawson, "A Social Gospel Portrait."

20. Julia Niebuhr Eulenberg, "Samuel Koch: Seattle's Social Justice Rabbi" (unpublished master's thesis, University of Washington, 1984), 59.
21. Molly Cone, Howard Droker, and Jacqueline Williams, *Family of Strangers: Building a Jewish Community in Washington State* (Seattle: University of Washington Press, 2003), 108.
22. William P. O'Connell, "Fifty Golden Years," *The Catholic Northwest Progress,* November 29, 1932, 24.
23. O'Connell, "Fifty Golden Years," 21–27.
24. Mark Matthews, quoted in *Seattle Times,* February, 3, 1902, 7; Dale Soden, *The Reverend Mark Matthews: An Activist in the Progressive Era* (Seattle: University of Washington Press, 2001), 68.
25. Mark Matthews, "The New City—Newly Discovered Seattle," *Sermonettes,* January–June, 1911. Mark Matthews Papers, University of Washington Libraries, Seattle. Matthews Papers are held at the University of Washington Libraries in Seattle, Washington, and consist primarily of scrapbooks and typescript sermons (hereafter cited as Matthews Papers).
26. Matthews Papers, "Tramp of the Ages," *Sermonettes,* January–July 1908.
27. Matthews Papers, "What Is Seattle's Moral Sentiment?" *Sermonettes,* July–December 1910.
28. Matthews Papers, "Christian Socialism," *Sermonettes,* September 1906–January 1907.
29. Gail Bederman, *Manliness and Civilization: A Cultural History of Gender and Race in the United States, 1880–1917* (Chicago: University of Chicago Press, 1995), 18.
30. Matthews Papers, "Wanted: More Man in Men," *Sermonettes,* 1907; see Clifford Putney, *Muscular Christianity: Manhood and Sports in Protestant America, 1880–1920* (Cambridge, MA: Harvard University Press, 2001), 11–44.
31. Matthews Papers, "Homeless Man," *Sermonettes,* January–July, 1909.
32. Matthews Papers, "Friendless Man," *Sermonettes,* January–July 1909.
33. Matthews Papers, "Penniless Man," "Heartless Man," "Conscienceless Man," "Childless Man," and "Christless Man," *Sermonettes,* January–July, 1909.
34. Scheck, "Transplanting a Tradition," 219.
35. Scheck, "Transplanting a Tradition," 220, 243, 246.
36. Scheck, "Transplanting a Tradition," 220.
37. Stephen Wise, *Challenging Years: The Autobiography of Stephen Wise* (New York: G. P. Putnam's Sons, 1949), 56.
38. Wise, *Challenging Years,* 57.
39. Dawson, "A Social Gospel Portrait," 40.
40. Eulenberg, "Samuel Koch," 83.
41. Richard C. Berner, *Seattle 1900–1920: From Boomtown, Urban Turbulence, to Restoration,* vol. 1 (Seattle: Charles Press, 1991), 189.
42. Scheck, "Transplanting a Tradition," 227.
43. Scheck, "Transplanting a Tradition," 223.
44. Matthews Papers, "Coffee or Coffin House—Which?" *Sermonettes,* 1907.
45. Matthews Papers, "Society's Crimes Due to a Diseased Nervous System," *Sermonettes,* 1907.
46. Soden, *Reverend Mark Matthews,* 80.
47. Boyer, *Urban Masses and Moral Order,* 112–120.
48. "Forty Years of the Young Men's Christian Association of Portland, Oregon 1869–1909," typescript in Historical Library, Young Men's Christian Association, Broadway, NY.

■ --

49. Putney, *Muscular Christianity*, 64–71.
50. For more detailed information on some of the activities of the Seattle YMCA in its early years, see Cassandra Tate, "Young Men's Christian Association (YMCA) of Greater Seattle—Part 2: Expansion, 1900–1930," History Link.org (accessed on April 13, 2015): http://www.historylink.org/_content/printer_friendly/pf_output.cfm?file_id=3099; for more specific information on Spokane's YMCA, see Lynn Gibson, "Spokane's YMCA: 125 Years of Building Strong Kids, Strong Families, and Strong Communities," 2009 Commemorative Booklet, n.p.
51. Ford Ottman, *J. Wilbur Chapman: A Biography* (Whitefish, MT: Kessinger Publishing, LLC, 1920, reprinted 2008); William G. McLoughlin Jr., *Modern Revivalism* (New York: Ronald Press, 1959); Dale E. Soden, "Anatomy of a Presbyterian Urban Revival: J. W. Chapman in the Pacific Northwest," *American Presbyterians: Journal of Presbyterian History* 64:1 (spring 1986), 49–57.
52. *Seattle Times*, April 18, 1905.
53. Richard P. Poethig, "Charles Stelzle and the Roots of the Presbyterian Industrial Mission," *Journal of Presbyterian History* 77:1 (spring 1999), 31–32.
54. *Seattle Times*, April 14, 1905.
55. Charles Stelzle, *A Son of the Bowery* (New York: George H. Doran Co., 1926), 215.
56. For an in-depth account of the Haywood trial, see *Big Trouble: A Murder in a Small Western Town Sets off a Struggle for the Soul of America* (New York: Touchstone, 1997); Carlos Schwantes, *The Pacific Northwest: An Interpretive History* (Lincoln: University of Nebraska Press, 1989, 1996), 324–325.
57. Matthews Papers, Scrapbook #8.
58. Matthews Papers, "The Emancipation of the Laboring Classes," *Sermonettes*, January–July 1910.
59. Matthews Papers, "Song of the Saw," *Sermonettes*, September 1906–January 1907.
60. Matthews Papers, Scrapbook #1.
61. Matthews Papers, "Bondage of the Pawn Shop," *Sermonettes*, 1906.
62. Boyer, *Urban Masses and Moral Order*.
63. Soden, *Reverend Mark Matthews*, 104–108.
64. *Seattle Times*, February 21, 1910.
65. Berner, *Seattle, 1900–1920*, 115.
66. Matthews Papers, "Seattle Needs the Sword for Tuesday," *Sermonettes*, January–July 1910.
67. Berner, *Seattle, 1900–1920*, 115–116; *Seattle Times*, February 9, 1910.
68. *Seattle Times*, October 23, 1910.
69. Sharon A. Boswell and Lorraine McConaghy, *Raise Hell and Sell Newspapers: Alden J. Blethen and the Seattle Times* (Pullman: Washington State University Press, 1996), 156; *Seattle Times*, October 23, 1910; Wappenstein's biographical description is found in Dorothy Miller Kahlo, *History of the Police and Fire Departments of the City of Seattle* (Seattle: Lumbermen's Printing Co., 1907), 75–76.
70. Boswell and McConaghy, *Raise Hell and Sell Newspapers*, 158–159.
71. Boswell and McConaghy, *Raise Hell and Sell Newspapers*, 159.
72. Boswell and McConaghy, *Raise Hell and Sell Newspapers*, 160; Clarence Bagley, *History of Seattle from the Earliest Settlement to the Present Time*, vol. 2 (Chicago: S. J. Clarke, 1916), 555.
73. *Seattle Post-Intelligencer*, October 17, 1910.
74. *Seattle Post-Intelligencer*, January 27, 1911.
75. Report to Mark Matthews from Burns agent, July 19, 1911, Box 2, Matthews Papers.

76. Matthews to Brainerd, January 24, 1911, Box 3, Erastus Brainerd Papers.
77. Burton J. Hendrick, "The 'Recall' in Seattle," *McClure's* 37 (October 1911), 660–663; Boswell and McConaghy, *Raise Hell and Sell Newspapers*, 60.
78. William R. Hunt, *Front-Page Detective: William J. Burns and the Detective Profession, 1880–1930* (Bowling Green, KY: Bowling Green State University Popular Press, 1990), 76–77.
79. *Seattle Post-Intelligencer* and *Seattle Times*, February 13–15, 1911.
80. *Seattle Post-Intelligencer* and *Seattle Times*, February 13–15, 1911.
81. *Seattle Times*, February 26, 1911.
82. *Town Crier*, February 25, 1911.
83. *Seattle Post-Intelligencer*, September 15, 1910.
84. Timothy Michael Dolan, *Some Seed Fell on Good Ground: The Life of Edwin V. O'Hara* (Washington, DC: Catholic University Press of America, 1992), 32.
85. Dolan, *"Some Seed Fell on Good Ground,"* 32.
86. Shaw, *Edwin Vincent O'Hara*, 38; Dolan, *Some Seed Fell on Good Ground*, 30–31.
87. Shaw, *Edwin Vincent O'Hara*, 42.
88. Shaw, *Edwin Vincent O'Hara*, 30.
89. Shaw, *Edwin Vincent O'Hara*, 45.
90. Shaw, *Edwin Vincent O'Hara*, 47–48
91. Shaw, *Edwin Vincent O'Hara*, 56.
92. Shaw, *Edwin Vincent O'Hara*, 56.

Chapter 4: Grand Crusades

1. *Spokesman-Review* (headline), February 11, 1909; (quotation) February 7, 1909.
2. Catherine Gilbert Murdock, *Domesticating Drink: Women, Men, and Alcohol in America, 1870–1940* (Baltimore: Johns Hopkins University Press, 1998), 4; see also W. J. Rorabaugh, *The Alcoholic Republic: An American Tradition* (Oxford, UK: Oxford University Press, 1979).
3. Norman Clark, *The Dry Years: Prohibition and Social Change in Washington* (Seattle: University of Washington Press, 1965), 9.
4. John Casswell, "The Prohibition Movement in Oregon, Part 1, 1836–1904," *Oregon Historical Quarterly* 39 (March 1938), 237–238.
5. Clark, *The Dry Years*, 21.
6. Casswell, "The Prohibition Movement in Oregon, Part 1," 245.
7. Clark, *The Dry Years*, 22.
8. Casswell, "The Prohibition Movement in Oregon, Part 1," 245.
9. Clark, *The Dry Years*, 28–29.
10. Casswell, "The Prohibition Movement in Oregon, Part 1," 251.
11. Casswell, "The Prohibition Movement in Oregon, Part 1," 254.
12. Casswell, "The Prohibition Movement in Oregon, Part 1," 255.
13. Clark, *The Dry Years*, 57; see also Dale E. Soden, "The Woman's Christian Temperance Union in the Pacific Northwest: The Battle for Cultural Control," *Pacific Northwest Quarterly* 94 (fall 2003), 197–207.
14. Olympia Minutes, 1883–1897, Woman's Christian Temperance Union, Washington State Historical Society, Tacoma.
15. "Welcome Addresses, Delivered at Miss Frances E. Willard's Reception Held in Yesler's Hall, Seattle, W.T., June 27, 1883," 10–11, Proceedings of the First Mass

■ ──

Temperance Convention of Western Washington, Washington State Historical Society, Tacoma.

16. "Welcome Addresses," 11.
17. "Welcome Addresses," 11.
18. Murdock, *Domesticating Drink*, 9.
19. "Welcome Addresses," 11.
20. Clark, *The Dry Years*, 50.
21. Clark, *The Dry Years*, 46.
22. Clark, *The Dry Years*, 82.
23. John Casswell, "The Prohibition Movement in Oregon, Part 2, 1904–1915," *Oregon Historical Quarterly* 40 (1939), 67.
24. Casswell, "The Prohibition Movement in Oregon, Part 2," 64.
25. Casswell, "The Prohibition Movement in Oregon, Part 2," 85–87.
26. Daniel Okrent, *Last Call: The Rise and Fall of Prohibition* (New York: Scribner, 2010), 97.
27. *Spokesman Review*, November 30, 1908.
28. *Spokesman Review*, December 26, 1908.
29. Dale Soden, "Billy Sunday in Spokane: Revivalism and Social Control," *Pacific Northwest Quarterly* 79 (January 1988), 15–16.
30. *Bellingham Morning Reveille*, January 12, 1910.
31. Norman Clark, *Mill Town: A Social History of Everett, Washington, from Its Earliest Beginnings on the Shores of Puget Sound to the Tragic and Infamous Event Known as the Everett Massacre* (Seattle: University of Washington Press, 1970), 95–97, 107–110.
32. Casswell, "Prohibition in Oregon, Part 2," 75.
33. Casswell, "Prohibition in Oregon, Part 2," 75–76.
34. *Oregonian*, January 6, 1912.
35. *Oregon Journal*, August 8, 1912; *Oregonian*, October 27, 1912.
36. Casswell, "Prohibition in Oregon, Part 2," 77.
37. Casswell, "Prohibition in Oregon, Part 2," 78–79.
38. Clark, *The Dry Years*, 109.
39. Wilfred P. Schoenberg, S. J., *A History of the Catholic Church in the Pacific Northwest 1743–1983* (Washington DC: Pastoral Press, 1987), 483.
40. Clark, *The Dry Years*, 110.
41. Matthews, quoted in Clark, *The Dry Years*, 66.
42. Clark, *The Dry Years*, 112–113.
43. Casswell, "Prohibition in Oregon, Part 2," 80.
44. Casswell, "Prohibition in Oregon, Part 2," 81.
45. Clark, *The Dry Years*, 36.
46. Clark, *The Dry Years*, 141.
47. Clark, *The Dry Years*, 147.
48. Clark, *The Dry Years*, 237.
49. John C. Burnham, *Bad Habits: Drinking, Smoking, Taking Drugs, Gambling, Sexual Misbehavior, and Swearing in American History* (New York: New York University Press, 1993), 28.
50. Murdock, *Domesticating Drink*, 160.
51. Murdock, *Domesticating Drink*, 170.
52. Heather Lee Miller, "From Moral Suasion to Moral Coercion: Persistence and Transformation in Prostitution Reform, Portland, Oregon, 1888–1916" (unpublished MA thesis, University of Oregon, 1996), 25.

53. David Pivar, *Purity Crusade: Sexual Morality and Social Control, 1868–1900* (Westport, CT: Greenwood Press, 1973), 81; Miller, "From Moral Suasion to Moral Coercion," 16–17.
54. Miller, "From Moral Suasion to Moral Coercion," 19.
55. *Oregonian*, June 12, 1888.
56. Miller, "From Moral Suasion to Moral Coercion," 24–26.
57. Miller, "From Moral Suasion to Moral Coercion," 38–39.
58. *Oregonian*, September 22, September 29, October 6, and November 11, 1894.
59. Miller, "From Moral Suasion to Moral Coercion," 48.
60. Miller, "From Moral Suasion to Moral Coercion," 48.
61. Miller, "From Moral Suasion to Moral Coercion," 50.
62. Jef Rettmann, "Business, Government, and Prostitution in Spokane, Washington, 1889–1910," *Pacific Northwest Quarterly* 89:2, 82.
63. *Spokesman Review*, September 28, 1899.
64. *Spokesman Review*, October 5, 1899.
65. Rettmann, "Business, Government, and Prostitution," 83.
66. E. Kimbark MacColl, *The Shaping of a City: Business and Politics in Portland, Oregon 1885 to 1915* (Portland: Georgian Press Co., 1976), 402.
67. MacColl, *The Shaping of a City*, 402.
68. MacColl, *The Shaping of a City*, 403.
69. MacColl, *The Shaping of a City*, 403.
70. MacColl, *The Shaping of a City*, 403.
71. MacColl, *The Shaping of a City*, 410.
72. MacColl, *The Shaping of a City*, 412.

Chapter 5: Tolerance and Intolerance

1. Daniel Liestman, "To Win Redeemed Souls from Heathen Darkness: Protestant Response to the Chinese of the Pacific Northwest in the Late Nineteenth Century," *Western Historical Quarterly* 24:2 (May 1993), 194; Murray Morgan, *Puget's Sound: A Narrative of Early Tacoma and the Southern Sound* (Seattle: University of Washington Press, 1979), 239–240.
2. Liestman, "To Win Redeemed Souls," 194.
3. Elizabeth McLagan, *A Peculiar Paradise: A History of Blacks in Oregon, 1788–1940* (Portland: Georgian Press, 1980), 25–26.
4. Egbert S. Oliver, "Obed Dickinson and the 'Negro Question' in Salem," *Oregon Historical Quarterly* 92 (spring 1991), 7.
5. Oliver, "Obed Dickinson," 6.
6. Oliver, "Obed Dickinson," 8; McLagen, *Peculiar Paradise*, 53.
7. Oliver, "Obed Dickinson," 5.
8. Oliver, "Obed Dickinson," 10.
9. Oliver, "Obed Dickinson," 11.
10. Oliver, "Obed Dickinson," 18.
11. Richard White, *"It's Your Misfortune and None of My Own": A New History of the American West* (Norman: University of Oklahoma Press, 1991), 250; Carlos Schwantes, *The Pacific Northwest: An Interpretive History* (Lincoln: University of Nebraska Press, 1989), 124.
12. Shih-Shan Henry Tsai, *The Chinese Experience in America* (Bloomington: Indiana University Press, 1986), 26.

13. Liestman, "To Win Redeemed Souls," 184.
14. *Pacific Christian Advocate*, quoted in Liestman, "To Win Redeemed Souls," 191.
15. Liestman, "To Win Redeemed Souls,"191.
16. Lietsman, "To Win Redeemed Souls," 191.
17. Liestman, "To Win Redeemed Souls," 192.
18. Tsai, *The Chinese Experience in America*, 70.
19. Liestman, "To Win Redeemed Souls," 194; Jules Alexander Kalin, "The Anti-Chinese Outbreak in Tacoma, 1885," *Pacific Historical Review* 23:3 (August 1954), 276.
20. Liestman, "To Win Redeemed Souls," 195.
21. Liestman, "To Win Redeemed Souls," 195.
22. Liestman, "To Win Redeemed Souls," 195.
23. Mildred Tanner Andrews, *Seeking to Serve: The Legacy of Seattle's Plymouth Congregational Church* (Dubuque, IA: Kendal Hunt Publishing Co., 1988), 25.
24. Liestman, "To Win Redeemed Souls," 200–201.
25. Dale Soden, *The Reverend Mark Matthews: An Activist in the Progressive Era* (Seattle: University of Washington Press, 2001), 78–79.
26. McLagan, *Peculiar Paradise*, 92–93.
27. Quintard Taylor, *The Forging of a Black Community: Seattle's Central District from 1870 through the Civil Rights Era* (Seattle: University of Washington Press, 1994), 37.
28. Taylor, *Forging of a Black Community*, 38–39.
29. Taylor, *Forging of a Black Community*, 37–38.
30. Dwayne Anthony Mack, *Black Spokane: The Struggle for Civil Rights in the Inland Northwest* (Norman: University of Oklahoma Press, 2014), 6–7.
31. *Spokane Chronicle*, July 6, 1921.
32. Joseph Franklin, *All Through the Night: The History of Spokane Black Americans 1860–1940* (Fairfield, WA: Ye Galleon Press, 1989), 106–109.
33. Kimberley Mangun, *A Force for Change: Beatrice Morrow Cannady and the Struggle for Civil Rights in Oregon 1912–1936* (Corvallis: Oregon State University Press, 2010), 118.
34. Kimberley Mangun, "'As Citizens of Portland We Must Protest': Beatrice Morrow Cannady and the African American Response to D.W. Griffith's 'Masterpiece,'" *Oregon Historical Quarterly* (fall 2006), 382–409.
35. *Morning Oregonian*, August 30 1915.
36. Mangun, "As Citizens We Must Protest,'" 394–396.
37. Mangun, "As Citizens We Must Protest,'" 403; Quintard Taylor Jr., "Susie Revels Cayton, Beatrice Morrow Cannady, and the Campaign for Social Justice in the Pacific Northwest," in *The Great Northwest: The Search for Regional Identity*, ed. William G. Robbins (Corvallis: Oregon State University Press, 2001), 41.
38. Eckard Toy, "The Ku Klux Klan in Eugene, Oregon, during the 1920s," in *The Invisible Empire in the West: Toward a New Historical Appraisal of the Ku Klux Klan of the 1920s*, ed. Shawn Lay (Urbana: University of Illinois Press, 2004), 161.
39. Toy, "Ku Klux Klan in Eugene," 155–156.
40. Toy, "Ku Klux Klan in Eugene," 155.
41. David Tyack, "The Perils of Pluralism: The Background of the Pierce Case," *American Historical Review* 74 (1968), 78–79.
42. Toy, "Ku Klux Klan in Eugene,"154; Kenneth T. Jackson, *The Ku Klux Klan in the City, 1915–1930* (Chicago: Ivan R. Dee, Inc., 1967, 1992), 197–198.
43. David A. Horowitz, "The Klansman as Outsider: Ethnocultural Solidarity and Antielitism in the Oregon Ku Klux Klan of the 1920s," *Pacific Northwest Quarterly* (January 1989), 12–20.

44. Mangun, *A Force for Change*, 140–143.

45. Toy, "Ku Klux Klan in Eugene," 156.

46. Kelly J. Baker, *Gospel According to the Klan: The KKK's Appeal to Protestant America, 1915–1930* (Lawrence: University of Kansas Press, 2011), 9.

47. Toy, "Ku Klux Klan in Eugene," 171–172.

48. Toy, "Ku Klux Klan in Eugene," 172–173.

49. Baker, *Gospel According to the Klan*, 18.

50. David A. Horowitz, ed., *Inside the Klavern: The Secret History of a Ku Klux Klan of the 1920s* (Carbondale: Southern Illinois Press, 1999), 71; Baker, *Gospel According to the Klan*, 9.

51. Toy, "Ku Klux Klan in Eugene,"153.

52. Toy, "Ku Klux Klan in Eugene," 153.

53. Horowitz, *Inside the Klavern*, 16.

54. David A. Horowitz, "Order, Solidarity, and Vigilance: The Ku Klux Klan in La Grande, Oregon," in *The Invisible Empire in the West: Toward a New Historic Appraisal of the Ku Klux Klan of the 1920s*, ed. Shawn Lay (Chicago: University of Illinois Press, 1992), 201.

55. Allison, quoted in Mangun, *A Force for Change*, 140; Allison is also described in some detail in Lawrence J. Saalfeld, *Forces of Prejudice in Oregon 1920–1925* (Portland: Archdiocesan Historical Commission, 1984), 14–16.

56. Horowitz, "Order, Solidarity, and Vigilance," 188.

57. Horowitz, "Order, Solidarity, and Vigilance," 202.

58. Horowitz, *Inside the Klavern*, 12.

59. Horowitz, *Inside the Klavern*, 13.

60. Christine Taylor, ed., *Abundance of Grace: The History of the Archdiocese of Seattle 1850–2000* (Strasbourg, France: Editions du Signe, 2000), 62.

61. *Auburn Globe-Republican*, January 12, 1923.

62. *Auburn Globe-Republican*, March 23, 1923.

63. *Kent Advertiser-Journal*, July 19, 1923.

64. Kingston J. Pierce, *Eccentric Seattle: Pillars and Pariahs Who Made the City Not Such a Boring Place After All* (Pullman: Washington State University Press, 2003), 205–206.

65. *Auburn Globe-Republican*, August 8, 1924.

66. *Auburn Globe-Republican*, August 15, 1924.

67. Baker, *Gospel According to the Klan*, 93.

68. Tyack, "Perils of Pluralism," 75.

69. Tyack, "Perils of Pluralism," 75.

70. Jackson, *Ku Klux Klan in the City*, 206.

71. Thomas J. Shelley, "The Oregon School Case and the National Catholic Welfare Conference," *Catholic Historical Review* 75 (July 1989), 439–457; Paula Abrams, *Cross Purposes: Pierce v. Society of Sisters and the Struggle over Compulsory Public Education* (Ann Arbor: University of Michigan Press, 2009).

72. Mark Matthews, *Sermonettes*, 1924, Matthews Papers, University of Washington Libraries.

73. David M. Buerge and Junius Rochester, *Roots and Branches: The Religious History of Washington State* (Seattle: Church Council of Greater Seattle, 1988), 197.

Chapter 6: Justice on the Rise

1. Steven Lowenstein, *Jews of Oregon 1850–1950* (Portland: Jewish Historical Society of Oregon, 1987), 176.
2. Jill K. Gill, *Embattled Ecumenism: The National Council of Churches, and the Trials of the Protestant Left* (DeKalb: Northern Illinois University Press, 2011), 23–45.
3. Christine Taylor, ed., *Abundance of Grace: History of the Archdiocese of Seattle 1850–2000* (Strasbourg, France: Editions du Signe, 2000), 72.
4. Minutes of the Executive Committee, Greater Portland Council of Churches, September 1930 to June 1931, files in office of the Ecumenical Ministries of Oregon, Portland.
5. Report of the Commission on Social and Industrial Betterment, January 11, 1932; Executive Minutes, Greater Portland Council of Churches, files in office of the Ecumenical Ministries of Oregon, Portland.
6. Minutes of the Executive Committee of Greater Portland Council of Churches, September 1936 to June 1937, files in office of Ecumenical Ministries of Oregon, Portland.
7. Molly Cone, Howard Droker, and Jacqueline Williams, *Family of Strangers: Building a Jewish Community in Washington State* (Seattle: University of Washington Press, 2003), 199.
8. Quoted in Cone, Droker, and Williams, *Family of Strangers*, 199.
9. Lowenstein, *Jews of Oregon*, 193.
10. Lowenstein, *Jews of Oregon*, 193.
11. David M. Buerge and Junius Rochester, *Roots and Branches: The Religious Heritage of Washington State* (Seattle: Church Council of Greater Seattle, 1988), 207.
12. *Time Magazine*, April 30, 1934.
13. Buerge and Rochester, *Roots and Branches*, 208–209.
14. John C. Cort, "The Catholic Worker and the Workers," *Commonweal*, April 4, 1952, 636; Keith D. Barger, "Hearing the Cry of the Poor: The Catholic Worker Communities in Oregon and Washington 1940 to the Present" (unpublished BA thesis, University of Portland, April 1992), 1–2.
15. Anonymous, "Poor People," *Commonweal*, June 23, 1950, 272.
16. Barger, "Hearing the Cry of the Poor," 8.
17. Barger, "Hearing the Cry of the Poor," 13.
18. Ray Abrams, *Preachers Present Arms* (Scottsdale, PA: Herald Press, 1933).
19. Dale Soden, *The Reverend Mark Matthews: An Activist in the Progressive Era* (Seattle: University of Washington Press, 2001), 186.
20. Jessie Kinnear Kenton, "New Beginnings, New Leadership, 1930–1939," in *Generation to Generation: The Story of the Church Council of Greater Seattle 1919–1995* (Olympia: Pan Press, 1996), 10–12.
21. Kenton, "New Beginnings, New Leadership," 15–16.
22. Kenton, "New Beginnings, New Leadership," 16.
23. Jessie Kinnear Kenton, "Changing Values in Ecumenical Strategy in the Greater Seattle Area 1919–1984 (MA thesis, San Francisco Theological Seminary 1985), 16–17.
24. Mark Matthews, "The Fury of Egypt," the *Presbyterian*, April 14, 1938, 3.
25. Lowenstein, *Jews of Oregon*, 175.
26. Lowenstein, *Jews of Oregon*, 176–177.
27. Harry H. Stein, *Gus J. Solomon: Liberal Politics, Jews, and the Federal Courts* (Portland: Oregon Historical Society Press, 2006), 45.

28. Lowenstein, *Jews of Oregon*, 178.

29. Lowenstein, *Jews of Oregon*, 179; Stein, *Gus J. Solomon*, 37–43.

30. Lowenstein, *Jews of Oregon*, 180.

31. Lowenstein, *Jews of Oregon*, 182.

32. Lowenstein, *Jews of Oregon*, 183; Albert F. Gunns, *Civil Liberties in Crisis: The Pacific Northwest 1917–1940* (New York and London: Garland Publishing, Inc., 1983).

33. Mark Matthews, "Racial Prejudice Un-American," *Annals of the American Academy of Political Science* 93 (January 1921), 69–72.

34. Douglas Dye, "For the Sake of Seattle's Soul: The Seattle Council of Churches, the Nikkei Community, and World War II," *Pacific Northwest Quarterly* 93:3 (summer 2002), 127.

35. Dye, "For the Sake of Seattle's Soul," 127–128.

36. *Seattle Times*, June 5, 2013.

37. Dye, "For the Sake of Seattle's Soul," 129.

38. Dye, "For the Sake of Seattle's Soul," 130.

39. Dye, "For the Sake of Seattle's Soul," 131.

40. Schmoe, quoted in Ellen Eisenberg, "'As Truly American as Your Son': Voicing Opposition to Internment in Three West Coast Cities, *Oregon Historical Quarterly* 104:4 (2003), 555.

41. Murphy, quoted in Eisenberg, "'As Truly American as Your Son,'" 555.

42. Eisenberg, "'As Truly American as Your Son,'" 555.

43. Thompson, quoted in Eisenberg, "'As Truly American as Your Son,'" 555.

44. Gill, quoted in Eisenberg, "'As Truly American as Your Son,'" 555.

45. Dye, "For the Sake of Seattle's Soul," 131.

46. Dye, "For the Sake of Seattle's Soul," 131.

47. Eisenberg, "'As Truly American as Your Son,'" 556–557.

48. Eisenberg, "'As Truly American as Your Son,'" 557.

49. Azalia Peet, quoted in Eisenberg, "'As Truly American as Your Son,'" 542.

50. Eisenberg, "'As Truly American as Your Son,'" 547.

51. Eisenberg, "'As Truly American as Your Son,'" 561.

52. Emery Andrews Papers, Box 1, Folder 1, Special Collections, University of Washington Libraries, Seattle.

53. Dye, "For the Sake of Seattle's Soul," 131; Christine Taylor, ed., *Abundance of Grace*, 76–77; see James Sakamoto correspondence with Father Tibesar, Sakamoto Papers, Box 2, File 40, Manuscripts and Special Collections, University of Washington, Seattle; see also Madeline Duntley, "Japanese and Filipino Together: The Transethnic Vision of Our Lady Queen of Martyrs Parish," *U.S. Catholic Historian* 18 (winter, 2000), 74–98; *Seattle Times*, June 5, 2013.

54. Linda Popp Di Biase, "Neither Harmony nor Eden: Margaret Peppers and the Exile of the Japanese Americans," *Anglican and Episcopal History* 70:1 (2001), 101–103.

55. Di Biase, "Neither Harmony nor Eden," 108–109.

56. Di Biase, "Neither Harmony nor Eden," 112–113.

57. Arthur Barnett Papers, Box 1, Folder 1, Special Collections, University of Washington Libraries, Manuscripts and Special Collections; *Seattle Times*, October 25, 2003.

58. Dye, "For the Sake of Seattle's Soul," 132.

59. Dye, "For the Sake of Seattle's Soul," 132.

60. Eisenberg, "'As Truly American as Your Son,'" 563.

61. Robert G. Kaufman, *Henry M. Jackson: A Life in Politics* (Seattle: University of Washington Press, 2000), 36–37.

■ ---

62. Dye, "For the Sake of Seattle's Soul," 132.
63. *Seattle Post-Intelligencer*, January 24, 1945.
64. Dye, "For the Sake of Seattle's Soul," 133.
65. Dye, "For the Sake of Seattle's Soul," 134.
66. Church Council of Greater Seattle Papers, Minutes, July 19, 1945, Box 15, Folder 2, Special Collections, University of Washington Libraries.
67. Dye, "For the Sake of Seattle's Soul," 134.
68. Dye, "For the Sake of Seattle's Soul," 135.
69. Harry Stein, *Gus Solomon*, 80–82.
70. Linda Tamura, *Nisei Soldiers Break Their Silence: Coming Home to Hood River* (Seattle: University of Washington Press, 2012), 148–154.
71. Tamura, *Nisei Soldiers*, 169–170; Burgoyne letter in Tamura, *Nisei Soldiers*, 249.
72. *Pacific Citizen*, April 19, 1947.
73. *Hood River County Sun*, February 14, 1947.
74. Roger Daniels, *Concentration Camps USA: Japanese Americans and World War II* (New York: Holt, Rinehart and Winston, 1971), 162.
75. Dwayne Anthony Mack, *Black Spokane: The Civil Rights Struggle in the Inland Northwest* (Norman: University of Oklahoma Press, 2014), 33; *Spokesman Review*, November 15, 1944.
76. Mack, *Black Spokane*, 33.
77. Mack, *Black Spokane*, 85–86.
78. Mack, *Black Spokane*, 97, 102.
79. Quintard Taylor, *The Forging of a Black Community: Seattle Central District from 1870 through the Civil Rights Era* (Seattle: University of Washington Press, 1994), 170–71; Johanna McClees, "Christian Friends for Racial Equality: A Unique Approach to Race and Religious Relations in Seattle" (unpublished BA thesis, University of Washington, 2001), University of Washington Manuscripts, Archives, and Special Collections, University of Washington Library.
80. Pauline Anderson Simmons Hill and Sherrilyn Johnson Jordan, *Too Young to Be Old: The Story of Bertha Pitts Campbell* (Seattle: Peanut Butter Publishing, 1981), 35–38.
81. McClees, "Christian Friends for Racial Equality," 3–4.
82. McClees, "Christian Friends for Racial Equality," 51.
83. "Racial Equality Bulletin," Christian Friends for Racial Equality, Manuscripts and Special Collections, University of Washington, Seattle.
84. McClees, "Christian Friends for Racial Equality," 36.
85. Taylor, *Forging of a Black Community*, 170–171.
86. Stuart John McElderry, "The Problem of the Color Line: Civil Rights and Racial Ideology in Portland, Oregon, 1944–1965" (unpublished PhD dissertation, University of Oregon, 1998), 98; Clow, quoted in *Oregonian*, October 2, 1942.
87. McElderry, "Problem of the Color Line," 86–87.
88. McElderry, "Problem of the Color Line," 132.
89. McElderry, "Problem of the Color Line," 129–130.
90. McElderry, "Problem of the Color Line," 144.
91. McElderry, "Problem of the Color Line," 149.

Chapter 7: *The Right Gathers Itself*

1. Charles Pierce LeWarne, *Utopias on Puget Sound 1885–1915* (Seattle: University of Washington Press, 1975), 3.
2. See Robert Wuthnow, *The Restructuring of American Religion: Society and Faith Since World War II* (Princeton, NJ: Princeton University Press, 1988), 3–13.
3. See Lisa McGirr, *Suburban Warriors: The Origins of the New American Right* (Princeton, NJ: Princeton University Press, 2001); Allan J. Lichtman, *White Protestant Nation: The Rise of the American Conservative Movement* (New York: Atlantic Monthly Press, 2008); Daniel K. Williams, *God's Own Party: The Making of the Christian Right* (Oxford, UK: Oxford University Press, 2010), 1–48.
4. Lichtman, *White Protestant Nation*, 74–81.
5. June Melby Benowitz, *Days of Discontent: American Women and Right-Wing Politics, 1933–1945* (Dekalb: Northern Illinois University Press, 2002), 16.
6. Benowitz, *Days of Discontent*, 17; Lichtman, *White Protestant Nation*, 85.
7. Norman P. Grubb, *Modern Viking: The Story of Abraham Vereide, Pioneer in Christian Leadership* (Grand Rapids, MI: Zondervan Publishing House, 1961), 47–51.
8. Jeff Sharlet, *The Family: The Secret Fundamentalism at the Heart of American Power* (New York: HarperCollins, 2008), 108.
9. Grubb, *Modern Viking*, 52.
10. Sharlet, *The Family*, 109.
11. Sharlet, *The Family*, 110.
12. Grubb, *Modern Viking*, 56–57; Lichtman, *White Protestant Nation*, 199–200.
13. For a more critical view of Langlie's role and what Langlie represents, see Sharlet, *The Family*, 116–120. Sharlet asserts that the "God-led" politician, the kind that Vereide was trying to cultivate, adopted a more reactionary agenda than does Langlie's biographer. See George W. Scott, "Arthur B. Langlie: Republican Governor in a Democratic Age" (unpublished PhD dissertation, University of Washington, 1971), 1–31, 106–141.
14. Grubb, *Modern Viking*, 60; Lichtman, *White Protestant Nation*, 199.
15. Lichtman, *White Protestant Nation*, 199–200; for Jeff Sharlet, Vereide provided the foundation for what would be a largely secret organization in Washington, DC, called "The Family." This group, led by Doug Coe, continues to host prayer breakfasts and in private preaches a gospel of "biblical capitalism" and American exceptionalism.
16. David Jepson, "Old-Fashioned Revival: Religion, Migration, and New Identity for the Pacific Northwest at Mid-Twentieth Century," *Oregon Historical Quarterly* 107:3 (fall 2006), 356–357; James N. Gregory, *The Southern Diaspora: How the Great Migrations of Black and White Southerners Transformed America* (Chapel Hill: University of North Carolina Press, 2005).
17. Jepson, "Old-Fashioned Revival," 358; Gregory, *The Southern Diaspora*, 204–209; From 1940 to 1950, Washington State's population surged by 37 percent to 2.38 million and added another 20 percent to reach 2.85 million from 1950 to 1960. Oregon's population grew by 40 percent from 1940 to 1950 and 16 percent from 1950 to 1960 to reach 1.77 million. Southern Baptist numbers increased significantly in the Northwest. In 1940, there were an estimated 57,000 Baptists and 230 Baptist-affiliated churches in Washington and Oregon. By 1948, the next year for which data are available, those numbers had grown to 77,000 members and 435 churches. By 1967, Southern Baptists claimed 152,000 members and 862 churches—a 267 percent increase in adherents and a 375 percent increase in churches since 1940.

■ ———

18. Lichtman, *White Protestant Nation*, 123.
19. Lichtman, *White Protestant Nation*, 123.
20. Lichtman, *White Protestant Nation*, 123–124.
21. Lichtman, *White Protestant Nation*, 124.
22. Lichtman, *White Protestant Nation*, 125.
23. Lichtman, *White Protestant Nation*, 125.
24. Thomas Bergler, "Christian Youth Groups and the Middle-Class Culture of Crisis, 1930–1965" (unpublished PhD dissertation, University of Notre Dame, 2001), 6.
25. Lichtman, *White Protestant Nation*, 125–126.
26. Author interview with Doug Ross, January 26, 2010.
27. Author interview with Doug Ross, January 26, 2010.
28. Bergler, "Christian Youth Groups," 104–170.
29. Bergler, "Christian Youth Groups," 105–106.
30. Bergler, "Christian Youth Groups," 111.
31. Newspaper clippings, *Spokane Daily Chronicle*, Northwest Christian archives, Colbert, WA.
32. *Oregonian*, July 23, 1950.
33. *Oregonian*, July 23, 1950.
34. *Seattle Times*, August 1, 1951.
35. *Seattle Times*, September 3, 1951; for further analysis of Billy Graham's early attention to Communism, see Williams, *God's Own Party*, 21–24.
36. Quotation in Christine M. Taylor, ed., *Abundance of Grace: The History of the Archdiocese of Seattle 1850–2000* (Seattle: Archdiocese of Seattle, 2000), 107.
37. Lorraine McConaghy, "No Ordinary Place: Three Postwar Suburbs and Their Critics" (unpublished PhD dissertation, University of Washington, 1993), 342.
38. McConaghy, "No Ordinary Place," 342–343.
39. Lichtman, *White Protestant Nation*, 197; McGirr, *Suburban Warriors*, 54.
40. McConaghy, "No Ordinary Place," 330–331.
41. *Whitworthian*, February 13, 1959, Whitworth University Library, Spokane, WA.
42. *Seattle Times*, February 12, 1962.
43. *Seattle Times*, February 13, 1962.
44. *Seattle Times*, February 14, 1962.
45. *Seattle Times*, February 15, 1962.
46. *Seattle Times*, February 17, 1962.
47. McConaghy, "No Ordinary Place," 339; *Bellevue American*, February 8, 1962, and February 15, 1962.
48. McConaghy, "No Ordinary Place," 338.
49. McGirr, *Suburban Warriors*, 53.
50. McConaghy, "No Ordinary Place," 308–309.
51. McConaghy, "No Ordinary Place," 308.
52. McConaghy. "No Ordinary Place," 342–343.
53. McConaghy, "No Ordinary Place," 309.
54. McConaghy, "No Ordinary Place," 331.
55. McConaghy, "No Ordinary Place," 332.
56. McConaghy, "No Ordinary Place," 333.
57. McConaghy, "No Ordinary Place," 333.
58. McConaghy, "No Ordinary Place," 335.
59. McConaghy, "No Ordinary Place," 339–351.
60. *Oregonian*, June 20, 1963.

61. *Oregonian,* June 20, 1963.
62. *Oregonian,* June 20, 1963.

Chapter 8: Trying to End Segregation

1. *Seattle Post-Intelligencer,* November 10, 1961.
2. Author interview with Samuel McKinney, July 25, 2004; *Seattle P-I,* November 9, 1961; *Seattle Times,* November 11, 1961; Dale E. Soden, "The Role of Religious Activists in the Seattle Civil Rights Struggles of the 1960s," *Pacific Northwest Quarterly* (spring 2013), 55–71.
3. David Chappell, *A Stone of Hope: Prophetic Religion and the Death of Jim Crow* (Chapel Hill: University of North Carolina Press, 2004), 3; other treatments of the role of the black church as well as the Southern Christian Leadership Conference in the early history of the Civil Rights Movement include Aldon D. Morris, *The Origins of the Civil Rights Movement: Black Communities Organizing for Change* (New York: Free Press, 1984); Adam Fairclough, *To Redeem the Soul of America: The Southern Christian Leadership Conference and Martin Luther King Jr.* (Athens: University of Georgia Press, 2001); Paul Harvey, *Freedom's Coming: Religious Culture and the Shaping of the South from the Civil War through the Civil Rights Era* (Chapel Hill: University of North Carolina Press, 2005); and Jonathan Rieder, *Gospel of Freedom: Martin Luther King, Jr.'s Letter from Birmingham Jail and the Struggle that Changed the Nation* (New York: Bloomsbury Press, 2013).
4. *Seattle Times,* June 25, 1963.
5. *Seattle Times,* February 14, 1998.
6. Author interview with John Hurst Adams, July 17, 2012; Seattle CORE papers, Box 2, folder clippings, Special Collections, University of Washington Libraries; *Seattle Times,* January 9, 1968; Larry Samuel Richardson, "Civil Rights in Seattle: A Rhetorical Analysis of a Social Movement" (unpublished PhD dissertation, Washington State University, 1975).
7. *Oregonian,* June 3, 1963; *Oregon Journal,* June 1, 1963.
8. For biographical details on Jackson's life, see Elizabeth McLagen, unpublished paper, "Notes Toward a Biography: The Papers of John Hiram Jackson," John H. Jackson Papers, Portland Community College Archives/Records Center, Sylvania Campus.
9. Author interview with Loreda Graham, August 23, 2012.
10. Joan Singler, Jean Durning, Bettylou Valentine, and Maid Adams, *Seattle in Black and White: The Congress of Racial Equality* (Seattle: University of Washington Press, 2011), 17–20; author interview with Joan Singler, June 7, 2011.
11. Singler et al., *Seattle in Black and White,* 35–45.
12. Singler et al., *Seattle in Black and White,* 37.
13. Seattle CORE Papers, "Report on Selective Buying Campaign," January 15, 1962, Box 1, unnumbered folder, General Correspondence, Special Collections, University of Washington Libraries; Seattle CORE Papers, Conference, August 17, 1963, Box 3, folder "Seattle Core Workshop, 1963"; Seattle CORE Papers, letter, Rev. E. S. Brazill to Edward Singler, January 19, 1962, Box 1, unnumbered folder, General Correspondence, 1962, Special Collections, University of Washington Libraries.
14. Quoted in August Meier and Elliot Rudwick, *CORE: A Study in the Civil Rights Movement 1942–1968* (New York: Oxford University Press, 1973), 189; Quintard Taylor Jr., *The Forging of a Black Community: Seattle's Central District from 1870 through the Civil Rights Era* (Seattle: University of Washington Press, 1994), 190–233.
15. "Walt Hundley," last modified April 9, 2011, Mary Henry History Link: http://www.historylink.org/index.cfm?DisplayPage=output.cfm&file_id=3173.

16. Ivan King, *The Central Area Motivation Program: A Brief History of a Community in Action* (Seattle: Central Area Motivation Program, 1990), 5–12.

17. Seattle Opportunities Industrial Center (SOIC) Records, Box 1, "Final Historical Summary," Special Collections, University of Washington Libraries.

18. *Seattle Times*, July 19, 1966; SOIC received a $2.1 million grant to build a $3.8 million center that trained more than 1,800 students a year by 1978. However, the center could not survive the funding cuts from the Reagan administration in the 1980s. SOIC applied for bankruptcy in 1986. See SOIC Records, Box 1, "Final Historical Summary," Special Collections, University of Washington Libraries.

19. *Oregon Journal*, December 29, 1961; *Eugene Register-Guard*, December 30, 1961.

20. *Oregon Journal*, December 29, 1961.

21. Stuart John McElderry, "The Problem of the Color Line: Civil Rights and Racial Ideology in Portland, Oregon, 1944–1965" (unpublished PhD dissertation, University of Oregon, 1998), 295–296.

22. Employee surveys, Box 6, Files 9-10, Metropolitan Interfaith Commission on Race, Stella Maris Papers, Oregon Historical Research Library.

23. McElderry, "Problem of the Color Line," 296–297.

24. McElderry, "Problem of the Color Line," 300.

25. McElderry, "Problem of the Color Line," 301–303.

26. Taylor, *Forging of a Black Community*, 194.

27. Stuart McElderry, "Building a West Coast Ghetto: African–American Housing in Portland, 1910–1960," *Pacific Northwest Quarterly* (summer 2001), 137.

28. Singler et al., *Seattle in Black and White*, 104–107.

29. "Conference on Race and Religion," Archbishop Thomas Connolly Official #1963-F, May 31, 1963, Officials, Archives of the Catholic Archdiocese of Seattle.

30. *Seattle Times*, June 6, 1963.

31. *Seattle Times*, June 15, 1963.

32. *Seattle Times*, June 30, 1963.

33. *Seattle Times*, July 2, 1963.

34. *Seattle Times*, July 2, 1963.

35. Singler et al., *Seattle in Black and White*, 225.

36. *Seattle Times*, August 10, 1963.

37. *Seattle Times*, August 10, 1963.

38. Georgia State Assembly Resolution, Senate Resolution 546, March 14, 2007.

39. Author interview with Samuel McKinney, June 18, 2012; author interview with John Adams, July 17, 2012.

40. *Seattle Times*, October 15, 1963; October 25, 1963; *Seattle Times*, October 26, 1963.

41. Singler et al., *Seattle in Black and White*, 120.

42. *Catholic Northwest Progress*, March 9, 1964.

43. Singler et al., *Seattle in Black and White*, 122.

44. *Portland Oregonian*, June 24, 1963.

45. *Portland Oregonian*, June 25, 1963.

46. McElderry, "Problem of the Color Line," 340–345.

47. McElderry, "Problem of the Color Line," 350.

48. Greater Portland Council of Churches statement, January 13, 1964, box "Social Action Legislation," file PCC Public Housing, Ecumenical Ministries of Oregon Archives, Patton House, Portland.

49. Robert Bonthius letter to Oregon's US senator, Wayne Morse, April 1, 1964, charging that HAP was tainted with racial bias. Morse read the letter into the Congressional Record on March 23, 1964, box "Social Action Legislation," file PCC Public Housing, Ecumenical Ministries of Oregon Archives, Patton House, Portland.
50. *Portland Oregonian*, November 17, 1973.
51. *Portland Oregonian*, May 2, 1963; McElderry, "Problem of the Color Line," 372.
52. *Portland Oregonian*, May 2, 1963.
53. *Portland Oregonian*, May 14, 1963.
54. McElderry, "Problem of the Color Line," 375.
55. Ethan Johnson and Felicia Williams, "Desegregation and Multiculturalism in the Portland Public Schools," *Oregon Historical Quarterly* (spring 2010), 13–15.
56. Paul Wright, "Statement to the School Board of School District No. 1 by the Portland Citizens Committee on Racial Imbalance in the Public Schools, November 16, 1994," box Social Action Legislation, file "Race and Education," Ecumenical Ministries of Oregon Archives, Patton House, Portland.
57. *Oregon Journal*, March 24, 1965. See Johnson and Williams, "Desegregation and Multiculturalism," 6–37.
58. "Statement by Albina Ministerial Association in Opposition to Appropriation of Funds by State and Federal Government for use in Portland's Segregated Public Elementary Schools," box Social Action Legislation, file "Race and Education," Ecumenical Ministries of Oregon Archives, Patton House, Portland.
59. McElderry, "Problem of the Color Line," 386.
60. Author interview with Charles Johnson, June 22, 2013.
61. Taylor, *Forging of a Black Community*, 197.
62. Doris Pieroth, "With All Deliberate Caution: School Integration in Seattle, 1954–1968," *Pacific Northwest Quarterly* 73 (April 1982), 52.
63. Frances Owen, quoted in Doris Pieroth, "With All Deliberate Caution," 53.
64. Pieroth, "With All Deliberate Caution," 52.
65. Singler et al., *Seattle in Black and White*, 151.
66. Pieroth, "With all Deliberate Caution," 56; see CORE minutes, February 17, 1966.
67. Singler et al., *Seattle in Black and White*, 161.
68. *Seattle Times*, March 20, 1966; Singler et al., *Seattle in Black and White*, 156–174.
69. *Seattle Times*, March 19, 1966.
70. *Seattle Post-Intelligencer*, March 18 and 25, 1966; *Northwest Catholic Progress*, March 25, 1966.
71. *Seattle Times*, March 20, 1966; *Seattle Post-Intelligencer*, March 27, 1966.
72. Singler et al., *Seattle in Black and White*, 161.
73. *Seattle Times*, March 19, 1966.
74. *Seattle Post-Intelligencer*, March 27, 1966.
75. Pieroth, "With All Deliberate Caution," 57.
76. *Seattle Times*, April 1, 1966.
77. *Seattle Times*, March 18, 1966.
78. *Portland Oregonian*, October 28, 1966; C-CAP Activities and Projects, 1965–1968, "Special Meeting Report-Black Power Conference," October 28, 1966," Box 4/2, Stella Maris House Collection, Oregon Historical Research Library.
79. *Seattle Times*, April, 20, 1967.
80. *Seattle Post-Intelligencer*, May 5, 1967.
81. *Seattle Post-Intelligencer*, May 5, 1967.
82. *Seattle Post-Intelligencer*, May 5, 1967.

83. *Seattle Times*, September 5, 1967.

84. Pieroth, "With all Deliberate Caution," 59.

85. Pieroth, "With all Deliberate Caution," 59.

86. Jeffrey Gregory Zane, "'America Only Less So?' Seattle's Central Area, 1968–1996" (unpublished PhD dissertation, University of Notre Dame, 2001), 106–107; *Seattle Times*, March 7, 1968, 11–12.

87. *Seattle Times*, February 28, 1968; *Seattle Post-Intelligencer*, March 7, 1968; quote from Pieroth in interview with Roberta Byrd.

88. Pieroth, "With all Deliberate Caution," 59–60.

89. *Seattle Times*, April 5, 1968.

90. *Seattle Times*, April 5, 1968.

91. *Seattle Times*, April 8, 1968.

92. Taylor, *Forging a Black Community*, 208.

93. Pieroth, "With all Deliberate Caution," 61.

Chapter 9: The Christian Right Strikes Back

1. *Ellensburg Daily Record*, July 9, 1977.

2. *Ellensburg Daily Record*, July 9, 1977.

3. *Spokesman Review*, July 11, 1977.

4. Author interview with Karen Frasier, January 18, 2013.

5. Allan J. Lichtman, *White Protestant Nation: The Rise of the American Conservative Movement* (New York: Atlantic Monthly Press, 2008), 321.

6. Lichtman, *White Protestant Nation*, 323.

7. *Oregonian*, May 21, 1968.

8. *Oregonian*, May 21, 1968.

9. *Oregonian*, May 19, 1968.

10. *Oregonian*, May 19, 1968.

11. *Oregonian*, May 24, 1968.

12. *Seattle Times*, May 13, 1976.

13. *Seattle Times*, May 13, 1976.

14. Lichtman, *White Protestant Nation*, 345.

15. Lichtman, *White Protestant Nation*, 345–346.

16. Lichtman, *White Protestant Nation*, 343–344.

17. James K. Wellman Jr., "Sectarian Entrepreneurs," in *Religion and Public Life in the Pacific Northwest: The None Zone*, eds. Patricia O'Connell Killen and Mark Silk (Walnut Creek, CA: AltaMira Press, 2004), 87.

18. James K. Wellman Jr., *Evangelical vs. Liberal: The Clash of Christian Cultures in the Pacific Northwest* (New York: Oxford University Press, 2008), 155–188; Wellman, "Sectarian Entrepreneurs," 79–105.

19. Wellman, *Evangelical vs. Liberal*, 165–177.

20. See Hartford Institute for Religion website http://hirr.hartsem.edu/megachurch/database.html.

21. *Eugene Register-Guard*, February 12, 1994.

22. *Seattle Times*, September 1, 2007.

23. In 2014, Mark Driscoll, at the height of his power and influence, found himself at the center of several controversies. One issue involved the use of church tithes to hire a firm and buy copies of one of Driscoll's books in order to increase sales: see *Seattle Times*, August 3, 2014; another controversy revolved around complaints about

Driscoll's leadership style. Additional charges of bullying and shunning of churchgoers eventually led to his resignation from Mars Hill: see *Seattle Times*, August 8, 2014.

24. Daniel T. Rodgers, *Age of Fracture* (Cambridge, MA: Belknap Press of Harvard University Press, 2011), 145.

25. Barry Hankins, *American Evangelicals: A Contemporary History of a Mainstream Religious Movement* (Lanham, MD: Rowman and Littlefield, 2008), 119–122.

26. Lee Moriwaki, "Promise Keepers Returning," *Seattle Times*, April 24, 1996.

27. Mark Driscoll and Grace Driscoll, *Real Marriage: The Truth about Sex, Friendship & Life Together* (Nashville: Thomas Nelson Publishing, 2012), 5.

28. Driscoll and Driscoll, *Real Marriage*, 8; Janet Tu, "Pastor Mark Packs 'em In," *Pacific Northwest Magazine: Seattle Times*, November 30, 2003.

29. Mark Driscoll, *Confessions of a Reformission Rev.: Hard Lessons from an Emerging Missional Church* (Grand Rapids, MI: Zondervan Press, 2006), 40.

30. Tu, *Seattle Times*, November 30, 2003.

31. Driscoll, *Confessions of a Reformission Rev.*, 26.

32. Molly Worthen, "Who Would Jesus Smack Down?" *New York Times*, January 11, 2009.

33. Worthen, *New York Times*, January 11, 2009.

34. Worthen, *New York Times*, January 11, 2009.

35. Driscoll, *Confessions of a Reformission Rev.*, 66–67.

36. Mark Driscoll, August 21, 2005, "Genesis 46: 1–47:12," sermon available at http://www.marshillchurch.org.

37. Driscoll, *Confessions of a Reformission Rev.*, 131–132.

38. Wellman, "Sectarian Entrepreneurs," 81.

39. William M. Lunch, "The Christian Right in the Northwest: Two Decades of Frustration in Oregon and Washington," in *The Christian Right in American Politics: Marching to the Millennium*, ed. by John Green, Mark Rozell, and Clyde Wilcox (Washington, DC: Georgetown University Press, 2003), 236.

40. Lon Fendall, *Stand Alone or Come Home: Mark Hatfield as an Evangelical and a Progressive* (Newberg, OR: Barclay Press, 2008), 39.

41. Vernon Bates, "Rhetorical Pluralism and Secularization in the New Christian Right: The Oregon Citizens Alliance," *Review of Religious Research* 37:1 (September 1995), 48.

42. Lunch, "Christian Right in the Northwest," 247.

43. Lunch, "Christian Right in the Northwest," 248.

44. Bates, "Rhetorical Pluralism," 57.

45. Lunch, "Christian Right in the Northwest," 249.

46. Patricia O'Connell Killen, "Religious Futures in the None Zone," in Killen and Silk, *Religion and Public Life*, 176–177.

47. See Oregon Family Council website at http://www.oregonfamilycouncil.org/.

48. See Oregon Right to Life website at http://www.ortl.org/.

49. John Fortmeyer, "Rift Develops among Oregon Evangelicals on Anti-Abortion Strategies," *Christian News Northwest*, November 2005.

50. *Christian News Northwest*, February 2009.

51. Lunch, "Christian Right in the Northwest," 238.

52. Lichtman, *White Protestant Nation*, 345;

53. Washington State Chapter of Concerned Women of America, website at http://www.cwfa.org/states/washington/.

54. Lunch, "Christian Right in the Northwest," 250.

55. Krista Kapralos, "Death with Dignity: Combatting Religious Opposition to Physician-Assisted Suicide," *Religion Dispatches*, May 15, 2009; John C. Hughes, *Booth*

Who? A Biography of Booth Gardner: Washington's Charismatic 19th Governor (Centralia, WA: Gorham Printing, 2010), 261–266.

56. *Seattle Times*, March 29, 2004.
57. *Seattle Times*, May 2, 2004.
58. *Seattle Post-Intelligencer*, January 8, 2008.
59. Janet Tu, "Religious Right: 'A Leaderless Army,'" *Seattle Times*, July 21, 2009.
60. *Seattle Times*, July 21, 2009.
61. *Seattle Times*, October 24, 2009.
62. Wellman, *Evangelical vs. Liberal*, 271.

Chapter 10: Liberal Dreams and Ecumenical Activists

1. *Seattle Times*, May 9, 1979.
2. *Catholic Northwest Progress*, May 11, 1979.
3. *The Source* (Monthly newspaper of Church Council of Greater Seattle), June 1982, Box 22, Church Council of Greater Seattle, University of Washington Manuscripts and Special Collections.
4. See Jill K. Gill, *Embattled Ecumenism: The National Council of Churches, the Vietnam War, and the Trials of the Protestant Left* (Dekalb: University of Northern Illinois Press, 2011), 3–19.
5. Author interview with Reverend Jonathan Nelson, June 7, 2011; *Seattle Times*, July 29, 2011.
6. David Wilma, "Rabbi Raphael Harry Levine," HistoryLink.org, 2005; David M. Buerge and Junius Rochester, *Roots and Branches: The Religious Heritage of Washington State* (Seattle: Church Council of Greater Seattle, 1988), 243–245.
7. Rabbi Raphael H. Levine, *To Love Is to Live: Building Bridges of Understanding* (Seattle: Peanut Butter Publishing, 1994), 164–165.
8. Father William Treacy, *Love Bears All Things: Bridging Troubled Waters* (Seattle: Peanut Butter Publishing, 1994), 150–151.
9. *Seattle Times*, November 21, 1976; Levine, *To Love Is to Live*, 168.
10. Levine, *To Live Is to Love*, 169.
11. Buerge and Rochester, *Roots and Branches*, 216.
12. Levine, *To Love Is to Live*, 168.
13. Ann LaGrelius Siqueland, *Without a Court Order: The Desegregation of Seattle's Schools* (Seattle: Madrona Publishers, 1981), 62–66.
14. Siqueland, *Without a Court Order*, 65.
15. Siqueland, *Without a Court Order*, 66.
16. Siqueland, *Without a Court Order*, 66.
17. Siqueland, *Without a Court Order*, 170.
18. *Philadelphia Inquirer*, September 9, 1978.
19. Ethan Johnson and Felicia Williams, "Desegregation and Multiculturalism in Portland Public Schools," *Oregon Historical Quarterly* (spring 2010), 26.
20. *Oregon Journal*, August 27, 1979.
21. Johnson and Williams, "Desegregation and Multiculturalism," 27–33.
22. William B. Cate, "Launching the New Council, 1970–1978," in *The Story of the Church Council of Greater Seattle 1919–1995*, ed. Church Council of Greater Seattle (Olympia: Pan Press, 1996), 86.

23. Cate, "Launching the New Council," 86.

24. "A Public Declaration to the Tribal Councils and Traditional Spiritual Leaders of the Indian and Eskimo Peoples of the Pacific Northwest," available at http://www. evergreen-abc.org/resources/resources.php.

25. Archbishop Thomas Connolly, "California Grape Workers' Strike," Official 1968-14, August 29, 1968, RG415 Officials, Box 5, Archives of Catholic Archdiocese of Seattle.

26. William B. Cate, *The One Church in This Place: A View from the Ecumenical Underside* (Seattle: Institute for Ecumenical Studies of the Northwest Theological Union, 1991), 5–6.

27. *Oregonian*, December 17, 2010.

28. Gary L. Atkins, *Gay Seattle: Stories of Exile and Belonging* (Seattle: University of Washington Press, 2003), 97–98, 109.

29. Cate, "Launching the New Council," 104.

30. *Catholic Northwest Progress,* July 1, 1977.

31. For a much fuller description of the role that Archbishop Hunthausen played in discussions regarding gay rights and sexual orientation see John McCoy, *A Still and Quiet Conscience: The Archbishop Who Challenged a Pope, a President, and a Church* (Maryknoll, New York: Orbis Books, 2015. McCoy also describes at great length the opposition to Hunthausen's position among the Catholic hierarchy including Cardinal Joseph Ratzinger who later became Pope Benedict XVI.

32. Cate, "Launching the New Council," 104–105.

33. Rodney Romney, "Homosexual Issues," Box 1, Folder 10, Whitworth University Archives and Special Collections, Spokane, WA.

34. *Oregonian*, June 30, 2012.

35. *Oregonian*, October 8, 2009; *Oregonian*, September 13, 2009.

36. Cate, "Launching the New Council," 84–85.

37. Brian Casserly, "Confronting the U.S. Navy at Bangor, 1973–1982," *Pacific Northwest Quarterly* (summer 2004), 130–139; "Radical Christian, Quaker, and Feminist Roots," quoted in Casserly, "Confronting the U.S. Navy," 135.

38. Casserly, "Confronting the U.S. Navy," 136.

39. John A. McCoy, *A Still and Quiet Conscience: The Archbishop Who Challenged a Pope, a President, and a Church* (Maryknoll, New York: Orbis Books, 2015), 1–105.

40. Frank A. Fromherz, "Archbishop Raymond Hunthausen's Thought and Practice in Society and Church: A Sociohistorical & Ethical Case Study of Nonviolence" (PhD dissertation, Graduate Theological Union, 1990), 70-105; Cate, *The One Church in This Place,* 54.

41. *Seattle Times* May 18, 1977, and June 22, 1977.

42. Cate, *The Church in This Place,* 6; Interview, Reverend Jonathan Nelson, November 15, 2002; Casserly, "Confronting the U.S. Navy," 136.

43. McCoy, *A Still and Quiet Conscience,* 22–23.

44. Cate, *The One Church in This Place,* 7.

45. *Seattle Times*, August 12, 1982, and August 13, 1982.

46. Author interview with Reverend Jonathan Nelson, June 7, 2011.

47. *Seattle Times*, September 3, 2010, *Tocaoma News Tribune*, March 6, 2015 and March 14, 2015.

48. Brian Casserly, "Puget Sound's Security Codependency and Western Cold War Histories, 1950–1984," *Pacific Historical Review* 80:2 (May 2011), 286.

49. See policy statements, Washington Association of Churches 2002, (files, Washington Association of Churches, Seattle); Ecumenical Ministries of Oregon Statement on

■ ——

Iraq, October 4, 2002, Ecumenical Ministries of Oregon Archives, Portland.

50. *Seattle Post-Intelligencer*, October 10, 2002.

51. *Seattle Times*, November 9, 2002.

52. *Oregonian*, November 17, 2002.

53. *Portland Tribune*, January 17, 2003.

54. Mark Silk and Andrew Walsh, *One Nation Divisible: How Regional Religious Differences Shape American Politics* (Lanham, MD: Rowman & Littlefield Publishers, 2008), 140.

55. *Seattle Times*, November 2, 2006.

56. Washington Association of Public Policy Principles, available at http://thewac.org/advocacy/public-policy-principles/.

57. Author interview with Tony Lee, July 28, 2002; author interview with Ned Dolesji, August 15, 2002.

58. Author interview with Reverend Tony Robinson, August 23, 2002; http://plymouthchurchseattle.org/; Mildred Tanner Andrews, *Seeking to Serve: The Legacy of Seattle's Plymouth Congregational Church* (Dubuque, IA: Kendall/Hunt, 1988), 197–219.

59. Lutheran Community Services in the Northwest website: http://www.lcsnw.org/index.html.

60. *Seattle Times*, January 15, 2007.

61. William Cate, "Launching a New Council," 82–83.

62. *Seattle Times*, August 25, 2009.

63. Patricia O'Connell Killen, "Faithless in Seattle? The WTO Protests," *Religion in the News* 3:1 (spring 2000), 12–14.

64. *Seattle Times*, February 22, 2001.

65. Press release, February 27, 2002, Washington Association of Churches, files, Faith Action Network, Seattle.

66. Earth Ministry website: http://earthministry.org/about.

67. Catharine Albanese, *Nature Religion in America: From the Algonkian Indians to the New Age* (Chicago: University of Chicago Press, 1990).

68. Mark A. Shibley, "the Promise and Limits of Secular Spirituality in Cascadia," in *Cascadia, The Elusive Utopia: Exploring the Spirit of the Pacific Northwest*, ed. Douglas Todd (Vancouver, BC: Ronsdale Press, 2009), 35.

69. Shibley, "The Promise and Limits of Secular Spirituality," 40–41.

70. Shibley, "The Promise and Limits of Secular Spirituality," 41.

71. Silk and Walsh, *One Nation Divisible*, 140–147.

Conclusion

1. Mark Matthews, "The Tramp of the Ages," Sermonettes, January–July 1908, Mark Matthews Papers, University of Washington Libraries, Seattle.

2. See Mark A. Shibley, "Secular but Spiritual in the Pacific Northwest," in *Religion and Public Life in the Pacific Northwest: The None Zone,* ed. Patricia O'Connell Killen and Mark Silk (Walnut Creek, CA.: AltaMira Press, 2004), 155–167; Mark Silk and Andrew Walsh, *How Regional Religious Differences Shape American Politics* (Lanham, MD: Rowman & Littlefield Publishers, 2008), 135–155.

3. Silk and Walsh, *Regional Religious Differences*, 147–151.

4. *Time Magazine*, January 26, 2015, 45–48.

5. Don Mackenzie, Ted Falcon, and Jamal Rahman, *Getting to the Heart of Interfaith* (Woodstock, VT: Skylight Paths Publishing, 2009).

BIBLIOGRAPHY

MANUSCRIPTS

Andrews, Emery. Emery Andrews Papers, University of Washington Libraries, Seattle.
Barnett, Arthur. Arthur Barnett Papers, University of Washington Libraries, Seattle.
Christian Friends for Racial Equality, University of Washington Libraries, Seattle.
Church Council of Greater Seattle Papers, University of Washington Libraries, Seattle.
Ecumenical Ministries of Oregon Archives, Portland, Oregon.
Jackson, John H. John H. Jackson Papers, Portland Community College Archives.
Japanese-American Clippings, United Methodist Church, Oregon-Idaho Annual
    Conference, Salem, Oregon.
Maris, Stella. Stella Maris Papers, Oregon Historical Society Research Library, Portland.
Matthews, Mark. Mark Matthews Papers, University of Washington Libraries, Seattle.
Men's Resort File, First Presbyterian Church, Portland Archives.
Official Archives of the Catholic Archdiocese of Seattle, Seattle.
Romney, Rodney. Rodney Romney Papers, Whitworth University Archives, Spokane.
Sakamoto, James. James Sakamoto Papers, University of Washington Libraries, Seattle.
Seattle CORE Papers, University of Washington Libraries, Seattle.
Seattle Opportunities Industrial Center Records, University of Washington Libraries,
    Seattle.
Woman's Christian Temperance Union of Western Washington, Washington State
    Historical Society, Tacoma.
Young Women's Christian Association, University of Washington Libraries, Seattle.

INTERVIEWS WITH AUTHOR

John Hurst Adams, July 17, 2012
Ned Dolesji, August 15, 2002
Karen Frasier, January 18, 2013
Loreda Graham, August 23, 2012
Charles Johnson, June 22, 2013
Tony Lee, July 28, 2002
Samuel McKinney, July 25, 2004, and June 18, 2012
Reverend Jonathan Nelson, November 15, 2002, and June 7, 2011
Reverend Tony Robinson, August 23, 2002
Doug Ross, January 26, 2010
Joan Singler, June 7, 2011

NEWSPAPERS AND MAGAZINES

Auburn Globe-Republican
Bellevue American
Bellingham Herald
Bellingham Morning Reveille
Boise Weekly
Catholic Northwest Progress
Christian News Northwest
Daily Journal of Commerce
Ellensburg Daily Record
Eugene Oregon Register-Guard
Hood River News
Kent Advertiser-Journal
Kitsap Herald
Morning Oregonian
New York Times
Oregonian

Oregon Episcopal Churchman
Oregon Journal
Pacific Christian Advocate
Philadelphia Inquirer
Portland Oregonian
Portland Tribune
Seattle Argus
Seattle Post-Intelligencer
Seattle Times
Seattle Town-Crier
Spokane Daily Chronicle
Spokesman Review
Time Magazine
Walla Walla Statesman
Whitworthian

OTHER DOCUMENTS

Annual Catalogue, 1894. University of Washington. Seattle, University of Washington Special
Collections and Archives.

Bibb, Thomas W., and Frederick E. Bolton. *History of Early Common School Education in
Washington Bulletin, 1934 No. 9.* Washington, DC: US Government Printing Office, 1934.

Catalogue of Gonzaga College for the College Year 1896–7. Spokane: Pigott & French, 1897.
Gonzaga University Archives, Spokane.

"Minutes of the Executive Committee, Greater Portland Council of Churches. September
1930 to June 1931." Files in office of the Ecumenical Ministries of Oregon, Portland.

"Minutes of the Executive Committee, Greater Portland Council of Churches. September
1936 to June 1937." Files in office of the Ecumenical Ministries of Oregon, Portland.

"Olympia Minutes, 1883–1897, Woman's Christian Temperance Union Records." Washington
State Historical Society, Tacoma.

Prichard, Valentine. "1906 Annual Report." People's Institute file, People's Institute, First
Presbyterian Church.

———. "Origin and Development of Settlement Work in Portland Including Free Medical
Work." People's Institute File, First Presbyterian Portland Archives, 1939.

"Report of the Commission on Social and Industrial Betterment, January 11, 1932,
Executive minutes to Greater Portland Council of Churches."
Files in office of the Ecumenical Ministries of Oregon, Portland.

Schwabacher, Emilie B. *A Place for Children: A Personal History of Children's Orthopedic
Hospital and Medical Center.* Seattle: Children's Orthopedic Hospital and Medical
Center, 1977.

"Welcome Addresses, Delivered at Miss Frances E. Willard's Reception Held in Yesler's Hall,
Seattle, W.T., June 27, 1883." Proceedings of the First Mass Temperance Convention of
Western Washington, Washington State Historical Society, Tacoma.

Whitworth College Catalogue, 1891–92. Tacoma: Whitworth College, 1902.

Wilson, Otto. *Fifty Years' Work with Girls 1883–1933: A Story of the Florence Crittenton Homes.* Alexandria, VA: National Florence Crittenton Mission, 1933.

THESES AND DISSERTATIONS

Barger, Keith D. "Hearing the Cry of the Poor: The Catholic Worker Communities in Oregon and Washington 1940 to the Present." BA thesis, University of Portland, April 1992.

Bergler, Thomas. "Christian Youth Groups and the Middle-Class Culture of Crisis, 1930–1965." Unpublished PhD dissertation, University of Notre Dame, 2001.

Bibb, Thomas William. "History of Early Common School Education in Washington." Unpublished PhD thesis, University of Washington, 1928.

Dawson, Jan C. "A Social Gospel Portrait: The Life of Sydney Dix Strong." Unpublished master's thesis, University of Washington, 1972.

Droker, Howard Alan. "The Seattle Civic Unity Committee and the Civil Rights Movement, 1944–1964." Unpublished PhD dissertation, University of Washington, 1974.

Engle, Nancy. "Benefiting a City: Women, Respectability and Reform in Spokane, Washington, 1886–1910." Unpublished PhD dissertation, University of Florida, 2003.

Eulenberg, Julia Niebuhr. "Samuel Koch: Seattle's Social Justice Rabbi." Unpublished master's thesis, University of Washington, 1984.

Fromherz, Frank A. "Archbishop Raymond Hunthausen's Thought and Practice in Society and Church: A Socio-Historical and Ethical Case Study of Nonviolence." Unpublished PhD dissertation, Graduate Theological Union, 1990.

Geddes, Elizabeth MacGregor. "Desegregation/Integration—Policies and Practices: Portland Public Schools, Portland, Oregon, 1970–1981." Unpublished EdD dissertation, Brigham Young University, 1982.

Mack, Dwayne Anthony. "Triumphing through Adversity: African Americans in Spokane, Washington, 1945–1965—A Social History." PhD dissertation, Washington State University, 2002.

McClees, Johanna. "Christian Friends for Racial Equality: A Unique Approach to Race and Religious Relations in Seattle 1942–1970." BA thesis, University of Washington, 2001.

McConaghy, Lorraine. "No Ordinary Place: Three Postwar Suburbs and Their Critics." PhD dissertation, University of Washington, 1993.

McElderry, Stuart John. "The Problem of the Color Line: Civil Rights and Racial Ideology in Portland, Oregon, 1944–1965." Unpublished PhD dissertation, University of Oregon, 1998.

Miller, Heather. "From Moral Suasion to Moral Coercion: Persistence and Transformation in the Prostitution Reform, Portland, Oregon, 1888–1916." MA thesis, University of Oregon, 1966.

Richardson, Larry Samuel. "Civil Rights in Seattle: A Rhetorical Analysis of a Social Movement." Unpublished PhD dissertation, Washington State University, 1975.

Scheck, John F. "Transplanting a Tradition: Thomas Lamb Eliot and the Unitarian Conscience in the Pacific Northwest, 1865–1905." PhD dissertation, University of Oregon, 1969.

Schlimgen, Veta R. "Defining Participation and Place: Women and the Seattle World's Fair of 1909 and 1962." MA thesis, University of Washington, 2000.

Scott, George W. "Arthur B. Langlie: Republican Governor in a Democratic Age." Unpublished PhD dissertation, University of Washington, 1971.

Zane, Jeffrey Gregory. "'America Only Less So?' Seattle's Central Area, 1968–1996." Unpublished PhD dissertation, University of Notre Dame, 2001.

BOOKS AND ARTICLES

Abrams, Paula. *Cross Purposes: Pierce v. Society of Sisters and the Struggle over Compulsory Public Education.* Ann Arbor: University of Michigan, 2009.

Abrams, Ray Hamilton. *Preachers Present Arms.* Scottsdale, PA: Herald Press, 1933.

Albanese, Catharine. *Nature Religion in America: From the Algonkian Indians to the New Age.* Chicago: University of Chicago Press, 1990.

Andrews, Mildred Tanner. *Seattle Women: A Legacy of Community Development.* Seattle: YWCA, 1984.

———. *Seeking to Serve: The Legacy of Seattle's Plymouth Congregational Church.* Dubuque, IA: Kendall Hunt, 1988.

———. *Washington Women as Path Breakers.* Dubuque, IA: Kendall Hunt, 1989.

———. *Woman's Place: A Guide to Seattle and King County History.* Seattle: Gemil Press, 1994.

Atkins, Gary L. *Gay Seattle: Stories of Exile and Belonging.* Seattle: University of Washington Press, 2003.

Bagley, Clarence. *History of Seattle from the Earliest Settlement to the Present Time.* Chicago: S. J. Clarke, 1916.

Baker, Kelly. *Gospel According to the Klan: The KKK's Appeal to Protestant America, 1915–1930.* Lawrence: University of Kansas Press, 2011.

Bates, Vernon. "Rhetorical Pluralism and Secularization in the New Christian Right: The Oregon Citizens Alliance." *Review of Religious Research* 37 (September 1995), 46–64.

Bederman, Gail. *Manliness and Civilization: A Cultural History of Gender and Race in the United States, 1880–1917.* Chicago: University of Chicago Press, 1995.

Benowitz, June Melby. *Days of Discontent: American Women and Right Wing Politics, 1933–1945.* Dekalb: Northern Illinois University Press, 2002.

Berner, Richard C. *Seattle 1900–1920: From Boomtown, Urban Turbulence, to Restoration.* Seattle: Charles Press, 1991.

Blair, Karen, ed. *Women in Pacific Northwest History.* Seattle: University of Washington Press, 2001, rev. edition.

Blocker, Jack S., Jr. *"Give to the Winds Thy Fears": The Woman's Temperance Crusade, 1873–1874.* Westport, CT: Greenwood Press, 1985.

Blue, Dana, and Patti Harris. *A Century of Turning Hope into Reality: A 100-Year Retrospect of Children's Home Society in Washington State.* Dana Blue, researcher and contributing writer; Patti Harris, contributing writer and project coordinator; Esme Ryan, editor. Seattle: Children's Home Society, 1996.

Bordin, Ruth. *Frances Willard: A Biography.* Chapel Hill: University of North Carolina Press, 1986.

Boswell, Sharon A., and Lorraine McConaghy. *Raise Hell and Sell Newspapers: Alden J. Blethen and the Seattle Times.* Pullman: Washington State University Press, 1996.

Boyer, Paul. *Urban Masses and Moral Order in America, 1820–1920.* Cambridge, MA: Harvard University Press, 1978.

Bragg, L. E. *More Than Petticoats: Remarkable Washington Women.* Helena, MT: Falcon Publishing, 1998.

Brandt, Patricia, and Lillian A. Pereyra. *Adapting in Eden: Oregon's Catholic Minority 1838–1986.* Pullman: Washington State University Press, 2002.

Buerge, David M., and Junius Rochester. *Roots and Branches.* Seattle: Church Council of Greater Seattle, 1988.

Carpenter, Joel A. *Revive Us Again: The Reawakening of American Fundamentalism.* New York: Oxford University Press, 1997.

Casserly, Brian. "Confronting the U.S. Navy at Bangor, 1973–1982." *Pacific Northwest Quarterly* (summer 2004), 130–139.

— — —. "Puget Sound's Security Codependency and Western Cold War Histories, 1950–1984." *Pacific Historical Review* 80 (May 2011), 268–293.

Casswell, John. "The Prohibition Movement in Oregon: Part I, 1836–1904." *Oregon Historical Quarterly* 39 (1938), 237–261.

— — —. "The Prohibition Movement in Oregon: Part II, 1904–1915." *Oregon Historical Quarterly* 40 (1939), 64–82.

Cate, William B. "Launching the New Council, 1970–1981." In *The Story of the Church Council of Greater Seattle 1919–1995.* Edited by Church Council of Greater Seattle, Olympia: Pan Press, 1996.

— — —. *The One Church in This Place.* Seattle: Institute for Ecumenical Studies of the Northeast Theological Union, 1991.

Chase, Cora G. *Unto the Least: A Biographical Sketch of Mother Ryther.* Seattle: Shorey Book Store, facsimile reproduction, 1972.

Clark, Malcolm H., Jr. "The War on the Webfoot Saloon." *Oregon Historical Quarterly* 58 (1957), 4–11.

Clark, Norman. *The Dry Years: Prohibition and Social Change in Washington.* Seattle: University of Washington Press.

— — —. *Mill Town: A Social History of Everett, Washington, from Its Earliest Beginnings on the Shores of Puget Sound to the Tragic and Infamous Event Known as the Everett Massacre.* Seattle: University of Washington Press, 1970.

Cone, Molly, Howard Droker, and Jacqueline Williams. *Family of Strangers: Building a Jewish Community in Washington State.* Seattle: University of Washington Press, 2003.

Cook, Sharon Anne. *"Through Sunshine and Shadow": The Woman's Christian Temperance Union, Evangelicalism, and Reform in Ontario, 1874–1930.* Montreal: McGill-Queen's University Press.

Cort, John C., "The Catholic Worker and the Workers." *Commonweal* (April 4, 1952), 636.

Courtwright, David T. *Violent Land: Single Men and Social Disorder from the Frontier to the Inner City.* Cambridge, MA: Harvard University Press, 1996.

Crabtree, Margaret, Priscilla Gilkey, and Terren Roloff, eds. *The Deaconess Story 1896–1996.* Spokane: Deaconess Medical Center.

Crowley, Walt, David W. Wilma, and the HistoryLink Staff. *Hope on the Hill: The First Century of Seattle Children's Hospital.* Seattle: University of Washington Press and History Ink/History Link, 2010.

Daniels, Roger. *Concentration Camps USA: Japanese Americans and World War II.* New York: Holt, Rinehart and Winston, 1971.

Deichmann Edwards, Wendy J., and Carolyn De Swarte Gifford, eds. *Gender and the Social Gospel.* Urbana: University of Illinois Press, 2003.

Divine, Jean Porter. *From Settlement House to Neighborhood House 1906–1976: An Historical Survey of a Pioneering Seattle Social Service Agency.* Seattle: Neighborhood House, 1976.

Dodds, Gordon B. *The American Northwest: A History of Oregon and Washington.* Arlington Heights, IL: Forum Press, 1986.

Dolan, Timothy Michael. *Some Seed Fell on Good Ground: The Life of Edwin V. O'Hara.* Washington, DC: Catholic University of America, 1992.

Driscoll, Mark. *Confessions of a Reformission Rev.: Hard Lessons from an Emerging Missional Church.* Grand Rapids, MI: Zondervan Press, 2006.

Driscoll, Mark, and Grace Driscoll. *Real Marriage: The Truth about Sex, Friendship & Life Together.* Nashville, TN: Thomas Nelson, 2012.

Duntley, Madeline. "Japanese and Filipino Together: The Transethnic Vision of Our Lady Queen of Martyrs Parish," *U.S. Catholic Historian* 18 (winter 2000), 74–98.

Dye, Douglas. "For the Sake of Seattle's Soul: The Seattle Council of Churches, the Nikkei Community, and World War II." *Pacific Northwest Quarterly* 93:3 (summer 2002), 127–136.

Earley, James. *The University of Puget Sound 1888–1988: On the Frontier of Leadership.* Tacoma: University of Puget Sound, 1987.

Edwards, G. Thomas. *The Triumph of Tradition: The Emergence of Whitman College 1895–1924.* Walla Walla, WA: Whitman College, 1992.

Eisenberg, Ellen. "'As Truly American as Your Son': Voicing Opposition to Internment in Three West Coast Cities." *Oregon Historical Quarterly* 104 (2003), 542–563.

Elliott, Eugene Clinton. *A History of Variety Vaudeville in Seattle: From the Beginning to 1914.* Seattle: University of Washington Press, 1944.

Epstein, Barbara Leslie. *The Politics of Domesticity: Women, Evangelism, and Temperance in Nineteenth-Century America.* Middletown, CT: Wesleyan University Press, 1981.

Fendall, Lon. *Stand Alone or Come Home: Mark Hatfield as an Evangelical and a Progressive.* Newberg, OR: Barclay Press, 2008.

Fishburn, Janet Forsythe. *The Fatherhood of God and the Victorian Family: The Social Gospel in America.* Philadelphia: Fortress, 1981.

Franklin, Joseph. *All through the Night: The History of Spokane Black Americans 1860–1940.* Fairfield, WA: Ye Galleon Press, 1989.

Frykman, George A. *Creating the People's University: Washington State University, 1890–1990.* Pullman: Washington State University Press, 1990.

Gardner, Nancy G. "The Woman's Christian Temperance Union: A Woman's Branch of American Protestantism." In *Re-Forming the Center: American Protestantism, 1900 to the Present.* Edited by Douglas Jacobsen and William Vance Trollinger Jr. Grand Rapids, MI: William B. Eerdmans, 1998.

Gates, Charles M. *The First Century at the University of Washington 1861–1961.* Seattle: University of Washington Press, 1961.

Gates, Charles M., and Dorothy O. Johansen. *Empire of the Columbia: A History of the Pacific Northwest,* 2nd edition. Seattle: University of Washington Press, 1967.

Giboney, Ezra P., and Agnes Potter. *Life of Mark A. Matthews.* Grand Rapids, MI: William B. Eerdmans, 1948.

Gifford, Carolyn De Swarte. "'The Woman's Cause Is Man's'?: Frances Willard and the Social Gospel." In *Gender and the Social Gospel.* Edited by Wendy J. Deichmann Edwards and Carolyn De Swarte Gifford. Urbana: University of Illinois Press, 2003.

Gill, Jill K. *Embattled Ecumenism: The National Council of Churches, the Vietnam War, and the Trials of the Protestant Left.* DeKalb: University of Northern Illinois Press, 2011.

Gleason, Philip. *Contending with Modernity: Catholic Higher Education in the Twentieth Century.* New York: Oxford University Press, 1995.

Gray, Alfred O. *Not by Might: The Story of Whitworth College, 1890–1965.* Spokane: Whitworth College, 1965.

Gregory, James N. *The Southern Diaspora: How the Great Migrations of Black and White Southerners Transformed America.* Chapel Hill: University of North Carolina Press, 2005.

Grubb, Norman P. *Modern Viking: The Story of Abraham Vereide, Pioneer in Christian Leadership.* Grand Rapids, MI: Zondervan Publishing House, 1961.

Gunns, Albert F. *Civil Liberties in Crisis: The Pacific Northwest 1917–1940.* New York and London: Garland, 1983.

Haarsager, Sandra. *Organized Womanhood: Cultural Politics in the Pacific Northwest 1840–1920.* Norman: University of Oklahoma Press, 1997.

Hall, Esther Mumford. *Seattle's Black Victorians 1852–1901.* Seattle: Ananse Press, 1980.

Handy, Robert, ed. *The Social Gospel in America, 1870–1920.* New York: Oxford University Press, 1966.

Hankins, Barry. *American Evangelicals: A Contemporary History of a Mainstream Religious Movement.* Lanham, MD: Rowman & Littlefield, 2008.

Hart, Patricia Susan. *A Home for Every Child: The Washington Children's Home Society in the Progressive Era.* Seattle: University of Washington Press, 2010.

Hendrick, Burton J. "The 'Recall' in Seattle." *McClure's* 37 (October 1911), 660–663.

Hill, Pauline Anderson Simmons, and Sherrilyn Johnson Jordan. *Too Young to Be Old: The Story of Bertha Pitts Campbell, a Founder of Delta Sigma Theta Sorority, Inc.* Seattle: Peanut Butter Publishing, 1981.

Hitchman, James. *Liberal Arts Colleges in Oregon & Washington, 1842–1980.* Bellingham: Western Washington University, 1981.

Hopkins, Charles. *The Rise of the Social Gospel in American Protestantism, 1865–1915.* New Haven, CT: Yale University Press, 1940.

Horowitz, David A., ed. *Inside the Klavern: The Secret History of a Ku Klux Klan in the 1920s.* Carbondale: Southern Illinois Press, 1999.

———. "The Klansman as an Outsider: Ethnocultural Solidarity and Antielitism in the Oregon Ku Klux Klan of the 1920s." *Pacific Northwest Quarterly* (January 1989), 12–20.

———. "Order, Solidarity, and Vigilance: The Ku Klux Klan in La Grande, Oregon." In *The Invisible Empire in the West: Toward a New Historical Appraisal of the Ku Klux Klan of the 1920s.* Edited by Shawn Lay. Chicago: University of Illinois Press, 1992.

Hunt, William R. *Front-Page Detective: William J. Burns and the Detective Profession, 1880–1930.* Bowling Green, KY: Bowling Green State University Popular Press, 1990.

Jackson, Kenneth T. *The Ku Klux Klan in the City, 1915–1930.* Chicago: Ivan R. Dee, 1967.

Jeffrey, Julie Roy. *Converting the West: A Bibliography of Narcissa Whitman.* Norman: University of Oklahoma Press, 1991.

Jepson, David. "Old-Fashioned Revival: Religion, Migration, and New Identity for the Pacific Northwest at Mid-Twentieth Century." *Oregon Historical Quarterly* 107 (fall 2006), 354–381.

Johnson, Ethan, and Felicia Williams. "Desegregation and Multiculturalism in the Portland Public Schools." *Oregon Historical Quarterly* 111 (spring 2010), 6–37.

Johnston, Robert D. *The Radical Middle Class: Populist Democracy and the Question of Capitalism in Progressive Era Portland, Oregon.* Princeton, NJ: Princeton University Press, 2003.

Kahlo, Dorothy Miller. *History of the Police and Fire Departments of the City of Seattle.* Seattle: Lumbermen's Printing Company, 1907.

Kalin, Jules Alexander. "The Anti-Chinese Outbreak in Tacoma, 1885." *Pacific Historical Review* 23:3 (August 1954), 271–283.

Kapralos, Krista. "Death with Dignity: Combatting Religious Opposition to Physician-Assisted Suicide." *Religion Dispatches,* May 15, 2009.

Kenton, Jessie Kinnear. "New Beginnings, New Leadership, 1930–1939." In *Generation to Generation: The Story of the Church Council of Greater Seattle, 1919–1995.* Olympia: PanPress, 1996.

Kershner, Jim. "Segregation in Spokane." *Columbia Magazine* 14:4 (winter 2000–2001), 38–44.

Killen, Patricia O'Connell. "Faithless in Seattle? The WTO Protests." *Religion in the News* 3:1 (spring 2000), 12–14.

Killen, Patricia O'Connell, and Mark Silk, eds. *Religion & Public Life in the Pacific Northwest: The None Zone.* Walnut Creek: AltaMira Press, 2004.

Lavender, David. *Land of Giants: The Drive to the Pacific Northwest 1750–1950.* Lincoln: University of Nebraska Press, 1979.

Lentz, Sister Dorothy, S. P. *The Way It Was in Providence Schools.* Montreal: Sisters of Providence, 1978.

Levine, Rabbi Raphael H. *To Love Is to Live: Building Bridges of Understanding.* Seattle: Peanut Butter Publishing, 1994.

Lichtman, Allan J. *White Protestant Nation: The Rise of the American Conservative Movement.* New York: Atlantic Monthly Press, 2008.

Liestman, Daniel. "To Win Redeemed Souls from Heathen Darkness: Protestant Reponse to the Chinese of the Pacific Northwest in the Late Nineteenth Century." *Western Historical Quarterly* 24:2 (May 1993), 179–201.

Lotz, David W., Donald W. Shriver, John Frederick Wilson, and Robert T. Handy. *Altered Landscapes: Christianity in America, 1935–1985.* Grand Rapids, MI: Eerdmans, 1989.

Lowenstein, Steven. *The Jews of Oregon 1850–1950.* Portland: Jewish Historical Society of Oregon, 1987.

Lukas, J. Anthony. *Big Trouble: A Murder in a Small Western Town Sets Off a Struggle for the Soul of America.* New York: Simon & Schuster, 1997.

Luker, Ralph E. *The Social Gospel in Black and White: American Racial Reform, 1885–1912.* Chapel Hill: University of North Carolina Press, 1991.

Lunch, William M. "The Christian Right in the Northwest: Two Decades of Frustration in Oregon and Washington." In *The Christian Right in American Politics: Marching to the Millennium.* Edited by John Green, Mark Rozell, and Clyde Wilcox. Washington, DC: Georgetown University Press, 2003.

MacColl, E. Kimbarck. *The Growth of a City: Business and Politics in Portland, Oregon 1915–1950.* Portland: Georgian Press, 1979.

— — —. *The Shaping of the City: Business and Politics in Portland, Oregon 1885 to 1915.* Portland: Georgian Press, 1976.

Mack, Dwayne A. *Black Spokane: The Civil Rights Struggle in the Inland Northwest.* Norman: University of Oklahoma Press, 2014.

Mackenzie, Don, Ted Falcon, and Jamal Rahman. *Getting to the Heart of Interfaith.* Woodstock, VT: Skylight Paths Publishing, 2009.

Mangun, Kimberley. "'As Citizens of Portland We Must Protest': Beatrice Morrow Cannady and the African American Response to D. W. Griffith's 'Masterpiece.'" *Oregon Historical Quarterly* (fall 2006), 382–409.

— — —. *A Force for Change: Beatrice Morrow Cannady & the Struggle for Civil Rights in Oregon, 1912–1936.* Corvallis: Oregon State University Press, 2010.

Marsden, George M. *Fundamentalism and American Culture: The Shaping of Twentieth Century Evangelicalism, 1870–1925.* New York: Oxford University Press, 1980.

Matthews, Mark. "The Fury of Egypt." *Presbyterian* (April 14, 1938), 3.

— — —. "Racial Prejudice Un-American." *Annals of the American Academy of Political Science* 93 (January 1921), 69–72.

Mathews, Shailer. "Social Gospel." In *A Dictionary of Religion and Ethics.* Edited by Shailer Mathews and G. B. Smith, 416–417. New York: Macmillan, 1921.

McCann, Sharon. "Dave Willis' Passion for Preservation." *American Profile*, May 6, 2001.

McCoy, John A. *A Still and Quiet Conscience: The Archbishop Who Challenged a Pope, a President, and a Church*. MaryKnoll, New York: Orbis Books, 2015.

McDowell, John Patrick. *The Social Gospel in the South: The Woman's Home Mission Movement in the Methodist Episcopal Church, South, 1886–1939*. Baton Rouge: Louisiana State University, 1982.

McElderry, Stuart. "Building a West Coast Ghetto: African-American Housing in Portland, 1910–1960." *Pacific Northwest Quarterly* 92 (summer 2001), 137–148.

McElroy, Paul. *Bridging the Divide: The History of the Urban League of Metropolitan Seattle*. Seattle: Seattle Urban League, 2005.

McGirr, Lisa. *Suburban Warriors: The Origins of the New American Right*. Princeton, NJ: Princeton University Press, 2001.

McKenzie, Michael. "James Harvey Wilbur: Man on the Move." *Willamette Journal* (2003), 51–55.

McLagan, Elizabeth. *A Peculiar Paradise: A History of Blacks in Oregon, 1788–1940*. Portland: Georgian Press, 1980.

McLoughlin, William Gerald. *Modern Revivalism: Charles Grandison Finney to Billy Graham*. New York: Ronald Press, 1959.

Meier, August, and Elliot Rudwick. *CORE: A Study in the Civil Rights Movement, 1942–1968*. New York: Oxford University Press, 1973.

Miranda, Gary, and Rick Read. *Splendid Audacity: The Story of Pacific University*. Seattle: Documentary Book Publishers, 2000.

Morgan, Murray. *Puget's Sound: A Narrative of Early Tacoma and the Southern Sound*. Seattle: University of Washington Press, 1979.

———. *Skid Road: An Informal Portrait of Seattle*. New York: Viking Press, 1951.

Murdock, Catherine Gilbert. *Domesticating Drink: Women, Men, and Alcohol in America, 1870–1940*. Baltimore: Johns Hopkins University Press, 1998.

Myers, Gloria E. *A Municipal Mother: Portland's Lola Greene Baldwin, America's First Policewoman*. Corvallis: Oregon State University Press, 1995.

Nordquist, Philip A. *Educating for Service: Pacific Lutheran University, 1890–1990*. Tacoma: University of Puget Sound, 1990.

O'Connell, William P. "Fifty Golden Years." *Catholic Northwest Progress* (November 29, 1932), 21–27.

Okrent, Daniel. *Last Call: The Rise and Fall of Prohibition*. New York: Scribner, 2010.

Oliver, Egbert S. "Obed Dickinson and the 'Negro Question' in Salem." *Oregon Historical Quarterly* 92 (1991), 4–40.

Ottman, Ford. *J. Wilbur Chapman: A Biography*. Kessinger Publishing, 1920, reprinted 2008.

Pascoe, Peggy. *Relations of Rescue: The Search for Female Moral Authority in the American West, 1874–1939*. New York: Oxford University Press, 1990.

Paul, Rodman. *The Far West and the Great Plains in Transition 1859–1900*. New York: Harper & Row, 1988.

Peiss, Kathy. *Cheap Amusements: Working Women and Leisure in Turn-of-the-Century New York*. Philadelphia: Temple University Press, 1986.

Pierce, J. Kingston. *Eccentric Seattle: Pillars and Pariahs Who Made the City Not Such a Boring Place after All*. Pullman: Washington State University Press, 2003.

Pieroth, Doris H. *The Hutton Settlement: A Home for One Man's Family*. Spokane: The Hutton Settlement, 2003.

— — —. "With All Deliberate Caution: School Integration in Seattle, 1954–1968."
Pacific Northwest Quarterly 73 (April 1982), 50–61.

Pivar, David. *Purity Crusade: Sexual Morality and Social Control, 1868–1900.*
Westport, CT: Greenwood Press, 1973.

Poethig, Richard P. "Charles Stelzle and the Roots of the Presbyterian Industrial Mission."
Journal of Presbyterian History 77:1 (spring 1999), 29–44.

"Poor People." *Commonweal* (June 23, 1950), 272.

Pope-Levison, Priscilla. "Emma Ray in Black and White: The Intersection of Race, Region
and Religion." *Pacific Northwest Quarterly* 102 (summer 2011), 107–131.

Porter, Samuel C. "The Pacific Northwest Forest Debate: Bringing Religious Back
In?" *Worldviews: Environment, Culture, Religion* 3 (1999), 3–32.

Putney, Clifford Wallace. *Muscular Christianity: The Strenuous Mood in American
Protestantism, 1880–1920.* Cambridge, MA: Harvard University Press, 2001.

Ray, Emma J. Smith, and L. P. Ray. *Twice Sold, Twice Ransomed: Autobiography of Mr. and Mrs.
L. P. Ray.* Chicago: Free Methodist Publishing House, 2000.

Rettmann, Jef. "Business, Government, and Prostitution in Spokane, Washington, 1889–1910."
Pacific Northwest Quarterly (spring 1998), 77–83.

Rodgers, Daniel T. *Age of Fracture.* Cambridge, MA: Belknap Press of Harvard University
Press, 2011.

Rorabaugh, W. J. *The Alcoholic Republic: An American Tradition.* New York: Oxford University
Press, 1979.

Saalfeld, Lawrence J. *Forces of Prejudice in Oregon, 1920–1925.* Portland: Archdiocesan
Historical Commission, 1984.

Scheck, John F. "Thomas Lamb Eliot and His Vision of an Enlightened Community. In *The
Western Shore: Western Country Essays Honoring the American Revolution.* Edited by Thomas
Vaughan. Portland: Oregon Historical Society, 1976.

Schoenberg, Wilfred P. *A History of the Catholic Church in the Pacific Northwest 1743–1983.*
Washington, DC: Pastoral Press, 1987.

Schwantes, Carlos. *The Pacific Northwest: An Interpretive History.* Lincoln: University of
Nebraska Press, 1989.

Schwarz, Fred. *Beating the Unbeatable Foe: One Man's Victory over Communism, Leviathan, and
the Last Enemy.* Washington, DC: Regnery Publishing, 1996.

Sevetson, Donald J. *Atkinson: Pioneer Oregon Educator.* CreateSpace, 2011.

— — —. "George Atkinson, Harvey Scott, and the Portland High School Controversy of
1880." *Oregon Historical Quarterly* 108 (2007), 458–473.

Sharlet, Jeff. *The Family: The Secret Fundamentalism at the Heart of American Power.*
New York: Harper Collins, 2008.

Shaw, James Gerard. *Edwin Vincent O'Hara: American Prelate.* New York: Farrar, Straus and
Cudahy, 1957.

Shelley, Thomas J. "The Oregon School Case and the National Catholic Welfare Conference."
Catholic Historical Review 75 (July 1989), 439–457.

Shibley, Mark A. "The Promise and Limits of Secular Spirituality in Cascadia." In *Cascadia,
the Elusive Utopia: Exploring the Spirit of the Pacific Northwest.* Edited by Douglas Todd.
Vancouver, BC: Ronsdale Press, 2009.

Shideler, John C. *A Century of Caring: The Sisters of Providence at Sacred Heart Medical Center.*
Spokane: Sacred Heart Medical Center, 1986.

Silk, Mark, and Andrew Walsh. *One Nation, Divisible: How Regional Religious Differences Shape
American Politics.* Lanham, MD: Rowman & Littlefield, 2008.

Singler, Joan. *Seattle in Black and White: The Congress of Racial Equality and the Fight for Equal Opportunity.* Seattle: University of Washington Press, 2011.

Siqueland, Ann LaGrelius. *Without a Court Order: The Desegregation of Seattle's Schools.* Seattle: Madrona Publishers, 1981.

Soden, Dale. "Anatomy of a Presbyterian Urban Revival: J. W. Chapman in the Pacific Northwest." *American Presbyterians: Journal of Presbyterian History* 64 (spring 1986), 49–57.

— — —. "Billy Sunday in Spokane: Revivalism and Social Control." *Pacific Northwest Quarterly* 79 (January 1988), 10–17.

— — —. *The Reverend Mark Matthews: An Activist in the Progressive Era.* Seattle: University of Washington Press, 2001.

— — —. "The Role of Religious Activists in the Seattle Civil Rights Struggles of the 1960s." *Pacific Northwest Quarterly* 104 (spring 2013), 55–71.

— — —. "The Woman's Christian Temperance Union in the Pacific Northwest: The Battle for Cultural Control." *Pacific Northwest Quarterly* 94 (fall 2003), 197–207.

Stein, Harry H. *Gus J. Solomon: Liberal Politics, Jews, and the Federal Courts.* Portland: Oregon Historical Society Press, 2006.

Stelzle, Charles. *A Son of the Bowery.* New York: George H. Doran Co., 1926.

Stevenson, Louis. *The Victorian Homefront: American Thought and Culture 1860–1880.* New York: Twayne Publishers, 1991.

Szasz, Ferenc. *Religion in the Modern American West.* Tucson: University of Arizona Press, 2000.

Szasz, Margaret. *Education and the American Indian: The Road to Self-Determination, 1928–1973.* Albuquerque: University of New Mexico Press, 1974.

Tamura, Linda. *Nisei Soldiers Break Their Silence: Coming Home to Hood River.* Seattle: University of Washington Press, 2012.

Tate, Cassandra. *The Triumph of "The Little White Slaver."* New York: Oxford University Press, 1999.

Taylor, Christine, and Patricia O'Connell Killen. *Abundance of Grace: The History of the Archdiocese of Seattle 1850–2000.* Edited by Christine Taylor. Original research by Patricia O'Connell Killen. Seattle: Archdiocese of Seattle, 2000.

Taylor, Quintards Jr. *The Forging of a Black Community: Seattle's Central District from 1870 through the Civil Rights Era.* Seattle: University of Washington Press, 1994.

— — —. "Susie Revels Cayton, Beatrice Morrow Cannady, and the Campaign for Social Justice in the Pacific Northwest." In *The Great Northwest: The Search for Regional Identity.* Edited by William G. Robbins. Corvallis: Oregon State University Press, 2001.

Toll, William. *The Making of an Ethnic Middle Class: Portland Jewry Over Four Generations.* Albany: State University of New York Press, 1982.

Toy, Eckard. "The Right Side of the 1960s: The Origins of the John Birch Society in the Pacific Northwest." *Oregon Historical Quarterly* 105 (summer 2004), 260–283.

— — —. "Robe and Gown: The Ku Klux Klan in Eugene, Oregon, during the 1920s." In *The Invisible Empire in the West: Toward a New Historical Appraisal of the Ku Klux Klan of the 1920s.* Edited by Shawn Lay. Urbana: University of Illinois Press, 2004.

Treacy, Father William. *Love Bears All Things: Bridging Troubled Waters.* Seattle: Peanut Butter Publishing, 1994.

Tsai, Shih-Shan Henry. *The Chinese Experience in America.* Bloomington: Indiana University Press, 1986.

Tyack, David B. "Bureaucracy and the Common School: The Example of Portland, Oregon, 1851–1913." *American Quarterly* 19 (fall 1967), 475–498.

— — —. "The Kingdom of God and the Common School: Protestant Ministers and the Educational Awakening in the West." *Harvard Education Review* 36 (fall 1966), 447–469.

— — —. "The Perils of Pluralism: The Background of the Pierce Case."
American Historical Review 74 (1968), 75–79.

Victor, Frances Fuller. *The Women's War on Whiskey; Or, Crusading in Portland.* Portland: Geo.
H. Himes, Steam Book and Job Printer, 1874.

Weaver, J. Dudley, Jr. *A Legacy of Faith: First Presbyterian Church Portland, Oregon 1854–2004.*
Aloha, OR: Beachwalker Press, 2004.

Wellman, James K., Jr. *Evangelical vs. Liberal: The Clash of Christian Cultures in the Pacific
Northwest.* New York: Oxford University Press, 2008.

— — —. "Sectarian Entrepreneurs." In *Religion & Public Policy in the Pacific Northwest:
The None Zone.* Edited by Patricia O'Connell Killen and Mark Silk, 79–105.
Walnut Creek, CA: Altamira Press, 2004.

White, Richard. *"It's Your Misfortune and None of My Own": A New History of the American
West.* Norman: University of Oklahoma Press, 1991.

White, Ronald C., Jr., and C. Howard Hopkins. *The Social Gospel: Religion and Reform in
Changing America.* Philadelphia: Temple University Press, 1976.

Williams, Daniel K. *God's Own Party: The Making of the Christian Right.*
Oxford, UK: Oxford University Press, 2010.

Wise, Stephen. *Challenging Years: The Autobiography of Stephen Wise.*
New York: G. P. Putnam's Sons, 1949.

Wuthnow, Robert. *The Restructuring of American Religion: Society and Faith since World War II.*
Princeton, NJ: Princeton University Press, 1988.

WEBSITES

American Family Association: http://www.afa.net/Detail.aspx?id=31.

Centerstone: http://center-stone.org/about/history.

Data base of Megachurches in United States: http://hirr.hartsem.edu/megachurch/
database.html.

Earth Ministry: http://earthministry.org/about/mission-history.

Ecotrust website: http://www.ecotrust.org.

Faith Action Network: http://fanwa.org/?s=legislative+principles&.x=0&.y=0.

Joe Fuiten: http://www.joefuiten.com/news/.

Lutheran Community Services: http: //www.lcsnw.org/index.html.

Mother Rhyther (History Link): http://www.historylink.org/index.cfm?DisplayPage=output.
cfm&file_id=546.

Oregon Family Council: http://www.oregonfamilycouncil.org/.

Oregon Right to Life: http://www.ortl.org/.

Portland YWCA 1901–2001: http://womhist.alexanderstreet.com/portywca/intro.htm.

Rabbi Raphael Harry Levine (History Link): http://www.historylink.org/index.cfm?
DisplayPage=output.cfm&file_id=7299.

Walter Hundley (History Link): http://www.historylink.org/index.cfm?
DisplayPage=output.cfm&file_id=3173.

YMCA of Greater Seattle (History Link): http://www.historylink.org/index.cfm?
DisplayPage=output.cfm&file_id=3099.

INDEX

Clinton, Gordon, 166
Clise, Anna, 37
Clise, James, 37
Clow, Jesse James, 136–137, 161–162, 164
Coalition against Hate Crimes, 225
Coe, Doug, 269n15
Coffee Club (WTCU), 27
Color and Democracy (DuBois), 137
Colson, Charles, 208
Colwell, David, 219, 233
Committee to Aid Relocation, 129
common schools. *See* public schools
Communism, Christian church opposition
    to, 141, 146–147, 148, 150–155, 190
Communism on the Map (film), 152
Communist Party, 121, 152
complementarianism, 195–196
Concerned Women for America (CWA),
    191, 205
Conference on Race and Religion (1963),
    166–167
Congregational Association, 91
Congregationalists, x, 11, 44, 70, 74, 245
    See also specific churches, church leaders and
    organizations
Congress of Industrial Organization (CIO),
    143
Congress of Racial Equality (CORE),
    162–163, 175, 181
Connolly, Thomas, 166, *167*, 169, 176, 215,
    222
Connor, Bull, 166
conservative Christians. *See* Christian right
    activism
Consumer League, 31, 46, 47
Cook, Richard A., 156
Corbett, Helen Ladd, 29–30
Cotterill, George, 54
Council Against Intolerance in America, viii
Council for Jewish Women, 22, 32–33, 38,
    46
Council of Church Women, 134
counterculture (1960s), 190
Courtwright, David, 4
Covenant Celebration Church, 194–195
Crittenton, Charles Nelson, 26
Cruzan, J. A., 94
Crystal Cathedral, Southern California, 194
cult of domesticity, 21
Curtis, C. C., 106–107

Daisy Williams Apartment Court, 170
Daniels, Rees P., 33
Daniels, Roger, 133
Darrow, Clarence, 58, 77

Daughtry, Don, 218
Day, Dorothy, 116–117
Deaconess Hospital, 24
Deaconess movement, 24
Deady, James, 117
Death with Dignity Act (1994), 203
Deer Lake Irrigated Orchards Company, 98
DeJonge, Dirk, 121
DeJonge v. Oregon (1937), 121
DeLashmutt, Van B., 84
denominationalism, 245
deParrie, Paul, 204
desegregation. *See* school desegregation
Devin, William, 144
Dickinson, Obed, 92–93, *93*
Dilling, George, 61, 62
divorce, 191, 196, 205
Dix, Dorothea, 54–55
Dobson, James, 191, 205, 207, 208
domesticity, cult of, 21
domestic skills education, 30
domestic violence, 82, 235
Donnelly, Ignatius, 46
Dore, Fred, 114
Douglass, Jim, 227, 228
Douglass, Shelley, 227, 228
Douglass, Walter, 143–144
Drake, Harvey, Jr., 233–234
Drakeford, John, 153
Driscoll, Grace, 197
Driscoll, Marc, 195, 197–199, 274n23
DuBois, W. E. B., 137
Dunn, Frederick, 103

Earth Ministry, 237–238
EastLake Community Church, 247
East Shore Unitarian Church, 166
ecumenical liberal activism, 211–240, 244,
    245–246
    antinuclear arms race, 211–212
    antiwar initiatives, 226–231
    civil rights, 217–226
    economic and social justice, 231–236
    environmental issues, 236–239, 244
    farmworker rights, 222
    gay rights, 224–225
    global economic injustice, 235–236
    hate crimes, 225
    influence of *Challenge* tv show on Seattle,
    214–216
    Native American fishing and sacred sites,
    221–222
    refugee immigrants and Sanctuary
    Movement, 222–224
    school desegregation, 217–221
    undocumented workers, 223

Morse, Wayne, 171
Mother Gamelin, 22
Mother Joseph, 22–24, *23*, 248
Mount Zion Baptist Church, Seattle, 97,
135, 158, 161, 163–164, 178, 180
Mt. Olivet Baptist Church, Portland, 97,
136–137, 161, 162, 178, 220
Muir, John, 238
Multnomah County Schools, Oregon
first free public high school, 10
Munger, Robert B., 176
municipal reform, 84
Murdock, Catherine Gilbert, 82–83
Murphy, John, 62
Murphy, U. G., 123–124
Murray, Cecil, 218–219
muscular Christianity, 51–53, 143–144
Muslims/Islam, 223, 230, 238
Myers, Gloria, 37

Nace, I. George, 131
Nakajo, Kenneth, 127
National Association for the Advancement
of Colored People (NAACP), 98, 99,
121, 134, 136, 137, 138, 162, 164–165,
170–175, 177–178, 181, 218, 219
National Association of Evangelicals
(NAE), 146–147, 149, 156, 208
National Catholic Conference, 203
National Conference of Catholic Charities,
114, 232–233
National Conference of Christians and Jews,
129, 131, 138, 215
National Consumers' League, 64
National Council for Jewish Women
(NCJW), 32–33
National Council of Churches, 113
National Education Association, 9–10
National Organization of Women (NOW),
205
National Prohibition Party, 25
National Right to Life, 204
National Woman's Suffrage Convention
(1909), 78
Native Americans
apology to by churches, 221–222
attempts to prohibit alcohol
consumption by, 68–69
treaty-based fishing rights, 221
Nature religion, 238–239, 244
Neal's Three-Day Drink Habit Cure, 79
Neighborhood House, 31–32
Neighbors in Need, 234
Nelson, Jon, 211–212, 213–214, 221, 225,
228, *229*, 248
Nelson, Juni, 211

Nelson, Roscoe, Sr., 112, 113, *120*
Newton, Huey, 178
nondenominational Protestants, xi, 193–194,
234, 245
*See also specific churches, church leaders and
organizations*
"None Zone" (Killen), xi–xii
Nordquist, Philip, 14
Nordstrom, 163
Northern Pacific Railroad, 71
Northwest Christian Schools, 149
Northwest Hospital, 234–235
Northwest Oriental Evangelization Society,
123
Northwest Towers, 170–171
nuclear arms race, 211–212, 226–230

Oakley, E. C., 95
Ockenga, Harold John, 146
O'Dea, Edward, 48, 114
Office of Economic Opportunity, 163
O'Hara, Edwin Vincent, 46–47, 63–65, *63*,
66, 248
Olcott, Ben, 102
Old Time Gospel Hour (Falwell tv series), 192
Oliver, Paul, 234
100% Americanism, 100, 103, 105–108
O'Neill, Minnie Beard, 24
Operation Abolition (film), 152
Opportunity Bake Shop, 116
Oregon (state)
anti-abortion organizations, 204
Ballot Measure 51, 203
Child Labor Commission, 46, 54
child labor laws, 54
civil rights law (1953), 162
Compulsory Education Law (1922),
107–109
criminal syndicalism law, 121
Death with Dignity Act (1994), 203
demographics of, 101–102
gay rights legislation, 201–202
Industrial Welfare Commission, 47
Initiative 36 (2004), ban on same-sex
marriage, 202–203
Ku Klux Klan, influence in, 101–103
laws prohibiting cruelty to animals and
children, 53
laws prohibiting ownership of land by
noncitizens, 130–131
legalized abortion, 188, 201
Oregon Minimum Wage Act (1913), 64
physician-assisted suicide, 244
Prohibition law (1914), 74, 80
southern migration to, 145, 269*n*17
statehood (1857), 91